P9-DNB-221

The growing interest in hermeneutics as a theory of interpretation in the human sciences makes this book timely and useful to a wide range of readers in the fields of literature, sociology, philosophy, and history. Some of the liveliest current issues before philosophical hermeneutics are examined in the articles gathered here. For example, they include arguments for the necessity of a hermeneutic approach, reflections on the unity of the hermeneutic enterprise, questions about the limits of hermeneutics, and inquiries into its phenomenological roots and affiliations. These issues are central to a variety of concerns, ranging from semiotic theories of language to meaning and intention in philosophy and the social sciences.

This major anthology of work by a group of internationally recognized scholars both reflects some of the excitement which hermeneutics has aroused and augments it. Contributors are Emilio Betti, Anthony Giddens, Fred Dallmayr, William H. Dray, Rex Martin, Paul de Man, Hans-Georg Gadamer, J. N. Mohanty, Hubert Dreyfus, Richard Palmer, Gerald Bruns, Gary Stonum, John O'Neill, and Gayatri Spivak.

Gary Shapiro is professor of philosophy at the University of Kansas. Also at the University of Kansas, Alan Sica is associate professor of sociology.

. . . . .

Hermeneutics

. . . . .

. . . . .

The University of Massachusetts Press

. . . . .

Hermeneutics

Questions and Prospects

. . . . .

Edited by Gary Shapiro and Alan Sica

Amherst, 1984

"Hermeneutics and Social Theory" originally ap-
peared in Anthony Giddens, *Profiles and Critiques*
(London and Balingstoke: Macmillan; Berkeley and
Los Angeles: University of California Press, 1983),
© Anthony Giddens. Reprinted by permission.

The excerpt from Emilio Betti, *Teoria generale della
interpretazione*, is reprinted by permission of
Gemma Betti.

. . . . .

Acknowledgments

. . . . .

The essays in this collection are meant to be representative both of the best current work on the nature of interpretation and of the necessity for such work to go beyond narrow disciplinary interests. We were aided in bringing the essays together by several institutions and individuals. The Rockefeller Foundation and the Center for Humanistic Studies at the University of Kansas enabled a number of the contributors to present initial versions of their papers to one another at a conference in April 1981 which had the same title as this book. Since then, many of these papers have been revised to take into account the exchange of views that took place. The other essays in the book are intended to reflect the broad range of hermeneutical alternatives that are now being actively explored.

For their assistance with various stages of this project we are grateful to the Rockefeller Foundation for its support; to Richard De George, Director of the Center for Humanistic Studies, and Gretchen Nolle of its staff for their enthusiasm and practical help; to the Matchette Foundation for making possible the forum at which Hans-Georg Gadamer and J. N. Mohanty presented earlier versions of their papers; and to Anthony C. Genova and Scott McNall, Chairs of the Philosophy and Sociology Departments at Kansas, for their aid in marshaling resources. The typing and preparation of the manuscript would have been impossible without the support of the Office of Research, Graduate Studies and Public Service, at the University of Kansas and the fine and patient work of Sharon Cox, Janice Criss, and Aurora Ripley. Finally, Dick Martin and Pam Campbell of the University of Massachusetts Press gave invaluable advice in the preparation of the collection for publication.

Contents

. . . . .

Introduction

Gary Shapiro and Alan Sica

. . . . .

John Steinbeck once said, perhaps when feeling like Hemingway, that critics are the eunuchs of literature, grouped around the bed in envious awe, while a complete man and his partner demonstrate the art of loving. Neither Steinbeck nor Hemingway is as much esteemed now as he has been, neither taken as an exemplar of intellectual precision, nor even as a writer of the first rank in much of his oeuvre. And today when "literature" here and in Europe is viewed as a setting for invention or artistry, the names that surface are Roland Barthes, Jacques Derrida, Michel Foucault, Paul de Man, Harold Bloom, perhaps Susan Sontag or George Steiner, each of whom gladly plays the eunuch (*pace* Sontag), but with such grace and energy that literature itself seems left behind. The ascendancy of critique, of observation—in literature, philosophy, and social science—and the supplanting of traditional work in the bed of creativity, have become an ordinary fact of life, not only in France (where Sartre's Flaubert outshines Flaubert), but in the Anglo-American sphere as well. Notable critics, like Wayne Booth, Denis Donoghue, Gerald Graff, Geoffrey Hartmann, Frank Lentricchia, and W. J. T. Mitchell, satisfy a felt need by gently guiding former readers of literature through today's surrogate, academic criticism.[1] E. M. Forster is remembered as a *theorist* of the novel, Balzac's short stories as fitting subjects for Barthes's scalpel. The world is upside down, again, and our book does nothing to right it.

One need no longer apologize, then, for moving with so many in the *Geisteswissenschaften* toward overt concern for interpretive, hermeneutic theory, leaving temporarily aside what before was confidently called "substantive" work. For example, essays included here treat Foucault and Barthes as themselves substantial, as primary intellectual forces. That neither has created a system of philosophy or work of literature as usually defined matters little, for what they have achieved currently means more. Along with Emilio Betti, Hans-Georg Gadamer, Paul Ricoeur, Derrida, and others, they have long labored in hope of *reducing* confusion, of rationalizing somewhat the irrational, not enlarging it—as great artists inevitably must. Whether respecifying the nature and history of the social sciences, or, with Barthes, penetrating mass culture through semiotics, the goal has consistently been to illuminate the hermeneutic act, by exemplifying it, at its most universal.

It may seem specious to view Derrida (who hangs over this volume unacknowledged, the absent but necessary guest) as dedicated to systematically reducing confusion or perplexity among readers. The same might be said of Foucault. Yet aside from the autochthonous tangles of their metatheories, their linguistic reconstructions, the desire remains to clear a new opening, free of classical debilities, in the *ultimate* interest of improved knowing; a twist upon Heidegger's gambit. This is particularly, even doctrinally, true of Betti and, despite his own hesitations regarding Schleiermacher's and Dilthey's "Romantic" hermeneutics, also of Gadamer. Ricoeur, as Gadamer notes in his essay here, seeks a middle ground between textual clarification and ontological query. Even Jacques Lacan's unique intervention within psychoanalytic theory, as captious as it appears to some, can be seen as an addition to a new hermeneutical literature, bridging the cultural sciences with ambitions suppressed since the nineteenth century. All are remorseless theoretical voyagers, and as such alienate and antagonize readers more accustomed to "readable," Arnoldian criticism.

The suspicion persists, even among the sophisticated, that "substance" is often played with strictly for show; that while Eliot actually illuminated Dante for readers lacking medieval Italian, de Man uses the *Iliad* to test his prowess, to prove rather than to clarify.[2] The critic as artist is heavily upon us, which, more to the point here, also means that hermeneutics becomes artful, if not art itself. Even though Hartmann argues that "literary criticism is neither more nor less important today than it has been since the Renaissance," he can shortly add, without irony, "there are, we sometimes feel, too many sources, and they are not as pure and distinct as they seemed to be."[3] Eliot refused to the end to grant critical genius equal ranking with literary creation, and turned the tables by insisting that the only indispensable critical activity took place as the artist selectively mixed his own impulses with those of the past. Yet who would ask today if de Man or Derrida write with any less calculating virtuosity or density than Samuel Beckett, John Hawkes, or Thomas Pynchon?

The appeal is different, of course. But how different? Is there not a response to *Gravity's Rainbow* and, say, to de Man's *Blindness and Insight* or Barthe's *S/Z* that, taken together, can be contrasted with the joint effect of Wolfe's *Of Time and the River* and Eliot's *Sacred Wood*? We draw no substantive parallels, but do see in these older works (even Eliot's) an almost lyrical form of exposition striving to embrace and sustain the reader. The newer stream has no such aims. Beginning with Hawkes's earliest novellas thirty-five years ago, serious fiction sets out to capture an audience by baffling it. And given the rationalization of culture, no one could have been much surprised when literary critics dropped the pose of avuncular, all-knowing helpmate, and took on the robes of mystagogue or poet-pretender. If Bloom's solo through new terrain, or old ground renewed, is the extreme case for criticism as baffling, autogenic act, he is not that far afield from many others. He has as much in common as a critic and intellectual with, say, R. P. Blackmur, as has Walter Abish (*Alphabetical Africa*) with E. M. Forster. Is it too early to know who, if anyone, will profit from this efflorescence of critical innovation—the artist, the critic, the reader in search of aid, or the publisher, riding waves of academic euphoria? And the waves roll in more quickly all the time. Before structuralism was assimilated in this country, poststructuralism had become the byword. Given the heated search for the new, will "posthermeneutics" soon be with us, before an even rudimentary grip on the elements of the approach have been managed? Perhaps this volume, as varied as its essays are, can help brake premature dismissal of a field introduced by Aristotle and, today, inescapable in social theory, epistemology, axiology, philosophy of history, aesthetics, and literary criticism. Hermes has arrived here now, so we must let him speak.

Philosophical hermeneutics

Hermeneutics is not as rigorous a philosophical method as Husserlian phenomenology or linguistic analysis are thought to be. It is more a philosophical movement or tendency—though not a school—not unlike existentialism, in that it designates a set of general concerns rather than a body of doctrine. Though absorbed with the theory and practice of interpretation, it offers no determinate criteria for the achievement or recognition of apodictic understanding. Following Gadamer (who revived philosophical hermeneutics in Europe, then America), we view hermeneutics as a type of philosophical activity or praxis, the effort to understand what is distant in time and culture (like Plato's *Dialogues*), or obscured by ideology or false consciousness (like the sexual or economic roots of human behavior). The broad hermeneutical aim is to make such understanding meaningful for life and thought.

Affinities exist between hermeneutics and Dewey's pragmatism, as well as with Wittgenstein's novel remaking of language. Richard Rorty suggests that we think of hermeneutics as edification rather than construction:

The attempt to edify (ourselves or others) may consist in the hermeneutic activity of making connections between our own culture and some exotic culture or historical period, or between our own discipline and another discipline which seems to pursue incommensurable aims in an incommensurable vocabulary. But it may instead consist in the "poetic" activity of thinking up such new aims, new words, or new disciplines, followed by, so to speak, the inverse of hermeneutics: the attempt to reinterpret our familiar surroundings in the unfamiliar terms of our new inventions.[4]

From another tradition Karl-Otto Apel sees pragmatism, Marxism, and existentialism as "the three philosophies that really function" since each has "taken up as a topic of thought the great problem of humanity thrust into an unfinished world, the mediation of theory and praxis with regard to an uncertain future."[5] Hermeneutics might seem less vital than these philosophies because of its interest in the past. Yet this tendency is modified by efforts to understand the past in light of the present's exigencies, with an eye toward emerging values. Heidegger's deep hermeneutic of early Greek philosophy illustrates such excavation of the past for the sake of an orientation to the unknown. He believed that the ancients saw the world as untransparent to knowing, since what makes it up is the knowable *and* the absent or concealed. Probing the inescapable tension between the two is what gives the Greek intellect its permanence. Heidegger applies this insight toward correcting the hubris of Western thought, forever seeking total knowledge and control.

Some of the liveliest issues currently before philosophical hermeneutics are examined in these essays. They form a rough sequence, including an argument for the necessity of a hermeneutic approach (Betti), reflections on the unity of the hermeneutic enterprise (Gadamer), questions about the limits of hermeneutics (Dreyfus and Palmer), and an inquiry into its phenomenological roots and affiliations (Mohanty). Emilio Betti's *Teoria Generale della Interpretazione* (2 volumes) is a monument in the field, though its author is known to English readers mainly through reports of his differences with Gadamer. Betti insists that interpretation must seek objective validity. He views Gadamer's as a dangerously relativistic approach since, for him, present and practical concerns ("application") must always govern hermeneutic work. Gadamer's account of interpretation, in contrast, is descriptive, not prescriptive; he is trying "to envisage in a fundamentally universal way what *always* happens."[6]

In this newly translated selection from the beginning of Betti's treatise, a more fundamental level of hermeneutics is disclosed, upon which he and Gadamer might concur. Betti criticizes naturalistic and behavioristic accounts of signs and signification in grounding a hermeneutic "understanding" which is more than "explanation." Among Continental hermeneutic theorists, Betti's use of such Anglo-American ideas is unusual. Unburdened by the immanent critique lodged against such ideas by Wittgenstein and others, Betti proceeds in connecting his traditionalist, almost Diltheyan approach to interpretation with streams of thought for which Gadamer found no use. Susan Noake's forthcoming translation of Betti's complete *Teoria* should stimulate interest in a thinker who masterfully joins his own tradition with that more familiar to Anglo-American philosophers.

Hans-Georg Gadamer's "The Hermeneutics of Suspicion" clarifies the history and current state of interpretive theory. Unlike Paul Ricoeur, he does not recognize two antipodal tendencies in interpretation: a "hermeneutics of respect," preserving the richness and integrity of its subject, and a "hermeneutics of suspicion" that demystifies cultural phenomena distorted by ideologies of class, sexual repressions, or the will to power. Gadamer argues that Ricoeur's hermeneutical technique can well be joined with Husserlian phenomenology and Heideggerian thought. In *Truth and Method* he identifies the interpreter's goal as achieving a fusion of horizons with the examined text, a fusion that is possible despite anomalies of emphasis or structure. Gadamer proceeds with this project of reconciliation, in contrast to his mentor, Heidegger, by minimizing the uncanny (*unheimlich*) dimension of interpretive experience. Heidegger sees human beings as "always already" hermeneutical, with individual existence and one's relation to the past fissured by uncanny alterations between authentic understanding of *Dasein* and the impersonal standpoint of "they say" (*das Man*); or between the conventional reading of a text and the way it may challenge one's whole life. Gadamer contains this irruption of the uncanny through the security of tradition and a shared moral concern, watched over by an Aristotelian practical wisdom.

Hubert Dreyfus explores a darker Heideggerian development in "Beyond Hermeneutics: Interpretation in Late Heidegger and Recent Foucault." He distinguishes two levels of hermeneutics in *Being and Time*. The first articulates the essential structures (care, equipment, and so on) of everydayness in human existence, while the second tears away the disguises we use to avoid the sensation of being ungrounded, uncanny, and radically finite. This second hermeneutic is directed especially toward guilt, death, and the chance for resolute or authentic existence. Dreyfus believes Heidegger abandoned his earlier view that all human beings understand preontologically that we are shaped by our social practices, but are otherwise ungrounded. An existential hermeneutic would therefore be of no value for those who lacked this preontological understanding of existence, which in *Being and Time* is attributed to *Dasein*. According to Dreyfus, Heidegger later saw the modern world as dominated by technological reality and its social practices. Since this technological consciousness is determinant, modern life cannot be saved by a hermeneutic like Gadamer's. Dreyfus asks: "How can there be a dialogue between the living and the dead? How could a fusion of horizons be possible when the only horizon that works now and determines truth for us is the technological horizon?" He sees Foucault's work as complementing Heidegger's by distinguishing between the overall structure of social discourse and the incomplete views held by those caught up in it, as in its social practices.[7]

Dreyfus forces us to re-examine Gadamer's departure from Ricoeur, in seeking continuity throughout hermeneutic practice, and in assimilating Heidegger to an ancient rhetorical tradition. Dreyfus confronts once again the uncanny, unsettling features of existence as framed by Heidegger. Yet Dreyfus's approach, perhaps owing to its schematic clarity, leads to other questions. As Richard Palmer suggests, interpretation as practiced by the older Heidegger and by Foucault is not altogether different from the hermeneutics of *Being and*

Time, or from that which Gadamer found in the rhetorical and humanistic tradition. Something may also have been omitted from Dreyfus's social interpretation of both early and late Heidegger. Surely the assimilation of Heidegger with Foucault seems feasible, since the latter has proposed a broad analysis of our social discourses and practices regarding medicine, insanity, punishment, and sexuality. Yet Heidegger speaks as if technological domination is part of Being itself, a long, fateful development in which man is not the only agent. His prophetic readings of Hölderlin and Trakl, and the posthumously published interview in which he declares that "only a god can save us," focus on Being, rather than man, as the likely agent of change. Maybe Dreyfus is taking Gadamer's approach by interpreting Heidegger vis-à-vis the pressing concerns of those in advanced industrial society, who live under technological domination and other accoutrements of one-dimensionality. Thus one enters into dialogue with a thinker or text in hope of illumination, but only after the interpreter articulates the limits of his own approach with respect to what is interpreted.

J. N. Mohanty, at some remove from Dreyfus, asks whether in philosophical hermeneutics there is anything absent from classical phenomenology. Mohanty's "Transcendental Philosophy and the Hermeneutic Critique of Consciousness" assays the complex relation between Husserl and Heidegger, which was also a task for Gadamer. Mohanty clarifies that relation by proposing Heidegger's critique of Husserl as analogous to Hegel's of Kant. He refuses to construe continental philosophy as a series of "overcomings," Hegel over Kant, Nietzsche over Schopenhauer, and so on. Instead he shows that the unsettled issues between Kant and Hegel adumbrate those between Husserl and Heidegger regarding hermeneutics, such that "phenomenology and hermeneutics stand in a peculiar dialectical relationship to each other." From this perspective Mohanty analyzes three questions about that relationship: the constitution of temporality, the problematic project of total objectification, and what Gadamer has called the "relentless inner tension between illumination and concealment."

The last of these issues has prompted the most comment within contemporary hermeneutics. Betti rejects such a tension since it endangers a hermeneutics capable of yielding "valid" meanings. Gadamer accepts the tension, yet finds relief from its uncanniness in certain continuities and the fruits of practical wisdom, while Dreyfus explores its tragic implications. As a phenomenologist, Mohanty asks how the principle can be legitimated. He rejects that hermeneutic circle (and Heidegger's associated obsession with *aletheia* in the pre-Socratics) that would ground the principle by hermeneutic reference to early Greek thought, revolving around the idea of truth as "undisclosedness." For Mohanty phenomenology is an open, self-revising project, like hermeneutics, and each can find stimulus and correction in the other. Whatever happens to be momentarily invisible to the phenomenologist (such as "operative" concepts or practices) can later become a fitting subject of hermeneutical reflection, which might in turn prepare the way for further phenomenological analysis. Husserl's *The Crisis of the European Sciences,* partly a response to Heidegger on the question of the *Lebenswelt,* would be especially susceptible to such an approach. Mohanty thus reminds us that the major philosophical movements of this century, including linguistic analysis, have described themselves as forms of philosophical activity and practice, not as closed systems. Husserl claimed that phenomenology was a "strict science," not because it led to unimpeachable results, but because its methods, like those of the natural sciences, allowed for constant revision and reflection. Thus he saw himself as a "perpetual beginner."

Mohanty's qualified defense of phenomenological method may remind us that Gadamer used the title *Truth and Method* ironically, to contrast hermeneutical openness to the truth with the arbitrary limitations of all precise methods. As T. W. Adorno argues in his critique of Husserl, methodical thinking is always a variant of a metaphysics of presence (or what Anglo-American philosophers might call a "foundationalism"): "method, the regulated 'way,' is always the lawlike consequence of a successor to something earlier. Methodical thinking also demands a first, so that the way does not break off and end up being arbitrary. For it was devised against that. The procedure was so planned from the beginning that nothing could disturb it."[8] Is the self-enclosured impermeability of rigorous method compatible with a hermeneutics inclusive of historically and culturally divergent sources? Other doubts about Mohanty's optimism surface, perhaps analogous to those Dreyfus expresses about Gadamer's "fusion of horizons."

Phenomenological reflection seeks absolute forms of experience. Hermeneutics evaluates "texts," either actual writings or the sort embedded in social practices—what Foucault calls "discourses." The true heir to Heidegger's concern with the uncanny may be Jacques Derrida. His departure from classical phenomenology *and* hermeneutics pointedly occurs in his two books on Husserl, *Speech and Phenomena* and *The Origin of Geometry*, where he identifies the gap between pure thought and text in Husserl's work as emblematic of a general, untameable uncanniness. For Derrida, Husserl's need to embrace writing, textuality, and the historicity they make up reveals a basic ambiguity in his thought. A fruitful dialectic between phenomenology and hermeneutics—oriented toward the fusion of horizons—may be jeopardized by a fundamental difference beyond reconciliation.

Paul de Man's "Phenomenality and Materiality in Kant" offers a perspective on just such a radical form of interpretation. Well known as a senior member of the Yale or deconstructive school of literary criticism, de Man's program has differed from many of his American colleagues who have been primarily interested in applying deconstruction to literary works. De Man himself has stressed the philosophical importance of deconstruction. Moving from writers whose work has an obvious literary component (like Nietzsche and Rousseau) to others whose writings appear more explicitly philosophical (like Hegel and Kant), de Man aims to show that even classic texts made up of explicit philosophical logic are based upon a linguistic or tropological structure. To suggest that this is so in the case of Kant and the sublime, as he does in his essay here, is rich in implications. First, it casts doubts on the success of the champion of "normal" philosophy in having used and developed a strictly autonomous form of philosophical discourse. De Man's claim is that we can make sense of significant transitions in Kant's work only by appealing to an implicit tropological scheme. Second, by focusing attention on the topic of the sublime, de Man reminds us that the stress that he and others of his school have placed on discontinuity and difference is not a completely novel development in aesthetics and criticism. As the antithesis of the harmonious experience of beauty, the Kantian sublime, like deconstructive difference, articulates a model for understanding art quite distinct from the traditional (Aristotelian to New Critical) paradigm of organic unity.

De Man's project of deconstructing the philosophical text is an ambitious one bound to be controversial. Kant scholars may want to raise questions about the details of his reading; for example, one might try to undercut de Man's questioning of the transition from the mathematical to the dynamical sublime by claiming that the latter represents Kant's most fundamental concern, the former being added as an afterthought. Nevertheless, it is important not to lose sight of the larger issue that de Man raises—the question of whether philosophy's claim to an autonomous rationality and coherence can be supported even on the immediate level on which its basic documents are produced and read. This question, raised in modern times by Kierkegaard and Nietzsche, shows signs of becoming a central issue in the current form of philosophy's traditional need to reflect upon its own practices and products. These signs are also evident in contemporary concerns with literature.

Literature and hermeneutics

Until recently, literary criticism in the English-speaking world honored the purity of its object while resisting the demands of theory, especially if it were foreign. New Criticism, for a time the paradigmatic form among Anglo-American academics, ritually warned its followers to attend "the poem itself," to turn to it repeatedly for nourishment and inspiration. It distrusted peripheral sources, holding the integrity and autonomy of the work itself as paramount. Though overtly denying a philosophical grounding, its critical practice followed several theoretical fashions prevalent in the early part of the century; treating the object of inquiry as pristine, for instance, is hoary empiricist dogma. European theorists also adopted this methodological atomism, reinforcing an aversion to easy classifications (as in Benedetto Croce's denial of the reality of genres). Or, like Kant, they held absolute the irreducibility of the aesthetic to the conceptual. Concern with the isolated text gave the critic a trim field of inquiry, handily lending itself to the search for metaphor, image, or irony.

Of course, the critical world was hardly monolithic. For instance, Erich Auerbach's *Mimesis* and Ernst Curtius's *European Literature and the Latin Middle Ages* located literature within history, which gave these books their "European" flavor. Frye's *Anatomy of Criticism* argued powerfully for applying as generic concepts romance, comedy, tragedy, and satire. Moreover, Frye saw the text under analysis as related to others, while also expressing a specifiable tie with the social world. Nevertheless, it was still possible to do "normal" criticism— like Kuhn's "normal science"—with barely a glance at historical or systematic forms of literary awareness.

By the 1970s all was changed. Incursions of foreign enthusiasms—hermeneutics, structuralism, semiotics, deconstruction, and others—seriously challenged the critical hegemony of the "pure" text. Today this heterodoxy itself forms the traditional, having been assimilated to older patterns of criticism. The need for synthesis may have arrived. Geoffrey Hartmann tried demonstrating how Arnold, Pater, and Eliot might join Nietzsche, Lévi-Strauss, and Derrida in a new republic of letters. Like that earlier republic, the new one hopes to educate broadly, combining the Anglo-American penchant for teachable technique with the European devotion to *Bildung*, or formative culture. Such catholicity may fail, but excitement runs high when responsible writers dare to sidestep the weakening excesses of either Anglo-American empiricism or European esotericism.

The essays here put to use some of the strongest voices now heard in the new republic of letters. They include a call to re-evaluate the usefulness of biblical hermeneutics (Bruns), a debate on breaking down the barrier between literature and criticism (O'Neill and Spivak), and a postmodern meditation on the banality of some contemporary revivals of rhetoric (Stonum).

Bruns is closest to hermeneutics in Gadamer's sense. The thinkers of his concern interpreted the Bible, viewing accomplished interpretation as essential to understanding Scripture. Since the Bible has prompted the largest single hermeneutic enterprise, the history of that venture may aid analysts of other texts. We should note that Philo, Origen, and Augustine did not pursue a *method* of analysis (the goal of New Criticism *and* structuralism), but rather practiced textual meditation. As Bruns says, they cared less about a text's meaning than its teaching. They submitted to the authority of a text on the basis of their faith. Yet faith (like Heidegger's "fore-understanding") is not irreducible; it, too, enters the hermeneutic circle, seeking deeper understanding from the text. Bruns believes contemporary critics could well pursue truth rather than method. Gadamer would seem to agree, given the irony of the title *Truth and Method*, his repudiation of the facile certainty that comes from applying a strict method to every text. Proponents of a nontheoretical (even antitheoretical) *Geisteswissenschaften*, such as Roger Shattuck, are dismayed by the worship of analytical technique. They should be pleased with Bruns's reminder about textual meditation, since it counteracts the blind scientism that has accompanied the Americanization of semiotics, structuralism, poststructuralism, and so on. American literary critics have too often ridden the new wave of European thought in vain hopes of replacing stale methods.

But the concepts of "method" and "methodology" can be treacherous. Methodology as unvarying procedure may wrap the critic protectively, shielding him from serious challenges the text might make to his established views. The etymology of "method," on the other hand, points to a way or path to which a logos (or logos barbarized, as "science") has not been attached. A responsible critic will follow a selected path even if hacked out of the woods uncertainly. As Heidegger noted, many paths through the forest may cross, or strangely disappear into the brush, at that point when they yield illumination. The reactionary response to these European ideas—the belief that no help can come from "dialogue" with the text—undercuts the most vital current thinking. Threatened traditionalists will refuse to acknowledge the major concerns and questions of the day; those attracted by the prospect of universal methodology will be suspicious of alleged eclecticism. If, as Bruns suggests, our engagement with texts is a matter of faith seeking understanding, methodologists are ignorant of faith as such, while traditionalists refuse to employ understanding in more complete form.

John O'Neill's "Homotextuality: Barthes on Barthes, Fragments (RB), with a Footnote" stands out in form from the other essays. O'Neill's is a tribute to Barthes, an attempt to re-create the style of the very personal *Roland Barthes* by Barthes himself. After experimenting with various critical approaches to literature, Barthes focused on the plurality and undecidability of the text (notably in *S/Z*), and described reading as analogous to bodily and sexual experience (in *The Pleasure of the Text*). These two themes were combined and personalized in *Roland Barthes*, a work of aphorisms and musings, exploring the tension between a conventional unitary personality (the standard formula for autobiography) and the pluralizing activities of reading and writing which lead to constant shifts in perspective and emphasis.

O'Neill explores the interconnections of desire and language, of public writing and private life, by referring to *RB*. Barthes's writing and O'Neill's homage to it (both in his "Fragments" and "Footnote") are realizations of Marx's materialism and Freud's questioning of the autonomous, idealized Western subject. Beyond the antinomies of production and consumption, of rational and irrational, Barthes finds the play of writing and of the body. Play, as Gadamer has also observed, cannot be localized in an isolated subject; we say that we are "in play," not that play is in us. O'Neill distances himself in play, from the lofty seriousness of most hermeneutic work. Breaking down the distinction between the readerly and writerly text (which Barthes discusses in *S/Z*) is taken as a creative, liberating transgression of restrictive dualisms and outmoded categories. Fragmentation, such as O'Neill's, following Barthes's, refuses to concoct a false unity, assimilable to conventional perspectives. Writing becomes a series of pleasures, an alternation of *plaisir* (pleasure) and *jouissance* (bliss), as the eroticized body experiences that which lies outside the numbing economics of everyday life.

So Barthes and O'Neill deconstruct traditional, rigid modes of reading and writing. This may be the comic branch of deconstruction, cousin to Hegel's "Bacchanalian revel where not a member is sober" and Nietzsche's joy in the Dionysian. It proposes a liberated praxis, nearly within our reach if only the old ways can be set aside. And doesn't the history of literary criticism *and* of social mores (especially those regarding bodily pleasure) document an accelerating tendency to overthrow all rigid codifications? To this vision Gayatri Spivak replies rather soberly. She is suspicious of a leap into a textual and sexual utopia which may reproduce, in new forms, some of the same problems that inspired the escape. Spivak's critique is reminiscent of Marx and Engels's response to utopian socialism. They saw it as a premature attempt to realize a goal requiring work, dedication, and a grappling with resistant materials (what Hegel called "the labor of the negative"). Moreover, such prematurity runs the danger of all idealism, even when carried out in the name of the bodily and the material, i.e., to rely upon a privileged category that can blind us to the true heterogeneity of the world and the conflicts that make it up. Her deconstruction does not plot an escape from all oppositions, but offers "a morphology for disclosing complicities in place of oppositions." Rather than privileging the body over the mind, for example, such a practice will aim at showing what is false and misleading in the opposition of the two, unmasking their unsettling dialectic.

In this respect, as in others, deconstruction owes something to Nietzsche's "genealogy": the patient tracing of manifold links and incestuous connections, in place of the idealistic search for origins, or revolutionary delusions that the totally new is possible. Thus Spivak draws attention to problems of power, domination, and institutional forces vis-à-vis Barthesian writing, leading to a reading of his texts quite different from O'Neill's, and to a critique of the images of male and female implicit in the latter's essay. She believes O'Neill has produced a "homogenized" version of Barthes's text (consider the title, "Homotextualities"), eliminating the tension, struggle, and sense of institutional realities that she finds there. Thus, the darker version of deconstruction compels one to locate Barthes's seductive texts within the larger social and sexual economies of the era, and in so doing to resist his charms.

Both tragic and comic deconstruction partake of Heidegger's insight, that inquiry into texts is at once the analyst's self-inquiry. This is also the theme of Gary Stonum's "Surviving Figures" which analyzes the romantic tenet that "the letter killeth, but the spirit giveth life." If literal meaning is common and conventional, the romantic poet and his critical followers (Stonum names Ricoeur, de Man, and Bloom) contradict convention, seeing figurative language as a vital antidote to the banal. (This has much in common with O'Neill's portrayal of mind and body, and the continuous versus the erotically fragmented text.) A trope, or figurative expression, is etymologically a turning away or deviation from the usual, and as such offers us the chance to avoid or transform the mundane. But Stonum wonders if critics who so value linguistic deviation might not be caught by a dialectic destructive of just what they esteem. Tropes are classified, systematized, and explained. What was vibrant is thematized and analyzed; as a romantic poet wrote, "we murder to dissect." Tropology, as a universal science of figurative discourse, will transform the glorious anxiety of poetry into the merely calculable. To counter this, Stonum holds that figurative language is by its nature underdetermined by language and context. He illustrates this with an alternative to de Man's reading of a richly figurative passage from Proust.

Accepting Stonum's argument, one wonders what the alternative might be to modern tropology. Perhaps a negative theology of the figurative could be devised, limited to observing that any given trope is always "not this and not that." Yet here a historical, hermeneutic treatment of critical forms and styles is surely needed. How else to evaluate the long supremacy of rhetoric, its rapid demise after romanticism, then its new life as tropology? Here are hints of Bruns's opposition between a meditative approach to texts and the wish to master them. But these are less timeless modes of literary perception as forms of human activity, arising within particular social and intellectual contexts. This rage for order that Stonum detects in modern tropology is part of Heidegger's world of *Gestell*, that is, the form of life that regularizes, calculates, and controls all being. If so, the hope of reviving poetic language or practicing a negative theology of the figurative may be sadly quixotic. We must be mindful of this, not because Heidegger's dissection of social life (or the present manifestation of Being) is beyond question, but because hermeneutics's grander task finds itself there—the attempt to understand ourselves through dialogue with history. As the contributors to this volume variously point out, literary interpretation will be informed by history, or merely become a repeated technique, indifferently applied.

Social science and hermeneutics

   Anthony Giddens writes: "Today . . . real and profound convergences of interest and problems are occurring across broad spectra of intellectual life. Social theory is at the very center of these convergences, having both to contribute to and to learn from them." If social theory is taken to mean the type advanced by Giddens—and many today would argue that his style of theorizing is the most propitious—then he is probably correct. For the last dozen years, in nearly as many books, Giddens has charted a new course in his field. He has served as the major single conduit of relevant ideas between the Continent and England, and thus to the United States. Before other social theorists knew much about Habermas, Foucault, Lévi-Strauss, Gadamer, Paci, Lacan, and now Derrida and Kristeva (to name but the most famous), Giddens had already devised ways to include them in social theory, in addition to the unprecedented incorporation of Heidegger. Though the comparison may not withstand close scrutiny, since the two diverge in certain key enthusiasms (e.g., for Freud), one is apt to think of Giddens as England's answer to Habermas. Just now, for instance, both are engaged in dissimilar critiques of historical materialism.

   The essay in this volume speaks more compactly to the nature of a "hermeneutically informed social theory" than much of Giddens's recent work, though he began explicitly using contemporary hermeneutics in the mid-1970s. He followed intently the Habermas-Gadamer debate of the late 1960s, concluding that Gadamer probably surfaced in better shape but with ideas too "historicized" to benefit social theory as much as they have. In fact, Giddens evaluated Gadamer, Ricoeur, and Betti as a preliminary to sidestepping them, finally returning for his interpretive canons to Peter Winch's Wittgenstein, in very modified form. Giddens is not as interested in the problem of "prejudice" as was Habermas when he read *Truth and Method,* and neither did he fully accept Ricoeur's idea that social action could be interpreted as a text. Rather he harked back to Winch's intervention, that language and the social rules it facilitates must be taken seriously, that social actors are not dopes, but repositories of complex linguistic and interactional knowledge. This is the root of Giddens's interest in hermeneutics, and as such is quite apart from Gadamer's or even Habermas's. What is special, though, about Giddens's approach to theories of interpretation is his skillful adaptation of various fragments to his own purpose. For instance, from Ricoeur he took the interesting (and, as Dallmayr suggests, potentially problematic) notion of "virtual" reality; from Heidegger came the importance of "presencing" and incorporating time-space explicitly in social theory in a way not recently done; and from Derrida, a virtuoso hermeneuticist in his own right, he thematized the Husserlian fascination with the Other, with *differance* as a creative force in understanding.

"Hermeneutics and Social Theory" is a handy summary of Giddens's theory of structuration, something he assembled over a decade. In marching toward his own goal, he has tried to overcome many hindrances: the "orthodox consensus"; Winch's special hermeneutic of social life; Dilthey's alleged shortcomings, as well as Gadamer's, in defining hermeneutics in social thought; needless rigidities in Lévi-Strauss, Schutz, Weber, and many others. He quite consciously practices *Aufhebung,* which ties him to Habermas in that their bibliographies are equally vast. But Giddens refuses to use idealized models of life, and presents social existence in unvarnished terms, as the "play of differences" among contending forces, full of their own subjectivity and unresponsive to universal norms. He sees social actors as individuals, as capable and sophisticated. In fact in his effort to "recover the subject," even after its de-centering, he theoretically downgrades, de-hypostatizes social structure and social institutions radically. Structure becomes "rules and resources instantiated in social systems, but having only a 'virtual existence.'" That is, they exist only in the doing, just as "language" exists (for Ricoeur) only virtually, while speech carries on in fact, aware of its dependence upon rules, but always threatening their hegemony as it moves its own way in suiting ephemeral needs of speakers. Although fitting unintended consequences of action into his theory—which includes the unconscious, though not psychoanalytically taken—he rejects "function" and "systemic needs" completely. One might ask if he protests too much in distancing himself from earlier structural-functionalist thinkers, to whom, it is clear, he owes something.

But Giddens's real contiguity with others in this volume comes in the form of his "double hermeneutic." The first part of hermeneutic labors, in the social theory he favors, involves interpreting social action as the result of forces, needs, intentions, and cultural processes, in a Weberian sense. The subtler half comes in realizing that the language one uses in categorizing observable action is itself a human product, and as such full of its own wishes for what one might call intellectual supremacy. Giddens cannot accept either Winch's or Schutz's comments on this problem, but neither does he offer a definitive solution to the question of "adequacy" between theory and action, posed by Weber and others. Happily, though, he is aware that social theory, as part of a hermeneutic dialogue between social action and theories used to construe it, can contribute either to "forms of exploitative domination," or in "promoting emancipation."

In Fred Dallmayr we find an ideal respondent to Giddens's ideas. Dallmayr's *Twilight of Subjectivity: Contributions to a Post-Individualist Theory of Politics* (Amherst: University of Massachusetts Press, 1981) carefully dissects many of the writers who also interest Giddens. What makes Dallmayr's questioning of Giddens so stimulating is his very different goal: first, to supply political science, not sociology, with a general theory, and second, to discover if in the latest ideas from Europe lie hope for an emancipatory understanding and restructuring of the polity. Dallmayr seems fully aware of Giddens's general purpose, "incorporating the lessons of ontology and post-structuralism *without* abandoning concern with the 'knowledgeability' and accountability of actors; . . . of moving beyond subjectivist metaphysics *without* relinquishing some of its insights, and especially *without* lapsing into objectivism and determinism." These thorny traditional antinomies have not put Giddens off the scent of a theory capable of resolving them, and Dallmayr seems impressed overall with his moves between subjective Charybdis, objective Scylla, and the waystations in between.

Yet problems with this sort of program must arise. For Dallmayr, Giddens's "novel correlation of agency and structure"— the fruit of his theory of structuration and its double hermeneutic—seems "somewhat vacillating and ambivalent; . . . his approach seems reluctant at points to draw the full implications from the adopted perspective." The adoption Dallmayr refers to is from Derrida's usage of *"differance,"* "the structuring of structure," and seeing structure as "an absent set of differences," hence, the "virtual." As Dallmayr notes, Derrida was working not only ontic terrain in his Husserlian derivation, but ontological as well, which, almost by definition as a social theorist, Giddens is hardpressed to follow. He is virtually forced to evade the " 'transcendental' dimension" so much a part of Derrida's task. The upshot is that "virtuality" of structure as Giddens writes of it bears more substantial affinity with the antique manifest-latent dichotomy than with poststructuralist "advances." Dallmayr is also worried by Giddens's rather unreconstructed reliance upon Wittgenstein's theory of rules, particularly regarding "recursive social practices." It would seem that a proper hermeneutic of Giddens's work would require lexical analysis of both "virtual order" and "recursiveness," since they act as axes around which so much of his innovation turns. Dallmayr also finds uncertainty in Giddens's understanding of agency, where "the peculiar nexus of action and nonaction within agency itself" is left untreated, with the result that the theory of structuration cannot deal with such Heideggerian insertions as "suffering" and "caring." Finally, Dallmayr points to Giddens's proposition that social science is afflicted with data that answer back, with "interpretation of preinterpretation" as its major duty—as well as its opportunity. The problem here originates in Giddens's simultaneous acceptance of something like a "universal hermeneutics," while taking serious exception to the correlative claim that in hermeneutics lay solutions for social science at large. Dallmayr finds Giddens's tilting toward *verstehen* over *erklaeren* a weak response to this general issue, though, as before, he recognizes his courage in wrestling with this and related difficulties, while trying to save "the subject" in a theoretically defensible way.

W. H. Dray has been known for many years as an expert interpreter of historiography. In his essay in this book he analyzes four current modes of understanding the English Civil War, the Whig, Marxist, "social interpretation," and revisionist. Dray's essay is in some ways a relief from much of what precedes it in the book, since the language is clear, in English, and pertains to a historical episode famous enough to guarantee immediate reader sympathy. In all these, his work differs from many contemporary hermeneutic exercises, which rely upon neologisms, foreign terms of gnostic importance (*wirkungsgeschichtliche Bewusstsein, aletheia, differance, Sein, parole, ad nauseum*), and obscure referents, or common ones rendered mysterious. Dray is clearly of another camp, one that recalls a less self-conscious, less worried approach to interpreting events, social or textual. His is the clearest instance in the book of Anglo-American sensibility, its willingness to deal directly with the observable, or to hypothesize about the unobservable straightforwardly. There is no longing for invisible structure à la Lévi-Strauss, Foucault, or Althusser, nor for probing the motivations of historical actors at subterranean depth. Facts are taken either as definable as such or as prefactual, and therefore unworthy of inclusion in serious causal models. It is on this level, more or less, that Dray takes to task all four interpretive models for the Civil War. But he is especially rigorous in showing analytical sloppiness in two—the social interpretation school, exemplified by Lawrence Stone, and the Marxist.

By choosing to assay a series of historical events that add up to a set piece, Dray can deal directly with the problem of causes, their priority and relative weight, without suffering through endless conceptual or terminological preliminaries. Some, sensitive to current hermeneutic, semiotic, or poststructural debates, might argue that this conceals more than it reveals. But Dray's robust argument, particularly with Stone's account of the Civil War, seems well suited for this type of interchange, where what is knowable (that Charles lost his head) and what is unknowable (what Charles thought a half-hour before) take on meanings different from those in the "texts" more typically treated by hermeneuticists. Dray's game is to precisely define an event (how it is categorized by a given interpreter and whether the categorization fits, logically and historically, with others in the interpreter's toolkit) and then to check the results against those of competing interpretive schemes. By doing this he can nip at the heels of writers in all four camps, but most tellingly with Stone's "preconditions," "precipitants," and "triggers" of historical action, and with the Marxist struggle to define where and when bourgeois or proletarian elements figured in the Civil War.

Dray's general complaint repeats what historians have said to generalizers (theorists and social scientists, philosophers of history, and so on) for two centuries: how can one decide when a historical event begins, how it is constituted, what it accomplished, what actually transpired—and then, most critically, compare this heuristic to others, perhaps separated by centuries in time, sea changes in thought?

He chides Stone for admitting that "historians can only weight causes 'intuitively,' at any rate 'in the last resort,'" calling this an "embarrassment." But isn't this the kind of embarrassment "good" historians have always seemed to pull off when "poor" ones did not? The notion that "intuiting" differences is degenerate intellectual labor would only arise—as Heidegger and others explained—in an era in which intelligence is equated with demonstrable precision, something a historian can seldom deliver. Dray pursues other important theoretical issues, perhaps in spite of his credentials as a historian, such as the usefulness of "a theory of principled judgment with regard to the relative importance of causes"; the need to consider "enabling conditions" beyond the control of historical agents; the place of chance and coincidence in causal models; and—perhaps most interesting given Dilthey's place in hermeneutic history—the call to "read history forwards": "giving an account of it from the standpoints of the original agents." In the end though, Dray sticks to the historian's traditional side of the platform, letting a little theory go a long way and watching it carefully lest it throw aside or trample too many hard-won "facts" from the record.

Just as with Giddens and Dallmayr, Dray's critic is expertly conversant with the matters at hand. Rex Martin's own monograph, *Historical Explanation* (Ithaca: Cornell University Press, 1977) partakes of a formalist tradition more in keeping with American than Continental philosophy of history. The driving force behind such analyses is a sharp, insistent habit of mental experimentation in which one asks: If an event can be identified clearly, would its presence in history be felt differently with certain key components altered? Though formalized (e.g., "chance" is expressed as the "crossing of finite and independent causal chains"), Martin's cross-examination of Dray's interpretive effort seems to owe as much to Socratic inquiry as to formal logic. It may at first, for the uninitiated, seem shocking to watch the machinery of logical analysis at work on a phenomenon as historically mundane as the English Civil War. But Martin's handiwork pays off, since he is able to systematize Dray's argument, then crisply point out its strengths and weaknesses.

Martin sees Dray as most sympathetic with the revisionist posture. "Several causal paradigms" make it up, including an appreciation of chance in historical occurrence as well as unintended consequences; "agent or intentionalistic causation" as the dominant "explanation form" (what social theorists label "voluntarism"); a theoretical aspiration toward understanding "principled judgment"; and "Dravian abnormalism," the search for genuinely intrusive, disruptive events that are thus identifiable as the beginnings of causal chains. This way of summarizing Dray's critique of others and, at the same time, his own positive formulation, is leagues away from Dray's own discursive style or cognitive frame. But with this new language Martin can say things—can make interpretations—that Dray probably could not, setting aside the question of whether he would care to. For instance, "Always, though, such unintended effects are secondary in that if the agent had never done what he did intentionally, or tried to do, he would never have brought about what he did bring about, unintentionally, as an effect of what he did intentionally." Martin is comfortable with such reasoning because, one would think, he can easily imagine historical facts or events fitting into it, and thereby being uniquely illuminated. But, owing perhaps to a distantiation from Hegelianism, historicism, and other correctives to the healthy simplicity of positivism, formulations such as Martin's risk violating a hermeneutical proposition dating from Schleiermacher. The content of consciousness is historically variable, making what Dray calls "motive analysis"—which Martin does not mention, but relies upon nonetheless—a tricky business. Establishing "finite causal chains," "quasi-causal patterns," "intersecting chains," and the like requires as an a priori, some sort of *Nacherleben* or "reliving," a distinctly nineteenth-century prospect when viewed today, but no less difficult and necessary for being so. Dray accused Stone, in practicing "social interpretation," of covering his traditional historical technique with a veneer of social science terms, adding little to explanatory power. One wonders if the language of analytic causal analysis completely escapes a similar plight. Still, Martin produces in short compass what Dray left unsaid, a clear statement of the logic in play, and what can be expected of it; no mean hermeneutic achievement.

The essays in this volume are broad in their coverage of contemporary hermeneutics, but they hardly exhaust the field. Rather than delineating here the boundaries of interpretive theory as applied in numerous disciplines today, we ask the reader to consult the book's bibliography. It is a selective list of works in English, most of them quite recently published. By considering the range of topics within hermeneutics as suggested by the bibliography, one easily understands the appeal of this field for scholars interested in bringing together what is often left in pieces; the synthetic possibilities seem limitless.

· · · · ·

1

Philosophy and Hermeneutics

· · · · ·

complex and potentially rewarding than they could be. Both my interpretive biases—stressing Betti's Italianness and his juristic background—are supported by his autobiography, *Notazioni autobiogra-
fiche* (Padova: CEDAM, 1953). The *Teoria* was the product of a difficult moment in Italian culture, and it came from a scholar whose
lifework had been the study of legal institutions as both results and
causes of human events. In fact, the idea for the book, his crowning
achievement, grew out of the political persecution he experienced just
after World War II. The principal evidence of Betti's "suspect" politics—for which he was interned—were articles in the *Corriere della
sera* arguing that the Anglo-American legal tradition was more concerned with the defense of property than the enhancement of life, that
post-war Europe should not ally itself with this tradition, and that a
North Atlantic Treaty Organization should be rejected in favor of a
pan-European alliance. Finally, and most objectionable at the time, he
argued that the Soviet Union, if willing to abandon imperialist ambitions, should be part of such an alliance. Thus, reading Betti's *Teoria*
as a political document (though not a party document, for being a
party man was something he rejected) becomes quite necessary.

Betti also mentions that the *Teoria* was most influenced by the
famous Nicolai Hartmann as well as Adelchi Baratono, scarcely known
outside Italy, and for a time Betti's colleague. Baratono's chief philosophical task was elaborating a materialist epistemology. This, and
the concept of form underlying it, grounds Betti's entire project,
which must be seen as not simply a type of reworked German idealism, but as contributing to the development of Italian materialism.
Aspects of Betti's hermeneutics that seem to me most significant have
remained invisible to non-Italian readers. For example, Josef Bleicher's
account of Betti (*Contemporary Hermeneutics* [London: Routledge
and Kegan Paul, 1980], pp. 29–94), while useful and acute, nonetheless treats him as if he were a German writer, and a rather parochial
one at that, unaware of sources in languages other than German.
Handling Betti this way curiously skews Bleicher's narrative of the
development of hermeneutics, particularly post-Gadamerian. Crudely
put: Habermas criticized Gadamer for limiting the hermeneutic context to language, for omitting labor and domination. Habermas was
also criticized by Lorenzer and Sandkuehler for semi-idealism. These
critiques, of putative idealist flaws, go back to Gadamer's reaction to
Betti. This "first" gesture within recent hermeneutic debate is incor-
rect, for Betti's epistemology, and its materialist concept of form, is

. . . . .

The Epistemological Problem of Understanding As an Aspect of the General Problem of Knowing

Emilio Betti

. . . . .

Translator's introduction

Emilio Betti's *Teoria generale della interpretazione* is the prover-bial elephant; each blind man proclaiming the small part within his reach to be the entire beast. Betti's opus is indeed mammoth, a crea-ture unlike anything normally encountered in libraries and academies. It intimidates even its translator, for many reasons. First, Betti's is an Italian book—written in the language and published in Italy by a native scholar—something crucial to its interpretation. And yet the book is vigorously international by design. Betti proclaimed himself a European, politically and culturally, at a time when saying so was risky. His father stressed the study of English and German, and his knowledge of them gave him lifelong, intimate access to traditions many of his peers lacked. His hermeneutics has received far more at-tention in the Anglo-Saxon and German spheres than in Betti's home-land, where leading students of literary theory admit they have not read him. Nevertheless, the "Italianness" of his hermeneutics I find instructive, perhaps reflecting my apprenticeship in philology, not philosophy. This is consonant with Schleiermachian (traditional) her-meneutic principles, not so discredited today as some believe.

It is similarly important that Betti was a legal scholar and theor-ist. The obvious connection between law and hermeneutics does not in itself explain how Betti's project is the work of a jurist. Italian jurisprudence has been conspicuously philosophical in character since at least Vico's time. The *Scienza nuova* is solidly rooted in the law, in the kind of mind that makes the law its principal object of inquiry. For Vico law seemed the most human of all human products, more informative about social life than even art, literature, or music; more anything but idealist. This sort of accusation ignores his real originality.

Choosing a suitable excerpt from the *Teoria* has been difficult, since no single passage can adequately represent 950 pages. This translation opens Betti's introduction to the book, following a prolegomenon on objectivity in relation to mind, since he believes an adequate theory of interpretation must reckon with representational form. Betti's approach to this problem depends upon Baratono's notion of form, also drawing heavily on Peirce (cf. my "Hermeneutics and Semiotics: Betti's Debt to Peirce," *Proceedings 1982*, Semiotics Society of America). The translated excerpt is part of a chapter on representational forms; in the larger volume, it is followed by another on hermeneutic gnosiology, since Betti casts his theory in the role of interpreting mass culture, i.e., as hermeneutic sociology. A third introductory chapter details hermeneutic method. Chapters 4 through 9 rigorously treat three types of interpretation: recognitive, reproductive, and normative, and their subtypes. The *Teoria*'s last chapter covers the phenomenology of interpretation in relation to its historical development, emphasizing the role of interpretation in ethics and its socially integrative function.

The *Teoria* may initially seem of encyclopedic ambitions. In fact, Betti's treatment of interpretable materials is exemplary, not exhaustive. Questions may arise, of course, about his criteria of selection. For example, he treats music prominently, while touching lightly on literature (with the exception of drama), because his system is grounded in Baratono's sensist analysis of representational form. Thus, Betti's system obliges him to analyze sound, following the analogy to the Ciceronian topics. Systematic needs rather than comprehensiveness motivate his selection of interpreted objects and the weight he assigns each.

The excerpt presented here tends to support what I have urged in understanding Betti's hermeneutics. Not only is Baratono's concept of form introduced in the first sentence, but the paradox embodied there is also his. Along with the German influences normally associated with Betti's work, American language theory and semiotics also play their parts. Betti explores semiotics, but believes his subject matter carries him beyond its borders. In his hierarchy semiosis is the simplest, least interesting form of "linking." Betti's legal background is also evident, explicitly and implicitly, e.g., in explaining the relation of document to statement (the penultimate sentence of para-

graph 1 and especially *ivi*, n. 6). Betti's style is not as infected with
"legalese" as it may seem, for each word is used precisely. In the last
sentence of paragraph 1, Betti writes of mental endowment as *"trat-
tenuta, incorporata e fissata"* in its material support. Apparently
identical in meaning, each of these past participles designates a distinct state: cessation of movement, the integration of one thing in
another, and a final changelessness, the endpoint of a process. Betti's
"codifications," then, are not gratuitous.

A few remarks on the translation. Since Italian, rather like German is capable of more complex hypotaxis than English, the translation bears the mark of this discrepancy in its sentence structure. I
have often, for example, added "on the one hand . . . on the other,"
to help realize contrasts within a lengthy sentence, contrasts organized for the Italian reader by syntax (gender, number). There are
terminological problems, too. To translate *"spirito"* simply as "spirit"
is etymological literalism (an error common to English versions of
Croce); *"spirito"* is polyvalent: *nutrire lo spirito* means "nourish the
mind" in the Garzanti dictionary; *spirito pratico* is "practical tempera-
ment"; for *condizione di spirito*, "mood"; for *presenza di spirito*,
"presence of mind." I have followed Betti's usage (in translating
Peirce and other Anglo-Saxon writers into Italian) in the case of
spirito, as in several others. In section 1 c, Betti translates Peirce's
"some mind" as *uno spirito pensante;* I have also translated *spiritual-
ita* as "mind." Betti's terminology in section 1 c, for concepts of "context" or "linkage," is also difficult, as signaled by the punctuation in
the first sentence of the paragraph which opens: "Given that experience is characterized by the recurrence of phenomena [as links] in
chains (contexts). . . ." This paragraph defines "context," a word
Betti uses in English, in parentheses, in this first sentence; yet nowhere in this paragraph does he use the equivalent Italian word,
"contesto." Typically, he chooses a more concrete term than used by
the source he is employing (Ogden and Richard's *Meaning of Meaning*): *concatenazione* (linkage), based on *catena* (chain). His term is
actually closer to the Latin *contextus*, indicating linkage in discourse.
Though Betti's use of *concatenazione* throughout the passage is consistent, English usage at points dictates "chain," then "context," even
"link." *Concatenazione* is less abstract than *contesto* and conveys the
idea more forcefully.

About translating the notes: in the original the brief passage
translated here is accompanied by 150 of them. The stringent re-

quirements of publishing today do not permit reproducing these. In hoping to give the reader some notion of Betti's annotative style and the way it aids his argument, and to provide basic information about his sources where complete information had to be omitted, I translated the first eight notes in their entirety, then condensed each of the remaining notes for sections 1 and 1 a. For sections 1 b and 1 c, I have summarized the principal references, without mentioning a number of others.

This brief Introduction takes traditional hermeneutic form. I have treated the *Teoria* as a classic text, and commented on it primarily in relation to its author's biography, to its period and sources, without seriously analyzing or questioning its content. The history of the reception of Betti's text justifies this tack. Such elementary matters have been neglected, while the work has been dismissed as "romantic" and "psychologistic"—the criticism found in *Truth and Method*. Analytic arguments can be made in countering such opinions. But before the whole creature can be understood, it must become visible; meanwhile, a good many blind men have to encounter and name many different parts.

Susan Noakes

1. *The object of understanding. The concept of representational form.*

Whenever we find ourselves in the presence of sensible forms, through which another spirit, objectified in them, speaks to ours, calling upon our intelligence,[1] our interpretive activity begins to move, trying to understand what sense those forms have, what message they are sending us, what they mean to us. From living and fleeting speech to the motionless document and monument, from writing to the conventional sign, to the number and to the artistic symbol, from language that is articulated, poetic, narrative, deductive, to language that is not articulated, like that which is figured or musical,[2] from the statement to the silent gesture and to personal behavior, from physiognomy and the expression of the face to the direction of conduct and the manner of behavior,[3] everything that comes to us from another mind extends a call to be understood, a request and a message to our sensibility and our intelligence.[4] Certainly we must not confuse the various levels and dimensions in which these objectifications of mind present themselves to us. On the contrary, we should carefully keep the language and meaning, which alone interests us, distinct from the sounds that embody it, from the notations and the signs that fix it;[5] keep distinct the statement from the document the function of which is to represent that statement and to identify it, whether with respect to communication or to certification.[6] We must, in general, carefully keep ourselves from confusing, on the one hand, the support of perceptible material instrument, which—however evanescent or lasting it may be—belongs to the dimension of the physical world, which serves more or less as vehicle, with, on the other hand, the mental endowment entrusted to it; an endowment, with symbolic force, which is, so to speak, held fast, incorporated, and fixed in this material support; an endowment whose content of mind and thought belongs to a dimension radically different from that of the physical world.[7]

But on the other hand, and with equal force, we must always maintain (against the contrary prejudice, perennially reborn) this fundamental concept: that no interpretation can arise without a *representational form*.[8] In this expression the word "form" should be understood in the very broad sense outlined by my late lamented friend Adelchi Baratono,[9] as a unitary relationship of sensible elements, suited to preserve the mark of the one who has molded it or of the one who incarnates it (for example: the face of a person), and the qualification of "representational" function is to be understood in the sense that *another mind* different from ours and nonetheless intimately linked with ours must make itself recognizable to us through the form, calling upon our sensibility and intelligence.[10] The need for representational forms in which the mind of another is objectified, while it leads back to the dialectical antithesis between intimate being immanent in itself (*An-sich-sein*) and being recognizable to others (*Sein-für-Anderes*), elaborated by Hegel[11] as a necessary position of speculative thought, on the other hand is only an aspect of that fundamental need for recognizability (by other community members), which is obeyed by all the communicative and social life of beings endowed with mind.[12] Indeed (as should be obvious) it is only by means of representational forms, given in perception or capable of being evoked once again in memory, which present objectified the mind of another, that men achieve understanding of one another, making communal bonds among themselves and setting up communions of mind in their reciprocal relations.[13]

For a first and provisional classification of such representational forms, we can derive some suggestion of an analogy from the distinction made among the *res*, set forth in the Ciceronian topics, V, 26,[14] keeping in mind that we will have to make their relationship to one another clearer further on (sec. 3).

The distinction, which Cicero probably takes from the Greek academicians, may be adapted by analogy also to the representational forms which are the object of interpretation, provided that we are careful, on the one hand, to relate some of these forms to any perception whatever, not only those that are tactile or visible, but also the auditory ones, including within this category the figure of sound, whether articulated (le voces lingua figuratae) or musical (the "Tonbild," as some call it),[15] and, on the other hand, to relate others to the forms not given in present perception, but capable of being called back in memory (sec. 3), or in any case, purely intelligible as "notions" translatable in well-defined formulations, without material support (corpus) except that of written or oral tradition, always indispensable for the objectification of oneself in the dimension of the phenomenal world.

Leaving aside for later analysis both the structure of the symbol and the manner of being of the mental endowment entrusted to it, we must henceforward reject, as a return to the materialistic prejudice just now deplored, the tendency to conceive of the representational forms, and in particular of statements, as a sort of veil or packaging, with the shedding of which one would bring about something like a transmission and reception of the thought that would be found "enclosed" in it.[16] In fact, humans get to the point of understanding one another not by exchanging material signs of things or by setting out to produce exactly the same idea by means of some sort of exchange automatism, but rather by reciprocally putting into motion, each one of them, the same link from the chain of his own representations or conceptions, and—to adopt a figurative image[17]— by touching in each other the same string of each individual mental instrument, as if to sound a chord, so that ideas corresponding to those of the one who speaks or writes will be stimulated in the one who listens or reads.[18] Indeed the doors of the mind can be opened only from the inside,[19] through an inner spontaneity, and that which is received is only an incitation to vibrate in harmony with the stimulus, as a function of the energy that communicates its signifying or semantic value.[20] The evocative energy of the message that has been cast forth is not something innate in it for itself alone, but the fruit of collaboration on the part of the one who is called to gather it up; it depends, therefore, on its own suitable disposition, openness and sensitivity to such excitation, on its commitment and interest, and on the infinite variety of contingencies that can influence it.[21] The nexus of reciprocity between the message and the collaboration requested from the one who is called to gather it up recalls the image of the seed thrown on earth which the most various contingencies can make fecund or resistant, which is an image that comes up in the evangelist's parable of the sower.[22]

A sower went forth to sow. And when he sowed, some seeds fell by the wayside, and the fowls came and devoured them up. Some fell upon stony places, where they had not much earth; and forthwith they sprung up, because they had no deepness of earth; and when the sun was up, they were scorched; and because they had no root, they withered away. And some fell among thorns; and the thorns sprung up, and choked them. But other fell into good ground and brought forth fruit: some a hundredfold, some sixtyfold, some thirtyfold. Who hath ears to hear, let him hear.

(That is, understand).[23]

1a   The process of understanding: its triadic character. Although the phenomenon of language in relation to the problem of the symbol remains to be analyzed later, we can say at this point that the representational or semantic function in social life is entrusted above all to language, whether this language consists of words, that is, of discourse, or of other signs and expressive means: formulae, images, figures, and sounds. In the social sphere the instrument most used to display a thought and to communicate it to others is the *statement*. In statements, both the representational end and the reliance that is placed on the intelligence by a larger or smaller circle of addressees are more evident. Or perhaps what is more evident is the mediation entrusted to the representational instrument in the sense of reawakening the idea of that which is represented; and the interpretation becomes a collaboration that the addressee extends to the author of the statement, inasmuch as he is called upon to reawaken in his own mind the idea conceived and expressed by the mind of the author.[24]

Moreover, interpretation does not necessarily presuppose that

the thought be expressed in symbols with a view to a representational goal, with a communicative intent and an interest dependent
upon the life of relationship.[25] Even a "manifestation" devoid of such
interest and a behavior not in itself directed toward making a
thought recognizable to others[26] may be the object of interpretation,
when what is at issue is, in the case of such a "manifestation," the
derivation of the expressive value proper to it, its style of art or of
life, or, in the case of such a behavior, the drawing forth from this
behavior, seen as a sign or index, of a taking of position or an
orientation, which is *revealed* there, that is to say, the manner of
conceiving and of valuing with which it shows itself objectively to
be imbued.[27] In particular, there inheres in any form of practical
activity an *implicit*, or perhaps *symptomatic*, representational value,
insofar as one can infer from it, by indirect deduction,[28] an index
to the personality at work, its manner of conceiving and of understanding, which is betrayed there and which—for the interpreter—it
is a matter of digging out and of representing explicitly, while reflecting upon it.[29] Such a deduction may turn out to be difficult, or
even impossible, in the case of a single practical act, when one knows
neither the circumstances nor the antecedents nor the consequences,
which form together with that act the links in a chain; but when
these are known, at once a reference becomes possible to that whole
that is the personality of the author.

Interest in exploring the implicit representational value of practical behaviors arises with special intensity in the jurist and in the
historian, naturally with a difference in directions determined by
their different responsibilities. In the jurist the interest arises above
all in relation to the interpretation of mores and habits, of constitutional and administrative practice,[30] of legal agreements, for which
the behaviors in question may constitute the available evidence, or
the clarifying or unifying elements, that is, indices to a manner of
seeing, and symptoms of an authentic interpretation, which the authors of the behaviors themselves give with their action to the rule
they have actualized.[31] In the historian an analogous interest, but
differently oriented, arises from the fact that practical attitudes, by
the very absence of a conscious representational finality, are the most
genuine and sincere indices or symptoms which reveal the mentality
of the authors: the historian's interest arises in response to the task
of reconstructing from the line of conduct that is actually followed,
the real manner of conceptualizing and of understanding problems,

the theoretical statement of which can be weakened by the interference of tendencies that distort and by a lack of disinterestedness.
One must note, however, that even in the cases just now described,
the object of interpretation is nonetheless always the realization of
a thought that is revealed[32] objectively in a practical attitude, since
the practical attitude is valorized as an indirect, or rather implicit,
presentation (expression) or a given manner of thinking; so that this
attitude, considered under the heading of such symptomatic value,
can well be qualified as a representational form in the wide sense of
an objectification of mind, the sense that we have here adopted. It
is at this point that we enter into the field of hermeneutics, with a
distinction based on the criterion of the direct or indirect, explicit or
implicit, character of the representational function attributed to the
form: a distinction, through this identical criterion, comes back in
perfectly analogous forms in other fields. Thus, in the field of legal
agreements and acts, those concerned with civil law have intuited for
a long time the distinction between statement and actual behavior;[33]
in the field of proof, specialists in judicial procedure have intuited
the analogous distinction between representational proof (historical)
and critical proof (indiciary); in the material that is the source of historical cognition historians have delineated the difference between
representational sources passed on by written, oral, or figurative
tradition and remnants, vestiges, or surviving rudiments of the era
studied, the latter characterized by the absence of conscious aim at
any representational function and, in addition, by the correlation
that ties such fragments to the whole of the past age, of which it is
the index of recognition.[34]

   In response to a misunderstanding rather widespread among
jurists, one can never insist enough on the concept that in practical
behaviors, no less than in statements, the object of interpretation is
not the "will" as such, but always only the form, in which the will
is carried out and realized: that which has been said or that which
has been done.[35] The "will" can and will be, like the logical or
aesthetic sense, that which is inferred from the practical attitude
through interpretation; therefore it is not the object of interpretation, but rather one of its results, that is to say, one of the goals of
hermeneutic determination. When, therefore, one speaks, as often
happens, of interpreting the "will," because (1) one is alluding to the
outcome of the interpretive process and is using a phrase improperly,
because, on the one hand, the action is exchanged for the outcome

or because, on the other, at least in law, what is being designated is
the normative *vis ac potestas* (an entity not reducible to the psychological plane); or because (2) one is referring to the object and
is adopting an ambiguous formula, since rather than alluding to the
will it alludes elliptically to its objective carrying out in social life;
or because (3) if by "will" one means properly a pure internal
psychological entity, it leads one to think that the interpretation may
do without a representational form, which is absurd.

It is less likely that an analogous misunderstanding should arise
in fields other than law in which interpretation is called upon to
carry out its task. The works of art and of poetry which the human
mind has conceived and shaped, the extremely varied forms which
the genius and the hand of man have fashioned and modeled, the
remnants and surviving rudiments of the past of humanity, are all
objectifications of mind, which, since they were at their origin im-
printed or molded by a mind, thus depend on the collaboration of
another mind, which in the present may again find, know, and
awaken these forms.[36]

Whether, then, such an objectification of mind has stamped its
mark on a lasting material by means of which it has been preserved,
or whether—evanescent in itself, as practical behaviors in general
are—it survives only in the memory or in tradition,[37] does not make
an essential difference: in the case of either hypothesis the interpreter always finds himself confronted with representational forms
that are direct or indirect, immediate or mediate, of first or second
degree. It is not to such differences that we must call attention here,
but rather to what is constant in the interpretive process, to the
features that this process always presents, even in the variety of attitudes and nuances that this process assumes and must assume, in
conformity with the needs of the object to be interpreted and as a
function of the different purposes and problems that must arise,
according to the various orientations of the interest in understanding.
The position is always that of a mind to which come a message and
a stimulus from the objectification of another mind, whether personal and individually identifiable or *impersonal* and superindividual.[38] The relationship between one mind and another always has
a *triadic* character:[39] the interpreter is called upon to understand the
sense, whether it is intentional or objectively recognizable; that is,
he is called upon to communicate with the mentality of another
through the representational forms in which this mentality has ob-

jectified itself. Communication between the two is never direct, but always mediated by this intermediary term.

1b Understanding, as a psychological phenomenon. First of all, before examining in depth the process of understanding, it will be useful to characterize it negatively, delimiting it above all—from a phenomenological viewpoint—from other modes of event, insofar as it is considered a psychological phenomenon that is the object of knowledge like other phenomena; delimiting it, moreover—from the viewpoint of gnosiology—from other modes of knowing insofar as it is itself considered a process of knowledge, an epistemological process.

From the *phenomenological* viewpoint, understanding as a *psychological* phenomenon is to be differentiated essentially from any event that is ruled purely by the law of causality. And here at the outset it is necessary to reject the naturalistic theory of behavior or of so-called prelinguistic meaning, held by Anglo-American psychologists who are followers of the movement known as "behaviorism,"[40] and to reaffirm the conception of linguistic understanding delineated by Humboldt. For naturalistic theory, the crucial question is whether the (overt) activity provoked in the perceiver of the prelinguistic sign necessarily indicates the attribution of a signified, in the sense associated with the interpretation of signs. In an affirmative response to this question a weakness is inherent: it offers no sure discriminatory criterion for distinguishing interpretation and understanding from other habitual acts suggested by an illation, and it leads us to name any stimulus to which there is a habitual reaction—or from which an inference is habitually made—a "sign," that is, an index, and thus to identify any reaction and illation made in this way with the interpretive process. Then, holding that one can equate "causation and understanding or interpretation," and recognizing as the element characteristic of understanding the single fact that "recurrence of only a part of the context cause (*sic*) us to react in the way we reacted before," one falls into the error of taking as already proven exactly what remains to be proved: for the question is whether the evocative element is indeed sufficient to justify a causal theory of signification. When, finally, one asserts that an observable, directly *perceptible* quality of entities given by experience, something that would be intuited as constitutive of the datum of perception, is the signified, it is clear that then, too, we are trapped in a logical fallacy, using what still remains to be demonstrated as a basic assumption: indeed, the signified is not perceived, but rather understood: it is not something that is simply and passively transmitted from outside, but rather a constitutive element of a spontaneous process of knowing.

From the *gnosiological* viewpoint, understanding, as a process of *knowledge* aimed at the acquisition of specific knowledge—an epistemological process—is differentiated essentially from other modes of knowing, and above all in this way from *deduction by concepts* that are predefined or by the operations of calculation—which is the method proper to the mathematical sciences—as also from *induction* or *explanation from causes:* which is the method proper to the physical or, in general, the experimental sciences. This is not to deny that the internal progress of such sciences depends not only on a means of proceeding independent of speculation or of observation, but also on an elaboration of acquired knowledge, which moves in fact from a scientific interpretation of the doctrines that have been inherited, while in the final analysis looking, through a critical evaluation of them, to a deepening of their meaning or to a reexamination of their conclusions, in order to derive from them further developments. But this type of understanding—at least until it is confined within the limits of an interpretation—is subject to the logic of its own particular object, and its method does not extend beyond this particular area. On the other hand, in cases where knowledge does not have for its object predefined concepts like those of mathematics, or phenomena of the physical world governed by the law of causality, but instead objectifications of mind, it is clear that the method called for by that different object cannot be transferred from that of deduction by abstract concepts or of induction by natural causes. Here, for the precise position of the epistemological problem, there is no need to see in the objectification something (a logical entity) that is resolvable, with no residue, into abstract concepts, nor something (a natural entity) that is to be explained completely by means of causal links: rather, one must seek to intuit also in that which has objective value a subjective import, and the reference to a totality that does not lie in the background but is instead immanent and working according to its own law of autonomy. Also in cases in which the laws of causality (biological, psychological, sociological) come together to determine the genetic process of objectification, one thing must not be lost from view: the modification and subordination (*Ueberformung*) which the causal connection undergoes through the interference, superposition, or insertion of an energy or individual totality having its own center in itself. The job of the interpreter is not that of reducing the genesis of the objectification to the connection of causality, but that of identifying its elements, and of rediscovering in them an adequate reason.

In order to understand the essential gnosiological difference between the inductive process of explanation by cause and the interpretive process of understanding, it is necessary to reflect on the different evidence presented to the subject who is called upon to take notice of them by, on the one hand, a phenomenon of nature, and, on the other, an objectification of mind. The phenomenon of nature is simply a datum, existing and irreducible, which in itself lacks evidence, that is familiarity, because it cannot be connected to an interior experience proper to the subject called upon to know it; and exactly this relative lack of evidence, this *Uneinsichtigkeit* that characterizes it, imposes on the subject that is to know it the need to reconduct the immediate datum to some other term, which is to say to relationships among invariables, and these, in their turn, to other relationships that are similar, in such a manner as to drive back, and to reduce more and more the lack of evidence, which characterizes the phenomenon, without, however, ever succeeding in overcoming this lack completely, in penetrating it, and transforming it into a secure possession, without residues. In the measure, always relative, in which possession is attained, it is said, indeed, that the phenomenon has been "explained." The subjection of natural phenomena to physical-mathematical laws elaborated according to suitable logical evidence from the so-called exact sciences is based, rather—as we have seen with the crisis of those sciences—on a postulate. It is based on the prediction, which is to the highest degree verisimilar, that those laws—to be used as a vehicle and schema for naturalistic analysis—are to find factual confirmation in the causal links of the physical cosmos. But the indeterminism that is encountered in the physical cosmos, insofar as it evades a rigorous mechanical causality, even revealing the insufficiency of such causality to the exhaustive explanation of phenomena, does not have, beyond this negative characteristic, anything in common with the indeterminism that characterizes freedom in the world of mind. Indeed freedom, as the prerogative of any personal being, is not definable in a purely negative and atomistic sense as a freedom from any yoke and a lack of causality: freedom is essentially the power of self-determination, ruled by its own law of autonomy, for which— we must say with Nietzsche—it is not important to ask *frei wovon*, but rather *frei wozu*; and as such it is not a *posterius*, which comes after the causal connection, but on the contrary a *prius*, which stands beyond this connection and transcends it. While the objectification of mind springs from this interior power and must flow back to it as to its totality, the phenomenon of nature must be understood in its necessity by means of an explanatory process that proceeds from the lower degrees of the physical cosmos to the higher ones with an increasing degree of generalization.

It is true that the notion of a clear-cut difference between understanding and explanation by causes may easily be lost, either when one attributes to the expression "understanding," on the one hand, the same generic signified attributable to any act of comprehension (as happens in daily life, prior to scientific reflection), or when, on the other hand, the signified of intuitive comprehension, in which a connection already known, including one between natural phenomena, is rendered evident; or when, by an extension equally unwarranted, one qualifies as "understanding" even teleological consideration, oriented to the explanation of facts of life and of organic growth in relation to "final causes," products of the "end" or of "the constructive plane" or of "the morphological plane," by which these facts show themselves to have been shaped. When submitting styles of social structures and styles of civilizations to a teleological valorization, one is tempted to recognize in such styles modalities with which one might actualize an unconscious finality or an end conscious of organic life; modalities, in which one might express a specific content of the soul (*Seelisches*), not individual, but collective and superindividual. To give a few examples: in the field of economics, the technical processes of production and the forms of behavior between workers and entrepreneurs would have such a character; in the field of government life, the attitudes of the bureaucrats or of the authorities toward the subjects would have it likewise; and so on. To a multiplicity of final interconnections, produced by a conscious teleology, would correspond a multiplicity of expressive interconnections, in the style of which a supersubjective content of soul (*ein übersubjektivisch Seelisches*) would unconsciously reveal itself. With such a notion a psychologistic direction tends to transfer

into the field of sociology the investigation of expression pursued by
Klages in characterizing psychological types discoverable in individual psychology; and therefore seeks to translate into the dimension of the soul the phenomenon of unconscious production (as an
antithesis to reason and conscious teleology), which other sociolo-
gists, more correctly relying upon the phenomenological datum, seek
in the mental dimension on the objective plane of community. Here
it will be sufficient to point out how even this unwarranted extension of the psychological method of inquiry beyond the field of psy-
chophysical expression proper to an individual tends to obscure the
difference between the epistemological process of understanding and
other cognitive processes oriented toward explanation by means of
causes.

Whether, then, the epistemological process of understanding
might require for its proper orientation the elaboration and the use
of fundamental hermeneutic criteria, that is, of concepts that pertain
to the mental activity studied—whether they are artistic concepts,
like the "*Grundbegriffe*" of Wölfflin, or literary ones, like those of
the genres elaborated in poetics, or juridical ones, like those delineated by dogmatics, or sociological ones, like that of the ideal type
proposed by Max Weber—will appear, after a brief critical outline
(at sec. 6), from my exposition on technical interpretation (in chap. 5).
But I must point out already at this juncture the essential difference
between such concepts as these and the abstract ones of the mathematical sciences or the classificatory concepts of the natural sciences.
Abstraction or classification, by means of which these sciences operate, tends to degrade the single physical phenomenon either, in the
first instance, to a simple "case" of an extratemporal category and
of a law which—at least within certain limits—is universally assumed to be valid, or, in the second instance, to a mere exemplar of
an abstract type verifiable (here also, within certain limits) at any
time: the individuality of the phenomenon, in itself, is not of interest.
On the other hand, in the epistemology of understanding, the individuality of the objectification with its peculiar historical characteristics is never lost from view; and the concepts with which one seeks
to hold fast to it can only assist in the proper placing of the hermeneutic question. If, for simplicity's sake, one reduces the schema
of the hermeneutic judgment to a predicative judgment, in which a
significative qualification is attributed to a subject (constituted by the

objectification of mind), one must say that the postulated concepts or hermeneutic criteria serve either to identify the subject which is of interest, or to attain the proper qualification for it. That their role is that of instruments of orientation seems evident, for example, from the elaboration (which I will mention again later) of the *"kunstge-schichtliche Grundbegriffe"* on the part of Wölfflin, or of the *"Idealtypus"* on the part of Max Weber: by realizing and synthesizing into a type a few features encountered here and there in single historical phenomena according to the changing needs of the inquiry, they seek to facilitate intuition about it and to deepen understanding of it. But what is most important at this point is the discrimination of hermeneutics from semiotics.

1c Understanding as a gnosiologic process. Discrimination of understanding from other modes of knowing by means of signs. Semiotics as a general theory of signs. The intellectual movement that in America took hold under the name of "pragmatism" concerned itself with the study of signs in the realm of animal behavior. The orientation of semiotics in the direction of "behaviorism" was begun by C. S. Peirce,[41] who gathered together the fruits of earlier English studies aimed at the analysis of signs. Peirce explicitly links semiotic processes to processes that imply mediation ("intervention of a third," "thirdness") and often establishes an equation between the two. In his view, "all dynamical action, or action of brute force, physical or psychical, either takes place between two subjects, or at any rate is a resultant of such actions between pairs." But by semiotics he means, on the contrary, "an action, or influence, which is, or involves, a coöperation of *three* subjects, such as, a sign, its object, and its interpretant, this tri-relative influence not being in any way resolvable into actions between pairs." He then defines representation as "to stand for," or as "to be in such a relation to another that for certain purposes it is treated by some mind as if it were that other." Now, the entity that can stand in the place of another with respect to a certain effect or mental process (to be engendered in some mind), Peirce calls "representamen" (i.e., representational form), while that mental process, or thought, is called the respective "interpretant" (*a parte subiecti* or interpretive key), and the other entity, in the place of which it stands, the respective "object." For Peirce, then, the sign is a "representamen," of which the respective interpretive key ("interpretant") is the criterion of cognition which it solicits on the part of some mind.

But the behaviorists who were most committed to the naturalistic direction objected to this attempt to define the "sign" in terms of thought and of mind, on the grounds that it meant abandoning a solid foundation in events and behavioral situations. This would be the unfortunate result, in their view, of the adoption of an uncertain criterion of diagnosis, and of the fall into uncertainty caused by oscillation between defining the interpretive key in terms of thought (as a mental process) and looking for its locus in terms of externally recognizable habit. Moreover, they claimed that he fell into a circular argument and a *progressus ad infinitum* when he characterized the "representamen" as a "*triadic* term of reference to a second term, which is its object, with respect to a third term, qualified as its interpretant," and added that "this triadic reference is so made that the 'representamen' determines its 'interpretant' (as interpretive key) to place itself in the same triadic reference to the same object with respect to some ulterior interpretant" (as addressee).

In response to this it is said—without keeping in mind the possibility of an intermediary or reproductive interpretation—that, even given that signs may engender a series of semantic processes, this would not be a reason to include this capacity within the very notion of sign.

Others—such as C. K. Ogden and I. A. Richards—in studying "the understanding of the signified" or the problem of the signified, indeed, the signified as a problem (the meaning of meaning), have elaborated the so-called hermeneutic theory of context (context theory of meaning): according to which a sign acts upon the thinking mind because it is an integral element in a certain type of interpretive context, or part of a whole, and what is induced by its presence is what it signifies or represents. Hence the "peculiarity" of "interpretation" would consist (sec. 1 b) in the fact that the recurrence of a single part of the context (understood as part of a chain or totality) would, all by itself, provoke in us a reaction in the same sense in which we reacted previously to the entire context. One of these authors then defined the signified (meaning) as "delegated efficacy," but he did not specify in what manner the sign brings about this "delegated efficacy"; and it has been pointed out, on the contrary, that the emphasis on contextuality would be better justi-

fied by situating semantic processes in the context of events and behavioral situations, or modes of conduct: in which context both the
respects in which signs serve as surrogates representative of real
situations and the manner in which they acquire "delegated efficacy,"
or a reflex efficacy, borrowed from other factors, would have to be
explained.

Another follower of this direction—G. W. Cunningham—distinguishes five terms or factors in the psychological phenomenon of
signification (meaning-situation): (a) allusion or reference; (b) content which recalls the allusion (refers); (c) referent which is referred to by the allusive recall; (d) the perspective in view of which
the allusion holds; (e) the context (concatenation or totality), by
reason of which the allusion itself holds. Therefore, one would have
the phenomenon of signification when a content calls up by allusion
(refers to) a referent, in view of a perspective and by reason of a
context in which it is framed. The perspective would be given by a
mind and would imply a system of beliefs, personally supported or
in any case in effect: "for it seems fair to say that only in respect of
some body of beliefs may anything refer meaningfully to anything
else or be said to have meaning."

In the theory of signs or semiotics, signs are above all classified
from the point of view of the one who is called upon to interpret
them, as modes of signifying something (the object, or situation),
according to the differences discoverable in the behavior that they
normally prepare and elicit. The modes of signifying, that is of
functioning through the interpreter in one guise and direction rather
than another, can thus be distinguished according to whether the
signs have value for identifying, for naming, that is, for valorizing,
or for prescribing a line of conduct, whatever may be its origin, social
or otherwise. The criterion for this first classification seems to be
deduced from the *obligation* to *react* which signs place upon the
animal organism to which they come, subject to the goals toward
which they direct behavior in accord with the requirements of the
signified object. A second classification of signs is made from the
point of view (teleological) of one who brings them into being (in
short, of the speaker) and who, in framing them within a behavior
oriented toward their production (purposive behavior), takes as criterion the various propositions or results, with regard to which an
animal organism, consciously or unconsciously, puts them to work.
In this second category, the sign is qualified as "adequate" to the

extent that it is suited to reaching the end to which it is used: this qualification is relative, since it has meaning in relation to the specific end that is being considered. This classification of the uses of signs, that is of their functions, is complicated by the fact that almost any of an animal organism's needs can induce it to use signs as instruments for its own satisfaction.

Signs may serve as means to gain money, social prestige, power over others; to deceive, inform, or entertain; to reassure, comfort, or excite; to record, describe, or predict; to satisfy some needs and to arouse others; to solve problems objectively and to gain a partial satisfaction for a conflict that the organism is not able to solve completely; to enlist the aid of others and to strengthen one's own independence; to "express" oneself or to conceal oneself. And so on without end.[42]

Without stopping to go into other classifications deduced from the criterion mentioned, it will be enough here to mention what Morris finally proposes, discriminating among signs on the basis of their use: whether they are employed to mould the organism addressed to some object or situation, or to help it in its selective orientation toward a choice, or to stimulate a series of reactions along a certain line of behavior, or to organize within a given totality the interpretive behavior of signs received. Thus, four means of using signs are distinguished: moulding, valorizing, stimulating, organizing (that is, integration into a system).

   In order to clarify this point of view, it will be useful to examine the concept of "reference" that Ogden and Richards developed in their theory of signs, which others came to follow. The intentional direction noted in thought processes takes as its point of departure the premise that any quid which is thought has the peculiar trait of being oriented toward one entity rather than toward another: such an orientation of thought is called reference, logical relationship, or allusion. Now, the referring thought (thought of reference) uses symbols (or representational forms), with which (a) it stands in a relationship that may be called causal, insofar as it produces them, and that can be verified as to their precision or legitimacy. Moreover, the thought of reference (b) stands in a relationship to its referent (that is, the objectivity) that may be more or less direct, or indirect and mediated by means of a chain of semantic links or interposed sign situations. On the other hand, (c) between the symbol used and its referent (or preferably referend) there is no connection other than the indirect one of its being used by a mind to represent a referent. When a hearer (or interlocutor) hears what has been said, the symbols urge (cause) him either to carry out, on his part, a mental act of reference, or to take on an attitude that, depending on circumstances, will be more or less in agreement with (similar to) the act and the attitude of the speaker. Thus, he is stimulated to verify whether the relationship spoken of above under (a) is precise, correct, and legitimate as well, and whether that spoken of under (b) is adequate. In any case, between the symbol and the referent (or between representational form and the objectivity it indicates) there is not (cf. c) a direct connection, but only an indirect one, mediated by the other two (a and b), and then through the thinking mind; and when, for grammatical reasons, we assume as implicit a direct relationship, what is involved is simply an attributed relationship, elliptically indicated, not already operative. Only in the relationship (c) between symbol and referent, and always when the words are used in their enunciative (symbolic) semantic function, to communicate a judgment (statement)—not when they are used in their stimulating (emotive) function to express or excite feelings or attitudes—does the predicate of truth (credibility), and the posing of the question whether the judgment is true or false, have any meaning for this relationship. On the other hand, as to the relationship (a) between thought and symbol (which usually is a series of words in the form of a judgment or valorization), it must be said that the symbol is true, that is, credible, when it calls precisely for a reference that, in the relationship (b), is to be recognized as adequate. This occurs when the reference is fitted to provoke in a reasonable (suitable) interpreter a harmonious (similar) reference. The symbol is, however, not true but false when it calls for an incongruous or inadequate reference.

Given that experience is characterized by the recurrence of phenomena (as links) in chains (contexts) which are more or less uniform, it is clear that an "interpretation," understood as induction, is made possible solely by such recurrent contexts, and saying that something constitutes an "interpretation" (induction) amounts to saying that this something is the link in a psychic chain (context) of a certain type. This is really all the old theory of causes could legitimately maintain, and it is all that is necessary to construct a "theory of signs." Such psychic contexts recur every time we recognize or infer. Usually these contexts are in a particular manner interconnected to—or form wider connections with—contexts in the external world; so important is this feature that, if they do not interconnect, we say that we are mistaken. Now, the simplest terminology in which such a type of linkage may be affirmed is that of signs. At the basis of any "interpretation" lies the fact that, when part of an external context recurs in experience, this part, by virtue of its connection with a link in such a psychic chain—connected mental events that form a group, even though they are temporally separate one from another—is often, or sometimes, a "sign" of the rest of that external context (an element, that is, in its totality). In this formula, for "context" one must understand a series of entities—things or events—that stand interrelated one to another in a certain way and that have, each one of them, features recurring almost uniformly in other series of entities, also linked to one another by the same interrelationship.

On the other hand, the attempted reference of a sign to its alleged term may be true as well as false. One has, then, a false induction (misinterpretation). This helps explain how groundless beliefs arise: when irrelevant considerations or notions are introduced or, on the other hand, when relevant ones are left out. A consideration or an experience is regarded as relevant to an induction when it forms a part of the psychological context that ties together other contexts in the manner characteristic of the induction. It is irrelevant when it is not suited to such a linking. Of anyone who tries to reduce logic to psychology it may be said that, if our induction were to depend solely on psychological contexts without further instances of interference, it would follow that our value judgments or convictions, whether true or false, would always be justified: so that a psychologically unjustified induction would be the result of the interference of mistakes with those contexts.

The theory of symbols and of modes of understanding the signified, as it is described by Ogden and Richards, takes as its point of departure the premise that, every time we hear discourse, there arises spontaneously in us the inference that the person speaking refers to what we would ourselves have in mind if we used the words he is speaking. But words, in cases in which they cannot join up directly with and be supported by gestures, constitute rather imperfect, deficient, and unreliable means of communication. Even in private meditation, thought is drawn forward by the snares and treachery of its natural symbolic resources; but in dialogue, in any serious attempt to bring two individual opinions face to face, the latitude acquired by

language shows itself to a much greater degree. Even if we leave
aside pathological cases in which language is diverted from its semantic function (to communicate logical relationships by means of
symbols) and made an instrument of advancing practical purposes,
perhaps by lies and deceit, the paths through which verbal ingenuity
may be led are still extremely varied and the goals toward which it
may be adopted are a long journey off, while the honest listener or
the unprepared reader is not in a position to notice it. One thinks of
the pharisaic interpretation of biblical passages to support the capi-
talistic spirit, or of the misunderstandings involving two possible
meanings—one understood by the speaker and the other made obvious for the listener—or of war propaganda, in which the discourse
presented in the press or on the radio becomes an integral part of a
sort of mechanism of deceit: a kind of technique of misdirection of
which it has been justly remarked that, like any weapon used in war,
it has, alongside its gain, also its cost in the imbalance and disorder
which it leaves in time of peace, as an unhealthy residue in the consciousness. Nonetheless, though they set snares, the resources of
words are indispensable and irreplaceable for communication. What
is needed, according to Ogden and Richards, are not new words, but
rather a means of verifying words in their value as symbols, a means
of readily ascertaining, on any occasion, the term that is referred to
in a particular use that is made; in their view, an adequate theory of
definition should serve this purpose. But such a theory should in its
turn be based on a theory of signs, which would be derived and developed from observation of the behavior of persons different from
us, and not from our own introspection, except insofar as it is framed
by observation of others and subject to evaluation according to reliable criteria: since in general it would seem that we are better
judges of what others do than we are of what we do ourselves. Keeping in mind, then, the extreme importance of those signs that men
use to communicate with one another and that they use as instruments of thought, Ogden and Richards include them in the technical
category of "symbols," meaning by "symbols" words, constructions
of words, images, gestures, and other representations, such as draw-
ings or mimetic sounds.

   Therefore, reviewing critically the various modes of understanding and of defining the meaning of signs, and in particular of symbols,
Ogden and Richards list first of all (1) the definition that hypostatizes
the signified, seeing it in an "intrinsic property" discoverable in this or

that thing, and (2) the definition that hypostatizes the signified, seeing it in a special relationship not subject to analysis, whence something, A, is referred to something else, B. The other definitions proposed are linked to this second one, insofar as they tend to equate the signified with the relationship between A and B, when A signifies B (the relationship that Ogden and Richards call "reference"), that is, insofar as they aim to equate the signified with the referent, B (what they call "referent": it would be better to say "referend"). Thus, the following definitions may be distinguished; all of them, derived from the previously mentioned relationship, equate the signified (3) with the other words attached in the lexicon to the word in question; (4) with the "connotations" that characterize the word; (5) with the connotations hypostatized as "essence"; (6) with "an activity taken up (by us) toward objects and energetically projected into them like an alpha "particle" (here it is necessary to distinguish between sound as sensory datum and sound as signified, and also between these and the thing signified); (7) with an event understood or contemplated, or with an understanding or proposition that is to be put into effect (this duality gives rise to misunderstandings); (8) with the place in which the significative thing is lodged in the totality of a system, whatever nature the system may have (with which an equation is established: meaning = "significance," in the area of a system, the dimensions of which are more or less broad); in particular: (9) with the subsequent practical consequences that the event or the significative thing is capable of explaining in our future experience; or, (10) with the logical consequences that, from a theoretical perspective, are contained or implicit in a statement; finally, (11) with the feeling awakened by the use of language shaped as a stimulating instrument (as in oratorical discourse) or as a means of appealing to notions of value. Moreover, the following additional definitions may be distinguished; they concern the referents and equate the signified, respectively, (12) with the event or attitude that may be referred to a sign according to a predetermined relationship posited between one and the other (as in naturalistic inference or in the psychoanalytic explanation of the sense of dreams); (13) with the referent, to which the mental process of "reference" leads the sign to adapt according to the psychological contexts that tie together the links or elements in the contexts of the external world. In the simplest case, it is a matter of the recognition of mnemonic images provoked by a stimulus in virtue of learned associations; in more complex cases it is a matter of establishing at least provisional connections, by means of which the acquired mnemonic resource is shown to be more or less suited to the other similar experiences: there is an oscillation between the verifiable inductive diagnosis of a symptom and the conjecture that it suggests by means of successive "adaptations." Coming finally to the interpretation of symbols, one must keep in mind the possibility of understanding them in a double way as allusions, or "acts of reference," whether on the part of the one who is using them or of the one who is called upon to perceive and interpret them. With this double perspective in mind, the signified of a symbol may be equated (14) with that term to which the one who is using the symbol refers or ought to refer (according to an objective criterion), (15) with that term to which he himself (subjectively) believes he is referring, (16) with that term to which the one who is called upon to interpret the symbol must refer, that is, to which he refers or, for his own part, believes he refers, or yet again, believes that the one who uses it refers. As signs of the references of others, symbols are certainly more trustworthy than concomitant feelings; nonetheless even they may lead one off the track; thus they require a method of verification that diminishes the risk of discrepancy, guaranteeing the correctness, the uniformity and the stability of the allusion within the sphere of a social group. It is, however, naive to depend on definitions or on the use of dictionaries.

At the foundation of any human communication there are to be discovered certain logical postulates, without which it is impossible to elaborate a system of symbols. Where formal logic treats propositions as objects of thought distinct from symbols, a logic that is not purely formal and that governs the elaboration of symbols must, in the opinion of Ogden and Richards, seek to establish a series of criteria or canons to regulate its procedure according to the model of mathematics. The canons to be observed, in their opinion, are the following:

(1) A symbol stands for one and only one referent: that is, it represents that one alone. When a symbol seems to call for two or more referents, it is to be seen as two or more symbols to be differentiated one from another.

(2) Symbols that can, with no difference, be substituted for one another really indicate the same reference (the so-called canon of definition).

(3) The referent of a symbol abbreviated in an elliptical formula is also the referent of that symbol explained in its entirety: one

should, however, be careful to discover its proper explanation, seeking out the sign situation that justifies the allusion, when it is designated by a doubtful formula (thus, we know for certain what is said, when we know why it is said). In this regard Ogden and Richards attempt a critique of ontological conceptualism, insofar as it tends to admit fictive entities: hence, what they call the canon of actuality.

(4) A symbol evokes once again the term that it is actually used and destined to recall: certainly not that term that it ought to serve to recall when used more correctly, or that different term that is by chance understood by the interpreter or by someone who adopts it.

(5) No complex symbol can contain as constitutive elements symbols that require being set in the same logical place as itself (the so-called canon of compatibility).

(6) All possible referents form together an order so constructed that any single referent occupies a single logical place in that order (the so-called canon of individuality, meaning individuality of position): with which is always supposed a referent to which we are actually referring, not one which is only alleged or believed. The falsehood of an affirmation would be characterized by the erroneous belief by which we assign to the referent a logical position in which it is not placed, or, rather, we assume we are referring to a term different from that to which we are actually referring. The above six canons would guarantee the proper use of words in argumentation. For Ogden and Richards the ideal would be a "system of symbols founded on fixed and unalterable definitions": an ideal from which, for example, psychology and sociology are still distant.

Following the path of those who conceive of the semantic phenomenon in terms of a mental process, C. J. Ducasse[43] characterizes the interpretation he calls "semiotic" as the type of mental process resulting from the fact that the consciousness of something makes us become aware of something else linked to it; and he set himself against a unilateral vision of the "sign" in pure terms of public behavior to conceive of it in relation to behavior that is in general observable. For Ducasse, S (sign) is a sign of D (denotatum) for an interpreting subject in the measure in which the presence of S, conjointly with such propositions as the subject has nurtured and also the belief (diagnosis) that he finds himself in a given situation and with the prognosis, or believed perspective, that he is capable of actualizing those propositions by behaving in a certain manner, induces the subject to behave in that given manner. Therefore, the psychological phenomenon of interpretation is seen as a function not only of social behavior but also of three other variables which are psychic and therefore private in character: propositions, diagnostic belief, and prospective belief; these are variables of which the interpreting subject becomes conscious by means of introspection, but which are not recognizable to his fellows except by indirect means, through more or less tenuous inferences based on his verbal or operatory behavior. Social behavior, then, is not sufficient to show the phenomenon of interpretation; such behavior would need, rather, to be considered together with complementary hypotheses about psychic states, such as propositions and beliefs. To such a critique, followers of the rigidly behavioristic path reply that the appeal to propositions and beliefs would not serve to clarify the phenomenon in question, if what is involved are private mental states, not recognizable by objective (classificatory) observation, and that the real question is whether such states are in fact prior to the appearance of signs (as Ducasse maintains), or whether, on the other hand, the manifestation of belief and the disposition to respond in a certain way are not, rather, the same thing, that is, whether beliefs and dispositions are new elements resulting from the appearance of signs. What is important to emphasize is the embeddedness of signs in behavioral situations: even if it were demonstrated that every semantic process realizes itself in the context of beliefs and presupposes beliefs for its own possibility, nonetheless it would not be necessary to introduce this psychological term in the description of those events. Now, the entire discussion cited here, including the last-mentioned updating, is symptomatic, insofar as it shows that what interests and propels Anglo-American behaviorism is not at all the mental process of understanding in its gnosiologic problematic, but only the naturalistic observation of the *psychological* phenomenon of interpretive behavior. This is the theme common to the various schools of thought, underlying the nuances of each of them.

The tendency to translate all psychic facts into semantic phenomena characterizes this naturalistic orientation. Thus, according to the "sign-gestalt" of Tolman,[44] the figure so-named would result: (a) when types of situations and behavior events that provoke a response of the animal organism are encountered (sign-objects); (b) when there are, moreover, objects signified by such situations and events (significates); (c) when the manner in which the commerce with signs leads, on the basis of preceding experiences, to communication with the respective signifieds is also identified (relation of means to end). Viewed from this position, the sign is always a means (means-object), the signified is a goal (goal-object), and the semantic process constantly involves a given teleological relationship between communicating with given means and arriving at a goal. Any behavior would function with "sign-gestalts" acquired, formed, or corrected on the basis of the expectation that, in responding to the sign in a certain manner, would lead to a result more or less in conformity with certain needs, interests, and dispositions prevailing at the moment. The expectation in question is defined as a disposition (of an organism) to expect, as the normal result of given "signs" offered to immediate experience, certain typical "signifieds," insofar as they are linked to those by typical relationships of means to end. For the behaviorists, the problem of identifying the conditions the advent of which may be said to justify an expectation is then posed. To some behaviorists the concept of expectation seemed too elevated and anthropomorphic to be attributed to an animal organism. The response to this criticism has been that what is at issue is not a conscious process, but rather a directive criterion suited to explaining typical behaviors and their persistence, as long as corresponding conditions persist, which means explaining a certain organization or phenomenal set in an animal organism. The critics reply that "expectation" cannot designate a response anticipated upon the appearance of the sign: for this reason, "expectation," understood in the only sense relevant to a semantic process, would have to be translated into "interpretant" (interpretive key), understood as a verifiable disposition to react in a certain manner to the given situation, because of something else that is connected to it. Concurrently, the requirement of objective recognizability and verifiability must be maintained (as most orthodox behaviorists do); the psychological phenomenon of interpretation should satisfy this requirement in a naturalistic description, as an animal trait. Seen from this perspective, the "signifieds" do not partake of the behavior events except as objects, things that provoke a response in the only ways relevant to the ends of the behavior itself.

Perhaps this exposition will be enough to show—without need of going into a more extensive critique as to merits—that the problematic of the Anglo-American theory of signs, or semiotics, emerges from an interest essentially different from that which informs hermeneutic theory. What interests semiotics is the psychological phenomenon of animal behavior, insofar as it reacts to certain sign situations with attitudes that express inferences ("interpretations," in this very broad sense) and that are subject to naturalistic observation and quantitative evaluations. Symptomatic in its sincerity is the confession of an American psychologist who studies "personal documents": He points out that "in the German language there is a large literature on the process of understanding, but only a few discussions of the problem are available in English. In America there is antipathy (sic) toward the investigation of the nature of understanding because of the subjective and nonquantitative issues involved." On the contrary, what interests hermeneutic theory, and has always interested it from its origins, is precisely the mental process of understanding, with which one thinking mind answers the message of another mind which speaks to it through representational forms. And exactly this different interest orients scientific investigation, not toward the psychological phenomenon, but toward the epistemological process, thanks to which understanding is attained; that is, it orients the investigation toward the interpretive process: a process that must be interrogated with a problematic that is essentially gnosiologic.

. . . . .

The Hermeneutics of Suspicion

Hans-Georg Gadamer

. . . . .

In proposing to discuss the hermeneutics of suspicion, I clearly had in mind the usage of Paul Ricoeur; Ricoeur, who never opposes without somehow reconciling, could not avoid opposing—at least in a first approach—hermeneutics in the classic sense of interpreting the meaning of texts, to the radical critique of and suspicion against understanding and interpreting. This radical suspicion was inaugurated by Nietzsche and had its most striking instances in the critique of ideology on the one hand and of psychoanalysis on the other. Now it is necessary to examine the relationship between traditional hermeneutics, its philosophical situation, and this radical form of interpretation, which is almost at the opposite end of the spectrum of interpretation—because it challenges the claims to validity of ideas and ideologies. I should begin by saying that the problem of hermeneutical suspicion can be understood in a more radical or wider sense. Is not *every* form of hermeneutics a form of overcoming an awareness of suspicion? Husserl himself tried to found his own phenomenology on the basis of the Cartesian way of doubting the appearances or reliability of first impressions. That was a consequence of the modern sciences, so there is no question that the problem of suspicion has also *this* place in our context. Our efforts at understanding can be seen from the point of view of the suspicion that our first approach—as a prescientific one—is not valid and that consequently we need the help of scientific methods to overcome our first impressions. What is involved here, then, is the whole question of the foundations of our insights into truth.

This recalls the beginning of the hermeneutical discussion under the impact of the new sciences. Consider the position of Vico who, as a professor of rhetoric in Naples, defended the old tradition of encyclopedic higher education in face of the new approach by scientific method, which he called *critica*. *Rhetorica* and *critica* are two competing approaches, insofar as *rhetorica* is obviously based on common sense, on the probability of arguments insofar as they are well received and assured by appearances. On the other hand, the critical attitude stands against appearances, on the side of the new physics, with its insistence on method. So we have indeed two competing approaches: on the one hand, the arguments of persuasion, on the other, the arguments of logical cogency.

It is not irrelevant to recall this original situation of the late seventeenth and early eighteenth century before giving an account of the role of hermeneutics, because there is a deep inner convergence with rhetoric and hermeneutics. In the course of recent investigations I found a remarkable shift from the tradition of rhetoric to hermeneutics, closely connected, of course, to the new priority given reading over speaking, and to the Gutenberg era, and the Reformation, when people began to read the Bible in private, and no longer only in the religious service. At this moment interest shifted from the speaking and writing of speeches to the understanding of the written and to the interpreting of it. That happened with Melanchthon, a friend and follower of Luther in Wittenberg, who reintroduced the whole tradition of Aristotelian philosophy into the Protestant schools. In his lectures on rhetoric, he develops something at the beginning about the role of Aristotle and of speech; yet he also says that one needs rules, models, and good arguments (all the help of the rhetorical tradition) not only to give a good talk, but also in order to *read* and understand extended argumentation. Here we are at the turning point between rhetoric and hermeneutics.

Recently, it seems, some of my colleagues have been trying to "save my soul" from such dishonest things as rhetoric! They think that hermeneutics is no noble pursuit and that we must be suspicious of rhetoric. I had to reply that rhetoric has been the basis of our social life since Plato rejected and contradicted the flattering abuse of rhetoric by the Sophists. He introduced dialectically founded rhetoric as in the *Phaedrus*, and rhetoric remained a noble art throughout antiquity. Yet one wonders why today everybody is not aware of it. When one cannot convince people through the exchange of arguments, in a more or less dialogical form, one *needs* rhetoric. Even Socrates was not able to speak to a mass of listeners in the same way that he spoke with individuals in the dialogues. So he shifts to speaking mythically in such moments and in such situations. Without doubt there is a function of rhetoric that has to do with the extension and sharing of common and relevant insights. Even scientists would have less influence if they did not use rhetoric to capture the interest of the public.

It is not so surprising that, in the shift to a more literate culture, rhetoric was more or less replaced by hermeneutics, that is, by an interest in interpreting texts. It was in two fields especially that the change came about. In theology, it is obvious that the new claim of the Protestant Church was that its doctrines were based completely on the statements of the Holy Scripture and not on the voice of tradition as in the case of the Roman Catholic Church. Protestants therefore needed the art of interpretation. A similar problem arose in law, where there is a special problem of interpretation regarding the determinants of jurisdiction. How can we apply law so as to achieve as much justice as possible? The role of hermeneutics in jurisprudence was based on the realization that no general rule could ever cover all the particularities of legal experience and practice. Fitting a particular case under a general law is *always* an act of interpretation. The role of judges and rulers consists in finding that form of classification according to a rule that corresponds best to the aims of justice. This is a very old problem of equity. Recall that Aristotle introduces the topic of equity in connection with the phenomenon of justice. He says that equity does not lower the dignity of justice. The opposite rather is true, namely, that equity makes justice *just*. It is in the service of just decision that one reinterprets the law and finds the most adequate solution of the juristic problem.

It is well known that once the French Revolution had broken the self-evidence of the Greco-Christian humanistic tradition, the distance of this tradition appeared—and with it what we ordinarily call romanticism, the feeling that something has been lost. Nostalgia may seek it, but it is no longer the unquestionable basis of our thinking and feeling. Romanticism along with its nineteenth-century continuation reveals also that the eighteenth century was the last period in the Western world with an inner style. What followed was really a series of experiments in historicism, whose architectural manifestation was seen in imitation Gothic cathedrals for university buildings and Roman churches for railway stations. The last century to have a monolithic expression or mood was the eighteenth and this mood also gave a new relevance to the feeling for antiquity. The Romantics developed the ability to overcome the classics and to discover the charm of the past, the far, the alien: the Middle Ages, India, China, and so on. Hermeneutics may be defined as the attempt to overcome this distance in areas where empathy was hard and agreement not easily reached. There is always a gap that must be bridged. Thus, hermeneutics acquires a central place in viewing human experience. That was indeed Schleiermacher's intuition; he and his associates became the first to develop hermeneutics as a foundation, as the primary aspect of social experience, not only for the scholarly interpretation of texts as documents of the past, but also for understanding the mystery of the inwardness of the other person. This feeling for the individuality of persons, the realization that they cannot be classified and deduced according to general rules or laws, was a significant new approach to the concreteness of the other.

This is why Schleiermacher defined hermeneutics as the ability to avoid misunderstanding, because, as a matter of fact, that *is* the mystery of individuality. We can never be sure, and we have no proofs, of rightly understanding the individual utterance of another. However, even in the romantic era when this feeling for the individuality and the "closedness" of the individual became widespread, it was never doubted that *behind* a person's individuality something common and intelligible could be reenacted. Schleiermacher, too, was in this last respect an idealist, not in the silly sense that he denied the existence of the external world, but in the sense of affirming that our understanding is able to grasp the real kernel, and that there is an ultimate identity of the subjective approach and reality, a common rationality in consciousness and being. But in the modern epoch, which is the end of the romantic era, the new trend of the experimental sciences belongs to us all. This interest became an epistemological interest in *Erkenntnistheorie*. That means, in the first place, that we are no longer convinced and sure that there is an identity between the subjective approach and the fact; the problem then is that of justifying the mathematically symbolic constructions of nature. The purely epistemological question that occupied the nineteenth century was To what extent can we justify the validity of our scientific methods and procedures?

As a consequence, hermeneutics also came to have an epistemological importance: to what extent are we justified in assuming that we have a correct understanding of the texts? A whole system of rules and principles was developed and collected from experience in classics and theological learning, stemming from the conviction that

there is a certain set of principles that allows us to grasp the real idea
of the text. On this basis the philosophical interpreters of the so-
called historical school, especially Dilthey, developed the belief that
the humanities need and have their own psychological foundation and
hermeneutical methodology. Yet in the same epoch there is what I
mentioned before: the concept of interpretation that began its new
career under Nietzsche's banner. Remember the famous statement,
"There are no moral phenomena, there are only moral interpretations
of the phenomena." Nietzsche, a philologist by profession, captured
this concept of interpretation in a completely new and radical sense.
The "will to power" changes completely the idea of interpretation;
it is no longer the manifest meaning of a statement of a text, but the
text's and its interpreter's function in the preservation of life. The
extension of power—that is the real meaning of our all-too-human
insights and cognitions. This radical position forces us to attend to
the dichotomy of the belief in the integrity of texts and the intelligibility of their meaning, and the opposed effort to unmask the pretensions hidden behind so-called objectivity (Ricoeur's "hermeneutics of suspicion"). The latter alternative was developed in the critique
of ideology, in psychoanalysis, and in the thought inspired more or
less directly by Nietzsche's own work. This dichotomy is too sharp
to allow us to rest content with a mere classification of the two forms
of interpretation, either as simply interpreting statements following
the intentions of the author *or* as revealing the meaningfulness of
statements in a completely unexpected sense and against the meaning
of the author. I see no way of reconciling the two. I think even Paul
Ricoeur must in the end give up attempts to bring them together, because we have here a basic difference involving the whole philosophical role of hermeneutics. The question is, how thoroughly can the
role that hermeneutics plays in philosophy be seen or discussed in
light of this opposition?

  The thinker who introduced the concept of hermeneutics in philosophy, and not only in the methodology of the humanities, was
Heidegger. He placed hermeneutics in the center of his analysis of
existence in showing that interpretation is not an isolated activity of
human beings but the basic structure of our experience of life. We
are always taking something *as* something. That is the primordial
givenness of our world orientation, and we cannot reduce it to anything simpler or more immediate. Yet shouldn't we recognize that
there was also a hermeneutic moment *in* Husserl's analysis of the ex-

periences of consciousness? This could certainly be elaborated. I refer you to a well-known note of Oskar Becker, a common pupil of
Husserl and Heidegger, a friend of both (and an excellent scholar,
especially in aesthetics and in ancient mathematics); Becker wrote
that when *Being and Time* was published there was a certain mistaken tendency to think of it as something completely new and
external to Husserl's phenomenology, and Becker said that what the
book does accomplish is the elaboration of the dimension of hermeneutical experience internal to the framework of Husserlian phenomenology, and the determination, in a creative and remarkable
form, of the finite structure of human understanding and interpretation. So far this statement is not inconsistent with Husserl's decisive
insights. But there are questions. Is there not a real break by Heidegger also in other respects? We should first pay some attention to the
principle of phenomenology *"Zu den Sachen selbst,"* as opposed to
constructions and to everything that is not really evident by its own
givenness. Husserl overcame the dogmatism of an immanent consciousness, which must ask: How can we transcend ourselves and
make contact with the external world? This is obviously an epistemological theme. Husserl overcame this by demonstrating that consciousness is exactly intentionality, which means that we are *in* the
matter and not simply enclosed in ourselves. The primacy of self-
consciousness is an error, phenomenologically speaking. Self-consciousness occurs only insofar as there is a consciousness of objects.
That was clear to the Greeks and to Franz Brentano, who revived
Greek psychology and became Husserl's teacher.

So far the claim is to be faithful to givenness. Nothing should be
accepted but the given itself. Husserl always claimed that he was the
only real positivist, in the sense of taking things as they are given.
But does Husserl follow the rigor of his own principle *"Zu den
Sachen selbst"* in beginning his analysis of the evidence of our cognition by the standard model of sense perception? Is sense perception
something given or is it an abstraction that thematizes an abstract
constant of the given? Scheler, aided by his contacts with psychologists and physiologists of his epoch as with American pragmatism
and Heidegger, demonstrated with vigor that sense perception is
never given. It is rather an aspect of the pragmatic approach to the
world. We are always hearing—listening *to* something and extracting
from other things. We are *interpreting* in seeing, hearing, receiving.
In seeing, we are looking *for* something; we are just not like photo-

graphs that reflect everything visible. A real photographer, for instance, is looking for the moment in which the shot would be an interpretation of the experience. So it is obvious that there is a real primacy of interpretation.

Husserl refused to accept this analysis, even in late publications such as *Erfahrung und Urteil*. (Although the text of the latter was done by Landgrebe, it cannot be doubted that Husserl accepted it.) He rejected the entire claim and held that all interpretation is a *secondary* act. The first thing is to realize what is present for the senses, that is, sense perception. Another question that arises is how the other person is given for the ego. Husserl's answer is very complicated. He discussed the whole problem with great care, and I would not say that he did not succeed in careful description. But how is the difference between selves and other objects of perception articulated following Husserl? There is no doubt that he described it somewhat by saying "There is another." What is given there? There is something extended with a human shape, I lend to this object an ego in transferring my own ego into it. Husserl called this "transcendental sympathy," which means that I constitute what I see there as another person through a new act, based upon the primary givenness of the visual object. That is hard to accept, especially after the superb analysis that thinkers like Sartre or Merleau-Ponty have given of the role of the look and the other.

Also the problem of one's own body is a very precarious one for Husserl. There is no question that he did give marvelous descriptions of the structure of the intimate feeling of one's own body. I remember how he introduced this theme in his class. "What is the *absolute here*?" he would ask. "Not that, not that," pointing to the limbs. "*That* is the absolute here," indicating his chest, "the point of the coordinates, that is the *absolute here*." Of course, behind this amusing story we see the mathematician who tried to reach ultimate clarity in his position and certainty in his assumptions and who will warn us. Do not forget that there is a basic structure in spite of all these difficulties in his phenomenology of the other and in the other's givenness: first, something is given as extended in the space—without ego—and then the ego must be added. But is it given so? What is behind the dogmatism of this description? The problems are obviously not resolved in Husserl's analysis, which claims to work out the program of philosophy as a rigorous science, and to found all insight in absolute and apodictic evidence. The apodictic evidence of the ego, the old Cartesian argument, is the founding principle for the whole phenomenology. But now we will ask ourselves why Becker, when *Being and Time* was published, could write his mediating note: in *Being and Time* Heidegger interpreted himself as a transcendental phenomenologist. Of course, not without criticizing Husserl. He attacked the transcendental ego of Husserl as a fantastic stylization, and went on to look for a deeper foundation of the whole problem of a philosophy in "existence." And what he called "existence," this projecting thrownness, was indeed not consciousness. I was recently asked what difference it made that Heidegger introduced the term "care" (*Sorge*) to replace consciousness. He described existence as care. What is the difference between "consciousness" and "care"? One point is clear, consciousness is representing what is present for it, care is anticipation of the future. Heidegger obviously replaced "consciousness" with "care" to demonstrate that the present and the idea of presentation are not adequate to the temporal structure of human existence and its projecting character. But did it really make such a radical difference to replace consciousness by care? Must we not agree that to be *careful*, to care for something, is always the central character of care; but whoever is "caring for" is careful in doing so, and that means he is concerned with himself; in the same sense in which Husserl says (with Kant) that to be conscious of something is, for essential reasons, to be self-conscious. So one can ask whether Heidegger really broke through the immanentism of the Husserlian description of consciousness and self-consciousness by replacing it with care—or whether he simply concretized consciousness by care and temporality? I think that, because the answer is unclear, it was possible, when *Being and Time* had just come out, for readers like Oskar Becker to see it as simply a new variation and extension within the framework of phenomenology.

But there is something else that should be taken seriously: namely, that Heidegger was not fully satisfied with himself and did not remain at this point. After some years, he described it as a reversal of turning, *die Kehre;* he gave up the transcendental self-interpretation. What he gave up by that was the ideal of ultimate foundation. I remember very well how Heidegger said one day to me, "*Letzbegrundung*—what a strange idea!" But how can one give up ultimate foundation? Certainly, one cannot give it up if one insists on a narrow sense of rationality, of rigorous science in the sense of mathematics and its analogues. For transcendental phenomenology, which should fulfill Husserl's ideal of science, one needs apodictic evidence and a consistent development of all valid consequences from this evidence. But is that possible? I mean, does it explain the full claim of rationality to self-understanding? That is the philosophical problem. For it is certainly not enough to insert some concretized descriptions of intersubjectivity, of the body, of whatever it may be. The question at stake is, What is the relation of rationality as rigorous science to the rationality of life? And here I think that the ideal of foundation as an ultimate principle indeed misses the point. That is the reason why Heidegger did not remain with his earlier foundation. That is the reason why I tried to do something in the same direction. We had to seek for another self-interpretation, *not* for a foundation. By "self-interpretation of our doings," I mean not my or Heidegger's doings, but all our doings including, on the one hand, the rationality of sciences and, on the other hand, the rationality of practical reasoning.

Perhaps I can demonstrate that phenomenology is not identical with foundationalism. Think for a moment of the givenness of our life; the most telling form of this givenness is language. Of course, language is now of essential concern in modern philosophy. I think there are good reasons for this, but I am not convinced that philosophy of language or linguistics touches at all the decisive point of givenness. In language there is, first of all, both *langue* and *parole,* to use Saussure's distinction. The spoken word is something other than the system of symbols that constitutes language. Language *is not* itself a given, what is given is *parole,* the speaking word in its working reality. And that certainly involves a strange form of concealment. One should realize that a basic character of speaking is that it is completely forgetful of itself. Nobody could utter one sentence if he were completely aware of what he were doing. If I were to attempt such total awareness I would not find a second word after the first. And more than that: it would really prevent me from going beyond every utterance to the matters I would convey, and force me to keep what I am saying to myself. I would go mad if I were to make an attempt at complete thematization of saying in saying. I must say *something* in order to speak; when I do there is a forgetfulness of speech as a theme or topic. One could reply that speech exists in texts. Yes, certainly, but the texts are alien or brutal. How is this speech, the speaking word, really preserved in the written text? Is it completely the utterance of my mind? Are we not all acquainted with the alienation between what we said and what we had in mind? Is it not one of our leading experiences that the utterance is no longer mine? We must always look for the *real* meaning of an utterance. It is an error when our logician friends insist that we must "improve" Plato, in those areas that are contradictory or inconsistent, making his argumentations more coherent. That is a misunderstanding of what speaking is. Speaking is not logical deduction; it is, in a way, overcoming the word, and it produces something one has to interpret by the context in the boldest sense. The context here is not only the words but the whole life context.

That context, of course, is never given in its full extent. So interpretation seems to me very demanding, and, of course, a field of philosophical and philological activity. I know just one instance in which the interpretation of speech is not an additional supplemental moment, and in which we go to the essence of the matters themselves: that is dialogue. In dialogue we are really interpreting. Speaking then is interpreting itself. It is the function of the dialogue that in saying or stating something a challenging relation with the other evolves, a response is provoked, and the response provides the interpretation of the other's interpretation. In this way, we know (an old Platonic insight) that the real mode of givenness of speech starts with dialogue. It is no longer a system of symbols or a set of rules of grammar and syntax. The real act of work is appropriation in the common being of the speakers. I try in my own work to develop this point of view, on how language, not in the sense of *langue*, but in the sense of real exchange and work, manifests itself in the dialogue. In any form of dialogue, we are building up. We are building up a common language, so that at the end of the dialogue we will have some ground. Of course, not every dialogue is fruitful, but it should at least aim at being a dialogue. (Very often it is the opposite of that: two monologues following one upon the other.) Anyway, we are here describing language in its *givenness*, I mean in its actuality and not in the abstracting modes of a science of symbols. We are speaking about the *word* which is presenting itself to us in our exchange of speech, exactly what the Greeks called dialectic. It is the procedure of Greek thinking.

Let me give you an outline of what I have in mind, i.e., dialectic as the common ground. Dialectic does not claim to have a first principle. It is true: Plato as he appeared to Aristotle developed two "principles," the One and the Dyad. The Dyad was an indeterminate

Dyad and that meant openness for further determination. Is that "foundation" in the sense of Husserl's higher principle? These "principles" of Plato were not meant to yield an ultimate determinancy. I think Plato was well aware of this position when he said that philosophy is something for human beings, not for gods. Gods *know*, but we are in this ongoing process of approximation and overcoming error by dialectically moving toward truth. In this sense I could present a partial defense of the idea that the oldest heritage of philosophy is exactly its functionality, its giving an account, and that as such it cannot presume to have first principles. This suggests very well what I would have in the place of "foundation." I would call it "participation," because that is what happens in human life. That is, without any doubt, the excellence of the humanities, that we share a common world of tradition and interpreted human experience. The interpretation of the common world in which we participate is certainly not in the first place the objectifying task of methodical thinking. That may certainly be included, but it is not the raison d'être of our activity. When we are interpreting a text, it is not to prove "scientifically" that *this* love poem belongs to the genre of love poems. That is an objective statement and nobody can doubt it; but if that conclusion is the only result of investigating a poem, then we have failed. The intention is to understand *this* love poem, on its own and in its unique relation to the common structure of love poems. It is an absolutely individualized particular form, so that one participates in the utterance or message which is there embodied by the poet. Participation is indeed a better formulation of what is going on in our life experience than is the foundationalist account of the apodictic evidence of self-consciousness.

"Participation" is a strange word. Its dialectic consists of the fact that participation is not taking parts, but in a way taking the whole. Everybody who participates in something does not take something away, so that the others cannot have it. The opposite is true: by sharing, by our participating in the things in which we are participating, we enrich them; they do not become smaller, but larger. The whole life of tradition consists exactly in this enrichment so that life is our culture and our past: the whole inner store of our lives is always extending by participating.

I want to end with just one remark about what there is in the methodical character of such an approach, that I would call hermeneutic in its central sense. Let me refer to the practical philosophy of

Aristotle. Aristotle asks, "What is the principle of moral philosophy?" and he answers, "Well, the principle is *that*, —the thatness." It means, not deduction but real givenness, not of brute facts but of the interpreted world. Is not the question of Husserl's *Crisis* how we can rejoin and reconnect our efforts at rigorous science, including phenomenology as a rigorous science, with the historical conditions of our own place in the course of history? And so my thesis is: exactly because we give up a special idea of foundation in principle, we become better phenomenologists, closer to the real givenness, and we are more aware of the reciprocity between our conceptual efforts and the concrete in life experiences.

· · · · ·

Beyond Hermeneutics:
Interpretation in Late Heidegger
and Recent Foucault

Hubert Dreyfus

· · · · ·

Two of the most original and influential interpreters of the contemporary world, Martin Heidegger and Michel Foucault, both deny that what they are doing should be called hermeneutics. Foucault has always opposed hermeneutics, which he calls exegesis or commentary, as the mistaken attempt to get at a deep truth hidden in discourse. According to Foucault commentary seeks "the re-apprehension through the manifest meaning of discourse of another meaning at once secondary and primary, that is, more hidden but also more fundamental."[1] Hermeneutics thus "dooms us to an endless task . . . [because it] rests on the postulate that speech is an act of 'translation' . . . of the Word of God, ever secret, ever beyond itself." Foucault dismisses this approach with the remark: "For centuries we have waited in vain for the decision of the Word."[2]

Heidegger, unlike Foucault, once had high hopes for hermeneutics. In fact his use of hermeneutic analysis in *Being and Time* modernized this approach, which he took from Dilthey (who took it from Schleiermacher), and made the hermeneutic method a respectable subject of discussion in philosophy and the human sciences. But later Heidegger characterizes the hermeneutic circle as "superficial"[3] and he explicitly distances himself from his earlier commitment. "In my later writings," he informs us, "I no longer employ the term 'hermeneutics' . . . I have left an earlier standpoint . . . because [it] was merely a way-station along a way."[4] In his book on Nietzsche, Heidegger criticizes his earlier "hermeneutic-transcendental questions" as "not yet thought in terms of the history of Being."[5] Instead of continuing to claim he is practicing hermeneutic-transcendental phenomenology, later Heidegger prefers to say he is simply thinking.[6]

To understand what Heidegger wishes to leave behind, we must look in some detail at the two-stage hermeneutic analysis Heidegger introduces in *Being and Time*.

In the introduction to *Being and Time* Heidegger tells us: "The phenomenology of *Dasein* [human being] is *hermeneutic* in the primordial signification of the word, where it designates the business of interpreting."[7] Heidegger then sets out to show *why* phenomenology must be hermeneutic. He accepts Husserl's definition of phenomenology as a discipline that lets what is studied manifest itself as it is in itself, but he points out that Husserl's notion of an "original, intuitive" access to the phenomena must not be understood as a naive immediate beholding. Phenomena can be covered up; indeed, "just because the phenomena are for the most part *not* given, there is need for phenomenology."[8]

There are, Heidegger says, three kinds of covered-up-ness. These three forms of hiddenness are decisive for us because they lay out the kind of phenomena that are to be subjected to analysis in division 1 and division 2 of *Being and Time,* and foreshadow what Heidegger will later see as part of the subject matter of thinking, insofar as thinking is still concerned with what he later calls "the hermeneutic-relation."[9] The first form of covered-up-ness is simply being undiscovered—"neither known nor unknown." The second is being buried over. "This means that [the phenomenon] has at some point been discovered but has deteriorated to the point of getting covered up again." Last, but most crucial, is the attempt to pass off the phenomenon that has covered over the original phenomenon as itself the truth, i.e., to deny that anything has been covered up. Heidegger calls this full-fledged cover up "disguise," which suggests that the covering up was motivated by not wanting to see the truth. "This covering up . . . is the most dangerous, for here the possibilities of deceiving and misleading are especially stubborn."[10]

Being and Time is concerned with the first and third kinds of hidden phenomena: our everyday understanding of the world and the objects in it, and the meaning of human being. According to Heidegger the way of being of the world is so obvious it is unnoticed in the course of our everyday activity; the way of being of human beings, however, is so unsettling that, just because it is constantly sensed it is constantly disguised. (Moreover, the unnoticed structure of our everyday world is itself distorted by being used to help hide what human beings really are.) In both of the above cases what is hidden, although it is not directly manifest to the investigator, is already present implicitly, so that making it manifest does not require empirical science of a priori construction, but rather the appropriate sort of interpretive description. Thus "the meaning of phenomenological description as a method lies in *interpretation.*" Moreover, the above two forms of hiddenness require two different kinds of phenomenological-hermeneutic inquiry. Thus one approach is employed in division 1 of *Being and Time,* and another is introduced in division 2 of that same work. Each of these interpretive techniques has been elaborated and applied by contemporary writers who call their work hermeneutic. In the first division Heidegger elaborates what he calls "an interpretation of Dasein in its everydayness."[11] Heidegger notes that our everyday practices for coping with things, social institutions, and people embody an unnoticed but pervasive interpretation of the world, the things in it, and of what counts as a normal human being. This interpretation is not something cognitive that has been explicitly handed down to us, nor did we have to figure it out in order to acquire it. We are just socialized into it. Thus it is appropriate to say, as Heidegger does, that it is neither known nor unknown.

Since the idea of an interpretation in our practices, which is unnoticed but can be made manifest, plays such an important role in Heidegger's work from *Being and Time* until his last essay, it is important to bear in mind an example. A striking case is the contrasting interpretation in the child-rearing practices in the United States and Japan:

A Japanese baby seems passive. . . . He lies quietly . . . while his mother, in her care, does [a great deal of] lulling, carrying, and rocking of her baby. She seems to try to soothe and quiet the child, and to communicate with him physically rather than verbally. On the other hand, the American infant is more active . . . and exploring of his environment, and his mother, in her care, does more looking at and chatting to her baby. She seems to stimulate the baby to activity and to vocal response. It is as if the American mother wanted to have a vocal, active baby, and the Japanese mother wanted to have a quiet, contented baby. In terms of styles of caretaking of the mothers in the two cultures, they get what they apparently want. . . . a great deal of cultural learning has taken place by three to four months of age. . . . babies have learned by this time to be Japanese and American babies.[12]

This example of Japanese and American socialization suggests that our practices embody pervasive responses, discriminations, motor skills, and so on, which add up to an interpretation of what it is to be a person. The same is true of our interpretation of what it is to be an object, and what, in general, being means. With this example in mind it should be clear that the common understanding in our practices that Heidegger wants to reveal is not some theory, conception, or *Weltanschauung* that we have either explicitly in our minds or implicitly in our actions. Heidegger's view is thus the extreme opposite of the cognitivism one finds in Husserl, Chomsky, Piaget, Habermas, and the Foucault of *The Archaeology of Knowledge*. All these modern Kantians hold that our practices are caused by a belief system, innate rules, or some other deep structure. For Heidegger, however, our practices are simply skills picked up by imitation. Heidegger puts the important difference between cognitivism and hermeneutics quite clearly when he says that what he is interested in "is not an object of mental representation, but . . . the dominance of usage."[13]

Because man is constituted by the interpretation embodied in usage or custom, Heidegger calls man's relation to the meaning of his practices a hermeneutic relation. By emphasizing the fundamental importance of this special relation, Heidegger is able to undercut the subject/object relation.

Later Heidegger tells us that all notions of private experience that refer experience back to the "I" were "left behind when [he] entered into the hermeneutic relation. . . ."[14] In thus denying the philosophical importance of subjective experience and mental processing, Heidegger is squarely on the side of the pragmatists and that other great original thinker of the twentieth century, Ludwig Wittgenstein. Moreover, since the understanding in our practices is not an internalized set of rules or an implicit belief system, there is nothing behind the practices that can be made explicit in order to explain them. All there is is the interpretation *in* the practices and all one can do if one wants to understand a culture is offer an interpretation of this interpretation.

Heidegger distinguishes our "vulgar conception" of the meaning of our activity from the "primordial understanding" which is in our everyday practices but not noticed. This "primordial understanding" in everyday practices and discourse, overlooked by the practitioners but recognized when pointed out to them, is the subject of much recent hermeneutic investigation. Harold Garfinkel in sociology[15] and Charles Taylor in political science[16] explicitly identify themselves with this type of hermeneutic concern. An off-shoot of this sort of hermeneutics of the everyday is the application of the same method to other cultures (e.g., Clifford Geertz's brand of anthropology)[17] or to other epochs in our own culture (e.g., Thomas Kuhn's application of what he now explicitly calls the hermeneutic method to the understanding of nature presupposed by Aristotelian physics).[18]

Heidegger thinks of attempts to interpret *alien* discourse and practices such as we find in Geertz and Kuhn, as descendants of an earlier version of hermeneutics which presupposes his hermeneutics of everydayness. He quotes Schleiermacher's remark that hermeneutics is "the art of understanding rightly another man's language," and notes that "broadened in the appropriate sense [hermeneutics] can mean the theory and methodology for every kind of interpretation." He then adds that "in *Being and Time* the term 'hermeneutics' is used in a *still* broader sense" to mean "the attempt first of all to define the nature of interpretation." Heidegger thus claims to be doing a sort of hermeneutics that lays the basis for all other hermeneutics by showing that human beings are defined by a set of meaningful social practices. Moreover, Heidegger sees that this claim is itself an interpretation so that "hermeneutics, used as an adjunct word to 'phenomenology' does not have its usual meaning, methodology of interpretation, but means the interpretation itself."[19]

Thus hermeneutic phenomenology is an interpretation of human being which demonstrates what interpretation is and why it is the proper method for studying human beings. Moreover, such a demonstration is "transcendental" since it does not discuss what it means to be a human being in specific cultures or historical periods but attempts to lay out the general characteristics of self-interpreting being which apply at all times and all places. These structures, which have never been noticed and so are covered up in the first sense of hiddenness mentioned above, turn out according to Heidegger to be isomorphic with the structure of temporality. Moreover they reveal an unsettling groundlessness, which makes everyone dimly anxious and which the everyday practices, therefore, seek to disguise.

The interpretation that makes up division 1 of *Being and Time* thus turns out to be only a first step on the way to uncovering the meaning in human practices. This gives special importance to the circular nature of hermeneutic analysis. In general, the so-called hermeneutic circle refers to the fact that in interpreting a text one must move back and forth between an overall interpretation and the details that a given reading lets stand out as significant. Since the new details can in turn modify the overall interpretation, which can in turn reveal new details as significant, the circle is supposed to lead to a richer and richer understanding of the text. As adapted by Heidegger, the phenomenological-hermeneutic circle provides the premises for a stronger methodological claim: (1) since we must begin our analysis from within the practices we seek to interpret, our choice of phenomena is already guided by the shared understanding of being which has made us what we are; (2) since this understanding may well be a disguise and distortion, we cannot take our first interpretation at face value; so (3), we must be prepared to revise radically our first account on the basis of the phenomena that it reveals. Indeed, we should expect that the interpretation of everydayness arrived at in division 1 will have to be totally reinterpreted by a second round of interpretation in division 2. As Heidegger puts it: "Our analysis of Dasein . . . is not only incomplete; it is also, in the first instance, provisional. . . . It is rather a preparatory procedure by which the horizon for the most primordial way of interpreting Being may be laid bare. Once we have arrived at that horizon, this preparatory analytic of Dasein will have to be repeated. . . ."[20] Thus in Heidegger's hands the hermeneutic circle becomes a two-step downward spiral toward a deep truth. Just as Foucault warned in his general definition of commentary, besides the everyday meaning in our practices there turns out to be another meaning "at once secondary and primary . . . more hidden but more fundamental." In division 2 of *Being and Time* Heidegger turns to the hermeneutic unmasking of this concealed truth.

Division 2, then, does not take the interpretation of division 1 at face value, rather it sees it as being used in the motivated masking of a painful truth. Heidegger draws the moral: "Dasein's *kind of Being* thus *demands* that any ontological interpretation which sets itself the goal of exhibiting the phenomena in their primordiality, *should capture the Being of the entity, in spite of this entity's own tendency to cover things up.* Existential analysis, therefore, constantly has the character of doing violence whether to the claims of the everyday interpretation, or to its complacency and its tranquilized obviousness."[21]

Whatever the truth about our being turns out to be, it is clear that in division 2 Heidegger's method turns into what Paul Ricoeur has called a hermeneutics of suspicion.[22] In any such case of motivated distortion, whether one finds truth in the class struggle as revealed by Marx, or in the twists and turns of the libido as uncovered by Freud, some authority who has already unmasked the concealed truth (the therapist, the Marxist theorist) must lead the self-deluded participant to see it too. In *Being and Time* this enlightened authority, already present in each person's sense of his or her condition, is called the voice of conscience. Moreover, in any such case the individual must confirm the truth of the deep interpretation by acknowledging it, and since the real problem is the restrictions erected as defenses against the truth, the result of the participant's insight into this repression is supposed to be some sort of liberation. Marx promises the power released by the realization one's class is exploited; Freud extols the control gained from discovering the repressed secrets of one's sexuality; and Heidegger claims that the realization that nothing is grounded and that there are no guidelines gives *Dasein* increased aliveness and flexibility.

It is important to be clear what deep truth Heidegger claims to have ferreted out. It is not simply that human being is interpretation all the way down, so that our practices can never be grounded in human nature, God's will, or the structure of rationality. It is, in addition, a certain understanding of this condition as one of such radical arbitrariness and contingency, that every human being senses deep down that he is fundamentally strange (*unheimlich*)—that human beings are essentially rootless and can never be at home. This is precisely what everyday social practices cover up in busily making man at home and secure in the world. But this frantic everyday activity in which human beings seek to give their life some stable meaning is just what reveals everyday activity as a flight motivated by the "preontological understanding" each human being has of his or her ultimate meaninglessness.

Thus transcendental-hermeneutic phenomenology does not simply seek to lay out the general structure of self-interpreting being; rather it claims to force into view a substantive truth about human beings. The truth, hidden by all cultures at all times, is that man can never be at home in the world. Or, putting it in fancier ontological terms, *the* ultimate horizon for the understanding of human being is an empty "ecstatic" temporal field. Early Heidegger thus turns out to be a paradigmatic practitioner of the sort of deep hermeneutics Foucault defines and rejects. What unites these two thinkers is that, rather than continuing to use this version of the hermeneutic method in his later works, Heidegger rejects it for reasons quite similar to Foucault's. To highlight what Heidegger preserves and what he abandons when he turns away from the transcendental hermeneutics of *Being and Time*, we will first summarize his early view in six theses:

1. Human being is a self-interpreting activity. This is the hermeneutic relation.

2. This activity involves an understanding of what being means, and it is this understanding that opens a clearing in which human beings can encounter objects, institutions, and other human beings. All members of a society share a preontological understanding of this interpretation.

3. Everyday practices and everyday awareness take place inside this clearing that governs what everyday human activity takes for granted. These practices embody specific cultural ways of treating things as important or trivial, public or private, perceptual or imaginary, controllable or mysterious, all of which adds up to an understanding of what counts as real for us.

4. On some deep level every human being realizes that what counts as real in the everyday world is thus "merely" an interpretation. The deep truth is that there is no ultimate reality to which our practices do or should correspond. This is revealed to each individual in the experience of anxiety, but since this experience is unsettling, human beings try not to face it.

5. Thus human beings plunge frantically into their everyday practices and take them even more seriously in order to cover up the realization that they have no ultimate justification, and thus that human practices necessarily lack the sort of truth and ultimate seriousness that human life seems to demand.

6. By a double use of the hermeneutic circle, hermeneutic phenomenology strips away our disguises and makes manifest the preontological understanding of being as *unheimlich* which is hidden in each person's awareness and in our public practices, thus revealing the deep truth of our condition.

Of these six theses, later Heidegger preserves only the first three. That is, he keeps the idea that members of a culture all share an understanding of what counts as an object, a person, and so on, which can be brought out by a hermeneutic analysis. But Heidegger now distinguishes the specific understanding of what counts as real, which everyone brought up in the practices of a particular culture at a particular time shares, from the metaunderstanding that this public understanding is nothing more nor less than an interpretation. It was this metaunderstanding, viz., that the hermeneutic relation is the essence of reality, which, in *Being and Time* was supposed to be revealed to each human being in an ever-present but ever-repressed sense of anxiety. Later Heidegger rejects his earlier claim that every human being is dimly aware of the hermeneutic relation. This change is reflected in his reinterpretation of the phenomenon of anxiety.

Heidegger introduced his account of anxiety as a privileged revealing experience of man's rootlessness in *Being and Time*, and elaborated it in his lecture, *What is Metaphysics?* But after his "turning," in a new introduction to that lecture, he presents anxiety quite differently. He still holds that anxiety in its revelation of meaninglessness is no ordinary mood that can be explained and removed by psychology or psychoanalysis; it is now, however, presented as the experience of the "oblivion of being" uniquely characteristic of the modern age.[23] Moreover, the experience does not directly manifest this meaning. It is not a source of truth, preontologically available to each human being, which hermeneutic phenomenology can recover by violently wrenching away motivated disguises. We all feel an "immeasurable need," and, since it is painful, almost everyone flees it most of the time—but few grasp its significance. Insofar as there is a shared interpretation of anxiety in our practices, it is still misleading and superficial: viz., that anxiety is the result of urbanization, repression, or overwork—problems that sociology and psychology have not yet solved. But later Heidegger no longer attempts to uncover a deep understanding of what anxiety really means which this superficial understanding covers up. If there is no preontological understanding of the meaning of our understanding of Being, repeated turns of the hermeneutic circle will lead us nowhere. So, if anxiety is to reveal the meaningless of our age, it must be *given* an interpretation. Heidegger the thinker (not the phenomenologist with a preontological understanding of the meaning of being) follows Rilke in interpreting anxiety as a specific response to the rootlessness of the contemporary technological world.[24]

Anxiety is no longer interpreted, then, as a manifestation of the essential truth, accessible to all human beings, that since reality is relative to human practices, human beings can never find a foundation for their world, and so can never feel at home in it. On the contrary, Heidegger becomes interested in how the pre-Socratic Greeks were aware of the relation between custom and being, and yet free from modern anxiety and at home in their world. He even hopes to find hints of how we can once again be at home in ours. Directly contradicting his early emphasis on man's essential experience of not being at home, later Heidegger strives to give us "a vision of a new rootedness which someday might even be fit to recapture the old and now rapidly disappearing rootedness in a changed form."[25]

Heidegger thus abandons theses 4, 5, and 6. That is, he no longer holds that human beings have a preontological understanding of the deep but disguised truth that what counts as reality is relative to human practices. Some people—whom he now calls wanderers, thinkers, and poets—do realize that our practices determine what counts as reality and bring forth what counts as truth. Moreover, in at least one period of our culture, fifth-century Greece, this realization was captured in the language and practices as revealed by the fact that their word for truth was "aletheia" (unconcealedness). But this understanding is no longer for Heidegger a transcendental truth immanent in each human being and so no longer provides a criterion of success for hermeneutic interpretation.

Starting with his reinterpretation of anxiety as occasioned by our modern understanding of being, Heidegger attempted to show that each specific epoch in the development of our historical culture is a variation on a basic interpretation of reality as presence. Thus, for the early Greeks, reality was that which opened itself and took man into its presence where he was "beheld by what is . . . included and maintained within its openness and in that way borne along by it, to be driven about by its oppositions and marked by its discord."[26] For medieval Christians reality was God's presence which was to be accepted, endured, and interpreted like a text; while for modern man, starting with Descartes, reality was to be made present by man by being made to live up to his standards of intelligibility. Of course each of these understandings of being allows different sorts of beings to show up in the clearing. The Greeks encountered things in their beauty and power, and people as poets, statesmen, and heroes; the Christians encountered creatures to be enjoyed and dominated, and people as saints and sinners; and we moderns encounter objects to be controlled and organized by subjects in order to satisfy their desires or, most recently with the total triumph of technology, we experience everything including ourselves as *resources* to be enhanced, transformed, and ordered simply for the sake of efficiency and power.

Heidegger's constant movement back and forth between our epoch and other understandings of beings in our history, in order to bring out our understanding more clearly, recalls the movement back and forth between the whole and details characteristic of the hermeneutic circle, but now there is no attempt to find an ahistorical, hidden, deep truth. Gadamer's version of nontranscendental hermeneutics as a dialogue with other ways of understanding the world from our past, is an offshoot of this stage in Heidegger's thought. But unlike Gadamer, Heidegger is not interested in these past understandings for the truth they contain, if that means a truth we can take up and fuse into our own horizon. One cannot enter into dialogue with practices—especially practices that are no longer practices in any unified, focused, way. How can there be a dialogue between the living and the dead? How could a fusion of horizons be possible when the only horizon that works now and determines truth for us is the technological horizon? Heidegger did feel that there was something important to be learned from the Greek understanding of "things," but the way that understanding could help us is, according to Heidegger, much more indirect than providing us with some kind of truth we can incorporate. (We cannot go into this question here.)

Heidegger's main interest in the history of our understanding of being, in any case, is as a way of diagnosing how we arrived where we are so that we can begin to mitigate the effects of our current technological understanding of reality by no longer taking it as self-evident and inevitable. When a culture's understanding of being becomes unbearable, relativizing its convictions are a first step toward a cure.

Later Heidegger still holds that each of the ways of understanding reality in our past, along with the correlative sorts of real things that were thus revealed, was understood preontologically by each of the human beings involved and so could be made manifest by phenomenological-hermeneutic analysis—minus, of course, any transcendental, cross-cultural ahistorical claims. But, in fact, after his turn to thinking being historically, Heidegger developed new techniques of interpretation. Thus, while he still accepts theses 1 to 3, he no longer thinks the phenomenological-hermeneutic techniques of *Being and Time* are the best way to get at the hermeneutic relation. Instead of using the hermeneutic circle—going back and forth between a general account and specific details in order to elicit the understanding of being of a particular epoch from the everyday practices of that epoch—Heidegger now finds this approach "superficial." Perhaps it is ironically superficial precisely because of its claim to be able to dig deeper and deeper, but it is more seriously superficial because it does not take account of the fact that practices, in order to form a historical understanding of reality, must be *explicitly* shared. That is, they must be focused, organized, and held up to the practitioners. This function, which later Heidegger calls "truth setting itself to work," is performed by what Heidegger calls a work of art. The nearness of a god (e.g., the Hebrew Covenant), the sacrifice of a god (e.g., the Crucifixion), the act of a great political leader, or the words of a great thinker are other examples of this stabilizing and focusing event which one might call a cultural paradigm. In any such case "there must always be some being in the Open, something that is, in which the openness takes its stand and attains its constancy."[27] There is no such claim in the hermeneutic theory laid out in *Being and Time*.

Once Heidegger has this insight his interpretations no longer go back and forth between details and the whole; rather he concentrates on that specific entity that incarnates for a people and for the interpreter what being means during a specific epoch. In interpreting the practices of fifth-century Greece, Heidegger describes the appearance and functioning of the Greek temple, and comments on the teachings of the pre-Socratics. In interpreting the understanding of being that allows things to appear to *us*, Heidegger describes the hydraulic power station on the Rhine as a paradigm case of our technological drive to order and control: "The hydroelectric plant is set into the current of the Rhine. . . . The hydroelectric plant is not built into the Rhine River as was the old wooden bridge that joined bank with bank for hundreds of years. Rather the river is damned up into the power plant. . . . The river is now . . . a water power supplier. . . ."[28]

Thus far we have seen that Heidegger is still interested in both the general fact that human practices always embody an understanding of being, and in the specific understanding of being that our practices embody. We have also seen that his reflections have led him away from hermeneutic phenomenology because (1) the practices do not themselves necessarily contain concealed hints of their own role in establishing a clearing, and (2) even though the practices do provide the basis for an interpretation of the specific sort of clearing they produce, the hermeneutic circle does not turn out to be the best approach for making this meaning manifest.

We now turn to what (for this particular essay) is an even more important development in Heidegger's later thought: the realization that there is another meaning in our practices, not deep and disguised, but still not noticed, for whose interpretation the hermeneutics of suspicion is actually a hindrance. This level of meaning might be called the *significance* of any given understanding of being. On this level an account asks how a given understanding of being developed, what its cost is, and what can be done about it. Both the idea that all human practices hold a single repressed truth, which it is the job of hermeneutics to uncover, and the notion that the practitioners have a preontological understanding of the meaning of their current cultural practices only distract the thinker from seeking the significance of our present understanding of reality. It should be clear that most practitioners of technology have no understanding repressed or overt of what the technological practices are doing to them. Indeed, if they were asked, most members of this culture, especially its elite scientists and administrators, would say that things are getting better and better as science and technology succeed in getting everything under control. If there is any problem, they would say, it is that we cannot control our own technology, but if we can gain control before we are blown up or polluted to death, then an era of peace and general welfare will ensue. Anxiety has no special significance in this interpretation and will be eliminated when we have better drugs and better therapy.

Heidegger offers the counterinterpretation that the cost of control is precisely the problem; that our anxiety and neediness will only increase as we achieve the total mobilization of all beings. This reading of the significance of our modern understanding of being is not a phenomenological-hermeneutic unpacking of the deep meaning each practitioner represses, nor even a reading of the surface meaning of the practices the practitioners share whether anyone knows it or not. It is an interpretation arising from a shared distress, which attempts to single out the paradigms that focus for all of us the technological understanding of being in our current practices, and then to call attention to what those practices do to the quality of our lives.

Later Heidegger calls the way a particular understanding of Being comes to be and pursues its course, "its essence." Thus to understand the essence of technology is to understand how we got this way, how technology works, and what it does to us. Those familiar with Foucault will recognize a striking parallel to what Foucault calls "genealogy."

Foucault, like Heidegger, has always been interested in an intelligibility in human activity: not in the ideas subjects have in their minds, but what unifies their practices. In Foucault's early writing he sought his intelligibility in supposedly autonomous rules governing the production of discourse. Later, Foucault saw that discourse itself depends upon the nonlinguistic practices that it unifies. Using a notion of the body reminiscent of Maurice Merleau-Ponty's, he arrived at the view that these practices are not governed by abstractable rules nor represented in a subject's mind, but are directly taken up by docile bodies: "Power relations can materially penetrate the body in depth, without depending even on the mediation of the subject's own representations. If power takes hold of the body, this isn't through its having first to be interiorised in people's consciousness."[29]

Foucault's objection to hermeneutics in *The Birth of the Clinic* is that this sort of exegesis merely adds to the proliferation of discourse without getting at what is really going on. In that book, and his other early books including *The Archaeology of Knowledge*, his goal was not to add more discourse, but to find the rules that determined or controlled the discourse that there was.[30] In his two recent books, however, Foucault, like Heidegger, criticizes the hermeneutics of everydayness for its misplaced emphasis on the meaning that social practices have for the practitioners. It is not that social actors fail to understand the surface significance of what they are saying and doing, but that the practitioners do not know the effect of what they are doing; thus a hermeneutics of their preontological understanding is no help in understanding what is going on.

The rejection of the participant's own interpretation of the import of his actions, however, does *not* lead Foucault to the hermeneutics of suspicion, the view that participants do not have direct access to the meaning of their discourse and practices because our everyday understanding of things is a motivated cover up. On Foucault's analysis, this position still rests on the methodological assumption that there is an essential connection between everyday intelligibility and a deeper kind of intelligibility, which the everyday view covers up. Foucault accepts certain insights of both surface and depth hermeneutics. He agrees that in one obvious sense of meaning speakers know exactly what they mean. On the other hand, he agrees with the hermeneutics of suspicion that some surface behavior can be understood as a distortion of significances, which the subject senses but is motivated to disguise. Foucault's basic objection to the hermeneutics of suspicion is that these secrets are mistakenly supposed to be the true and deepest meaning of the surface behavior. Rather, Foucault seeks to demonstrate that the deeper meaning that the authority directs the participant to uncover in his practices itself hides another, more important meaning, which is not directly available to the participant. Here Foucault turns to another kind of interpretation he calls "genealogy," the study of the significance of the "micropractices" inscribed in our bodies.[31]

The participant can directly see what his everyday behavior means; he can be led to see deeper meanings masked by this everyday behavior; but what neither he nor the authority directing the hermeneutic exegesis can see is what the exegetical situation is doing to both of them, and why. Since the hidden meaning is not the final truth about what is going on, finding it is not necessarily liberating, and can, as Foucault points out, lead away from the kind of understanding that might help the participant resist pervasive practices whose only end is the efficient ordering of society.

An understanding that makes resistance possible can only be obtained by someone who shares the participant's involvement but distances himself from it and does the hard historical work of diagnosing the history and organization of our current cultural practices. The result is a pragmatically guided reading of the effect of present social practices which does not claim to correspond either to the everyday understanding of being in those practices nor to a deeper repressed understanding. In this sense Foucault's genealogical method, which he sometimes calls *déchiffrement*, is like Heidegger's "thinking."

In this essay I have distinguished three different ways of doing interpretation, each with its distinct subject matter, method, and goals. The hermeneutics of everydayness treats social practices as a text, and by circling back and forth between details and the whole, seeks to reveal the meaning in these practices; the hermeneutics of suspicion uses the same method to liberate the social participants by unmasking the deep meaning the everyday practices serve to suppress; finally, thinking or deciphering focuses on specific social phenomena in order to highlight what our current practices are doing to the quality of our lives, so as to alert us to the cost of the practices and open us to the possibility of change.

Foucault was always critical of the hermeneutics of suspicion (with the possible exception of his suggestion in *Madness and Civilization*, which I have not discussed here, that society attempts to cover up the total otherness of pure madness). Heidegger abandoned the hermeneutics of suspicion soon after the publication of *Being and Time*. Both thinkers reject the view that human subjects, or everyday social practices, can be understood as repressing a deep truth, both because such an interpretation cannot be made plausible and because it tends to obscure rather than illuminate the nature and dangers of our practices. Later Heidegger and Foucault are interested almost exclusively in assembling evidence that our current social practices manifest (and in no way repress) a general tendency or strategy whose effect is to turn nature and human beings into resources to be efficiently organized and used.

Heidegger and Foucault would both, therefore, accept one aspect of the hermeneutics of suspicion. They would agree that some people feel distress as a result of current technological and disciplinary practices, and that some people repress this distress, but both would deny that this distress is repressed because the society senses its true meaning and that current practices can therefore be understood as *motivated* by the attempt to cover up this malaise.

Heidegger holds that our current practices distort our historical way of being open to beings, and that our current distress thus reveals a truth about human beings. Poets and thinkers are acutely aware of this truth which need not be hidden or deep. Most people, however, do not understand the meaning of their distress. So late Heidegger can no longer account for our everyday practices in terms of a preontological understanding they work to repress. Rather, after his turn to thinking the history of being historically, Heidegger understands current practices as the gradual working out of the understanding of being as presence which begins with the pre-Socratics—an understanding that never served to hide some deep truth but was simply the way beings appeared at the beginning of our history.

Foucault is more radical. He denies any universal truth at all, and so gives no account of the source of our distress. According to Foucault, some people, such as Foucault himself, suffer from the current practices of social control and others do not. Everyone might retroactively view our current condition as deprived in the light of some future practices, but whatever social malaise there is cannot be understood as a reaction to a loss of our historical possibilities nor can our current disciplinary practices be understood as an attempt to cover up some general social distress.

The question remains: What stand does each of these thinkers take on the hermeneutics of everydayness? Do they reject it along with the hermeneutics of suspicion or practice it in some new form? Here our parallel breaks down. Heidegger continues throughout his work to interpret the understanding of being in our cultural practices. He gives up the idea that this understanding is preontologically given to each participant, but he looks to previous thinkers to help him trace the history of the technological understanding of being characteristic of Western society. He thus carries further and historicizes the hermeneutics of everydayness carried out and justified in division 1 of *Being and Time*. Heidegger would presumably endorse the hermeneutics of surface meaning found in the works of Kuhn, Taylor, Geertz, and Garfinkel. He might point out, however, that prior to their hermeneutic circling back and forth between details and whole, which is appropriate for a text, each writer attempts to find the social paradigm, appropriate for a culture, that manifests to the society and the investigator which details of the social practices are important. The interpretation, then, consists in taking some particular scientific achievement, political issue, or ritual as a case of "truth setting itself to work" and putting into words what this paradigm means for the practices it brings into focus.

Foucault's recent work is also organized around paradigms such as Bentham's panopticon model for prisons and the "meticulous rituals" of Christian and psychoanalytic confessional practices. But Foucault does not approach these social paradigms as ways of focusing the meaning of being in the practices, but merely as particular ways our present disciplinary institutions concentrate and further social strategies.

Thus both Heidegger and Foucault wish to determine the way our practices affect our lives. But for Heidegger the effect of the practices follows from their meaning, so he still seeks an understanding of the meaning of being in the practices in order to understand how they work. According to Heidegger we must understand that since the pre-Socratics our culture has equated "to be" with "to be present," in order to see why and how we have arrived at the "total mobilization of all beings." Thinking presupposes the hermeneutics of our everyday understanding of being.

Foucault, however, for whom all that is important about our micropractices is how they affect the people whose bodies and minds they form, is not interested in finding an understanding of being in our everyday practices. For him, such an understanding would in any case be seen as an effect of disciplinary power rather than the reverse. He thus by-passes a hermeneutics of everydayness and turns directly to a genealogy of strategies of social control.

.....

On the Transcendability of Hermeneutics
(A Response to Dreyfus)

Richard E. Palmer

. . . . .

The preceding essay by Hubert Dreyfus is tremendously suggestive. Not only does it propose a valuable typology of interpretive
strategies in Heidegger (which I hope to qualify somewhat), it also
links up meaningfully with the ongoing discussion today on the meaning and scope of hermeneutics in which he is playing a major role.
Concern with the meaning and scope of hermeneutics is not new to
Dreyfus, who participated with Richard Rorty and Charles Taylor in
a symposium organized by David C. Hoy on the theme: "What is
Hermeneutics?" at the 1979 annual meeting of the Society for Phenomenology and Existential Philosophy.[1] In his interesting earlier
paper, entitled "Holism and Hermeneutics," Dreyfus is aware both of
Taylor's view of hermeneutics as a field that holds great methodological significance for the human sciences[2] and of Richard Rorty's view
of hermeneutics as an alternative to the sort of philosophy that lays
epistemological foundations for everybody else to build on. The latter
view has thrown down the gauntlet for a direct and unavoidable confrontation between philosophy oriented to hermeneutics and philosophy in the analytic tradition.[3] For this reason, it must be considered a
landmark in the history of hermeneutics in America.

Although Dreyfus's present essay constitutes something like a
continuation of the earlier essay, there are important differences, also.
Let us look at the first essay briefly. In "Holism and Hermeneutics"
Dreyfus defends a hermeneutics rooted in social practices, which he
sees as growing out of Heidegger's interpretation theory of *Being and
Time*, against what he sees as a more modest claim, based on the hermeneutical circle, that all work in the interpretive social sciences is
necessarily circular, since it relies on preunderstandings to be understandable at all (Charles Taylor), as well as the claim advanced by

Rorty that hermeneutics should be defined as dealing with the problem of incommensurable discourses. Significantly, we are confronted here with three fairly distinct alternative definitions of hermeneutics, one based on the hermeneutical circle and preunderstanding—a tradition in hermeneutics—another based on Gadamer (among others), which emphasizes dialogue between worlds that are incommensurable and thus require translation, and the last, that of Dreyfus, which claims to be rooted in that specific kind of preunderstanding we find in *Being and Time* in which understanding stands in a concrete and opaque relational totality that is not in principle a set of rules or propositions but practices whose nature is never fully articulable in rational terms. At the end of his paper Dreyfus uses the solidity of this platform in the given and concrete social practices to attack the abstractness of Derridean poststructuralism, which denies any roots in facticity and asserts that language is just a play of differences. Now in his more recent essay, it is clear that Dreyfus has serious reservations about Heidegger's hermeneutical strategies in *Being and Time* and is seeking to supplement them with the standpoint of the later Heidegger. He is not giving up his view that Heidegger's hermeneutics in *Being and Time* has great value because it is rooted in social practices (contra Taylor and Rorty), but he now wishes to expose the limits of such a hermeneutics by showing why Heidegger himself felt a need to go beyond it. At the same time, he finds that Heidegger's implied denial of the earlier hermeneutics of *Being and Time* places him closer to the poststructuralist Foucault, so that one wonders whether Dreyfus would now feel quite so free to attack the "nihilistic relativism" he earlier found so objectionable in poststructuralist theory of text interpretation? In any case, I think it is fair to say that the present essay represents a further stage in Dreyfus's own effort to conceptualize hermeneutics, using the contrast between early and later Heidegger as his textual basis.

There are a number of issues one could raise with regard to this essay. First, how adequate is this analysis of the hermeneutical in *Being and Time*? (I find it somewhat schematic and couched in terms of "methods," "strategies," and "insights" that Heidegger supposedly had as he was writing *Being and Time*.) Second, in what sense is it fair to say that Heidegger came explicitly to "deny" that what he was doing was "hermeneutics"? (I find Dreyfus pushing Heidegger into denying things he did not explicitly deny but kept a resolute silence about.) Third, will the analogy between the view of interpretation in the later Heidegger and that in recent Foucault hold up? (I find the differences more significant than their common objection to modes of interpretation which merely disclose an implicitly held view.) Fourth, is Dreyfus's threefold typology logically coherent, or are there inconsistencies in it? (Is critique of the prevailing practices in the light of one Truth not also found in Heidegger's critique of technology? Is the insight that there is no ground or single Truth really assertable without contradiction as a Truth? Which comes closer to asserting a Truth that contradicts the prevailing view, this early thinking or the essential thinking of the later Heidegger?) Fifth—and the key issue, in my view—can one "go beyond" hermeneutics? Dreyfus's assertion of the transcendability of hermeneutics rests on the assumption that hermeneutics must be identified with a certain set of philosophical presuppositions. He, and Foucault (but not Heidegger), would like us to see hermeneutics as assuming there must be some kind of metaphysical Truth that stands behind and guarantees the text (as in theological hermeneutics), so interpretation has the task of revealing or reclaiming a hidden, sacred Truth. Or in Dreyfus's view of Heidegger, that in *Dasein's* being-in-the-world there is an implicit meaning in the fabric of one's everyday existence which a hermeneutics of *Dasein* will disclose, and further (in the second turn of the two-step downward spiral of interpretation), that a deeper analysis will disclose the call of conscience to exist authentically in the face of the ever-present eventuality of death.

Certainly if one conceives of hermeneutics in this way, then one can and should go "beyond hermeneutics." But I shall argue that hermeneutics need not and ought not be conceived in this way. I shall argue that Dreyfus is led by a Foucaultian conception of hermeneutics to "frame" Heidegger with a narrower conception than Heidegger's own text calls for. I shall, in fact, argue that Heidegger's thinking remains hermeneutical (that is, oriented to the explication of significant texts and works of art) from early to late, and that in fact when he enters into dialogue with a Japanese on the nature of language, and of man's relation to language and being, he has recourse to his early use of the term "hermeneutics" and then to a description of man as standing in a twofold relation to being on the one hand and language on the other. This he calls the "hermeneutical relation." But before presenting my arguments against the view that Heidegger went "beyond hermeneutics" (and thus, by implication, so ought we), let me first deal briefly with each of the other four questions I have posed.

First, how adequate is Dreyfus's analysis of the hermeneutical in *Being and Time*? While I find the contrast he is able to show between the two steps of the "two-step downward hermeneutical spiral" very illuminating, I feel that he neglects the theme of the essence of the hermeneutical in favor of an analysis of Heidegger's "hermeneutic method." The result is that we see an important contrast in the two phases of Heidegger's analytic of *Dasein*, but the *essence* of the hermeneutical remains unnoted. Yet Heidegger remarks later that "hermeneutics in *Being and Time* does not mean the art of interpretation (*Auslegungskunst*) nor the interpretation itself but rather the effort to determine the essence of interpretation first of all from the hermeneutical."[4] What is this essence of the hermeneutical? It is that things show themselves *from* themselves (speaking phenomenologically), or that one receives a *message* whose fateful character is not modified by our fears or hopes (speaking in terms of text interpretation). In either case, one "lets" things disclose themselves in their being. This is shown in the contrast between the existential-hermeneutical "as" in which things are "seen as" what they "are" (for us) and not in some abstract and distanced way—the "apophantic as." The hermeneutical *relates to* our being, but that relation is one in which one studiously avoids reductive, manipulative, abstractive procedures. This is the reason that Heidegger thinks he has found in phenomenological description the "method" in harmony with the essence of the hermeneutical, since it is supposed to let things show themselves *from* themselves.

I think Dreyfus has rendered a valuable service in distinguishing the two concepts of interpretation in *Being and Time* and articulating them in terms of his six theses. Certainly there is an important contrast between interpretation that discovers an implicit meaning (in a text, in a remark, or in one's social practices, but not just in social practices) and interpretation that places the interpretive text, remark, or practice in the context of a demand for authenticity, hears the call of conscience, and ultimately senses the anguish of human finitude. By using a term like "social practices" Dreyfus is able correctly to suggest that Heidegger's preunderstanding is like Wittgenstein's, a body of concrete practical abilities to do things; on the other hand, we should not lose sight of the fact that we understand from out of a "totality of involvements," a context of relationships that is far more inclusive than what is ordinarily meant by "social practices."

Making the object of hermeneutical understanding something

like "social practices" also enables Dreyfus to take the next step and suggest that simply rendering explicit the implicit meaning of these "practices" is manifestly not enough. One must take the second step and realize that everyday understanding has the tendency to cover things up. One cannot exhibit phenomena in their primordiality without doing violence to everyday interpretation. But Dreyfus puts a further cast on this second step in interpretation by saying that "Heidegger's method (now) turns into what Paul Ricoeur has called a hermeneutics of suspicion." Like Marx and Freud, who have also offered interpretations based on a critique of social practices, Heidegger too is giving us a "hermeneutics of suspicion" that does not take the social self-interpretation at face value but rather finds "another meaning in our practices" which is (according to Foucault) "at once secondary and primary, more hidden but more fundamental." This other meaning is the "painful truth" that for hidden reasons we cover up.

Now Dreyfus makes another interesting interpretive move. A hermeneutics of suspicion, he notes, rests on the prior assertion of a "deeper truth": in Marx, that of economic determinism; in Freud, libidinous drives; in Nietzsche, the will to power. "In any such case, some authority who has already seen the truth must lead the self-deluded participant to see it too." In Heidegger, then, there must be some such deeper truth. Heidegger, who was just trying to do phenomenological description of the being-in-the-world of *Dasein*, seems to have fallen into a metaphysical trap and is selling a deep Truth: man's everyday being (his "false consciousness," as the hermeneuts of suspicion would call it) is really "a flight motivated by the 'preontological understanding' each human being has of his or her own ultimate meaninglessness." Deep down, every human being knows he is fundamentally weird, says Dreyfus, which means "that human beings are essentially rootless and can never be at home." What is significant here, as Dreyfus notes, is that this is a transcendental analysis, not a historical one. It claims to force into our view a painful truth that Heidegger takes to be true for "all cultures at all times." Where can one go with such a view? One can explore the universal anxiety before such nothingness, as Heidegger did in *What is Metaphysics*? Or one can turn aside from a method of seeking the meaning of Being which is oriented to making universal claims—which is what he did after the turn.

So, according to Dreyfus, Heidegger decided he did not want to become a dealer in transcendental metaphysics, and he gave up his hermeneutic phenomenology. But hold on a minute! Wasn't Heidegger resisting the transcendental element in phenomenology when he made it hermeneutical? Is it Heidegger who wants to impose a Big Truth on his reader, or does he find—contrary to the essence of the hermeneutical, which is to try to receive what is as it shows itself, and also contrary to the essence of the phenomenological, which resists advance assumptions and does not posit a Truth behind phenomena—that he has become entangled in *transcendental* modes of thought? Is it not the search for *transcendental* structures in his analysis of the meaning of *Dasein's* being-in-the-world, in his interrogation of *Dasein's* sense of being-in-the-world, that doomed his results to take the form of universal statements (like science)? Heidegger found that the shape of his own questioning had preshaped his answer. Because his question about the meaning of Being had taken the form: "What is the *structure* of Being as it exists in the understanding of being that a human being has?" his answer came out as a *structure* of being: a temporalizing thrown project with a preontological understanding of the ungroundedness of his being. But the "structure" of Being is not necessarily the "meaning" of Being: so Heidegger had to continue his quest in another form: the interrogation not of *Dasein* as an abstract structure but the interrogation of art works and texts. One does not, however, necessarily go "beyond hermeneutics" by turning to the interpretation of texts!

This brings us to the second question: In what sense is it fair to say that Heidegger came to "deny" that what he was doing was "hermeneutics"? Dreyfus has a point in attempting to contrast the "hermeneutic method" of *Being and Time*, division 2, with what Heidegger later preferred to leave nameless. (It is questionable whether what Heidegger calls "thinking" can be conceived as a "method," although Dreyfus is able to give "thinking" a Heideggerian form, just as he gives hermeneutics a Heideggerian form; so that if Heidegger had moved on to still another stage, I suppose Dreyfus would say he had moved "beyond thinking," which makes about as much sense as talking about going "beyond hermeneutics" while all the time making the interpretation of texts and the meditation on interpretation the heart of one's thinking.) If one accepts Foucault rather than Heidegger as the guide to one's thinking about hermeneutics, and if one obstinately insists on identifying hermeneutics with the kind of bad metaphysics that Heidegger himself was continually denying (in fact, his efforts to use phenomenology and hermeneutics were specifically an effort to

escape the bad metaphysics associated with other approaches), then
certainly it is true that Heidegger does move beyond that sort of hermeneutics, as well as the quite different kind of hermeneutics we find
in *Being and Time*—hermeneutic phenomenology. But if one takes
one's bearings not from Heidegger's "two-step downward spiral" but
from his repeated efforts to point at the essence of the hermeneutical,
then Heidegger remains hermeneutical to the end. He simply pursues
the hermeneutical without naming it, becomes the text-interpretive
philosopher par excellence, meditates on the "eventing" of language
(the central problem in hermeneutics), and the hermeneutical placement of man in the world (without calling it hermeneutics). The fact
that he did not, after *Being and Time*, turn away from his guiding
question of the *meaning* of being and how being *discloses* itself to
man (even though he abandoned a transcendentally oriented way of
interrogating being) suggests that Heidegger is becoming *more* not
less hermeneutical, since hermeneutics is centered on the process of
being grasped by *meaning* in an event of disclosure. He abandons
transcendental modes of thought but he does not abandon the essence
of the hermeneutical. The fact that he prefers to abandon the terminology of his hermeneutic phenomenology in *Being and Time*
does not mean he is abandoning the basically hermeneutical character
of his own thinking. In my opinion, it is more accurate to say that
Heidegger abandoned one form of hermeneutics (that of *Being and
Time*) for another (the special kind of listening to texts and deconstructive dialogue with former thinkers) rather than to say that Heidegger is now "beyond hermeneutics" or "denies" that he is doing
hermeneutics any more.

       In his late dialogue with a Japanese, Heidegger sheds a great deal
of light on his association with the hermeneutical. He states there that
he purposely chose this term in *Being and Time* to avoid a philosophy
of language as "expression," which would take him back into a metaphysics of subjectivity. Rather, he wished to stay with *Erscheinung*,
the moment of appearing, and this term not as a metaphysical manifestation but as articulation, of "seeing as." And also, he calls for an
essential rather than specifically methodological sense of hermeneutics: the word goes back to Hermes, he points out, the messenger of
the gods who brings not just any message but fateful tidings. Such
a "message," however, is not analogous to the "painful truth" of
some explanatory principle like Marxian economic determinism or
Freud's libidinous foundation of all life; it is not some humanistic ex-

planatory hypothesis; it is a historical disclosure of who and what man is now in this epoch and what he is called to be. This is a *message*, however, not some universal, rational, deep Truth. It is more like a warning, or a beckoning to man. But according to Dreyfus, when Heidegger "starts thinking historically" (in terms of epochs of the self-giving of being), he is "beyond hermeneutics." He may be beyond what Foucault thinks hermeneutics is, but actually hermeneutics has traditionally concerned itself with the historical gap between epochs. Thus, all the while Heidegger is "thinking," he is also playing the messenger (the hermeneut of Being), and he is executing his thinking through a close and loving explication of texts! Clearly, Heidegger has not moved beyond the "hermeneutical" in some larger sense, although admittedly he is doing a different sort of philosophizing than he did in *Being and Time*. But does he *deny* that he is doing hermeneutics? What Heidegger did was to quietly drop the terminology of *Being and Time* in order to become less transcendental—and more hermeneutical! And when he turns, in the dialogue with a Japanese, to explain the essential thrust of his thinking, his view of language and of man in relation to language and being, he explicates not only his former use of the word hermeneutical but the word itself, and goes on to speak of man's "hermeneutical relation" to Being. I think Heidegger is urging us not to think of hermeneutics as a "method" or to come up with models of a "hermeneutic method" but to try to think the essence of interpretation from out of the phenomenon of the hermeneutical. I do not believe Heidegger ever gets definitively "beyond" meditating on the interpretation process that constitutes the existence of man.

Third, will the analogy between the view of interpretation in the later Heidegger and that in recent Foucault hold up? I do see some parallel between Foucault's effort to render explicit the implicit power relationships in the totality of involvements that make up our social practices and the early Heidegger's analysis in *Being and Time*, division 1; and possibly a little of the Heidegger that Dreyfus identifies with hermeneutics of suspicion, the great truth being the ubiquity of domination; but the modest hermeneutical stance of the later Heidegger, though it does not assert one big universal truth, seems to contrast with the relentless rational analysis Foucault focuses on everything from mental hospitals to the history of sexuality. Dreyfus's claim that Foucault rejects hermeneutics "for the same reason Heidegger does" rests on his questionable view that early Heidegger is "a paradigm practitioner of the sort of deep hermeneutics Foucault defines and rejects." We would argue, however, that the image of Heidegger as a paradigm practitioner of the sort of metaphysical hermeneutics Foucault has in mind unfairly limns Heidegger as a metaphysician, when in fact he was struggling against bad metaphysics. Heidegger does not so much reject the hermeneutical, we have said, as rather stops using the term hermeneutics for strategic reasons. These reasons are not, as Dreyfus and Foucault imply, because hermeneutics as such is *inherently* metaphysical, so that it must always assume a Big Truth which it is the task of interpretation to disclose. If this were so, a deconstructionist hermeneutics would be a contradiction in terms instead of something being practiced today in various forms by the "hermeneutical mafia at Yale"—Geoffrey Hartman, Harold Bloom, J. Hillis Miller, and Paul deMan. Rather, because he himself found he had loaded his project with the transcendental tendencies of Husserlian phenomenology, he decided to extricate himself from that project in order to pursue a course that was essentially more hermeneutical but without the term. But the kind of hermeneutics Foucault is defining and rejecting can only be identified with Heidegger by making him into a hermeneuticist of suspicion on all fours with Marx, Freud, and Nietzsche. Heidegger, however, is not doing social critique but fundamental ontology, a kind of phenomenological description. Whereas Heidegger is patiently and reticently seeking a means of access to the meaning of Being and trying not to define or explain it in advance (this is the heart of phenomenology and hermeneutics), Marx, Freud, and Nietzsche mount their social invectives on the basis of a positive explanatory principal (which Dreyfus says belongs to the more genealogical Heidegger of later days); but Heidegger's method (if we may call it such) is not somehow *based on* the Truth Dreyfus says it *produces:* that man is weird. Also this "truth" certainly lacks the positive explanatory power of such concepts as economic determinism, libido, or the will to power. The reason for this is probably that Heidegger is still trying to find the meaning of being, whereas the others have gone on to explain it according to a single Truth. I think a good deal more needs to be sorted out before one can simply accept the proposal that Heidegger in division 2 of *Being and Time* becomes a hermeneuticist of suspicion who understands everything in advance in terms of one big universal Truth; for both his phenomenological method and his emphasis on the hermeneutical are specifically directed against such a procedure.

This is a crucial issue for Dreyfus's argument, however, in that he
uses the image of Heidegger as a hermeneuticist of suspicion to prove
that Heidegger is doing the kind of hermeneutics (is even a paradigm
case?) "that Foucault defines and rejects."

The fourth question I suggested had to do with the logical coherence of the three typologies of interpretive stance that Dreyfus
has put forward on the basis of Heidegger. It is probably the case
that the categories would be valuable quite apart from their relative
applicability to or derivability from Heidegger. I believe this is so.
But I would myself prefer to define hermeneutics in such a way as to
include all three typologies—as well as Dreyfus's own efforts to reflect on the nature of interpretive strategies: Dreyfus, in my opinion,
is himself doing hermeneutics. (Does this mean he is a metaphysician,
or embracing one Big Truth? I think not.) I find the typologies quite
helpful in distinguishing kinds of hermeneutical stance—that is,
stance in relation to the task of interpreting actions, texts, or world.
My problem arises with the claim that the third type of interpretation
somehow goes "beyond hermeneutics." If I understand Dreyfus's argument correctly, the difference between the second and the third
interpretive stance is that because he is now "thinking historically"
Heidegger is no longer assuming that there can be "a truth which it
is the task of interpretation to disclose." However it may be with the
status of what is disclosed, I fail to see that "thinking historically"
suddenly and necessarily takes one "beyond hermeneutics." This is to
portray hermeneutics as a specific kind of ideology, a methodology
that simply cannot go on without assuming that texts contain Truth
(capital *T* indicates metaphysical truth, and, by the way, I don't think
Dreyfus is fair to the issue of truth in Heidegger in subtly slipping
in an ahistorical conception of it). How much is changed if we say
that interpretation discloses, or construes, or constructs, *meanings* instead of "truths"? As for the derivability of the three forms of interpretation as Dreyfus characterizes them from Heidegger, I have some
reservations. I see a great reticence in the ontologist Heidegger of
Being and Time to do anything like the social criticism one finds in
Marx, Freud, or Nietzsche. On the one hand, I can see traces of the
interpreter with the one Big Truth in *later* Heidegger, who argues that
modern man has forgotten being. Certainly, after Heidegger "starts
thinking historically" he does indeed speak about the weakness of
our epoch, the nature of technology, and so on. But it is paradoxical
that this very move toward historicism supposedly disqualifies Hei-

degger, according to Dreyfus's own typology, from being a hermeneuticist of suspicion, or indeed to be "doing hermeneutics" any
more, since he is not arguing on the basis of some Truth (or principle) applicable to all men everywhere. Nevertheless, I find Heidegger's critique of technology functioning with something more like the
explanatory power that the key principles in Marx, Nietzsche, and
Freud possessed. Also, I find in later Heidegger a positive side, a
vision of Utopia, if you wish (agrarian and anarchist though it may
be), that parallels the hermeneuticists of suspicion. Finally, I sense a
kind of "rootedness" in late Heidegger that is missing in Foucault. In
sum, the typology of three forms of interpretation Dreyfus proposes
seems to be coherent enough, but I find the paths of thought of Heidegger and Foucault resist easy classification into them.

My arguments above have already anticipated what may be said
with regard to the fifth question, which relates to whether one can go
beyond hermeneutics, or what sense of the meaning of hermeneutics
one would have to possess in order to make this type of claim. As I
said, I think there is little sense in roping off a certain kind of "historical" interpretation of texts and saying that this is not hermeneutical any more but "thinking." I prefer to view this postmetaphysical
kind of text interpretation as simply the next phase in the history of
hermeneutics, which has to adjust to the shifting philosophical currents of the age. I realize that both Derrida and Foucault find it helpful in clarifying the radicality of their rejection of origins and centered thinking to "define and reject" hermeneutics. In fact, a variation
of this issue is seen in the Gadamer-Habermas debate over the universal claim of philosophical hermeneutics in Gadamer's *Truth and
Method*.[5] Habermas's argument was that this universal claim tended
to accredit the prevailing preunderstanding in advance and led one
to talk about the "fruitfulness of prejudice" as Gadamer had (rather
polemically) done. Habermas argued that one must go "beyond
hermeneutics" in order to offer a critique of false consciousness. But
again I see this as a strategic move to highlight a difference, an effort
to go beyond the "ontological hermeneutics" of Gadamer. But if one
holds (as Gadamer does) that the history of hermeneutics is the history of all reflection on the interpretive experience man has as he
"reads" his world, then hermeneutics is not something one can out-
grow. One can quite legitimately find a given hermeneutical theory
or standpoint outmoded or wrongheaded, but not the effort to think
the essence of text interpretation itself.

Granted, hermeneutics has been given a special stamp by its theological history, its philological development in the nineteenth century, and the form it has taken in German philosophy (in Heidegger and Gadamer). But in Heidegger I see hermeneutics redefining itself in terms of "the business of interpretation itself" and in Gadamer hermeneutics makes universal claims to be the descriptive study of interpretation, namely, that which man does in his interpretive interaction with the world. Whatever Heidegger may have done in reference to labeling his own later thought, I believe few persons would deny that his thinking remains focused on the process of interpretation, that he continues to see man as situated between being and language in a "hermeneutical relationship" (as he himself calls it), and that his method does not stand in the abstract and transcendental tradition of Descartes, Kant, or even Husserl, but proceeds by explicating, interpreting, unfolding the meaning of texts. I do not find this posthermeneutical but essentially hermeneutical. I find a similar preoccupation with texts, writing, and phenomena in Derrida, and I consider his thinking to be a continuation of the history of reflection on text interpretation. His style and method, centered as they are on text interpretation, are also intertextual (some of his essays even remind one visually of Jewish texts, like the Talmud with its layers of commentary). So I prefer to say not that Derrida has somehow transcended hermeneutics but that he is putting forward an antimetaphysical hermeneutics, is suggesting a new way to understand writing and writtenness. His poststructuralist exegesis of texts is simply deconstructionist hermeneutics.

It may take some adjustment to think of hermeneutics in a way that is free of the ideological connotations that some persons would like to associate with it, but I think that to move in this direction is a logical continuation of developments in the thinking of both Heidegger and Gadamer. I see no particular need to equate hermeneutics with onto-theology, even if there is a markedly onto-theological dimension in hermeneutics to which some people would like to call our attention. Rather, I think popular usage already is moving in this direction with terms like "deconstructionist hermeneutics"— which, if we were to accept hermeneutics as the kind of thing Foucault "defines and rejects," would be a contradiction in terms. Manifestly it is not, and I have hopes that a broader, more general sense of the term will prevail.

. . . . .

Transcendental Philosophy and
the Hermeneutic Critique of Consciousness

J. N. Mohanty

. . . . .

I

Although the origins of transcendental philosophy lie possibly in antiquity and certainly in scholastic thinking, it is safe for my purpose to go back no further than Kant. It is not necessary to recall the more well-known features of Kantian transcendental philosophy. What interests me are not so much the overtly maintained doctrines but the deeper motivations, assumptions, and implied positions. To sum up a long and familiar story, one may begin by saying that, for Kant, the foundation of human knowledge lies in an *ahistorical, incorporeal,* and *formal* subjectivity whose structure is capable of being laid bare before the gaze of reflection. Being ahistorical, this structure, certainly its core, does not change and is invariant throughout cultural and historical variations. It is incorporeal, for body plays no a priori role for Kant in the possibility of knowledge. If anywhere, it is in the doctrine of "outer sense" that one may want to look for the role of body, but the opening sentences of ¶2 of the "Transcendental Aesthetic" says that outer sense is a property of the mind, as much as inner sense is. I also want to distinguish between "subjectivity" and "consciousness," thereby ascribing to Kant a conception of transcendental subjectivity that is wider than the concept of transcendental consciousness. Transcendental subjectivity may be taken as the title for the a priori structure of the human mind: it includes the a priori structure of sensibility as much as that of understanding. What, then, does he mean by "consciousness"? Of course, for him, to be conscious is to be conscious of an object. But it is also, pari pasu, to have synthesized the given representations under the concept of an object. In the very same act, it is also to judge. Consciousness therefore is synthesis. It is thought. It is conceptual, and *eo ipso* judgmental. Merely to *have* an intuitive representation is not as such to be conscious, unless and until such representations are brought under the unity of a concept, i.e., of an objective judgment. In this sense, one can say, following Kemp Smith, that for Kant consciousness is awareness of meaning, but it is also constitution of meaning. Since the *contents* of meanings derive from given representations, consciousness confers only the form (of unity). Kant, therefore, can say that "consciousness in itself is not a representation distinguishing a particular object, but a form of representation in general, that is, of representation in so far as it is to be entitled knowledge."[1] What is noteworthy in this is the close connection between the concepts of "consciousness," "synthesis," "concept," "judgment," and "form of unity," and also, eventually, "object." Let me call it the *formal* theory of consciousness.

The locution "unity of selfconsciousness" raises the question of whether Kant regarded consciousness as transparent in any sense. It might be thought that since he undoubtedly holds that the unity of selfconsciousness accompanies all our representations, all consciousness must also be selfconsciousness. However, we need to remember that in this context Kant speaks of a "necessary possibility," suggesting that all consciousness can be rendered selfconscious, and necessarily so. He even speaks of "degrees of consciousness," perhaps without realizing how such a position is compatible with the formal theory of consciousness. In any case, he belonged to a philosophical tradition that, at least in principle, believed that reflection can lay bare the total structure and content of consciousness. The very possibility of transcendental philosophy seems to rest on this assumption.

In fact, three other assumptions hang together with this one. If "reason" is the title for the formal structure of transcendental subjectivity, then these three assumptions are: (1) that pure reason is a perfect systematic unity in which the whole is for the sake of the parts, and every part for the sake of all the others; (2) that reason contains no self-contradiction; and (3) that reason can fully comprehend its own constituting functions.[2]

We have then a perfect example of what has been called philosophy of total reflection. Kant did not thematize reflection as a method but practiced it. This is part of that complaint that Hegel raised about Kant, namely, that Kant did not thematize the question of the possibility of that philosophical knowledge that the critiques deliver to us.

II

Just as all subsequently developed transcendental philosophies return to Kant, so do all critics of transcendental thinking return to Hegel's critique of Kant. Hegel holds that the Kantian philosophy is a phenomenology, by which he means that it is a knowledge of consciousness to the extent this knowledge is only *for* consciousness. But, of course, for Hegel, the truth of consciousness cannot be made transparent to consciousness itself. The point of view of consciousness is characterized by an externality, by an absolute opposition between consciousness and object, by the "given" that claims to set a limit to thought, and, in the long run, by the opposition between thought and reality. Kantian thinking remains imprisoned in these oppositions. While it claims to be a critique, it does not criticize its own presuppositions. These presuppositions are: the conception of knowledge as mediated by a medium or instrument, standing between the ego and the absolute as a distorting factor; an empirical conception of science as exemplified in the physics of his time; the conception of a complete, fixed, and formal knowing subject; the common-sense, sensualistic concept of the given; and an irremovable opposition between the subject and the reality. But underlying all these is the confidence that reflection can lay bare the structure of consciousness before the gaze of consciousness. If, however, "knowing is not the refraction of the ray, but the ray itself through which truth reaches us"[3]—i.e., if knowledge is not mediated by an instrument, if radical philosophizing cannot take for granted a historically handed-down concept of science, but must develop, for itself, and by its own autonomous effort, a satisfactory concept of science, if with the continuing critique of consciousness the conception of subjectivity itself is altered, and, ultimately, is to be overcome, once the point of view of consciousness is transcended through historical development, socialization of the individual, and reflection on both processes from the point of view of absolute knowledge—then phenomenology will make room for ontology, "The Science," i.e., Logic, will be the structure of the real.

Transcendental philosophy has learned one thing from Hegel:

namely, that its critique of knowledge has to be radical. It has to watch out for unknowledged presuppositions—contentual as well as methodological. It has also to account for its own possibility—something that Kant did not in the least worry about. But one still has to ask for the exact sense of radical philosophizing. In the context of Hegel, there are questions that need to be asked such as: Is it necessary for radical philosophizing that it should begin at an absolute point of beginning? If so, in what sense? Recall Kierkegaard's polemic against Hegel regarding the paradox of beginning. Furthermore, Is it necessary that *radical* philosophy, worthy of its name, should generate its own content and should have no subject matter given to it? Contrast the naivete of axiomatic deductive theory construction, which generates its own content but lacks radicalness. Is the Hegelian *science* as the self-development of the *concept*, but not as correlate of acts of thinking, of subjectivity, radical? Can the thinking-thought correlation be transcended and one term of that correlation hypostatized?

Pursuing this series of questions, may one not also ask: Is it necessary that a thinking fails to be radical if it recognizes its own limits? If it does not so recognize its origin, can it be said to account for its own possibility? May not the Hegelian critique of Kant be turned against Hegelian logic? But there is a surprising way the Hegelian may respond. He may point out that Hegel does not pretend to go beyond the appearances and posit an unknown thing-in-itself. Kant does that, and so it is Kant who transgresses the limits of reason, the very same limits that he posits. Hegel, on the other hand, needs nothing but the appearances in whom reason is immanent. It is, then, not the Kantian *sense* of limit, but the positing of unknowable things in themselves, that may be called in question. Just as it is not the Hegelian immanence of reason in phenomena but the hypostatization of the system that we are disputing.

Two things may still be said in defense of Hegel. It has been urged by many modern critics of transcendental *argument* that all that it proves is that a certain conceptual framework is necessitated by the way the world is structured for us. But since this is only a conceptual necessity—it has been argued—to demonstrate its reality, something more is required, namely some sort of verification procedure.[4] But what if the empirical basis is altogether rejected, as it was by Hegel? Shall we be left with a conceptual framework, internally consistent as well as inclusive in scope, but with no possibility of verification, and so no "reality"? The Hegelian, however, may turn this seemingly hopeless situation to his advantage and reply by beginning to point out that by rejecting the concept-intuition distinction he is also making it pointless to speak of alternative conceptual frameworks. He is, in fact, making it pointless to ask about the criterion of "applicability" of a conceptual framework. The criterion of its "reality" will be internal to the framework, and a conceptual framework will be "real" not if it *applies* or can be verified, but only if it satisfies its own internal claim, i.e., if it is, in truth, what it claims to be. This, in fact, is what the *Phenomenology* shows with regard to a whole series of "shapes of consciousness." The second point that the Hegelian will want to make is that, with the rejection of the concept-intuition distinction, the very concept of "concept" has undergone a radical change. A concept is no longer merely a set of common marks or a rule of synthesis, which in the absence of given intuitions is an empty shell. It is rather the concrete universal that, since it contains within it its own differentiations, already *posits* its own object—but does not wait for an alien given to assure it of its objectivity. It is *not* the same concept, the abstract universal, the empty form, which, Kant had argued, does not entail existence of its object, of which Hegel said that it posits its own object. It is rather the concrete universal, which is constituted by what has been called a network of inferential relations, which *posits* its own object. With the overcoming of the point of view of consciousness, the element of subjectivity is taken up into the concept; the concept, as it were, is the Fichtean ego, so that it is neither the act of consciousness nor the pure ego that posits; the object is rather posited by the concept. In effect, once the concrete universal is arrived at in thought, its objectivity is *eo ipso* guaranteed. All that in Kantian thought was rejected is taken up and internalized within the structure of the concept.

We can now more clearly see in what way the Hegelian phenomenology itself is a transcendental philosophy. If what a transcendental argument purports to show—as in the paradigmatic case of Kant's *Refutation of Idealism*—is that the skeptic cannot coherently deny the conceptual framework under consideration, i.e., without implicitly presupposing it, then we can say that a conceptual framework is transcendentally necessary if it cannot be coherently denied. The *Phenomenology* may then be represented as a series of succeeding conceptual frameworks, each with its own claim to truth—in fact each making claim to being transcendentally necessary. As reflection exposes the untenability of these claims, it at the same time presupposes an ultimate framework—Absolute Knowledge—which is true to its claim, and whose "reality" is guaranteed by the internal structure of the framework itself.

However, all is not well with this program. Hegel's project in the *Phenomenology* can succeed only if the criterion by which a shape of consciousness is criticized is internal to that shape. The entire series of critiques is intended to lead up to the final goal, i.e., Absolute Knowledge, the science itself. Closer examination reveals, to our disappointment, that Absolute Knowledge is presupposed in those criticisms, and the criterion that is used for the critique, far from being immanent to the shape being criticized, rather requires Absolute Knowledge. I will illustrate this with the help of only one example, a most crucial case at that: Hegel's critique of perceptual consciousness. Hegel begins thus: "Perception, on the other hand [i.e., contrasted with sense-certainty which "wants to deal with the this"] takes what exists for it to be a Universal."[5] This seems, at first, to be a somewhat strange description of what perceptual consciousness takes its object to be like. But Hegel has an important point: perception regards its object as what is capable of remaining *the same* in the midst of noetic variations. There is a certain stability and constancy that perceptual consciousness attributes to its object. In this sense, the object of perceptual consciousness has a universality, as contradistinguished from the allegedly unique singularity of the mere "this." In the same sense, Hegel goes on to say, the "I," who perceives, is also a universal. *I* can perceive it again, just as *it* can again be perceived by me as well as by others. While this much description is undoubtedly valid, Hegel proceeds to examine this *stability* and *constancy* in the case of the I and in the case of the object. Both are found to fail to satisfy the demands of reflection. The thing fails to demonstrate a unity that can hold together its various characteristics ("white," "cubical," "tart," etc.). All devices for keeping them together fail ("also," "insofar as," etc.). Phenomenology declares a discrepancy between what perceptual consciousness takes itself to be and what it is in itself, and moves on to the next higher shape of consciousness, i.e., scientific understanding.

In this telling criticism, I find that the criterion used is not internal to perceptual consciousness. Perceptual experience surely *intends* to apprehend its object totally, adequately, but it is also aware that it cannot. Perception "knows" its own perspectival character. The threat of failure and disappointment haunts it, without sublating its basic commitment to the world it encounters. *It* never suspects or abandons its object on the ground that the unity of the object, as presented in perception, is not up to the theoretical-reflective criterion of holding the diversity together in a unity in a manner that would be satisfying to reflection. A truly phenomenological description of perception would rather delineate the process by which the identical object is presented as the *noematic* nucleus around which various other components are structured. The unity of the perceived object is given through a plurality of noematic variations entering into a passive synthesis of identification. Hegel could bring out the inner dialectic of perceptual consciousness in the precise manner in which he does because he is using a criterion that has already been presupposed and whose genesis within perceptual consciousness is not apparent: the criterion that the truth is the whole. It is of course true that neither any particular perceptual consciousness nor its object is a systematically self-complete whole. Both contain intentional references beyond themselves, some of which are fulfilled in varying degrees, others, not fulfilled at all. There is no a priori guarantee that any of these intentional references will not be frustrated. And yet perceptions and perspectives do, on the whole, blend and cohere, though always under the threat of a possible collapse of that assurance. If perceptual consciousness is to be made intelligible in its own terms, then we are not obligated to go beyond it.

It may be said in reply to the above that the criterion of systematic wholeness is not extrinsic to thought, but precisely its moving spirit. To think means to be guided by this criterion. This monistic view of thinking is not itself borne out by phenomena. If to reflect on a form of consciousness is to carry it forward—by canceling its particularity and raising it to a higher form of wholeness—toward the goal of systematic wholeness, then, of course, the Hegelian move is evidently justified. But that is not the sort of thinking that abandons itself to the object or that watches the forms of consciousness arise and grow without interfering in the process—which is what Hegel claims to be doing in the *Phenomenology*.[6]

However, there are two fundamental insights we owe to Hegel, which transcendental philosophy can ill afford to do without. The first is the need for *an access* to the transcendental point of view. If the transcendental point of view is, in a sense, a reversal of the everyday, let us say, natural point of view, than how can we who live in the natural point of view ever make sense of the transcendental assertions such as Kant's to the effect that understanding makes nature possible? If Hegel's phenomenology, as providing such an access, fails—then some other mode of access needs to be found out. A radical philosophizing such as the transcendental is under an obligation to account for its own possibility.

The second fundamental insight we owe to Hegel—one that has survived the collapse of the Hegelian *system*—is that consciousness is hermeneutical. What Hegel shows, I think, in the *Phenomenology* is that every form of consciousness is also a certain way of understanding itself. It is a self-interpretation as well as an interpretation of the world. This interpretation need not be an explicitly elaborated system of propositions. It is the task of philosophy to provide such an elaboration. But even prior to such elaboration, a shape of consciousness is neither a diaphanous medium for manifesting its world, nor the purely formal unity which Kant thought consciousness to be. It is rather a *way of* apprehending its world; this "way of" not only constitutes the world but defines how the consciousness interprets itself to be. Thus, every shape of consciousness is implicitly philosophical.

This revolutionary position does *not* necessarily commit us to the further Hegelian thesis, exemplified in the *Phenomenology*, that every shape of consciousness, short of Absolute Knowledge, labors under a self-deception as to what it really amounts to, as to what its implications are, as to what precisely its *truth* is. Hegel's *Phenomenology*—which, borrowing Paul Ricoeur's expression, I would like to call phenomenology of *suspicion*—refuses to accept on trust the initial report of a form of consciousness as to what it is in truth. It claims to go deeper and discover what is claimed as its truth. In this regard, Hegelian phenomenology stands as the inspirer of both Marx and Freud. Now I want to acknowledge the Hegelian insight that consciousness is always hermeneutical, but I want also to incorporate it into a phenomenology of respect, as distinguished from what has been called a phenomenology of suspicion. A phenomenology of respect is methodologically committed to a respect for the given, and to undertake only such reflective analysis as is not repugnant to the *sense* of the given. It does not judge, but seeks to understand. The destiny of transcendental philosophy, then, as I see it, is to face the question:

Can a hermeneutical concept of consciousness and a phenomenology of respect be appropriated into a theory of transcendental subjectivity?

III

Phenomenology, as a transcendental philosophy, wants precisely to be able to do this. In fact, Husserl's philosophy, basically a philosophy of consciousness, appears to be the last hope for such a philosophy in a rather hostile and alien environment. Before we turn to its critics, we need to be very clear about Husserl's understanding of "transcendental" and also about what he means by "consciousness."

To begin with the first: Husserl consciously takes over the expressions "transcendental" and "transcendental philosophy" from Kant, and perceives himself as continuing, radicalizing, and perfecting the inner motivation in the Kantian program, but for him, unlike for Kant, "transcendent" is what is not included, as a real part, in consciousness. Everything worldly, the world itself, has the sense of being transcendent. Consciousness is *transcendental* in that it is necessarily presupposed by the sense of "transcendence" that the world has. The sense "transcendent being" is constituted within consciousness, which, therefore, is transcendental. The distinction between the transcendent and the transcendental is the distinction between the constituted and the constituting.

Where then does Husserlian phenomenology go beyond Kant? First, Kant does not see the full scope of the transcendental problem. He restricts it to the domain of *scientific* nature and to the correlative question regarding the possibility of pure physics and mathematics. He does not recognize that the vast domain of the perceived world, the life-world, on the basis of which physics comes into being, also needs transcendental sense investigation. In other words, Kantian inquiry begins with a higher-level accomplishment: namely, mathematical physics and the correlative ontic domain. But the everyday world of praxis and interest, the prescientific (and prepredicative) world in which we live, simply does not come upon the Kantian scene. Accordingly, the transcendental subjectivity that is revealed through the Kantian inquiry remains the formal principle that it is. Husserl, however, proceeds to lay bare the concrete life of consciousness in its multifarious nexus of intentionalities, intentional implications, and sense-constituting accomplishments. Transcendental investigation becomes *concrete* research.

What is lacking in Kant is found in the empiricist. Hume had raised concrete questions, genuinely transcendental in their import: questions about the genesis of *identity* and *objectivity* of things. In his answers also, he had achieved genuine insights into the way the life of consciousness constitutes these senses. But a sensationalistic and atomistic psychology and a blindness to intentionality as the essential structure of consciousness distort these insights, and lead to skeptical doubts, whereas genuinely transcendental philosophy is "neither openly nor covertly a skeptical decomposition of the world cognition and the world itself into fictions." Or, as Husserl writes: "It does not occur to transcendental philosophy to dispute the world of experience in the least, to take from it the least bit of *the* sense which it really has in the actuality of the experience. . . ."[7]

Kant shares with the empiricist, whom he seeks to overcome but is not able radically to do, not only this sensationalistic, atomistic psychology, but also a blindness to the *ideal objectivity* of the logical entities, senses, and truths. Although Kant does distinguish between formal logic and transcendental logic, he does not ask the transcendental question about formal logic, i.e., how subjectivity can in itself bring forth, a priori, formations that can be rightly called ideal objects? Kant, in Husserl's words, looks upon formal logic with a sort of naivete, "in its a priori positivity." Thus both with regard to prescientific life-world and the ideal objectivity of logical structures, Kant does not raise transcendental problems, so that his transcendental philosophy remains limited in scope to mathematical physics and its correlative: scientific nature.

This extension and deepening of the Kantian problem would not have been possible if Husserl had not, at the same time, developed a new theory of consciousness and a new theory of meaning. In recognizing the objectivating function as intrinsic to consciousness and the inner correlation between "concept," "judgment," and "object," Kant, in fact, had foreseen some of the consequences of both of those theories, without explicitly espousing any. In his theory of consciousness, Kant sought to retain a Humean psychological atomism alongside the theory of formal synthesis. His theory of meaning is more difficult to extract. One suspects that his theory should be somewhere between a referential theory, some sort of a verificationist theory, and a purely

logical theory according to which a concept, even apart from all sche-
mata, possesses a logical meaning, i.e., is a rule of synthesis in a unity
of representation. I suppose one would not be unfaithful to Kantian
texts if one distinguished between logical meaning (concepts as rules),
sensible meaning (the schema), and objective meaning (*objektive
Bedeutung*) or reference.[8]

What is thus implicit in Kant is made explicit by Husserl. Consciousness is intentional in the sense of being directed toward an object, such directedness not being a real relatedness to something real
(for the object of consciousness may also be a fiction). It is also intentional in the sense that every act of consciousness has its sense, which
is none other than the manner in which the object is intended or referred in it, regardless of whether the object is real, imaginary, or fic-
titious. Many numerically distinct acts may have identically the same
sense, many different senses may present one and the same object.
Both the sense and the object, then, are identities in difference, neither
therefore is a real component of a mental act. The sense is an ideal objectivity, to which one can return again and which one can share with
others. Insofar as an object is also identifiable and re-identifiable as
being the same, its identity is constituted by a structure of meanings,
for—in the domain of brute reality—nothing abides in the Heracli-
tean flux.

Since regardless of whether the object of an act is out there or
not, the act has its own sense and its own reference, the *ego-cogito-
cogitatum* constitutes a structure whose autonomy and self-complete-
ness is independent of the being or nonbeing of a world outside. Phenomenological *epoche*, for the first time, reveals the wonderful self-
completeness of this structure, of which each (the ego, the act, and
the sense) is a non-self-sufficient moment. However, this much can be
the theme for a phenomenological-descriptive psychology, without
requiring cultivation of the transcendental point of view. The transcendental point of view requires not only the bringing forth of all
hidden presuppositions (brought under the title "the world" and
its accepted, taken-for-granted being-sense), but investigation of
how these senses are constituted within the "purified" life of consciousness.

How then does Husserlian phenomenology compare with Hegel's? I have earlier characterized Hegel's as a phenomenology of suspicion. However, this affinity must be taken together with a deep

difference between the two modes of philosophizing. Hegel's reflections are intended to bring out the *truth* of the reflected upon, so that
in the *Phenomenology* he presents us with a series of forms or shapes
of consciousness arranged as lower and higher in a hierarchy in which
every succeeding member is the *truth* of the preceding one, and which
appears to have a closure in absolute knowledge. As contrasted with
this, a transcendental philosophy whose task is the clarification of
sense would be a phenomenology of respect. It is methodologically
committed to a respect for the given qua given, and to undertake only
such reflective analysis as is not repugnant to the sense of the given.
It does not judge, but seeks to understand. If a philosophical analysis,
for example, results in the thesis that we never perceive physical objects, or that there are no material objects, or no other minds, such
analysis conflicts with the senses of the acts of outer perception or of
the acts in which we come to apprehend the other person as an other.
Transcendental philosophy will not revise, but will rather exhibit the
structure of our experience. It will aim at a fresh *understanding* of the
world—by showing how the nexus of meanings, which is the world,
gets constituted—and likewise of our place in it, rather than at finding out a *truth* about the world that is to replace the ordinary and
scientific beliefs about it. The *epoche* about which I have been talking,
following Husserl, which, as it were, brackets, suspends, or rather
neutralizes our belief in the world, is *not* motivated by suspicion and
doubt as to the veracity of our world belief. Its purpose is not to free
natural consciousness of those elements that breed suspicion, or to
cancel its misleading self-interpretations in favor of a more adequate
philosophical interpretation. What it tries to do rather is precisely to
lay bare for the first time *what* its self-interpretation is, to reveal even
the fact that it consists in self-interpretations, and to exhibit, for the
first time, belief in the world as a belief, as an acceptance-phenome-
non. By this, we become reflectively aware of the sense of *mundaneity*
that attaches to natural consciousness, not denying or modifying it.
As the sense of mundaneity shows itself, and as reflection clarifies
how this sense constitutes itself, by that very achievement it becomes
transcendental. "Mundane" and "transcendental" do not designate
two different domains. The mundane constitutes itself within the
transcendental. Perhaps, it is more accurate to say that the transcendental apperceives itself as mundane.

V

What Hegel's critique is to Kant, Heidegger's is to Husserl. Both critiques are hermeneutical, both appeal to the interpretive nature, in one case, of consciousness, in the other of *Dasein*. I have argued that Hegel's phenomenology still retains transcendental philosophy. The same may be said, and has been said, of Heidegger's position in *SuZ*. In place of the Kantian conception of knowledge as judgment, Heidegger, following the lead of Husserl's intentionality thesis, wants to understand knowledge as an ontic relatedness to being by virtue of which an entity stands unconcealed and shows itself as it is in itself. Given this concept of knowledge, the conditions of its possibility lie not in a system of pure concepts or logical principles, but in that Being that brings entities to unconcealment. In other words, ontic knowledge is grounded in ontological knowledge. But how is ontology possible? Heidegger's answer is that ontological knowledge is grounded in that preontological understanding of Being that characterizes man's mode of being, i.e., *Dasein*. This mode of being is not that of an epistemological subject. *Dasein* is not consciousness. It is rather concrete human existence, ecstatic being-in-the-world, being-outside-of-itself, being-toward-death, caring and projecting future possibilities, constituting the world as a system of concerned references, and, by virtue of its own intrinsic temporality, making possible time with its dimensions of past, present, and future. It is such a being that replaces, in Heidegger's thought, the Kantian "I think," the Fichtean "ego," and the neo-Kantian logical subject. It is still the transcendental ground, for it is the source of all meaning, the ground of all knowledge—ontic and ontological. Even after the reversal, when Heidegger's thinking turns from the *Dasein*'s understanding of Being to Being's availability to *Dasein*, the thinking is transcendental in structure: the *Lichtung* of Being makes possible the *clearing* within which entities come to be unconcealed.

For the present, what directly concerns us is Heidegger's critique of the concept of "consciousness." Part of his critique lies in showing that man's primary relation to the world is not epistemic, but affective concern and caring. The other part consists in this, that if consciousness is intentionality, then the intentional relation must be grounded in something that is not itself intentional. In other words, Heidegger raises a question, which he says Husserl and other transcendental philosophers did not raise: What is the Being of consciousness? The condition of the possibility of intentionality lies, for him, in the original prepredicative nonconceptual *understanding* of Being which characterizes *Dasein*, or in what he calls the transcendence of *Dasein*.

A still more radical attempt to overcome the point of view of consciousness is made in the later writings, where the transcendental move takes the form of a history of Being. History of Being is in fact history of man's understanding of Being. A major phase in this history is the understanding of Being as consciousness, and so of human existence as subject and of the world as object. Heidegger can never think of consciousness except as representation, as the inner, as subjective. One often has the suspicion that the efforts of Husserl to overcome, in his developed thesis of intentionality, the representative theory of consciousness, or the attempts of the neo-Kantians to free our understanding of consciousness from subjectivity, were lost on him. In his critique, he continues to insist on the inevitably representational character of consciousness.

One of the merits Heidegger claims for his understanding of *Dasein* is that it undercuts the very possibility of the realism-idealism issue by making the question "Does the world exist in consciousness, or outside of consciousness?" pointless, inasmuch as *Dasein* is not consciousness but being-in-the-world.[9] Little does he recognize, much to our surprise, that a radicalized theory of consciousness as intentionality has exactly the same consequence. For if consciousness is intentional and so is directed toward the world, then it does not have an inner core where the things could have their habitation and it hardly makes sense to ask whether the world does or does not exist in consciousness.

I have earlier drawn attention to the Hegelian insight that consciousness is necessarily hermeneutical, that it both interprets itself and its world. Heidegger's philosophy radicalizes that thesis with regard to *Dasein*. *Dasein* is hermeneutical inasmuch as it is essentially characterized by a certain comprehension of Being—a comprehension that, however, is not theoretical-cognitive, but practical-affective, an understanding that philosophy needs to elaborate and conceptualize. He recognizes the "hermeneutical circle" that is involved, but advises us to plunge into the circle "for one just cannot step outside it." It may again be noted that this recognition of the interpretative-constitutive character (of *Dasein*) is *not* lacking in a fully developed phenomenology of consciousness as well. There is thus a remarkable *structural isomorphism* between theory of consciousness and theory of *Dasein*, and in spite of some of the great merits of several of Heidegger's specific analyses, his claim to have brought about a radical improvement over the consciousness philosophies is hardly justifiable.

If Heidegger's overcoming of the philosophy of consciousness is not to lie in a desire to save a realistic ontology (contrary to what commentators on Heidegger thought to be the case), for Husserl was already beyond the realism-idealism controversy, *then* we still have to look for the decisive Heideggerean critique. Here I will recall two versions of it.

Eugen Fink has popularized the distinction between the thematic and the operative concepts of a system, and has used it to argue that every philosophical system generates its own operative concepts—a point that is closely connected with the finiteness and situatedness of the philosopher.[10] Even here we should be aware of misunderstanding Fink's point. It is true that there will always remain open and unsolved problems for every system. But these are not Fink's "operative" concepts. Only those unsolved problems and dark regions deserve to be called "operative" that are generated or subtended by the movement of one's thought and the course of its thematization. Applied to Husserl's phenomenology, if the world and individual worldly objects constitute the themes of natural attitude, the attempt, through the *epoche,* to thematize this fact of the natural attitude, lays bare the operative presuppositions of that attitude: e.g., the acts of subjective experiencings through which a natural object comes to self-givenness. Husserlian phenomenology precisely thematizes these subjective acts of experiencing, but in doing so subtends its own operative concepts of "phenomenon," "constitution," "reduction," and "transcendental subjectivity"—concepts that cannot in principle be fully clarified within Husserl's philosophy. Fink notes that the Hegelian speculative proposition, Heidegger's hermeneutic circle, and Husserl's phenomenological reduction are all attempts to deal with this tension between thematic and operative concepts. Since this tension cannot be resolved, the program of a transcendental philosophy is destined to fail.

Time will not permit me to make a detailed examination of Fink's idea of "operative concept." I can only record my impression that Fink appears to have in mind several different, albeit related, things: first, there is the Heideggerean *Ungedachte,* not thought within the system but making possible what is thought precisely as it is thought; the *horizon of sense* within which the problems and the themes first become posited for a system; the *mode of access* that a

philosophical thinking uses to deal with its theme, by which is meant
not so much the method which may have been explicitly thematized
if the thinking is critical, but what makes such method first possible
in relation to the given theme; and fundamental concepts that are
necessary correlates of concepts that have been thematized. An example of the first, of course, is the concept of Being as enduring presence, and so a certain relation between Being and time with regard to
the dominant strand of Western metaphysics; an example of the second is the understanding of Being as object, within which the Kantian problematic first becomes possible; of the third, the mode of reflection Kant employs in the critiques and the mode of knowledge
that the critical philosophy itself gives, which, according to a standard
Hegelian critique of Kant, was never and cannot, in principle, be
thematized within the self-prescribed limits of Kantian epistemology;
and, finally, of the fourth, such conceptual phenomena as the necessary correlation between "rest" and "movement," "one" and "being,"
"identity" and "difference" brought out in Platonic dialectics.

For my purpose, I can only refer to Hans-Georg Gadamer's decisive reply: it is not "the limiting problem of a transcendental foundation" that can provide the stimulus to the turn from Husserl to
Heidegger.[11] As I understand it, the goal of transcendental philosophy
is not intended to be achievable "in one shot." In fact, it is an "infinite
task," the pursuit of which would involve progressive thematization
of all those things that are, at any given stage, unthought. The idea
of such a transcendental philosophical goal is not refuted by pointing
out that no particular researcher can achieve it, in his own work. The
decisive issue is whether it is even a legitimate goal.

As contrasted with Fink's critique, Gadamer's is more apprecia-
tive of the goal, the inner potentiality, and even the universality of
the transcendental-phenomenological research. Gadamer sees, for example, that Husserl's phenomenology goes beyond the realm of explicit objectification in its discovery of anonymous and horizon intentionalities. He recognizes that the thesis of correlation between noesis
and noema is as far beyond the opposition between realism and
idealism as Heidegger's position is. He recognizes that the problem of
intersubjectivity is not an unsurmountable barrier for Husserl's transcendental egological stance. Heidegger's critique, as he sees it, "presupposes the consistent carrying out of the transcendental thought of
Husserl's phenomenology, the result of a constant confrontation with
the attitude of phenomenological research."[12] To the extent I can see

it, Gadamer isolates three points where Husserl's program of phenomenological research needs to be overcome—one of them from
within, i.e., at the precise place where the transcendental constitution
analysis was to reach its goal, the two others at marginal corners, but
of equal importance.

The one that arises from within phenomenological inquiry lies,
according to Gadamer, in the problem of the self-constitution of temporality in its primal source of the present. One question he raises is,
can one still say that even here, "constitution" of temporality does
not amount to creation, as Husserl would not want to say of constitution in general? As far as I can see into this extremely difficult
matter, it is not a question of the *generation* of temporality out of
something that is not temporal, in which case one would be justified
to speak of creation, but it is tracing the origin of the higher-order
meanings of temporality back to that originary experience of the living present in which all temporal dimensions are given in their most
rudimentary form. We still have genesis of sense, but not real production. Gadamer also raises another question here: How is this
primal living present experienced? It has to be the end result of transcendental reflection, and yet does not transcendental reflection itself
come to be by virtue of that primal phenomenality? This problem, to
be sure, does not arise because of the objectifying thinking of constitutive phenomenology, for the primal living present is, for Husserl,
not a thematic, objectifiable experience. In fact, it presents a sort of
limit to that process of objectification. Any objectifying experience is
constituted, in the long run, Husserl often says, in this unthematized,
"enigmatic," self-experience. The problem that Gadamer succeeds in
revealing characterizes all transcendental philosophy. The thinking
that leads to the uncovering of the transcendental conditions of all
thinking and experience, must itself be subject to these conditions.
Such self-referentiality does not annul transcendental thinking, it
rather shows its transcendental nature.

The other two considerations which, according to Gadamer, provide just the occasions needed for escaping from the grips of Husserlian phenomenology are the realization that total objectification is
not possible, and what he, following Heidegger, calls "the interinvolvement of disclosure and concealment." As to the first, we have
already learned from Gadamer that Husserl *himself* did not regard all
intentionality as objectifying. Moreover, there is no reason, quite
apart from questions of Husserl exegesis, why the distinction between

actus signatus and *actus exercitus* (which he so fondly recalls from his student days with Heidegger)[13] should not find its rightful place within phenomenology. It is then to "the interinvolvement of disclosure and concealment" that we now turn.

What does this interinvolvement mean? In our present context, it seems to *imply* that neither can consciousness ever be fully transparent to itself nor can it ever totally grasp its object. For any disclosure, be it of itself or of another, must necessarily involve some concealment. There is one question about this allegedly necessary principle, which I cannot now discuss: this is the question, How is this principle legitimized? On what evidence does its alleged necessity rest? It is neither an a priori proposition nor an empirical generalization. For hermeneutic thinking in general, it cannot also be an essential truth, an intuitive induction, or a self-evident truth. Appropriate readings of ancient texts standing at the beginnings of Western thought cannot elevate it to a principle by which to evaluate all thinking.

There is a sense in which the proposition follows from the temporality, situatedness, and finiteness of human existence, not excluding the existence of the reflective, transcendental thinker. Phenomena such as the perspectival character of perception, even of all experience, the forgetting that goes with temporality, lack of omniscience, impossibility of adequate givenness, the opacity that lies at the heart of consciousness (Freud's unconscious and Marx's class interest)—all these are challenges to transcendental philosophy. In the concluding section I will briefly comment on them.

V I

We have noticed several challenges to the very possibility of such radical philosophizing. All these challenges are in fact challenges to the traditional concepts of consciousness as transparent, of reflection as capable of achieving total identity with the reflected upon, and of the reflecting philosopher as a transcendental ego raised, by that very act of reflection, above time, body, language, and history. If consciousness, both the reflecting and the reflected upon, is intrinsically hermeneutical, i.e., interprets both itself and its world, and if it cannot fully clarify to itself its own self-interpretations without further interpreting them, there will always be a zone of opacity in its very heart, a shadow, as it were, which it cannot eliminate by its luminousness. Add to this its temporality and historicity. Just as the reflected-upon consciousness carries with it retention of its past and protention of the yet-to-come so that the past enters into the structure of the present as much as expectation of the future does, and there is no bare "now" where reflection can achieve coincidence with the reflected upon, so also do reflective consciousness and philosophical meditation live on inherited historical traditions, without fully making clear to themselves how that tradition permeates them. That tradition itself is a structurally layered sedimentation of interpretations whose total unraveling is impossible, not on empirical but on a priori grounds. Being involved in the hermeneutic circle, philosophy can only interpret those interpretations. It is not temporality and history alone that limit the power of reflection; in another dimension, corporeality and language exercise similar constraints. How can the reflecting consciousness, embodied as it is and through embodiment integrated into the structure of the natural world, anymore than the reflected-upon consciousness, assume the stance of a worldless, incorporeal, pure transcendental ego for whom the real existence or nonexistence of the world makes no difference? If the existence of the world, *ex hypothesis,* can be put within brackets and the philosopher, freed from living participation in the world belief, "transforms" his reflecting consciousness to the transcendental, can he also cease to make use of a language? And if language is not merely an instrument of communication but shapes our thoughts and our world and embodies through its lexical as well as syntactical features sedimented interpretations of the community, can we say that, inasmuch as the philosopher uses it, he can ever be certain of that ideal of presuppositionlessness that transcendental philosophizing requires of him? These questions, all centering around the hermeneutic character of consciousness (or of human existence, as the hermeneutic philosophers prefer to say, suspecting the language of consciousness as carrying the conceptual load of a discredited tradition) are also connected with the findings of Marx and Freud; for, both in psychoanalysis and in the Marxist concept of ideology, the false consciousness, a wrong self-interpretation, conceals from consciousness its true nature if it does not present it with an inverted picture of itself. In both, the question of interpreting symbolism, of deciphering its significance, not piecemeal but in the context of a total system of interpretations, becomes of paramount importance. It is not surprising, then, that many see here the death of all consciousness philosophies and their replacement by a hermeneutic philosophy of human existence. How can the traditional philosophy of consciousness, with its historical rootedness in the metaphysics of light, account for one's errors about one's own conscious life to which psychopathology bears ample testimony? Basically, it becomes a question of the finitude of man. When, as in the wake of the breakdown of the Hegelian system, the finitude of man came to the forefront of philosophical consciousness, it was also felt that a transcendental philosophy was not *his*. A philosophy that lays bare the constitution of man and of the world within subjectivity could be only talked about but not realized, and a transcendental stance would be an act of bad faith, i.e., one that knows, but refuses to concede, that it is what it is not.

I want to contend, in response to these powerful challenges, that they do not destroy or weaken transcendental philosophy as such, but only the classical forms of it as formulated by Kant and German Idealism. What is still open is a phenomenological version of it, for phenomenology and hermeneutics stand in a peculiar dialectical relation to each other. We need to ask if the concept of transcendental subjectivity cannot be so formulated as to be able to comprehend all the recalcitrant phenomena: corporeality, historicity, and all the rest.

Let us begin with corporeality. Once we try to formulate the *sense* "body," we find that it is a many-layered noematic structure.[14] At least four such layers have to be distinguished: the body as physical object, the body as living organism, the body as expressive object, the body as cultural object. An account of the constitution of body as a sense structure has to exhibit the constitution of all these layers within that structure. Constitution of this complex sense structure of body leads back to acts and experiences that, at their most basic layer, may be brought under the title "body feeling" or bodily subjectivity. Body feeling and felt body are indeed not distinguished from each other. The felt body is not an object, presented to me; it is a mode of experiencing myself and ordering the world around me. It is not localized in the environment, for all localization and spatial orientation presuppose it. As lived from within, my hand's reaching out to a glass of water is directed toward the glass of water in the "how" of its givenness, and not the physicochemical process described by physiology. I move a thing with my body, but "I move myself" is prior to, and is presupposed by all "I can," it gives me the most elementary experience of possibility. In fact, the kinesthetic experience "I move myself" is involved in the constitution not alone of body as a sense structure, but also in the constitution of *nature*. The *sense* "material object" is constituted not merely in actually performed acts of *outer* perception, but also in the possibilities of performing such acts from other perspectives, which presuppose the subjective kinesthetic anticipation, "I can go round and look from the other side"; also necessary for constitution of the full sense of "materiality" is actual experience and anticipation of resistance—both presupposing the same "I move myself." Thus in the very structure of the transcendental subjectivity, as constituting both my body and nature, there is involved a stratum of corporeality. The transcendental character of corporeality—not of the thing called "body"—has to be recognized, in contrast to Kant.

Next, by "historicity" is to be understood not being in time, which, to be sure, belongs to natural events as well. What is meant, for one thing, is original temporality in the sense in which every moment of consciousness carries with it its temporal horizon of retentions and protentions. Even that is not enough: with *its temporal horizon*, to be historical needs to be built upon sedimented acquisitions from the past. It is this idea of sedimentation whose recovery through reflection seems to have presented serious problems for transcendental philosophy. What is being originally lived through becomes an abiding possession to which one can always return. Again, insofar as I belong to an intersubjective community, the sedimentations that I inherit were not instituted by me, but by others, my ancestors; they become my acquisitions to which I also can return. It is this living-present-sedimentation-inheritance-reactivation structure that constitutes historicity of the world in which we live, as well as of the consciousness through which the sense of that world becomes constituted.

What, then, is the problem for transcendental philosophy? There is, in fact, a nexus of problems. In the first place, a historical consciousness is *situated* in a particular moment, from which it cannot achieve the universal point of view that philosophy requires. Also, since the historical sedimentations need to be uncovered for full self-knowledge and the necessary presuppositionlessness, the latter are unattainable ideals, for those sedimentations cannot be fully uncovered, involved as we are—and necessarily so—in the hermeneutic circle. Furthermore, the world whose constitution would lead us to the transcendental domain is itself a historical phenomenon; with changes in the world (correlatively, in the conceptual framework), the structure of the constituting subjectivity needs to be different.

These anxieties lead us to ask what the element of truth is in the hermeneutic approach. Husserl had already pointed out that intentionality is not mere reference to an object, consciousness's being *of* an object, but that such reference is mediated by meaning that is conferred by consciousness. In other words, the intentional consciousness is meaning bestowing, and therefore interpreting (for what else is interpreting but conferring meaning?). However, Husserl had also realized that an *act* of consciousness is always inserted into a total *life* of consciousness, and in fact into a tradition and community, so that the meanings that mediate intentional reference are not creations *de novo* but in fact presuppose the context of meanings that are *available*. But at the same time Husserl insisted that we do perceive things that are nevertheless given. In other words, for him being given and being interpreted are descriptions of the same situation from two different levels of discourse. Hermeneutics and phenomenology coexist in his thought. Furthermore, what are in fact described in phenomenology are often nothing but interpretations that are uncovered and rescued from their anonymity.

It is then true that if thinking is hopelessly involved in the hermeneutic circle there would be an end to philosophizing. There would only be a historiography of changing conceptual frameworks, and even that may not be feasible. The possibility of philosophy surely requires that one can take a reflective stance in which one watches this circle itself, in which one can bring to light, without distorting, already sedimented interpretations (as Heidegger in such an exemplary manner does with regard to the concept of "thing"). We are really back with the problem of access to the transcendental point of view which so much concerned both Hegel and Husserl—the former in his account of "shapes" of consciousness, the latter in his theory of phenomenological *epoche*. It is true that a complete coincidence between reflection and the reflected upon is ruled out by temporality. But complete coincidence is too strong a requirement for philosophy, and its failure is too hasty a ground for skepticism.

What I am trying to say is perhaps something like this: it is true that the philosopher is a human being, entrenched in time and history. It is also undeniable that transcendental philosophy, by its very conception, is a philosophy from a radically critical standpoint. As such, it would seem as though the possibility of such philosophizing is a priori denied to man. But in drawing this conclusion, one overlooks two things. In the first place, it is not the case that the whole being of human consciousness is exhausted in its being in time and in its historicity. Second, it is not a matter of exclusive disjunction: *either* all at once, and without the least trace and risk of failure, one achieves the transcendental point of view, *or* one does not do so at all. Regarding the first: consciousness has both temporal and nontemporal aspects. In its nontemporal aspect, it is self-revealing, and this self-revelation is not an event which has its temporal horizon. Furthermore, the meanings that consciousness confers are logical unities, and retain an identity through time; one can return to them again. There is still something more to be hopeful about: if consciousness were nothing more than temporality and historicity, we could not know that very structure. We would not have been able to determine such an essential structure. A formal structure remains invariant amidst the temporal and historical flow. Moreover, we not only determine these eidetic structures, we also can, in reflection, relive in our consciousness the essential stadia in history. Heidegger does it in his thinking of Being; Husserl does it in reactivating the essential process by which Galilean physics originated. The fact that history can be relived in its essential structure, that sedimented acquisitions can be reactivated (otherwise they would not be acquisitions), shows that consciousness always transcends its own historicity, that it is not a perpetual dissipation of itself, but always gathers itself up: in its own transparency, in the logical meanings it secretes, and in its ability to relive and reactivate the past.

The exclusive disjunction, which is the ground of skepticism, is also mistaken. It is true that resolving to disconnect all presuppositions, to suspend belief in the world, to philosophize radically, is no guarantee that one has, once and for all, achieved the transcendental stance. There may be lurking unacknowledged presuppositions of which one is unaware. If one may not long tread on the razor's edge, it does not follow that one does not do so at all. The proof of the pudding lies in the eating. Transcendental philosophizing has been practiced. But it is a matter of continuing self-examination and self-criticism, which itself bears testimony to the actuality of the standpoint.

We cannot also avoid the question, Is the transcendental subjectivity nonlinguistic? If not, how can it help being contaminated by the hidden presuppositions, cultural as well as metaphysical, of any given language? Here again, my answer would be roughly on the same lines as in cases of corporeality and historicity. It is both linguistic and nonlinguistic. Language may be looked upon either as the linguistic system (*la langue*) or as speech (*la parole*). As the former, it is an objective system of lexical elements built out of an inventory of phonemes and syntactical and semantical rules. Such a system may be perceived diachronically or synchronically. At any given time, we are presented with a logical system with an ideal being of its own; at the same time, it is undeniable that the system had a genesis, a course of development, a history. Insofar as *this* is concerned, we have taken care of it in the context of our discussion of historicity in general. What I say of language would equally well be true of cultures in general: the objective structures are, in the long run, constituted in subjective acts. This thesis, I am aware, runs contrary to a predominant philosophy in continental Europe today. The structuralists have insisted on the priority of objective structures, so that in speaking, for example, I follow rules that I find rather than generate. Heidegger's thesis, that it is not I who speak but language that speaks through me, makes the same point. A detailed examination of this seemingly Hegelian thesis, to which Chomsky's findings about innate linguistic competence are perhaps marginally related, is not possible within the limits of this essay. For my present purpose, I can only state rather dogmatically that in any historical epoch, when I speak I take up language (lexical and formal) already constituted, which is true of any historical acquisition. But that which I inherit *was* constituted by acts of speaking. It is not the hypothetical first beginning of a language that we are after. It is rather the fact that what are today anonymous structures, appearing to be objective, self-subsistent entities, had their genesis in acts. One could formulate the same in the form of a counterfactual: were there no speaking consciousness, there would have been no language.

In according this primacy to speech, we are in the company of Husserl and Wittgenstein. But speaking, apart from being a rule-governed behavior, is an act of consciousness, it is an intentional act. Not only is speaking an act of consciousness, it has a universality that does not belong to any other sort of act, which is borne out by the fact that all other acts are "expressible." I may even go further and say that in speech the domain of consciousness is mapped onto itself. The speech act, in its relationship to nonlinguistic acts, consti-

tutes a most interesting structure, not merely of empirical consciousness but also of the transcendentally purified consciousness. If consciousness is permeated by linguisticality, it also always escapes it.
Consciousness of speaking, which accompanies speaking, is not linguistic (I do not say, "I am speaking"). And, as in the case of history,
reflection can reactivate the process of genesis and thereby neutralize
the anonymity that threatens the autonomy of consciousness.

It is time to gather together these thoughts and to see what conception of transcendental subjectivity emerges. A transcendental subjectivity that is to assure objective validity of scientific theories cannot itself be anything more than the bare logical form of thinking: it
becomes, in effect, the formal essence of empirical thought. A transcendental subjectivity that is to serve as the domain within which all
meanings have to have their genesis needs to be a *concrete* field of experience. It also needs to be *historical*, for meanings are constituted
on the foundation of other historically sedimented structures. Insofar
as all meanings are not conceptual, but even the perceived object has
a *perceptual* sense for the perceiver, such a transcendental subjectivity needs to contain, within its structure, a dimension of corporeality as well. It is also linguistic. Speaking consciousness constitutes
not only conceptual meanings but also intersubjectivity. However,
transcendental subjectivity has a dimension that *exceeds* corporeality,
historicity, and linguisticality. This is what makes *reflection* possible,
and hence also transcendental *philosophy*. But the dialectic of reflection and reflected upon makes *total* reflection impossible. The transcendental point of view cannot be achieved *all at once*, at one shot,
as it were from a pistol, to use Hegel's words; but, like liberty, it
needs constant vigilance. It is an on-going affair of philosophical self-
criticism.

· · · · ·

Phenomenality and Materiality
in Kant

Paul de Man

· · · · ·

The possibility of juxtaposing ideology and critical philosophy which is the persistent burden of contemporary thought, is pointed out, as a mere historical fact, by Michel Foucault in *Les Mots et les Choses*. At the same time that French idéologues such as Destutt de Tracy are trying to map out the entire field of human ideas and representations, Kant undertakes the critical project of a transcendental philosophy which, says Foucault, marks "the retreat of cognition and of knowledge out of the space of representation."[1] Foucault's ensuing historical diagnosis, in which ideology appears as a belated manifestation of the classical spirit and Kant as the onset of modernity, interests us less than the interplay between the three notions: ideology, critical philosophy, and transcendental philosophy. The first term of this triad, "ideology," is the most difficult to control and one may hope that the interrelationship with the two others might be of some assistance.

A possible starting point can be found in the introduction to the *Third Critique* in a difficult but important differentiation between transcendental and metaphysical principles. Kant writes as follows: "A transcendental principle is one by means of which is represented, a priori, the universal condition under which alone things can be objects of our cognition. On the other hand, a principle is called metaphysical if it represents the a priori condition under which alone objects, whose concept must be given empirically, can a priori be further determined. Thus the principle of the cognition of bodies as substances and as changeable substances is transcendental if thereby it is asserted that their changes must have a cause; it is metaphysical if it asserts that their changes must have an *external* cause. For in the former case bodies need only be thought by means of ontological predicates (pure concepts of understanding), e.g., as substance, in order to permit the a priori cognition of the proposition; but in the latter case, the empirical concept of a body (as a movable thing in space) must lie at the base of the proposition, although once this basis has been laid down it can be seen completely a priori that the other predicate (motion by external causes) belongs to the body."[2]

The difference between transcendental and metaphysical concepts that concerns us is that the latter imply an empirical moment that necessarily remains *external* to the concept, whereas the former remain entirely interconceptual. Metaphysical principles lead to the identification and definition, to the knowledge, of a natural principle that is not itself a concept; transcendental principles lead to the definition of a conceptual principle of possible existence. Metaphysical principles state why and how things occur; to say that bodies move because of gravity is to reach a conclusion in the realm of metaphysics. Transcendental principles state the conditions that make occurrence possible at all: the first condition for bodies to be able to change is that such a thing as bodies and motion exist or occur. The condition of existence of bodies is called substance; to state that substance is the cause of the motion of bodies (as Kant does in the passage quoted) is to examine critically the possibility of their existence. Metaphysical principles, on the other hand, take the existence of their object for granted as empirical fact. They contain knowledge of the world, but this knowledge is precritical. Transcendental principles contain no knowledge of the world or anything else, except for the knowledge that metaphysical principles that take them for their object are themselves in need of critical analysis, since they take for granted an objectivity that, for the transcendental principles, is not a priori available. Thus the objects of transcendental principles are always critical judgments that take metaphysical knowledge for their target. Transcendental philosophy is always the critical philosophy of metaphysics.

Ideologies, to the extent that they necessarily contain empirical moments and are directed toward what lies outside the realm of pure concepts, are on the side of metaphysics rather than critical philosophy. The conditions and modalities of their occurrence are determined by critical analyses to which they have no access. The object of these analyses, on the other hand, can only be ideologies. Ideological and critical thought are interdependent and any attempt to separate them collapses ideology into mere error and critical thought into idealism.

The possibility of maintaining the causal link between them is the controlling principle of rigorous philosophical discourse: philosophies that succumb to ideology lose their epistemological sense, whereas philosophies that try to by-pass or repress ideology lose all critical thrust and risk being repossessed by what they foreclose.

The Kant passage establishes two other points. By speaking of a *causal* link between ideology and transcendental philosophy, one is reminded of the prominence of causality in Kant's example, the focus on the internal or external *cause* of the motion of bodies. The example of bodies in motion is indeed more than a mere example that could be replaced by any other; it is another version or definition of transcendental cognition. If critical philosophy and metaphysics (including ideologies) are causally linked to each other, their relationship is similar to the relationship, made explicit in the example, between bodies and their transformations or motions. Critical philosophy and ideology then become each other's motion: if an ideology is considered to be a stable entity (body, corpus, or canon), the critical discourse it generates will be that of a transcendental motion, of a motion whose cause resides, so to speak, within itself, within the substance of its own being. And if the critical system is considered stable in its principles, the corresponding ideology will acquire a mobility caused by a principle that lies outside itself; this principle, within the confines of the system thus constituted, can only be the principle of constitution, the architectonics of the transcendental system that functions as the cause of the ideological motions. In both cases, it is the transcendental system, as substance or as structure, that determines the ideology and not the reverse. The question then becomes how the substance or the structure of a transcendental discourse can be determined. To try to answer this question from the inside of the Kantian text is the tentative purpose of this still-introductory and expository paper.

The second point to be gained from the same passage has to do with the aesthetic. Immediately after distinguishing between transcendental and metaphysical principles, Kant goes on to distinguish between "the pure concept of objects of possible subjective cognition [der reine Begriff von Gegenständen des möglichen Erfahrungserkenntnisses überhaupt]" and "the principle of practical purposiveness which must be thought as the idea of the determination of a free will" (ibid.); the distinction is a correlate of the prior more general distinction between transcendental and metaphysical principles. The distinction directly alludes to the division between pure and practical reason and corresponds to the major division in the corpus of Kant's works. One sees again how the *Third Critique* corresponds to the necessity of establishing the causal link between critical philosophy and ideology, between a purely conceptual and an empirically determined discourse. Hence the need for a phenomenalized, empirically manifest principle of cognition on whose existence the possibility of such an articulation depends. This phenomenalized principle is what Kant calls the aesthetic. The investment in the aesthetic is therefore considerable, since the possibility of philosophy itself, as the articulation of a transcendental with a metaphysical discourse, depends on it. And the place in the *Third Critique* where this articulation occurs is the section on the sublime; in the section on the beautiful, the articulation is said to be between understanding (*Verstand*) and judgment. In both cases, one meets with great difficulties but the motives for this are perhaps easier to perceive in the case of the sublime, possibly because reason is explicitly involved.

The complexity and possible incongruity of the notion of the sublime, a topic that no eighteenth-century treatise of aesthetics is ever allowed to ignore, makes the section of the *Third Critique* that deals with it one of the most difficult and unresolved passages in the entire corpus of Kant's works. Whereas, in the section on the beautiful, the difficulties at least convey the illusion of being controlled, the same can hardly be said of the sublime. It is possible to formulate with some clarity what the project, the burden, of the section might be, and equally possible to understand what is at stake in its accomplishment. But it remains very difficult to decide whether or not the enterprise fails or succeeds. The complication is noticeable from the very start, in the introduction that distinguishes between the beautiful and the sublime. From the point of view of the main theme of the *Third Critique*, the problem of teleological judgment or of purposiveness without purpose, the consideration of the sublime seems almost superfluous. "The concept of the sublime," says Kant, "is not nearly so important or rich in consequences as the concept of the beautiful and, in general, it displays nothing purposive in nature itself. . . ." "The idea of the sublime thus separates from that of a purposiveness of nature and this makes the theory of the sublime a mere appendix (*einen blossen Anhang*) to the aesthetic judging of that purposiveness . . ." (p. 167; 84). After that modest beginning, however, it turns out that this outer appendage is in fact of crucial importance, because instead of informing us, like the beautiful, about the teleology of nature, it informs us about the teleology of our own faculties, more specifically about the relationship between imagination and reason. It follows, in accordance with what was said before, that whereas the beautiful is a metaphysical and ideological principle, the sublime aspires to being a transcendental one, with all that this entails.

Contrary to the beautiful, which at least appears to be all of a piece, the sublime is shot through with dialectical complication. It is, in some respects, infinitely attractive but, at the same time, thoroughly repellent; it gives a peculiar kind of pleasure (*Lust*) yet it is also consistently painful; in less subjective, more structural terms, it is equally baffling: it knows of no limits or borders, yet it has to appear as a determined totality; in a philosophical sense, it is something of a monster or, rather, a ghost: it is not a property of nature (there are no such things as sublime objects in nature) but a purely inward experience of consciousness (*Gemütsbestimmung*), yet Kant insists, time and again, that this noumenal entity has to be phenomenally represented (*dargestellt*); this is indeed an integral part, the crux, in fact, of the analytics of the sublime.

The question becomes whether the dialectical incompatibilities will find, in the concept of the sublime, a possibility of resolution. A first symptom that this may not simply and unambiguously be the case appears in an additional complication that makes the schema of the sublime distinct from that of the beautiful. One can grant that it is methodologically as legitimate to evaluate the impact on us of the sublime, as pleasure or as pain, in terms of quantity instead of, as is the case with the beautiful, in terms of quality. But, if this is indeed the case, why then can the analytics of the sublime not be closed off with the section on the mathematical sublime, centered on quantity and on number? Why the need for another section, nonexistent in the area of the beautiful, which Kant calls the *dynamic* sublime, and of which it will be difficult to say whether it still belongs to the order of quantity or of quality? Kant gives *some* explanation of why this is needed, but this explanation raises more questions than it answers (sec. 24). The sublime produces an emotional, agitated response in the beholder; this response can be referred back to the needs of knowledge (in the mathematical sublime) as well as to the needs of desire (*Begehrungsvermögen*) (in the dynamic sublime). In the realm of aesthetic judgment, both have to be considered regardless of purpose

or interest, a requirement that can conceivably be met in the realm of
knowledge but that is much less easy to fulfill in the realm of desire,
all the more so since it is clearly understood that this desire has to be
considered in itself, as subjective manifestation, and not as an objectified knowledge of desire. And indeed, when we reach the section on
the dynamic sublime, we find something quite different from desire.
The need for the additional subdivision, as well as the transition from
the one to the other (from mathematical quantity to the dynamic) is
by no means easy to account for and will demand an avowedly speculative effort of interpretation, of which it is not certain that it will
succeed.

The antinomies at play in the mathematical sublime are clearly
defined and so are the reasons of their relevance for aesthetic judgment. The mathematical sublime starts out from the concept of number. Its burden is that of calculus, as one would expect in a philosopher whose master's thesis dealt with Leibniz: it is the burden of
realizing that finite and infinite entities are not susceptible of comparison and cannot both be inscribed within a common system of knowledge. As calculus the proposition is self-evident and, in the infini-
tesimal realm of number "the power of number," says Kant, "reaches
infinity" (p. 173; 89), it creates no difficulties: the infinitely large (or,
for that matter, the infinitely small) can be conceptualized by means
of number. But such a conceptualization is entirely devoid of phenomenal equivalences; in terms of the faculties, it is, strictly speaking, unimaginable. This is not, however, how the sublime has been
defined. The sublime is not mere quantity or number, still less the notion of quantity as such (*Quantum*). Quantity thus conceived, and
expressed by number, is always a relative concept that refers back to
a conventional unity of measurement; pure number is neither large
nor small, and the infinitely large is also the infinitely small: the telescope and the microscope, as instruments of measurement, are the
same instrument. The sublime, however, is not "the large" but "the
largest"; it is that "compared to which everything else is small." As
such, it can never be accessible to the senses. But it is not pure number either, for there is no such thing as a "greatest" in the realm of
number. It belongs to a different order of experience, closer to extension than to number. It is, in Kant's words, "absolute magnitude"
(*die Grösse*—or better, as in the beginning of the section, *das Grösste
schlechthin*), as far as consciousness can grasp it in an intuition (*so
weit das Gemüt sie in einer Anschauung fassen kann*) (p. 173; 90).

This phenomenalization cannot stem from number, only from extension. The sentence is another version of the original statement that the sublime is to be borderless (*unbegrenzt*) yet a totality: number is without limit, but extension implies the possibility of a determined totalization, of a contour. The mathematical sublime has to articulate number with extension and it faces a classical problem of natural philosophy. The fact that it is a recurrent philosophical theme does not make it any easier to solve, nor does it allow one to overlook the intricacies of the arguments by which the solution is attempted just because the burden of argument turns out to be familiar.

Kant tries to articulate number with extension by way of two demonstrations, the first epistemological, the second in terms of pleasure and pain. Neither of these arguments is truly conclusive. On the level of understanding, the infinity of number can be conceived as a purely logical progression, which is not in need of any spatial concretization. But, on the level of reason, this "comprehensio logica" is no longer sufficient. Another mode of understanding called "comprehensio aesthetica" is needed, which requires constant totalization or condensation in a single intuition; even the infinite "must be thought as entirely given, according to its totality" (p. 177; 93). But since the infinite is not comparable to any finite magnitude, the articulation cannot occur. It does not, in fact, ever occur and it is the *failure* of the articulation that becomes the distinguishing characteristic of the sublime: it transposes or elevates the natural to the level of the supernatural, perception to imagination, understanding to reason. This transposition, however, never allows for the condition of totality that is constitutive of the sublime, and it can therefore not supersede the failure by becoming, as in a dialectic, the knowledge of this failure. The sublime cannot be defined as the failure of the sublime, for this failure deprives it of its identifying principle. Neither could one say that, at this point, the sublime fulfills itself as desire for what it fails to be, since what it desires—totality—is not other than itself.

The same pattern returns with regard to pleasure and pain. It is clear that what the sublime achieves is not the task required by its own position (articulation of number and extension by ways of the infinite). What it achieves is the awareness of another faculty besides understanding and reason, namely the imagination. Out of the pain of the failure to constitute the sublime by making the infinite apparent (*anschaulich*) is born the pleasure of the imagination, which discovers, in this very failure, the congruity of its law (which is a law of failure) with the law of our own suprasensory being. Its failure to connect with the sensory would also elevate it above it. This law does not reside in nature but defines man in opposition to nature; it is only by an act of what Kant calls "subreption" (p. 180; 96) that this law is fallaciously attributed to nature. But is not this subreption a mirror image of another, previous subreption by which the sublime subreptitiously posits itself by claiming to exist by dint of the impossibility of its own existence? The transcendental judgment that is to decide on the possibility of existence of the sublime (as the spatial articulation of the infinite) functions metaphorically, or ideologically, when it subreptitiously defines itself in terms of its other, namely of extension and totality. If space lies outside the sublime and remains there, and if space is nevertheless a necessary condition (or cause) for the sublime to come into being, then the principle of the sublime is a metaphysical principle that mistakes itself for a transcendental one. If imagination, the faculty of the sublime, comes into being at the expense of the totalizing power of the mind, how can it then, as the text requires, be in contrastive harmony (p. 182; 97) with the faculty of reason, which delimits the contour of this totality? What the imagination undoes is the very labor of reason and such a relationship cannot without difficulty be said to unite both of them, imagination and reason, in a common task or law of being. Kant's definition of aesthetic judgment as what represents the subjective play of the faculties (imagination and reason) as "harmonious through their very contrast" remains, at this point, quite obscure. Which accounts, perhaps, in part for the fact that a further elaboration is needed in which the relationship between the same two powers of the mind will be somewhat less enigmatically represented; this can occur, however only after moving from the mathematical to the dynamic sublime.

The difficulty can be summarized in a shift in terminology that occurs later in the text but that directly alludes to the difficulties we already encounter in the mathematical sublime. In section 29, in the general remark upon the exposition of the aesthetic judgment, appears the most concise but also the most suggestive definition of the sublime as "an object (of nature) the representation [*Vorstellung*] of which determines consciousness [*Gemüt*] to *think* the unattainability of nature as a sensory representation (*Darstellung*) of ideas" (p. 193, 108; English italics mine). The key word, for our present purpose, in this quotation in which every word is rich in innumerable questions, is the word *"denken"* in the phrase "die Unerreichbarkeit der Natur als Darstellung zu *denken*." A few lines later, Kant speaks of the necessity "to think nature itself in its totality, as the sensory representation of something that lies beyond the senses, without being able to accomplish this representation objectively" [Die Natur selbst in ihrer Totalität, als Darstellung von etwas Uebersinnlichem, zu *denken*, ohne diese Darstellung *objektiv* zu Stande bringen zu können] (p. 194; 108. Italics Kant's). Still a few lines later, the word "*denken*" is singled out and contrasted with knowing: "die Natur als Darstellung derselben (d.h. die Idee des Uebersinnlichen) nicht *erkennen*, sondern nur *denken* können" (ibid). How are we to understand the verb "to think" in these formulations, in distinction from knowing? The way of knowledge, of *Erkenntnis*, has not been able to establish the existence of the sublime as an intelligible concept. This may be possible only by ways of *denken* rather than *erkennen*. What would be an instance of such thinking that differs from knowing? Was heisst denken?

Still in the mathematical sublime, in Section 26, next to the epistemology and the eudaemony of the sublime, appears another description of how an infinite quantity can become a sensory intuition in the imagination, or how, in other words, the infinity of number can be articulated with the totality of extension (p. 173; 89). This description, which is formal rather than philosophical, is a great deal easier to follow than the subsequent arguments. In order to make the sublime appear in space we need, says Kant, two acts of the imagination: apprehension (*apprehensio*) and comprehension or summation (*comprehensio aesthetica*), *Auffassung* and *Zusammenfassung* (p. 173; 90). Apprehension proceeds successively, as a syntagmatic, consecutive motion along an axis, and it can proceed ad infinitum without difficulty. Comprehension, however, which is a paradigmatic totalization of the apprehended trajectory, grows increasingly difficult as the space covered by apprehension grows larger. The model reminds one of a simple phenomenology of reading, in which one has to make constant syntheses to comprehend the successive unfolding of the text: the eye moves horizontally in succession whereas the mind has to combine vertically the cumulative understanding of what has been apprehended. The comprehension will soon reach a point at which it is saturated and will no longer be able to take in additional apprehensions: it cannot progress beyond a certain magnitude which marks the limit of the imagination. This ability of the imagination to achieve syntheses is a boon to the understanding, which is hardly conceivable without it, but this gain is countered by a corresponding loss. The comprehension discovers its own limitation, beyond which it cannot reach. "[The imagination] loses as much on the one side as it gains on the other" (p. 174; 90). As the paradigmatic simultaneity substitutes for the syntagmatic succession, an economy of loss and gain is put in place which functions with predictable efficacy, though only within certain well-defined limits. The exchange from part to whole generates wholes that turn out to be only parts. Kant gives the example of the Egyptologist Savary, who observed that, in order to perceive the magnitude of the pyramids, one could be neither too far away nor too close. One is reminded of Pascal: "Bornés en tout genre, cet état qui tient le milieu entre deux extrêmes, se trouve en toutes nos puissances. Nos sens n'aperçoivent rien d'extrême, trop de bruit nous assourdit, trop de lumière éblouit, trop de distance et de proximité empêche la vue. Trop de longueur et trop de brièveté de discours l'obscursit, trop de vérité nous étonne. . . ."[3] It is not surprising that, from considerations on vision and, in general, on perception, Pascal moves to the order of discourse, for the model that is being suggested is no longer, properly speaking, philosophical, but linguistic. It describes, not a faculty of the mind, be it as consciousness or as cognition, but a potentiality inherent in language. For such a system of substitution, set up along a paradigmatic and a syntagmatic axis, generating partial totalizations within an economy of profit and loss, is a very familiar model indeed—which also explains why the passage seems so easy to grasp in comparison with what precedes and follows. It is the model of discourse as a tropological system. The desired articulation of the sublime takes place, with suitable reservations and restrictions, within such a purely formal system. It follows, however, that it is conceivable only within the limits of such a system, that is, as pure discourse rather than as a faculty of the mind. When the sublime is translated back, so to speak, from language into cognition, from formal description into philosophical argument, it loses all inherent coherence and dissolves in the aporias of intellectual and sensory appearance. It is also established that, even within the confines of language, the sublime can occur only as a single and particular point of view, a privileged place that avoids both excessive comprehension and excessive apprehension, and that this place is only formally, and not transcendentally, determined. The sublime cannot be grounded as a philosophical (transcendental or metaphysical) principle, but only as a linguistic principle. Consequently, the section on the mathematical sublime cannot be closed off in a satisfactory manner and another chapter on the dynamics of the sublime is needed.

According to the principles of the quadrivium, the further extension of the system number-extension should have been motion, and we could have expected a kinetic rather than a dynamic sublime. But the kinetics of the sublime are treated at once, and somewhat surprisingly, as a question of *power:* the first word of section 28 (p. 184; 99) (on the dynamics of the sublime) is *Macht,* soon followed by violence (*Gewalt*) and by the assertion that violence is the only means by which to overcome the resistance of one force to another. A classical way to have moved from number to motion would have been by way of a kinetics of physical bodies, a study, as for example in Kepler, of the motion of heavenly bodies in function of gravity as acceleration. Gravity can also be considered a force or a power, next to being a motion—as in Wordsworth's line: "no motion has she now, no force"—and the passage from a kinesis to a dynamics of the sublime could be treated in terms of mathematical and physical concepts. Kant does not pursue this line of thought and at once introduces the notion of might in a quasi-empirical sense of assault, battle, and fright. The relationship between the natural and the aesthetic sublime is treated as a scene of combat in which the faculties of the mind somehow have to overpower the forces of nature.

The necessity of extending the model of the mathematical sublime, the system of number-extension, to the model of the dynamic sublime as the system number-motion, as well as the interpretation of motion as empirical power, is not accounted for in philosophical terms in the analytics of the sublime, nor can it, especially in its latter aspect (the empiricization of force into violence and battle), be explained by purely historical reasons. The only way to account for it is as an extension of the linguistic model beyond its definition as a system of tropes. Tropes account for the occurrence of the sublime but, as we saw, in such a restrictive and partial way that the system could not be expected to remain quiescent within its narrow boundaries. From the pseudo-cognition of tropes, language has to expand to the activity of performance, something of which language has been known to be capable well before Austin reminded us of it. The transition from the mathematical to the dynamic sublime, a transition for which the justification is conspicuously lacking in the text (sec. 28 begins most abruptly with the word "Power" [*Macht*]), marks the saturation of the tropological field as language frees itself of its constraints and discovers within itself a power no longer dependent on the restrictions of cognition. Hence the introduction, at this point in the text, of the concept of morality, but on the level of practical rather than pure reason. The articulation between pure and practical reason, the raison d'être of the *Third Critique*, occurs in the widening definition of language as a performative as well as a tropological system. The *Critique of Judgment* therefore has, at its center, a deep, perhaps fatal, break or discontinuity. It depends on a linguistic structure (language as a performative as well as a cognitive system) that is not itself accessible to the powers of transcendental philosophy. Nor is it accessible, one should hasten to add, to the powers of metaphysics or of ideology, which are themselves precritical stages of knowledge. Our question then becomes whether and where this disruption, this disarticulation, becomes apparent in the text, at a moment when the aporia of the sublime is no longer stated, as was the case in the mathematical sublime and in the ensuing general definitions of the concept, as an explicit paradox, but as the apparently tranquil, because entirely unreflected, juxtaposition of incompatibles. Such a moment occurs in the general remark or recapitulation (sec. 29) that concludes the analytics of the sublime.

The chapter on the dynamics of the sublime appears as another version of the difficulties encountered in the mathematical sublime rather than as their further development, let alone their solution. Except for the introduction of the moral dimension, hard to account for in epistemological or aesthetic terms, this chapter differs most from the preceding inquiry by concentrating on affect rather than on reason (as in the mathematical sublime) or on understanding (as in the analytics of the beautiful). The preeminence of the faculty of the imagination is maintained, as is the question of its relationship to reason, but this dialectic of reason and imagination is now mediated by affects, moods and feelings, rather than by rational principles. The change results in a restatement and refinement rather than in a transformation of the principle of the sublime. The admirably concise and previously quoted definition given at the beginning of the *General Remarks* benefits from the references to mood and to affectivity but does not differ in substance from similar developments that occurred in the preceding paragraphs. Nor is it, for all its controlled concentration, in essence less obscure than the previous formulations.

The chapter also contains, somewhat abruptly, a reminder that, in a transcendental aesthetic of judgment, objects in nature susceptible of producing sublime effects have to be considered in a radically nonteleological manner, completely detached from any purpose or interest that the mind may find in them. Kant adds that he had previously reminded the reader of this necessity, but it is not clear to what passage he alludes. He is rather restating a general principle that underlies the entire enterprise and that was first formulated, with all desirable clarity, at the onset of the analytics of the beautiful under the modality of quality (p. 116; 38). This time, however, Kant relates the principle of disinterestedness specifically to objects in nature and takes for his example two landscapes: "If, then, we call the sight of the starry heaven *sublime*, we must not place at the foundation of judgment concepts of worlds inhabited by rational beings and regard the bright points, with which we see the space above us filled, as their suns moving in circles purposively fixed with reference to them; but we must regard it, just as we see it [*wie man ihn sieht*], as a distant, all-embracing vault [*ein weites Gewölbe*]. Only under such a representation can we range that sublimity that a pure aesthetic judgment ascribes to this object. And in the same way, if we are to call the sight of the ocean sublime, we must not think of it as we ordinarily do, as implying all kinds of knowledge (that are not contained in immediate intuition). For example, we sometimes think of the ocean as a vast kingdom of aquatic creatures, or as the great source of those vapors that fill the air with clouds for the benefit of the land, or again as an element that, though dividing continents from each other, yet promotes the greatest communication between them; all these produce merely teleological judgments. To find the ocean nevertheless sublime we must regard it as poets do [*wie die Dichter es tun*], merely by what the eye reveals [*was der Augenschein zeigt*]—if it is at rest, as a clear mirror of water only bounded by the heavens; if it is stormy, as an abyss threatening to overwhelm everything" (p. 196; 110–11).

The passage is remarkable in many respects, including its apparent anticipation of many such passages soon to be found in the works of romantic poets and already present, in many cases, in their eighteenth-century predecessors. But it is just as necessary to distinguish it from these symbolic landscapes as to point out the similarities. The predominant perception, in the Kant passage, is that of the heavens and the ocean as an architectonic construct. The heavens are a vault that covers the totality of earthy space as a roof covers a house. Space, in Kant as in Aristotle, is a house in which we dwell more or less safely, or more or less poetically, on this earth. This is also how the sea is perceived or how, according to Kant, poets perceive it: its horizontal expanse is like a floor bounded by the horizon, by the walls of heaven as they close off and delimit the building.

Who, one may wonder, are the poets who thus perceive the world in an architectonic rather than in a teleological way and how can the architectonic then be said to be opposed to the teleological? How are we to understand the term *"Augenschein"* in relation to the other allusions to sensory appearance that abound in the attempts to define or to describe the sublime? It is easier to say what the passage excludes and how it differs from others than to say what it is, but this may well be in accordance with Kant's insistence (p. 195–96; 109) on the primarily *negative* mode of the imagination. Certainly, in our tradition, the first poet we think of as having similar intuitions is Wordsworth who, in the nest-robbing episode in *The Prelude*, evoked the experience of dizziness and absolute fright in the amazing lines: "The sky was not a sky / Of earth, and with what motion moved the clouds!" Here, too, the sky is originally conceived as a roof or vault that shelters us, by anchoring us in the world, standing on a horizontal plane, *under* the sky, reassuringly stabilized by the weight of our own gravity. But, if the sky suddenly separates from the earth and is no longer, in Wordsworth's terms, a sky *of* earth, we lose all feeling of stability and start to fall, so to speak, skyward, away from gravity.

Kant's passage is *not* like this because the sky does not appear in it as associated in any way with shelter. It is not the construct under which, in Heidegger's terms, we can dwell (*wohnen*). In a lesser-known passage from the *Logic* Kant speaks of "a wild man who, from a distance, sees a house of which he does not know the use. He certainly observes the same object as does another, who knows it to be definitely built and arranged to serve as a dwelling for human beings. Yet in formal terms this knowledge of the selfsame object differs in both cases. For the first it is mere intuition [*blosse Anschauung*], for the other both intuition and concept."[4] The poet who sees the heavens as a vault is clearly like the savage, and unlike Wordsworth. He does not see prior to dwelling, but merely sees. He does not see in order to shelter himself, for there is no suggestion made that he could in any way be threatened, not even by the storm—since it is pointed out that he remains safely on the shore. The link between seeing and dwelling, *sehen* and *wohnen*, is teleological and therefore absent in pure aesthetic vision.

Or, still in association with Wordsworth, one thinks of the famous passage from Tintern Abbey:

> And I have felt
> A presence that disturbs me with the joy
> Of elevated thoughts; a sense sublime
> Of something far more deeply interfused
> Whose dwelling is the light of setting suns,
> And the round ocean and the living air
> And the blue sky, and in the mind of man: . . .

The sublimity of the round ocean, horizon-bound as a vast dome, is especially reminiscent of the Kant passage. But the two invocations of sublime nature soon diverge. Wordsworth's sublime is an instance of the constant exchange between mind and nature, of the chiasmic transfer of properties between the sensory and the intellectual world that characterizes his figural diction, here explicitly thematized in the "motion and spirit that impels / All thinking things, all objects of all thoughts / And rolls through all things." No mind is involved in the Kantian vision of ocean and heaven. To the extent that any mind, that any judgment intervenes, it is in error—for it is not the case that heaven is a vault or that the horizon bounds the ocean like the walls of a building. That is how things are to the eye, in the redundancy of their appearance to the eye and not to the mind, as in the redundant word *"Augenschein,"* to be understood in opposition to Hegel's *"Ideenschein,"* or sensory appearance of the idea; *Augenschein,* in which the eye, tautologically, is named twice, as eye itself and as what appears to the eye.

Kant's architectonic world is not a metamorphosis of a fluid world into the solidity of stone, nor is his building a trope or a symbol that substitutes for the actual entities. Heaven and ocean as building are a priori, previous to any understanding, to any exchange or anthropomorphism which will allow Wordsworth to address, in Book 5 of *The Prelude,* the "speaking face of nature." There is no room for address in Kant's flat, third-person world. Kant's vision can therefore hardly be called literal, which would imply its possible figuralization or symbolization by an act of judgment. The only word that comes to mind is that of a *material* vision, but how this materiality is then to be understood in linguistic terms is not, as yet, clearly intelligible.

Not being part of trope or figuration, the purely aesthetic vision of the natural world is in no way solar. It is not the sudden discovery of a true world as an unveiling, as the a-letheia of Heidegger's *Lichtung*. It is not a solar world and we are explicitly told that we are not to think of the stars as "suns moving in circles." Nor are we to think of them as the constellation that survives at the apocalyptic end of Mallarmé's *Coup de Dés*. The "mirror" of the sea surface is a mirror without depth, least of all the mirror in which the constellation would be reflected. In this mode of seeing, the eye is its own agent and not the specular echo of the sun. The sea is called a mirror, not because it is supposed to reflect anything, but to stress a flatness devoid of any suggestion of depth. In the same way and to the same extent that this vision is purely material, devoid of any reflexive or intellectual complication, it is also purely formal, devoid of any semantic depth and reducible to the formal mathematization or geometrization of pure optics. The critique of the aesthetic ends up, in Kant, in a formal materialism that runs counter to all values and characteristics associated with aesthetic experience, including the aesthetic experience of the beautiful and of the sublime as described by Kant and Hegel themselves. The tradition of their interpretation, as it appears from near contemporaries such as Schiller on, has seen only this one, figural, and, if you will, "romantic" aspect of their theories of the imagination, and has entirely overlooked what we call the material aspect. Neither has it understood the place and the function of formalization in this intricate process.

The vision of heaven and world entirely devoid of teleological interference, held up here as a purely sublime and aesthetic vision, stands in direct contradiction to all preceding definitions and analyses of the sublime given in section 24 on until this point in section 29. Still in the condensed definition that appears in the same chapter the stress falls on the sublime as a concrete representation of ideas (*Darstellung von Ideen*). As in the Wordsworth passage from "Tintern Abbey" the articulation of physical motion with the movements of the affects and of practical moral judgment has to encompass natural and intellectual elements under one single unifying principle, such as the sublime. And there has been so much emphasis, from the start, on the fact that the sublime does not reside in the natural object but in the mind of man (*Gemütsbestimmungen*) that the burden of the argument, much rather than emphasizing the purely inward, noumenal nature of the sublime, becomes the need to account for the fact that it nevertheless occurs as an outward, phenomenal manifestation. Can this in any way be reconciled with the radical materiality of sublime vision suddenly introduced, as if it were an afterthought, at this point in the argument? How is one to reconcile the concrete representation of ideas with pure ocular vision, *Darstellung von Ideen* with *Augenschein?*

The analytics of the sublime (like those of the beautiful) are consistently stated in terms of a theory of the faculties combined, in the dynamics of the sublime, with a theory of moral affect. "A feeling for the sublime in nature cannot well be thought without combining therewith a mood of consciousness which is akin to the *moral*" (p. 194; 109). In the case of the beautiful, this moral component was also present, though in a much more subdued form. It manifested itself as the autonomy of aesthetic pleasure with regard to sensuous pleasure, a form of freedom and thus, in Kant's system where morality is always linked to liberty, at least potentially a form of moral judgment. But in the case of the sublime, the tie with morality is much more explicit, for morality is involved, not as play, but as law-directed labor [*gesetzliches Geschäft*] (ibid.). The only restriction that keeps the sublime from passing entirely into the camp of morality is that the faculty involved in it is not reason, or at least not an unmediated manifestation of reason, but that the sublime is represented by the imagination itself, as a tool of reason. In the laborious, businesslike world of morality, even the free and playful imagination becomes an instrument of work. Its task, its labor, is precisely to translate the abstractions of reason back into the phenomenal world of appearances and images whose presence is retained in the very word *imag*ination, *"Bild"* in the German *"Einbildungskraft."*

Why this incarnation of the idea has to occur is accounted for in various ways. It is, first of all, a quasi-theological necessity that follows necessarily from our fallen condition. The need for aesthetic judgment and activity, although it defines man, is the expression of a shortcoming, of a curse rather than of an excess of power and inventiveness. There would be no need for it "if we were creatures of pure intellect or even capable of displacing ourselves mentally in such a condition" (p. 197; 111). The same inherent inferiority of the aesthetic (or, more precisely, of the aesthetic as symptomatic of an inherent shortcoming in us) becomes visible with regard to moral judgment. Morality and the aesthetic are both disinterested, but this disinterestedness becomes necessarily polluted in aesthetic representation: the persuasion that, by means of their very disinterestedness, moral and aesthetic judgments are capable of achieving is necessarily linked, in the case of the aesthetic, with positively valorized sensory experiences. The moral lesson of the aesthetic has to be conveyed by seductive means which, as we know, can reach far enough to make it necessary to read "Kant avec Sade" rather than the reverse. Instead of purely intellectual beauty we can only produce the beauty of the imagination. How this occurs is the object of a crucial and difficult paragraph (p. 195; 109) in which the articulation of the imagination with reason, the assumedly "harmonious" relationship between reason and imagination wishfully promised at an earlier stage is described in greater detail.

The passage introduces what a few pages later will be defined as a modulation between two moods or affects, the passage from shocked surprise (*Verwunderung*) to tranquil admiration (*Bewunderung*). The initial effect of the sublime, of a sudden encounter with colossal natural entities such as cataracts, abysses, and towering mountains, is one of shock or, says Kant, astonishment that borders upon terror (*Verwunderung, die an Schreck grenzt*). By a play, a trick of the imagination, this terror is transformed into a feeling of tranquil superiority, the admiration one expresses for something or for someone one can afford to admire peacefully, because one's own superiority is not really in question. The better one thinks of him, the better one has to think of oneself. How enviable a peace of mind thus achieved in the recognition of another's worth as confirmation of one's own! Moral nobility is the best ego booster available—though Kant is not so blind as not to know of its cost in hidden terror.

He had not always held that the serenity of admiration, the tranquility of spent emotion is the highest of qualities. In the early, precritical essay on the sublime and the beautiful from 1764,[5] he had stated in peremptory fashion that the humor of the phlegmatic had to be rejected out of hand as having not the slightest possible relationship with beauty or sublimity, in any form or shape. It was said to be utterly devoid of any interest whatsoever. Its equivalent in terms of national stereotypes is that of the Dutch, described as a phlegmatized kind of German interested only in the dreariest of commercial and money-making activities. I have never felt more grateful for the fifty or so kilometers that separate the Flemish city of Antwerp from the Dutch city of Rotterdam. Considerations on feminine languor and passivity, unfavorably contrasted with male energy, make for equally difficult reading in the early Kant essay.

By the time of the *Critique of Judgment*, however, things have changed a great deal. "For [which seems strange] the absence of affection [apatheia, phlegma in significatu bono] in a mind that follows consistently its unalterable groundrules, is sublime, and in a far more outstanding way, because it is backed by the satisfaction of pure reason" (p. 199; 113). The tranquility thus achieved receives the predicate of nobility, of a morally elevated state of mind that will then subreptiously be transferred to objects and things such as "a building, a garment, literary style, bodily presence, etc." How is it, then, that the imagination can achieve the nobility of such loss of pathos, of such a serenity?

It does so by an essentially negative way, which corresponds philosophically to the elevation of the imagination from a metaphysical (and, hence, ideological) to a transcendental (and, hence, critical) principle. As long as the faculty of the imagination is considered empirically—and one is reminded that, in the late Kant, the presence of this empirical moment characterizes the metaphysical dimensions of the mind—it is free and playful, closer to what then in English is called "fancy" rather than what is called "imagination." By sacrificing, by giving up this freedom, in a first negative moment of shocked, but pleasurable surprise, the imagination allies itself with reason. Why this is so is not at once clear; in affective terms, it takes on the form of a reconquered mastery, a reconquered superiority over a nature of which the direct threat is overcome. The free, empirical reaction of the imagination, when confronted with the power and might of nature, is to indulge, to enjoy the terror of this very magnitude. Taming this delectable, because imaginary, terror—the assumption always being that the person is not directly threatened, or at the very least separated from the immediate threat by a reflexive moment—and preferring to it the tranquil satisfaction of superiority, is to submit the imagination to the power of reason. For the faculty that establishes the superiority of the mind over nature is reason and reason alone; the imagination's security depends on the actual, empirical physical situation and, when this situation is threatening, it swings toward terror and toward a feeling of free submission to nature. Since, however, in the experience of the sublime, the imagination achieves tranquility, it submits to reason, achieves the highest degree of freedom by freely sacrificing its natural freedom to the higher freedom of reason. "Thereby," says Kant, "it achieves a gain in power that is larger than what it sacrifices" (p. 195; 109). The loss

of empirical freedom means the gain in critical freedom that characterizes rational and transcendental principles. Imagination substitutes for reason at the cost of its empirical nature and, by this anti-
or unnatural act, it conquers nature.

This complicated and somewhat devious scenario accomplishes
the aim of the sublime. The imagination overcomes suffering, becomes a-pathetic, and sheds the pain of natural shock. It reconciles
pleasure with pain and in so doing it articulates, as mediator, the
movement of the affects with the legal, codified, formalized, and
stable order of reason. Imagination is not nature (for, in its tranquility, it determines itself as larger and mightier than nature) but,
unlike reason, it remains in contact with nature. It is not idealized to
the point of becoming pure reason, for it has no knowledge of its
actual predicament or of its actual strategies and remains pure affect
rather than cognition. It becomes adequate (*angemessen*) to reason
on the basis of its inadequacy (*Unangemessenheit*) to this same reason in its relation to nature. "In elevating this reflection of the aesthetic judgment to the point where it becomes adequate to reason
[*zur Angemessenheit mit der Vernunft*], without however reaching a
definite concept of reason, the object is nevertheless represented,
despite the objective inadequacy of the imagination, even in its greatest extension, to reason [*Unangemessenheit der Einbildungskraft
. . . für die Vernunft*] as subjectively purposive" (pp. 195–96; 109–
10)—and thus, we may add, as pertaining both to reason and to
practical judgment.

However complex this final formulation may sound, it is clarified and made persuasive by the road that leads up to it and that is
by no means unfamiliar. Even as uninspired a paraphrase as the
one I have given should reveal that we are hardly dealing with a
tight analytical argument (as was the case, for example, in the distinction between transcendental and metaphysical principles from
which we started out). What we have here is less authoritative but a
great deal more accessible. For one thing, instead of being an argument, it is a story, a dramatized scene of the mind in action. The
faculties of reason and of imagination are personified, or anthro-
pomorphized, like the five squabbling faculties hilariously staged by
Diderot in the *Lettre sur les sourds et les muets*,[6] and the relationship
between them is stated in delusively interpersonal terms. What could
it possibly mean, in analytical terms, that the imagination sacrifices
itself, like Antigone or Iphigenia—for one can only imagine this

shrewd and admirable imagination as the feminine heroine of a tragedy—for the sake of reason? And what is the status of all this heroism and cunning which allows it to reach a-pathia, to overcome pathos, by ways of the very pathos of sacrifice? How can faculties, themselves a heuristic hypothesis devoid of any reality—for only people who have read too much eighteenth-century psychology and philosophy might end up believing that they have an imagination or a reason, the same way they have blue eyes or a big nose—how can faculties be said to *act*, or even to act freely, as if they were conscious and complete human beings? We are clearly not dealing with mental categories but with tropes and the story Kant tells us is an allegorical tale. Nor are the contents of this tale at all unusual. It is the story of an exchange, of a negotiation in which powers are lost and gained in an economy of sacrifice and recuperation. It is also a story of opposite forces, nature and reason, the imagination and nature, tranquility and shock, adequacy (*Angemessenheit*) and inadequacy, that separate, fight, and then unite in a more or less stable state of harmony, achieving syntheses and totalizations that were missing at the beginning of the action. Such personified scenes of consciousness are easily identified: they are not actually descriptions of mental functions but descriptions of tropological transformations. They are not governed by the laws of the mind but by the laws of figural language. For the second time in this text (the first time being in the interplay between apprehension and comprehension in the mathematical sublime) we have come upon a passage that, under the guise of being a philosophical argument, is in fact determined by linguistic structures that are not within the author's control. What makes this intrusion of linguistic tropes particularly remarkable is that it occurs in close proximity, almost in juxtaposition to the passage on the material architectonics of vision, in the poetic evocation of heaven and ocean, with which it is entirely incompatible.

For we are now confronted with two completely different notions of the architectonic—a concept that appears under that name in Kant's own text. The architectonic vision of nature as a building is, in Kant, as we saw, entirely material, emphatically not tropological, entirely distinct from the substitutions and exchanges between faculties or between mind and nature that make up the Wordsworthian or the romantic sublime. But the architectonic is also at times defined by Kant, though not in the *Third Critique*, in entirely different terms, much closer to the allegory of the faculties and the tale of recovered tranquility we have just been reading, much closer as well to the *edle Einfalt* and *stille Grösse* of Winckelmann's neoclassicism. Near the end of the *Critique of Pure Reason,* a chapter entitled "The Architectonics of Pure Reason" defines the architectonic as the organic unity of systems, "the unity of miscellaneous cognitions brought together under one idea" and greatly favored, by Kant, over what he calls the "rhapsody" of mere speculation devoid of *esprit de système.* That this unity is conceived in organic terms is apparent from the recurring metaphor of the body, as a totality of various limbs and parts ("*Glieder,*" meaning member in all the senses of the word, as well as, in the compound "*Gliedermann,*" the puppet of Kleist's Marionettentheater). "The whole," says Kant, "is articulated [*articulatio—gegliedert*] and not just piled on top of each other—[*gehäuft*]; it can grow from the inside out but not from the outside in. It grows like an animal body, not by the addition of new limbs [*Glieder*] but, without changing the proportions, by making each individual member stronger and more efficient for its own purpose."[7] One will want to know what becomes of this Aristotelian, zoomorphic architectonic when it is being considered, in the *Third Critique*'s passage on heaven and ocean, in a nonteleological, aesthetic perspective. For one thing, it does not imply a collapse of the architectonic in the rhapsodic, a disintegration of the building; sea and heaven, as the poets see them, are more than ever buildings. But it is no longer at all certain that they are still articulated (*gegliedert*). After lingering briefly over the aesthetic vision of the heavens and the seas, Kant turns for a moment to the human body: "The like is to be said of the sublime and beautiful in the human body. We must not regard as the determining grounds of our judgment the concepts of the purposes which all our limbs serve [*wozu alle seine Gliedmassen da sind*] and we must not allow this unity of purpose to influence our aesthetic judgment (for then it would no longer be pure) . . ." (p. 197; 111). We must, in short, consider our limbs, hands, toes, breasts, or what Montaigne so cheerfully referred to as "Monsieur ma partie," in themselves, severed from the organic unity of the body, the way the poets look at the oceans severed from their geographical place on earth. We must, in other words, disarticulate, mutilate the body in a way that is much closer to Kleist than to Winckelmann, though close enough to the violent end that happened to befall both of them. We must consider our limbs the way the primitive man considered the house, entirely severed from any purpose or use. From the phenomenality of the aesthetic (which is always based on an adequacy of the mind to its physical object, based on what is referred to, in the definition of the sublime, as the concrete representation of ideas—*Darstellung der Ideen*) we have moved to the pure materiality of *Augenschein*, of aesthetic vision. From the organic, still asserted as architectonic principle in the *Critique of Pure Reason*, to the phenomenological, the rational cognition of incarnate ideas, which the best part of the Kant interpretation in the nineteenth and twentieth century will single out, we have reached, in the final analysis, a materialism that, in the tradition of the reception of the *Third Critique*, is seldom or never perceived. To appreciate the full impact of this conclusion one must remember that the entire project of the *Third Critique*, the full investment in the aesthetic, was to achieve the articulation that would guarantee the architectonic unity of the system. If the architectonic then appears, very near the end of the analytics of the aesthetic, at the conclusion of the section on the sublime, as the material disarticulation not only of nature but of the body, then this moment marks the undoing of the aesthetic as a valid category. The critical power of a transcendental philosophy undoes the very project of such a philosophy leaving us, certainly not with an ideology—for transcendental and ideological (metaphysical) principles are part of the same system—but with a materialism that Kant's posterity has not yet begun to face up to. This happens, not out of a lack of philosophical energy or rational power, but as a result of the very strength and consistency of this power.

What, finally, will be the equivalence of this moment in the order of language? Whenever the disruption asserted itself, in the passage in the nonteleological vision of nature and of the body and also, less openly but not less effectively, in the unexplained necessity of supplementing the consideration of the mathematical sublime with a consideration of the dynamic sublime, in the blank between section 27 and section 28 (as we refer to a blank between stanzas 1 and 2 of the Lucy poem "A slumber did my spirit seal . . ." or between parts 1 and 2 of the Boy of Winander poem), whenever, then, the articulation is threatened by its undoing, we encountered a passage (the section on apprehension, the section on the sacrifice of the imagination) that could be identified as a shift from a tropological to a different mode of language. In the case of the dynamic sublime, one could speak of a shift from trope to performance. In this case, the nonteleological apprehension of nature, a somewhat different pattern emerges. To the dismemberment of the body corresponds a dismemberment of language, as meaning-producing tropes are replaced by the fragmentation of sentences and propositions into discrete words, or the fragmentation of words into syllables or finally letters. In Kleist's text, one would isolate the dissemination of the word *"Fall"* and its compounds throughout as such a moment when the aesthetic dance turned into an aesthetic trap, as by the addition of one single mute letter which makes *"Fall"* (fall) into *"Falle"* (trap).[8] No such artful moments seem to occur, at first sight, in Kant. But just try to translate one single somewhat complex sentence of Kant, or just consider what the efforts of entirely competent translators have produced, and you will soon notice how decisively determining the play of the letter and of the syllable, the way of saying (*Art des Sagens*) as opposed to what is being said (*das Gesagte*)—to quote Walter Benjamin—is in this most unconspicuous of stylists. Is not the persuasiveness of the entire passage on the recovery of the imagination's tranquility after the shock of sublime surprise based, not so much on the little play acted out by the senses, but on the proximity between the German words for surprise and admiration, *"Verwunderung"* and *"Bewunderung"*? And are we not made to assent to the more than paradoxical but truly aporetic incompatibility between the failure of the imagination to grasp magnitude with what becomes, in the experience of the sublime, the success of this same imagination as an agent of reason, are we not made to assent to this because of a constant, and finally bewildering alternation of the two terms, *"Angemessen(heit)"* and *"Unangemessen(heit),"* to the point where one can no longer tell them apart? The bottom line, in Kant as well as in Hegel, is the prosaic materiality of the letter and no degree of obfuscation or ideology can transform this materiality into the phenomenal cognition of aesthetic judgment.

. . . . .

2

Literature and Hermeneutics

. . . . .

. . . . .

The Problem of Figuration
in Antiquity

Gerald L. Bruns

. . . . .

Well, if God has not a face, transcending as He does the peculiarities that
mark all created things . . . [then] the only thing left for us to do is to
make up our minds that none of the propositions put forward is literally
intended and to take the path of figurative interpretation so dear to philosophical souls.—Philo, "On the Posterity and Exile of Cain" (7.1–9)

The first thing that I should say about my subject is that from
the point of view of the ancients figuration is not a problem; that is,
the practice of taking one thing for (or as) another is not an epistemological problem, as it is for Enlightenment and Nietzschean
thinkers. Quite the contrary, it is a resource of understanding, which
means that it is a way of enlarging upon and even, in a manner of
speaking, a way of reinscribing what is written—in order to make
sense of it. I want to confine my attention here principally to three
major figures in the early history of interpretation: Philo of Alexandria (c. 20 B.C.–A.D. 40), Origen (c. 185–254), and Augustine (354–
430). And I want to address two questions to each of them: What
do you do when the text you are studying doesn't make sense? And:
When you have understood the text you are studying, what is it
exactly that you have understood? Is it a text, a meaning, a truth?
(And what if it makes greater sense to say that understanding has
themes rather than objects?)

Let me assume that the text in question is the Old Testament,
or, more accurately, the Septuagint in the case of Philo and Origen,
and the Vetus Latina or Old Latin version of the Septuagint in the
case of Augustine. This assumption is worth making because for
each of these thinkers the Holy Scriptures constituted an eminent but
profoundly abnormal text. Against the textual norms of Hellenic and

Roman culture, the Scriptures make their appearances as a practically unreadable book—a barbarous text. They are notoriously a book of *skandala* or stumbling blocks, a book filled with things offensive to reason that, to be overcome, require a searching meditation—and what requires to be searched is not only the text but the one who meditates as well. What we should understand at once, however, is that textual abnormality or textual scandal does not simply repose in the figurality of what is written. The opposite is true: recourse to the notion of figure, or to some equivalent concept such as allegory, symbol, or even catachresis, was for the ancients a way of normalizing the Scriptures. For once you have identified a scandal as a figure, you have already turned it into something you can deal with: something no longer scandalous, something that can be made sense of. Figure is the antidote of scandal. This was especially (or, anyhow, explicitly) so in the case of Augustine, who was the first major thinker to regard the Scriptures generically as a work of rhetoric, that is, as a work of figural eloquence with designs upon its audience.

We should also keep in mind that the ancients did not divide up what is written the way we do. For them, the crucial distinction in the understanding of what is written is not between the literal and the figurative but between the plain and the obscure, where what is technically figurative could very easily be plain in the obvious sense that what is written is often plainly or unmistakably a figure of speech. This is why Luther, among many others, preferred to speak of the grammatical rather than the literal sense of the Scriptures, since anyone who studied grammar—that is, anyone who knew how to read—would know a figure of speech when he saw one. The ruling distinction here would not be between the literal and the figurative but between the grammatical and the spiritual, where the spiritual has to do not only with what is written but also, and preeminently, with the way or spirit in which one reads. Spirituality is a hermeneutical rather than a textual category. Grammatically the Scriptures are often literally (that is, plainly) metaphorical.[1]

More important is the assumption shared by Philo and Origen, which is that very little of importance in the Scriptures is plain. That which is easy to understand is not worth understanding, except for those who can understand nothing else. "We must make up our minds," Philo says, "that [everything] is figurative and involves deeper meanings" ("That the Worse is Wont to Attack the Better," 167.7[Loeb]). The translation here needs to be untranslated. Philo's word for "figurative" in this case is *tropikoteron*, from the Greek word for turning. Everything, in other words, is to be taken as a trope—and here we can imagine a word or phrase that has to be (physically) turned in order to be understood. On the face of it, or in that portion that faces you, there is nothing to be found—nothing, anyhow, of much importance—but if you turn it slightly you will be able to glimpse what is hidden on its nether side. On the face of it, it is dark, but if you turn it you will begin to be enlightened by the luminous and philosophical face that had been turned away from you. It is as if the text possessed a front and a back (like a head) rather than an inside and an outside (like a mind).

Philo's word for "deeper meaning" here is *"huponoia,"* which he uses along with (but not quite interchangeably with) *"allegoria"* and *"symbolon."* Huponoia means a deeper, higher, or additional thought—but it means more: on the nether side of what is written, or in that portion that is dark or contrary to reason, there is something more for the mind, namely, philosophy, divine wisdom, the truth. *"Huponia"* is not a word for meaning; indeed, it is not clear that Philo had a word for meaning, or that he felt the need or lack of such a word. In one of his treatises on the Cain and Abel story, Philo says that his purpose is merely to treat certain "unfamiliar terms" [*ton onomaton asunethes*] in order "to give as clear an account as I can of the underlying philosophy" [*ten emphainomenon philosophian*] ("On the Birth of Abel and the Sacrifices Offered by Him and by His Brother Cain," 1.6–8). The "unfamiliar terms" are not necessarily or technically figurative; you simply may not have seen them before—or heard them used in this way before. Like Aristotle (*Rhetoric*, 1404b), Philo divides what is written into the strange and the familiar, where the one is often understood to conceal the other, or where a familiar word is made strange by unfamiliar usage (or by unfamiliar interpretation). The Scriptures are *huponoiac* in the sense of being, on the face of it, strange or alien, but if you turn them, you will discover what is familiar to you, namely, philosophy, wisdom, and so forth. Hence Philo proceeds in good Platonic fashion by making the Cain and Abel story recognizable as something worth studying or worth reflection—something worth a second thought. "It is a fact," he says, "that there are two opposite and contending views of life, one which ascribes all things to the mind as our master . . . , the other which follows God. . . . The first of these views is figured by Cain, who is called Possession, because he thinks he possesses all things; the other by Abel, whose name means 'one who refers (all things) to God.' Now both these views or conceptions lie in the womb of the single soul" (2.1–9). If you take the story this way, and are a man of wisdom, you will know what you are reading.

Here we should know that the word for "figured" in this passage is *"ektuposis,"* "to make distinct"—literally to make plain what is obscure by deepening the outline, as when you cut into a piece of wood, making shadows to heighten visibility. Cain is thus a perfect illustration of the paradox of figuration: he does not obscure the principle of self-love, rather he darkens it to make it more distinct, or to show it for what it is—to those who know how to take him in this way. For Philo, figures do not conceal in and of themselves; rather, to take a word or expression (a name or a number) as a figure, that is, in another or higher sense, is to make it plain—to bring it into the open or into the light, whereas to take anything literally is simply to leave it in the dark (as if not to take it at all). The same is true in the case of Abel, "whose name means 'one who refers (all things) to God'": the word "means" here is a translation of *"hermeneuetai,"* that is, interpreted or understood (as).[2] Normally we would not think of using the word "meaning" as a synonym for "interpretation"—yet, on reflection, that is exactly what our modern conception of meaning was made for, namely, to stand in place of interpretation and, in effect, to objectify the way a word or phrase can be taken by figuring it (the way it is taken) as a textual entity: something that inhabits a text independently rather than in virtue of any understanding of it. The concept of meaning, after all, is just what is required as soon as one begins imagining texts as objects toward which one is to adopt an analytic attitude.

Philo, however, clearly did not take analytically the distinction between what goes on in a text and what occurs when a text is taken in a certain way. This is why the practice of allegorizing a text seemed normal to him in a way that it cannot seem normal to us. Allegory is simply the art of taking a text now in one way, now in another. A good illustration of Philo's practice is to be found in his several interpretations of the Cherubim and the flaming sword mentioned in Genesis 3:24. "I suggest," he says, "that they are an allegorical figure [*huponoion*] of the revolution of the whole heaven" ("On the Cherubim," 21.3–4)—and Philo then goes on to explain how they can be taken in this way. However, they can, he says, be taken a second way as well: "on another interpretation the two Cherubim represent the two hemispheres" (25.5–6)—and a second explanation follows. "But there is a higher thought than these," he says. "It comes from a voice in my own soul [*logon para psuches*], which oftentimes is god-possessed and divines where it does not know. This thought I will record in words if I can" (27.1–4). What we have here is a complicated hermeneutical situation, one that needs to be characterized in terms of meditation rather than in terms of reading, since it is clear that the intelligibility of the text cannot be isolated from that which occurs to the reader in the course of his meditations upon what is written. Allegory is not a *method* of interpretation; it is not any sort of formal approach to the text. It is a form of mental or spiritual life, or a way of practicing philosophical contemplation. *Huponoia* is not reducible to a textual entity because it cannot be abstracted from the course of reflection in which it makes its appearance. Naturally the modern reader of Philo is worried about the status of the text in allegorical reflection, but the point is that the text in this case cannot be figured as an objective entity that is subjected to some sort of mental operation. On the contrary, the concept of *huponoia* seems to presuppose a Platonistic theory of knowledge as the recognition of what is already known to you. An allegorical reading of the Law is in this respect not the introduction of something alien into the Law but rather the recognition in it of what you know to be true. *Huponoia* presupposes a memory-based epistemology, not an epistemology of subjects and objects and methods for certifying their correspondence.

It needs to be stressed, however, that the practice of allegorical interpretation does not presuppose that the text for study is without a life and reality of its own. For example, Philo frequently uses the word *hermeneia* to characterize what speech does to thought. The uttered word, Philo says, "sounds and speaks and interprets [*hermeneuei*] our thoughts" ("That the Worse is Wont to Attack the Better," 127.2–3); that is, speech brings what is hidden into the open or into the light. The spoken word is not (as it is in Aristotle's *Peri hermeneias*) a sign or representation of thought; it is not a term in a logical relation but is an instance of disclosure, as when "the sound produced by the voice and the other organs of speech takes the thoughts into its hands like a midwife, and brings them forth to the light" (127.8–128.1)—as if in the fullness of time. On this model, the interpreter stands with the text in a relation that is more phe-

nomenological than logical. To interpret what is written is to speak
for it. One naturally thinks here of Plato's *Phaedrus* and the complaint against the muteness of writing. It is useless to interrogate
what is written, Socrates says, because letters will not answer back
(275d–e). Interpretation, as Philo understands it, tries to overcome
this muteness of the letter. To be an interpreter of the text is to be
answerable for it; it is to say what the text does not say and perhaps
is not able to say. The Cherubim and the sword of flame are not able
to speak for themselves except in a literal way (that is, by means of
letters); they are not self-disclosing or self-interpreting. They make
sense grammatically but not hermeneutically. Only in a meditation
upon what is written can they begin to emerge. To know what a text
means in this sense (as Philo appears to think of it) would be to know
the things a text would say if it were able to speak.

Our epistemological bias in favor of objects of analysis makes it
difficult for us to imagine that figuration might not be regarded as a
textual or even as a linguistic phenomenon. We will say, without a
second thought, that figuration is a form of synonymy and, therefore, a certain kind of meaning, that is, a certain kind of correspondence between terms. Thus it can only be with some rough approximation that we will be able to comprehend Philo—and this holds for
Origen as well—for whom figuration belongs to the categories of
mystery and prophecy. The notion of mystery is one of the regulating
ideas of Philo's conception of the Law, that is, of what it is that needs
to be studied and interpreted. "I myself was initiated under Moses
the God-beloved into his greater mysteries," Philo says in the treatise
"On the Cherubim" (49.1–3), and it is under the authority of Moses—
that is, in the name of Moses—that he claims to instruct us as to
what the Law teaches concerning the nature of virtue (42.1–47.5).
Origen, for his part, says that the Holy Spirit, in composing the
Scriptures, was "preeminently concerned with unspeakable mysteries" [*aporreton musterion*]—and "unspeakable" is precisely the
right word, for a mystery is just that which is not self-disclosing or
self-interpreting but that which has to be entered into.[3] A mystery
in Eastern antiquity is something that cannot be expressed plainly
and perhaps cannot be put into words at all. "*Musterion*" is the
Greek word for secret ceremony, but what is interesting is that the
word does not derive from any ceremonious content or sacramental
knowledge but from *mustes*, that is, "one who is initiated": and
mustes means, literally or, rather, etymologically, "one who keeps his

eyes shut" (presumably until told to open them) and also, secondarily, "one who keeps his mouth shut" as well—someone who does not betray secrets, but also one who does not speak plainly, if at all. *Mustes* is related to *murmur*, that is, to make a sound without saying anything, and also to *mute* and *myopic*. To murmur is evidently to practice the mystic way of speaking.

It is not surprising, then, that the word "mystery" defines for Origen (as, on occasion, it does for Philo) not only the content of the Scriptures but also the way they are to be understood. Mystery is not only a liturgical and epistemological but also a hermeneutical concept. For Origen, to understand is to be initiated into what is hidden or obscure. To understand anything (no matter what: a natural object, a text, justice, the will of God) is to be let in on it. Most of us think of understanding on the model of seeing, or as a form of representation (placing something before the mind's eye), but for Origen understanding is as much a process of initiation as a process of seeing—and thus it implies the mediation of teaching. For Origen, the Scriptures are not composed for those who can only understand things that are plainly put to them; rather, Origen characterizes the proper reader of the Scriptures as "the man who is capable of being taught" [*unamenos didachthenai*]—someone who "might by 'searching out' and devoting himself to the 'deep things' revealed in the spiritual meaning of the words [*tois bathesi tou nou dia ton lexeon eatoun epidous*] become partaker of all the doctrines of the Spirit's counsel" (p. 282; *Patrol.* 11,372A). No doubt the crucial question is: How do you know when you are one who is capable of being taught, that is, taken into God's confidence and made privy to his secrets? Origen's answer can be paraphrased as follows: When you know that something is wrong with what you are reading—that is, when you discover that what is written is garbled, contradictory, unbelievable, or even when it contains an obvious scribal error—*then* you know that it is trying to speak to you, or (more accurately) that it is trying to draw you into its secrets. After all, if everything were plain, nothing would be required to be studied; everything would be commonplace—much would be known, but little would be understood. Scripture is written for those who know a contradiction when they see one, and who also know how to resolve a contradiction by reading in a certain way, that is, in a way not expressed in the text, a way left unspoken, perhaps even a way that must remain unspeakable.

What you have here, by the way, is Origen's theory of scriptural abnormality. The Scriptures are written in such a way as to command the attention of those who are connoisseurs of reason—those capable of being initiated into what is hidden. As Origen says, the Holy Spirit, in composing the Scriptures, "has arranged for certain stumbling blocks and barriers and impossibilities [*skandala kai proschommata kai adunata*] to be inserted in the midst of the law and the history, in order that we may not be completely drawn away by the sheer attractiveness of the language [*tes lexeos elkomenoi to agogon akraton echouses*], and so either reject the true doctrines absolutely, on the ground that we learn from the scriptures nothing worthy of God, or else by never moving away from the letter [*grammatos*] fail to learn anything of the divine element" (p. 285; *Patrol.* 11, 373B). Notice what is being said here! The Scriptures are not meant to be rhetorically captivating (although we could succumb to them that way); they are a *purposefully scandalous text*—we are meant to be scandalized, not enchanted, when we read. Imagine God composing on purpose, or as part of his providence, a deliberately muddled text! But this, of course, is exactly what Socrates, for example, would have recognized as a rhetoric of bewilderment: to catch the attention of anyone, and to get him thinking or to move him to reflection, one must not spellbind him with words but confuse him with questions. He who knows that he knows understands very little. Those who take no offense at what is written—who are merely delighted by it—will rest satisfied with absurd tales and impossible injunctions, and so miss the whole point; but "the man who is capable of being taught" will take offense at absurdity and will feel compelled to search the Scriptures for what is not offensive—not philosophically trivial or, what amounts to the same thing, not inconsistent with a meaning worthy of God.

The concept of teaching here is quite important. To understand Scripture is not to understand what it *means* but what it *teaches*. Origen did not have a word for meaning—or, rather, for him meaning is the same as naming, but Scripture is not a book of namings; it is a book of teachings [*dogmata*], where the notion of teaching is to be understood as the initiation of one "who is capable of being taught." All teaching is by nature recondite, since it involves taking out and putting back again that which is to be understood, namely (in this case), the whole of what can be learned, from the nature of God to the nature of evil and all of what goes on in between.

An obscure and scandalous way of writing is thus a way of teaching the secrets of what is written without giving them away or betraying them as secrets—without demystifying the mystery. It was on this scriptural model of figuration that Moses Maimonides composed his *Guide of the Perplexed,* a twelfth-century work of scriptural exegesis (by a master for his disciple), in which, however, the truth of what is written is not made plain but is to be glimpsed in a flash before it is hidden again.[4] The exegete here is an accomplice in obscurity or scriptural reserve: a conspirator of the spirit. For example, the *Guide* is composed in Arabic but is inscribed in Hebrew characters, and so outwits two sorts of audience. Moreover, at the outset Maimonides identifies the seven ways in which a writer may contradict himself; he then explains that in composing the *Guide* he has taken care to contradict himself according to the fifth and seventh modes. This means that in reading the *Guide* you must not be scandalized by its contradictions, since these are designed to compel you to search the text for what it really teaches, namely, not the secrets of the Law exactly, but the ways of entering into them. Thus every misunderstanding of what is written may be a sign that there is something more for the mind, or that understanding (if it is able) can now occur. And in the unlikely event that it does occur, that is, in the event that you should actually come to understand something, it is also a sign that you are to keep quiet about it (1:17–20).

I mentioned that for Origen figuration was a category not only of mystery but of prophecy as well. Prophecy here is a hermeneutical rather than an epistemological concept; that is, it defines how something is to be taken, not any sort of visionary experience. In this event the secrets of the Law are understood to have been transmitted in a recondite or secret way, not indefinitely, but only until the appointed time, sometimes called "the end of time" or, on the analogy of pregnancy and birth, "the fullness of time," which frequently turns out to be the present time, or the time of the interpreter, when the secrets are to be brought forth by proclamation, and so disclosed to all the people. Thus, to this way of thinking, the Gospel stands in relation to the Law and the Prophets as a plain version of what is obscure, since that which was hidden in types of shadows, parables, and prophecies, now stands revealed: namely, Christ, who understands himself, and who makes sense of himself to others, as the secret of the Law and the promise of the Fathers. In a homily in *Joshua,* Origen writes:

Here is my thought: If, when Moses is read to us, "the veil of the letter is lifted" (II Cor. 3:15), and we begin to understand that "the Law is spiritual" (Rom. 7:14) . . . it is because it is the Lord Jesus who reads it to us; it is he who recites it in the hearing of all the people. . . .

Jesus, therefore, reads the Law to us when he reveals to us the secrets of the Law. For we who are of the catholic Church, we do not spurn the law of Moses but accept it, so long as it is Jesus who reads it to us. Indeed, we can only possess a correct understanding of the Law when he reads it to us, and we are able to receive his sense and his understanding. Did not he adopt his thought who said, "We have the thoughts of Christ in order to have the things of God about which we speak" (I Cor. 2:12–13, 16); and also those who said, "Did not our hearts glow when he was talking to us on the road and explaining the Scriptures to us," when "he began with Moses and all the Prophets and explained the passages all through the Scriptures that referred to himself?" (Luke 24:32, 27–28).[5]

Christ is here a sort of hermeneutical personality who appropriates the Scriptures to himself in order to make his appearance as a certain way of understanding them. As he says in John 5:46, "if you believed Moses, you would believe me, because it was about me that he wrote." Christ is a self-interpreting mystery, a self-opening secret.

In the Gnostic tradition there is a wonderful variation on this idea. That which is written is not only obscure in itself (since only a certain order of events can make it plain); it is *literally* to be kept hidden, as if, for example, in jars in the desert, and is not to be brought out until the pleroma, or the fullness of time. Thus *The Gospel of the Egyptians* explains that it is "the book which the great Seth wrote, and placed in high mountains on which the sun has not risen"; and, again, "The great Seth wrote this book with letters in one hundred and thirty years. He placed it in the mountain that is called Charaxio, in order that, at the ends of the times and the eras . . . it may come forth and reveal this incorruptible, holy race of the great savior and those who dwell with them."[6] Time, after all, is the greatest exegete. Only time can bring things into the open, just as, of course, it can close them up again, leaving us once more in the dark.

This whole mysterious and prophetic way of thinking about plainness and obscurity alters and, in a sense, begins to grow familiar to us—normal to our way of thinking—as soon as we transfer it from the desert to the city, or, more to the point, from Alexandria to Rome, and so bring it under the control of rhetoric, which is, in its

Latin sophistication, the discipline in which figuration is given a name we recognize.[7] Yet figuration is still not, strictly speaking, the sort of linguistic and textual concept that we take it to be.

Here the appropriate text for study is Augustine's *On Christian Doctrine*. Like every writer before him, Augustine divides the Scriptures into plain and obscure portions, but he does so in an entirely new way. Obscurity, for example, now assumes a pragmatic function in the art of winning over an alienated and even contemptuous audience: "Many and varied ambiguities deceive those who read casually," Augustine says; "indeed, in certain places they do not find anything to interpret erroneously [that is, they cannot even misread the text], so obscurely are certain sayings covered with a dense mist." And here is the point: "I do not doubt," Augustine says, "that this situation was provided by God to conquer pride by work and to combat disdain in our minds, to which those things which are easily discovered [that is, commonplace] seem frequently to be worthless" (2.6.7.1–8 [Robertson]). Obscurity, in other words, is just Scripture's way of overturning the cultured prejudices that stand in the way of the understanding of it. Here it is well to remember that Augustine's first response to the Scriptures was to find them appalling as something foreign and primitive: "they seemed to me unworthy [*indigna*] to be compared to the stateliness of Ciceronian eloquence [*Tullianae dignitati*]. For my pride fled from the temper of their style, nor was my sharp vision able to penetrate into their interior" (3.5.8–11 [Loeb, which I have altered slightly]). There is no doubt that in *On Christian Doctrine* Augustine is addressing those who have had, or who are likely to be troubled by, a similarly disagreeable scriptural experience: "those who think like me," he says (4.6.9.5)—those who will find the *sermo humilis*, the low or humble utterance, a stumbling block.[8]

In *On Christian Doctrine*, however, Augustine's purpose is not to defend the humility of the Scriptures against Ciceronian norms of style; rather, it is to argue that the Scriptures already (in their way) fulfill these norms, and are only obscure because of the artfulness of their composition. Thus a healthy portion of Book 4 is devoted to a figural analysis of "the eloquence of the Prophets, where many things are obscured by tropes" (4.7.15.14–15). Scripture is on its own a figuratively inscribed document (the Vetus Latina being slightly more figurative, and therefore more obscure, than the original, that is, than Jerome's translation from the *hebraica veritas*). To be sure, it is not a product of schooling and is even "rustic" in its fashion—but "what

more than this eloquence," Augustine asks, "could sober ears require?" (4.7.17.1–2). What is important about this way of thinking,
however, is that the traditional distinction between the plain and the
obscure has been redescribed as a distinction between the plain and
the *adorned,* or between that which is expressed openly (namely, the
doctrine of charity), and that which is dressed or concealed in the artful vocabulary of the figures (namely, and also, the doctrine of charity). There is no longer, as there was for Origen, a distinction between
esoteric and exoteric teachings, or between secret wisdom and Christian proclamation (although Augustine does, when the occasion suits
him, make use of this distinction); instead, Scripture in many places,
and particularly in the New Testament, exhibits its teachings plainly
and with inescapable clarity. It is just that elsewhere, particularly
(although not exclusively) in the Law and the Prophets, it inscribes
these same teachings figuratively, that is, obscurely, but with a native
eloquence. This means that interpreting or expounding the Scriptures
becomes a matter of reading the obscure in terms of the plain; it becomes a matter of allowing Scripture to speak for itself, and to shed
light on its own darkness.[9]

    I said that in Augustine's thinking figuration is still not a lin-
guistic or textual phenomenon. To be sure, the Scriptures are, in
their obscure portions, figurally composed, but what is of importance
to Augustine is the way the Scriptures are to be taken, not how they
were made. This distinction between what the Scriptures are in themselves and how they are to be taken is what we must keep in mind
when we read the following famous passage:

    To [the] warning that we must beware not to take figurative or trans-
ferred expressions as though they were literal, a further warning must be
added lest we wish to take literal expressions as though they were figurative. Therefore a method of determining whether a locution is literal or
figurative must be established. And generally this method consists in this:
that whatever appears in the divine Word that does not literally pertain
to virtuous behavior or to the truth of faith you must take to be figurative.
Virtuous behavior pertains to the love of God and of one's neighbor; the
truth of faith pertains to a knowledge of God and of one's neighbor.
(3.10.14.1–11)

Here we have a superb way to illustrate the difference between the
hermeneutical and the analytical attitude, or, if you wish, between a
hermeneutics rooted in tradition and a hermeneutics rooted in analysis. This amounts at first glance to a distinction between ancient and

modern hermeneutical attitudes, but this distinction also prevails between the philosophical hermeneutics of Hans-Georg Gadamer and
the analytical tradition that extends from Spinoza and the seventeenth
century and Schleiermacher in the nineteenth to the objectivist hermeneutics widely supported in our own time. Augustine's method of
determining the difference between the literal and the figurative rests
not upon an unprejudiced analysis of the text but upon the application of the traditional Christian "rule of faith," whereby scriptural
texts are to be taken as they stand when they are consistent with
apostolic teachings and in another sense when they appear at odds
with or indifferent to these teachings. The text is not to be taken as
it is in itself but only at it has been appropriated and transmitted
within a particular tradition of understanding.

A question worth considering is whether Augustine's hermeneutical method is really a method at all and not simply a special instance
of what characterizes every hermeneutical situation. Isn't it the case
that the prior appropriation of a text within a particular tradition of
understanding is something that must necessarily take place if there
is to be any understanding of the text at all? This, at least, would be
Gadamer's position.[10] Such a position presupposes the historicity of
all understanding, whence there can be no such thing as an unprejudiced hermeneutical analysis of a text but only its appropriation
within a particular, historical hermeneutical practice. Thus the tradition of Spinoza and Schleiermacher, which seeks to comprehend a
text in itself, that is, in terms of an original or originating intention,
is only another way of appropriating texts and providing for the
understanding of them—a tradition that has provided the regulating
concepts of modern biblical and literary criticism. The point is that
all hermeneutical positions are rooted in one or another tradition of
understanding—one or another tradition that hands down normative
practices for determining authoritative interpretations. The question
of what counts as authoritative is always historically contingent; that
is, it is never purely logical but is always relative to prevailing cultural norms. This is why, in order to understand the nature of interpretation, one must study its history. It is not enough to adopt a hermeneutical position, not even a position that offers the promise of an
objective and disinterested understanding of what is written; one
needs always to be open to the history in which one's position happens to emerge.

I want to be more precise about Augustine's conception of the relationship between literal and figurative expressions. In the passage above, Augustine's distinction is not quite the same as the Pauline distinction between *gramma* and *pneuma*,[11] nor, again, is it the same as the medieval distinction between the *sensus literalis* and the *sensus spiritualis*. Augustine's word for literal is *"proprius,"* that is, that which is one's own, or that which is proper or peculiar to itself.[12] The literal sense in this case would be simply the sense that Scripture expresses on its own, that is, plainly and of itself, whereas the figurative sense would be that which Scripture does not express of itself but only if and when it is so taken by the one who reads. In other words, figuration remains for Augustine a thoroughly hermeneutical concept, even though it has now also taken on an explicitly rhetorical meaning in his conception of how the Scriptures artfully deal with a disdainful or contemptuous audience.

It is worth knowing, however, that in the passage above Augustine does not use the word "sense" (nor any word for meaning) but speaks only of proper and figurative locutions. The word *"sensus"* turns up (along with *"voluntas"* and *"sententia"*) in Book 12 of the *Confessions*, where Augustine wrestles with the question of how the words of Moses are to be taken when it is no longer possible to say how Moses wanted to be understood—"behold how confidently I affirm, that in thy incommutable Word thou has created all things visible and invisible: but can I so confidently affirm that Moses had not another meaning than this when he wrote, In the beginning God made heaven and earth? No. Because though I see this to be certain in thy truth, yet I cannot so easily see in his mind, that he thought just so in the writing of it" (12.24.9–15 [Loeb]). Augustine's counsel is that we should not claim to know what Moses thought, only to assume that he could not have written anything false or contrary to reason—or contrary to the law of charity. Moreover, Augustine says, we should take the Scriptures to be a fountain that produces many streams, "whence every man may draw out for himself such truth as he can upon these subjects, he, one observation, and he, another, by larger circumlocutions of discourse" (12.27.7–8). Here exegesis is not simply decipherment; it is also enlargement or embellishment, not in the sense that what is extraneous or secondary is introduced as a textual supplement, but rather in the sense that what is understood is never simply reducible to a grammatical intention. The doctrine of charity, for example, would thus be not so much the goal of scriptural understanding as its point of departure, because the doctrine defines the spirit in which the Scriptures are to be taken; that is, what the doctrine of charity defines is just the presupposition of a Christian reading of the Scriptures. Augustine's attitude is, once more, hermeneutical rather than analytical. The question is not what Scripture means in itself (as if on a presuppositionless reading) but how it is to be understood—and the point is that, granting the presupposition of charity, it is capable of being taken in diverse senses:

> So now, when another shall say, Moses meant as I do [*hoc sensit, quod ego*]: and another, Nay, the very same as I do: I suppose that with more reverence I may say: Why meant he not as you both mean, if you both mean truly? And if there be a third truth, or a fourth, yea, if any other man may discover any other truth in those words, why may he not be believed to have seen all these: he [that is, Moses], by whose ministry God, who is but One, hath tempered these holy Scriptures to the meaning of many, that were to see things true, and yet diverse [*per quem deus unus sacras litteras vera et diversa visuris multorum sensibus temperavit*]. (12.31.1–8)

When you have understood the Scriptures, what exactly have you understood? You may (or may not) have understood Moses, depending on what he himself understood. It is not clear that you have understood a *text*, because for Augustine the understanding of the Scriptures is not so much the recovery of a meaning as it is the discovery of a truth. To understand the Scriptures is not simply to grasp an idea that is intrinsic to them; rather, it is that the Scriptures are able to disclose to you what would otherwise remain hidden in the mind of God, namely (speaking only in the most general way), how things were in the beginning, how they came to be as they are now, and how things will come to pass in the end. The interesting point here is that these mysteries, so far from being incomprehensible to the many, are accessible to every sort of understanding—capable of being taken now in one sense, now in another. For Augustine, the Scriptures are more rhetorical than philosophic. This means that, whereas for Origen the Scriptures are closed to everyone but a single category of reader, for Augustine they open to a heterogeneous audience. The Scriptures are a public rather than a secret text; the truth has been tempered to a plurality of understanding.

On the question of the relation of meaning and understanding there is another text by Augustine that should be considered. It is from the chapter on *significatio* in the treatise *On Dialectic*, and it is part of Augustine's effort to produce a technical vocabulary for talk-

ing more rigorously about the signification of words—for it was
plain to him that the traditional rhetorical notions of *res* and *verba*
were insufficient for the sorts of discrimination required in logic:

> When, therefore, a word is uttered for its own sake, that is, so that some-
> thing is being asked or argued about the word itself, clearly it is the thing
> which is the subject of the disputation and inquiry; but the thing in this
> case is called a *verbum*. Now that which the mind not the ears perceives from
> the word and which is held within the mind itself is called a *dicibile*. When a
> word is spoken not for its own sake but for the sake of signifying something
> else, it is called a *dictio*. The thing itself which is neither a word nor the con-
> ception of a word in the mind, whether or not it has a word by which it can
> be signified, is called nothing but a *res* in the proper sense of the name. There-
> fore, these four are to be kept distinct: the *verbum*, the *dicibile*, the *dictio*,
> and the *res*. *Verbum* both is a word and signifies a word. *Dicibile* is a word;
> however, it does not signify a word but is understood in the word and con-
> tained in the mind [*Quod dixi dicibile, verbum est, nec tamen verbum, sed
> quod in verbo intelleqitur et animo continetur, significat*]. *Dictio* is also a
> word, but it signifies both the first two, that is, the word itself and what is
> brought about in the mind by means of the word. *Res* is a word which signi-
> fies whatever remains beyond the three that have been mentioned.[13]

What is of importance here is *"dicibile,"* which is a word for meaning, not in the sense of naming or reference—that is, not in the sense
of a correspondence between *verbum* and *res*—but in the hermeneutical sense of that which is understood when a word is used. *Dicibile*
is a word for meaning in the sense of being a word for the understanding of a word. *Dicibile* is not any sort of entity intrinsic to the
word; it is simply the word as understood.

  Augustine's word for meaning helps me to make my final point,
which is that the ancients may seem to us analytically naive, but this
may be only because hermeneutically they were extraordinarily sophisticated—connoisseurs of understanding. This is not an idea many
will be able to accept. What I mean is that there are two attitudes
that we can take toward the ancients, but because we are taught to
believe that history is the history of error we are likely to be already
fixed in our views. Thus, on the one hand, we can (and almost always
do) adopt an enlightened—or, I should say, an Enlightenment—attitude, in which case the ancients will appear to us benighted for their
failure to treat figuration and understanding problematically. On the
other hand, however, we can refuse to assume that the ancients were
also primitives, and we can ask what would happen if we tried to

study the topics that enflame us within the history of their thinking. I'm not talking about replacing what Geoffrey Hartman calls our "negative thinking" with the "incorporative and reconciling" motive of much ancient reading.[14] Such a shift in thinking could not be within our capacity. It could be, however, that the study of the ancients can help us understand why we are not capable of thinking of figuration, for example, except in the most skeptical way—valuing the figures for their negative virtues. For what distinguishes us from the ancients is precisely our Enlightenment habit of reducing everything to epistemological categories, in which case figuration becomes a problem for us because we find ourselves able to think of it only as a mental or linguistic or textual operation—not something that we learn to practice but something that goes on in spite of ourselves and screws up every conceivable effort we make to represent things as they are.[15] The study of the ancients thus becomes enlightening for the light that they throw upon us, because they call vivid attention to the historicity of our concerns, and also perhaps to our blindness in this regard. History appears as a history of error only to the extent that we are closed off from it.

The ancients, indeed, may be one up on us. What if, as they believed, representation is not at issue in the matter of figuration, at least not in any interesting way? What if the matter were hermeneutical rather than epistemological, such that questions of meaning were only ways of posing questions of understanding, or of how something is to be taken? What would matter in such an event is not the accuracy of representation (its rigor, its reproducibility, whether it can be counted as knowledge) but applicability to a situation. In this event the question is not how does figuration work (or what does it interfere with) but what does it enable us to do? The ancients would say simply that figuration enables us to understand what is written; that is, it provides us with a way of understanding that which, otherwise, we would have to do without. Figuration is the alternative to not understanding anything; it is that which goes on whenever understanding occurs. The ancients would not have been impressed by our modern or enlightened practice of withholding our understanding from what is written on the grounds that understanding is not to be trusted (owing to the infiltration of figures); they would have seen at once that this suspicion is rooted not in a desire for knowledge but in a fear of authority: that is, we are simply not willing to allow anyone the authority of judging what a text means, because judging won't do. We want certainty—a certainty that will withstand not only second thoughts and better arguments but also new circumstances and new sources of understanding. We want understanding to be free of the contingencies of its occurrence, and so we defer it endlessly by means of every sort of methodological contrivance— semiotics, deconstruction, readerly aesthetics, psychoanalysis, Marxist critiques, and so on—seeking now in this method, now in that, *the* analysis that will abolish the as structure of understanding (that is, its historicity) once for all. A *furor methodologicus* has replaced the *furor allegoricus,* as if understanding were to be found in the operation of mental hardware.

The ancients—were we actually to study them[16]—would encourage us to think of interpretation on the model of a social practice rather than as a certain type of mental operation. After all, as a description of a mental operation, allegory is strange indeed, and it would have seemed strange even to someone like Philo. As a description of how to overcome the strangeness of a philosophically abnormal text, however, allegory is no more odd than any social custom no longer current among us, and constituted perfectly rational behavior in an age every bit as advanced as ours.

Homotextuality: Barthes on Barthes,
Fragments (RB), with a Footnote

John O'Neill

. . . . .

Fragments (RB)

Why fragments? Passages. Images. Texts. Paragraphs. Stars. Con-
stellations. Turning up for their own sake; for the sake of it—the
pleasure of *ID*.

Woven. Written. Without design. Uncopied. Copious. Words. Some-
body is writing. Whose body?
Write about yourself. Whenever was that? The child's body amid
larger bodies. Surrounded, seen, handled, hungered, caressed, cross.
Other bodies, every body, some bodies, no bodies. Mother there,
father gone, grandmother, grandfather. Incorporate. Prehistory.

Proper talk. Gossip. Piano. Woman's talk. Programmes. Contracts.
Bills. The dead body of language. Boredom. Silence. Retreat. Waiting.
Generation. Acting. Illness. Records. The written body. Ritual of
science. Dangers of childhood. Parents. Absence. Custom.

When is the body my body? Death. Sickness. Family photos. Childhood. Vacations.

Paradoxical. Contrary. Cut outs. Fragments. Free, discreet, generous
texts. Dislocation. Mutations. Text on text. Language on language.
Without a center. Without repetition. Abolition. Language. Society.
Bourgeois contract. Political discourse. Sacrifice. Public bodies. Literary bodies. Mythologies.

Decomposition. Play. Perversion.

Writing as surplus value. Seminal play. The spume. Irrigation. Ink.
Writing upon writing, text upon text. Barthes on Barthes. Page upon

page; word without end. The play within the play. By degrees, transgression. Foreground/background. Gendered. Dialectics. Dissolution of paradigms, of sexual and semantic conflict into fragments, shimmers, slips and drifts.
Improvisation of meaning and sexuality:
"Who knows if this insistence on the plural is not a way of denying sexual duality? The opposition of the sexes must not be a law of Nature; therefore, the confrontations and paradigms must be dissolved, both the meanings and the sexes be pluralized: meaning will tend toward its multiplication, its dispersion (in the Theory of the Text) and sex will be taken into no typology (there will be, for example, only *homosexualities,* whose plural will baffle any constituted, centered discourse, to the point where it seems to him virtually pointless to talk about it)" (RB).

Sowing words. Sowing seed. Polysemy. Proliferation. A sea of ink. Pen. Man. Ship. Floating. Cruising. Adrift. Butterfly. La Papillon.

Theory of literary fragments: Limitations. Openings, desire, foreplay. Promiscuous starts without the traps of conclusion, contracted consummation. Jottings from nowheres, *hors-texte.* Condensations. Scraps of my life; daily narcissisms:
"Production of my fragments. Contemplation of my fragments (correction, polishing, etc.). Contemplation of my scraps (narcissism)" (RB).

He wanted to write himself in RB. But always there crept in the maxims. Were these to reassure others that this fragmentary creature had, after all, a bottom nature? Or were they there to appease his own fears, to calm his passion for extravagance by catching himself in words that hang upon him like old clothes? To wrap himself in a patchwork, a quilt of rhapsodic thoughts, starting from no center, at all costs avoiding a scene.

To really write RB he would need to get past his mirror image, to slip past his mother. But he cannot do this because RB is the blind spot from which all this is seen. To see himself in depth is a task he poses for others. This book (RB) is therefore only the book of the self's resistance to his own life—a novel without a proper name. To the extent that it subverts even this achievement, it does so by occasionally shrugging off its own corpus in favor of the writer's working body—such as it is:

> To write the body
> Neither the skin, nor the muscles, nor the bones nor
> the nerves, but the rest: an awkward, fibrous, shaggy,
> raveled thing, a clown's coat (RB)

Literature's two bodies: one whole, a corpse with integrity, respected; the other fragmented, teasing and tormented; delirious, drifting in a tide of words. But with a vision of the feminine flood; cycle of life; therefore waiting, voyeur:

No object is in a constant relationwhip with pleasure (Lacan appropos of Sade). For the writer however, this object exists: it is not the language: it is the *mother tongue.* The writer is someone who plays with his mother's body (I refer to Pleynet on Lautréamont and Matisse): in order to dismember it, to take it to the limit of what can be known about the body: I would go so far as to take bliss in a *disfiguration* of the language, and opinion will strenuously object, since it opposes "disfiguring nature." (*The Pleasure of the Text,* p. 37)

Barthesian fragments: textual cuts, circumcisions; women's robes; flowing, feminized. Writing, bleeding on the virgin page; cave artist of the womb's passages. (See Bruno Bettelheim, *Symbolic Wounds: Puberty Rites and the Envious Male* [New York: Collier Books, 1962]; Geza Roheim, "Aphrodite, or the Woman with a Penis," in *The Panic of the Gods and Other Essays,* ed. Werner Muensterberg [New York: Harper and Row, 1972], pp. 169–205.)

Literary labor, conceived in envy of speechless fertility. Speak, mother, to tell me who I am. Silence, waiting. Therefore *literary couvade:* reenter the mother's body through the inking watch, germinate words, words, words. Risk of birth, risk of death to heal the polemic of language. Seek literary bliss: resurrection of the fragmentary, broken text. Writer's body in the grip of its own myth. Logos of literary pregnancy: to take hold of the new body's beginnings. Flesh, smile, language. Mother. Home. But wait. Begin a watch, daily zigzag upon the page to keep the wound open.

A Footnote[1]

We read books with our bodies. We write with our bodies too. Because we do so, we read and write our bodies as conversible, storyable experiences of living, loving, waiting, sensing ourselves and one another. We live, then, between two bodies: the *literary body* that reads and writes that other *body of literature* so that we can hardly know one apart from the other. Poets celebrate this; novelists, essayists, and critics make hard work of it. At least, this was so until writers discovered themselves as poets. They did not, of course, admit this readily. The discovery could at first be attributed to language itself. That is to say, the poetic, playful, and pleasurable in language could be said to be of language: the autonomy of language thereby found as an infantile pleasure, heteronomous. In this way, literary pleasure could be contained by literary work: a division of literary labor. This is perhaps a necessary arrangement. We do not, and should not, easily abandon the work of realism through which we have fashioned so much of the world and ourselves. What is done is done. Moreover, we have built this world much as we have fenced our fields, built our homes and all the other machinery of our living. Indeed, we rightly celebrate these achievements in the realisms of our science and literature. Yet, the life of the arts and sciences cannot be confined to retailing their achievements. Where this happens, interpretation tends to become a dead weight. In the arts and sciences there must therefore be periods of rejection, innovation, and iconoclasm.

Everything Barthes wrote exploited and subverted the formats that fasten the literary body to outworn ideologies of production and consumption. Like Rabelais, he was a literary transvestite,[2] trying anything, one costume after another, one body after another, dividing, multiplying himself, in pursuit of pleasure: "So far as much of the best, of the most original in modern art and literature is autistic, i.e., unable or unwilling to look to a reality of 'normality' outside its own chosen rules, so far as much of the modern genius can be understood from the point of view of a sufficiently comprehensive, sophisticated theory of games, there is in it a radical homosexuality."[3]

Barthes's literary principles were ludic rather than destructive: unmasking, unveiling, undressing—but never exceeding the striptease itself. He had a dread of dead language and of the social institutions that make literature a corpse rather than a living body of filiations and flashes that articulate the sheer pleasures of reading and writing. He struggled to generalize writing, to de-oedipalize the text. Childlike, he wished to set afloat all specific languages, to unmoor interpretation from its literary models, to let it drift pleasurably in the mother tongue. In other words, always more words, Barthes im-

provised a further state in the *physiology of literature,* lodging interpretation once and for all in the *literary body:*[4]

Apparently Arab scholars, when speaking of the text, use this admirable
expression: the certain body. What body? We have several of them; the
body of anatomists and physiologists, the one science sees and discusses:
this is the text of grammarians, critics, commentators, philologists (the
pheno-text). But we have also a body of bliss consisting solely of erotic
relations, utterly distinct from the first body: it is another contour, another
nomination; thus with the text; it is no more than the open list of the fires
of language (those living fires, intermittent lights, wandering features
strewn in the text like seeds and which for us advantageously replace the
"semina aeternitatis," the *"zopyra,"* the common notions, the fundamental
assumptions of ancient philosophy). Does the text have a human form, is
it a figure, an anagram of the body? Yes, but of our erotic body. The
pleasure of the text is irreducible to the physiological need. (RB)[5]

To understand this conception of the literary body, we cannot, of
course, hang on to an unrevised conception of language, mind, and
embodiment. When we speak of the autonomy of language and literature we should be careful not to reintroduce the very separation that
this notion is intended to heal with respect to the instrumentalist
conception of language and embodiment. We do not have language at
our disposal. As embodied beings we live in language. As such we
have no privileged position with respect to language, any more than
we have with respect to time, indeed, it is this double bind that is
properly understood in the recognition of the autonomy of language.
Yet we are not caught in the web of language like helpless flies. We
achieve a certain distance with respect to it; thus the polarities of
synchrony and diachrony may be taken as vibrations in the web,
points at which the code turns into a message. We may use the linguistic web to see ourselves caught in it and struggling to be free
from it; the web thereby having served its purpose. Thus in the
theater of Artaud, Brecht, Ionesco, and Beckett the voice is no longer
used in order to repeat or enact a thought, as though the body were
merely the soul's servant. Speech is rather an originary gesture that
sets the body thinking as it is forced to do, for example, when confronted with alien things, madness, and otherwise exotic cultures.
Thus Beckett can employ only Mouth or Voice or Footsteps, and
Brecht can bring forth thought from color, because they create meaning for an embodied community which is deprived of its audience/
viewer transcendence by these very effects/affects. The mind is

bracketed in such theater; only the body can anticipate the action. Not, of course, the Cartesian body, atrophied by its superior mind, no better than the debris that surrounds and eventually overwhelms our living. Rather, the gestural body, before the spectacle, before the conventions of language and the conformist text. The gest as gist; the meaning thereby deeded in a public act available to anyone present: corporate community.

The web of language is therefore both a necessary structure and a temporary event; metalanguage as the pact between language and the writer that provides the space within which he can maneuver. A writer's language, like his body, carves out a virtual space in which neither words nor objects ever have any absolute closure, but rather release each other in exhaustible systems of meaning which he brings to recognition through style, that is to say, in practical sketches of his world. None of this is necessary for a disembodied mind. But the writer dwells in language precisely because he or she is an embodied being; familied and thereby social. Our *embodied presence* to the world and others is the wedge of *difference* that generates and elides time and distance but without any totalization of the histories and geographies of language and perception.[6]

Barthes called for a thoroughly structuralist approach to literature, as in his own study of fashion,[7] or in Lévi-Strauss's studies of myth.[8] Yet he regarded literature as an endless interrogation, a fracturing, Orpheus-like forbidden to look back upon the truth to which it believes itself allied. He considered literary realism hopelessly inarticulate about its necessary choices; in short, it cannot tell of its alliance with the unreality of language through which it works its very realism.[9] Barthes also rejected the mythology of scientific discourse. He regarded its objectivism and realism as rhetorical achievements that affect the neutrality of science in a referential code whose grammatical decoys—absence of first-person referee/third-person agency—can just as well be appropriated in literary discourse. From the other side, literary discourse, so far from being a purely subjective achievement, can be analyzed in terms of objective units of discourse, intelligible progression and resolution, as well as conventional taxonomies and classification of things, persons, and events that fulfill its sense and expressivity. In Barthes's view, however, structuralism is not exempt from taking a stand on its own use of language. In other words, structuralism is neither presumptively nor uniquely on the side of the scientific mode of discourse. Indeed,

Barthes considered it necessary for structuralism to comprise its analytic intent with its historist experience of language, in order to accommodate its own lateness:

In short, structuralism will be just one more "science" (several are born each century, some of them only ephemeral) if it does not manage to place the actual subversion of scientific language at the center of its programme, that is, to "write itself." How could it fail to question the very language it uses in order to know language? The logical continuation of structuralism can only be to rejoin literature, no longer as an "object" of analysis but at the activity of writing, to do away with the distinction derived from logic which turns the work itself into a language-object and science into a meta-language, and thus to forego that illusory privilege which science attaches to the possession of a captive language. (RB)[10]

By turning to the activity of writing, we once again confront the options of subjective and objective discourse, and with the artificiality of the dominance of scientific over nonscientific language once released from the constraints of the hierarchical conventions of realism and objectivism, the writer is obliged to explore the pleasure of the text without any sense of its frivolity or constrained pedagogy. Indeed, it is the task of structuralism to reveal to science the scandal of language, namely, that after so many years of abuse it still remains sovereign, and is no longer in need of the technical alibis furnished to science by the humanities in its seeming defense.

The fragmentary mode that Barthes chose for his own work was designed to show by incongruity the design of "real" books, to reveal the material format of consequential thought, the idea flowing through the words in sustained narrativity punctuated with reasonable stops and starts; essential paraphrase. Above all, literary realism subordinates detail to a general schema, guaranteeing the reader will always know where he is and what to look for; everything worked out. Hence the importance of literary genres for the orderly passage of truth in kinds. These two movements come together in the activity of structuralism—*a movement of deconstruction in order to reproduce the function of structure: the production of meaning and value.*[11] The benefit of this notion is that it undercuts literary positivism inasmuch as the latter sacrifices the productive intention of the work to the establishment of its external biographical and circumstantial facts. Positivist history paradoxically rejects the lived, embodied historicities of literature by locating the author's intention and sources in formative influences found elsewhere and otherwise than the author conceived them. It misses the radical *literary deformation* or *misreading*[12] through which a work acquires "sources" as embodied "resources" and thereby structures itself. As such, the work must first be interpreted from within, and then as an attempt to put meaning in the world as one of its languages or styles.

Every literary work is caught in this tension between language and literature, that is, between literature as the parasite of language and as its life-giving transfusion of new meaning and intelligibility. Barthes contrasted language and style. For the writer, language is not so much an instrument of expression as a horizon, a setting of familiar bodily experiences within which he speaks much like anyone else. Literature and his style, that is, his specific carnal imagery, vocabulary, and timing: "Thus under the name of style a self-sufficient language is evolved which has its roots only in the depths of the author's personal and secret mythology, that subnature of expression where the first coition of words and things takes place, where once and for all the great verbal themes of his existence come to be installed" (RB).[13] It is in this corporeal infralanguage that Barthes discovered his own writing, as well as that of Michelet and Racine. To be consequent, he could hardly work in any other fashion if he were to realize the project of *Barthes by Barthes*. Style, then, is the corporeal bond between the man and his text—what I am calling, therefore, *homotextuality*. It is sounded in the writer's personal myths which work in him like the four humors, or in those places where his flesh and the world experience the metamorphosis of expression and carnal being.[14]

Barthes had no patience with the claim that literature expresses anything else than language; there is no prelinguistic expression. No first words. The author's job is to work with language that has already been used, stereotyped, and settled a thousand times, layer upon layer of convention, law, and common sense. Hence *fragmentation* offers at least one device for blocking meaning until it overflows this very artifice in whatever direction it cares to take.[15] Inasmuch as the *author* sinks himself in the tautological resonances of languages upon language, he loses himself and the world in the task of writing which somehow—not as sheer instrument or material—restores both the world and himself. Thus an author can never present a doctrine, or evidence, or even commitment, since the literary labor involved in their production obliges him more heavily to their flawed creation: "an author is a man who wants to be an author" (RB).

Like Montaigne earlier, Barthes "rolled around" in his literary body, enjoying its moments, its slackness, its dispersions—essential diaspora—its tastes, its moods, its rejections, as well as its loves, even when impossible. It is with this in mind that we must understand Barthes's choice of writing *fragments* rather than books. Literary fragments reveal the writer the way a woman's dress reveals her body. The pleasure is in the artful choice, arrangement, moment, movement—understatement. He played with texts as women play with dress, multiplying their bodies, each woman every woman, shimmering—other woman. Barthes found his own passion for fragmentation in other writers. In Sade, Fourier, and Loyola, he discovered the same pleasure in segmentation (the body of Christ, the body of the victim, the human soul). He intended nothing transcendental in this trinity: merely three fetishisms of the text, pleasuring word upon word through an excess of classification:

our three authors deduct, combine, arrange, endlessly produce rules of assemblage; they substitute syntax, *composition* (a rhetorical ignation word) for creation; all three fetichists, devoted to the cut-up body, for them the reconstitution of a whole can be no more than a summation of intelligibles; nothing indecipherable, no irreducible quality of ejaculation, happiness, communication: nothing that is not spoken. . . . (RB)[16]

No official reading; Barthes sought only the man in the text. Like Montaigne he had no other physics; no other metaphysics. No concern, then, with the official sites and alibis of literary interpretation: history, class, biography. Look only for the excess in writing: the stolen goods of literature. The necessary method, therefore, is to unglue the text, fragment it; to let socialism, faith, and evil through the net (for others to fish) catching smaller pleasures in the text—a method he hoped for and which he applied to himself as well as to Sade, Fourier, Loyola, and Michelet:

were I a writer, and dead, how I would love it if my life, through the pains of some friendly and detached biographer, were to reduce itself to a few details, a few preferences, a few inflections, let us say: to "biographemes" whose distinction and mobility might go beyond any fate and come to touch, like Epicurean atoms, some future body, destined to the same dispersion; a marked life, in sum, as Proust succeeded in writing his in his work, or even in a film, in the old style, in which there is no dialogue and the flow of images (that *flumen orationis* which is perhaps what makes up the "obscenities" of writing) is intercut, like the relief of hiccoughs, by the barely written darkness of the intertitles, the casual eruption of another

signifier: Sade's white muff, Fourier's flowerpots. Ignatius's Spanish eyes
(RB).[17]

Thus he materialized the problem of biography. That is to say,
he cut into the hermeneutical problem by going for the *humoral
imagination* that furnishes the thematic unities in an author's work,
whether of Michelet or of himself. His readings, therefore, are like
the palmist readings, finding repetitive themes in auguries of the flesh
and matter, condensations of living. Thus he gave to Michelet's vast
corpus a carnal history, discovering an incessant metamorphosis between the historian's working, suffering, animal, fluid body, and the
ravages of the body-politic suffering the history of France.[18] The
rhythms of the history of France held Michelet in the same obsession
as the rhythm of life he worshipped in the female cycle. History appeared to him like a living body whose trajectory ran through all
sorts of intermediate stages of life, matter, vegetation, character, and
spirit, culminating in the moralization of nature. At its highest point,
therefore, history appeared to Michelet to reproduce itself in a gendered struggle between Grace, the women—at times sleepy (Turkey),
or bored (Napoleon), or playful (Richelieu)—and Justice, the forceful
male (Satan, Luther, the Revolution). Just as the grand principles of
history are sexualized in Michelet's discourse, so all the major figures
of history are bodily types, dry, cold, ruled by the basic humors of
the world's body. For this reason, the most enduring historical figures
are women. Their bodies are historical bodies: eternal rhythm of
blood and life, magic and religion; dominance and submission. The
highest unity of history is therefore prefigured in the androgyne, the
marriage of the heart and reason, and realized in the revolutionary
deliverance of the people.

We shall not enjoy any work of Barthes's without first perusing
the table of contents from which its pickings are offered. And we
would miss the feast if we were to insist upon ordering the items
into a menu *fixe*. The items are ordered alphabetically as in an ency-
clopedia precisely because they obey no order. They constitute a
treasury of discourse, of endless little chats for anyone who picks out
an item. Only a madman—a nerveless reader—would use Barthes's
text in an orderly fashion. As with titles, so with books. Barthes
never wrote one. He started many, enjoyed the foreplay, postponed
consummation. Hence book on book—*metabook*—permitting the
reader to choose a passage, proceed at his own pace; stops, starts,

gaps, flashbacks, abridgments, footnotes—above all, never saying anything that cannot as well be said later at another turn; reader and writer waiting for another, like lovers: "The libertine body, *of which language is a part*, is a homeostatic apparatus that maintains itself: the scene requires justification, discourse, this discourse inflames, eroticizes; the libertine 'cannot hold out': a new scene begins, and so on, *ad infinitum*" (RB).[19] Barthes explains his procedures as the only way a literary lover can proceed with any hope of finding a listener, or reader. The lover discourses, runs ahead of himself to where he and his lover will be, carried upon *futures of speech* that indeed embody his love like a dancer's feet. The lover's discourse, therefore, is exclamatory rather than descriptive of what loving he experiences. The lover's discourse is a hallucination of his feelings toward the beloved whom he always beholds otherwise: "Amorous *dis-cursus* is not dialectical; it turns like a perpetual calendar, an encyclopaedia of affective culture (there is something of Bouvard and Pecuchet in the lover)" (RB).[20] Thus Barthes points out that his discourse draws languorously upon books, conversations, friends, and his own life but without any authoritative purpose. For if he were to proceed in anything but a fragmentary fashion, he would encounter the institutional sirens of the love story and, worse still, of the philosophy of love. Consequently, he chooses "an *absolutely insignificant* order," namely, that of titles in an alphabetic order; foreclosing the will to possess his lover. (See Figure 1.)

In such tokens, the writer like a lover abandons any concern with integrity. This would be an impossible demand upon the reader's own passion. Like lovers, both reader and writer want to get to their satisfaction any way they can, on each occasion this way rather than that, skipping within an order motivated by pleasure. Barthes's fragmentary method therefore consciously provides for the same literary liberties to be taken with his text as he himself took with other texts. Literary pleasure cannot be controlled any more than a lover's discourse; it awaits the reader's picking:

Tmesis, source or figure of pleasure, here confronts two prosaic edges with one another; it sets what is useful to a knowledge of the secret against what is useless to such knowledge; Tmesis is a seam or flaw resulting from a simple principle of functionality; it does not occur at the level of the structures of languages but only at the moment of their consumption; the author cannot predict Tmesis: he cannot choose to write *what will not be read*. And yet, it is the very rhythm of what is read and what is not read

Figure 1:

A. *Lover's Discourse,* Fragments. The table of contents is disturbed by the English translation and the page sequence which upsets the left/right, down/up, arrangement. Fortunately, this effect restores the disorder invited by the alphabetical arrangement.

CONTENTS

that creates the pleasure of the great narratives: has anyone ever read Proust, Balzac, *War and Peace,* word for word? (Proust's good fortune: from one reading to the next, we never skip the same passages.) (RB)[21]

Only the lover is caught in the act of discourse, in figures articulated according to varying moods, hours, places, memories—the need to integrate them being specifically absent; as though a lover could discourse upon what love is finally. If we still need to ask what made Barthes write, we should see in our own question nothing else than a sign of fatigue which the writer does not know: writing made him write; as love makes a lover's talk. He was feminized by writing, wore it like a wound: "A gentle hemorrhage which flows from no specific point in my body." As a writer he could double himself like a hermaphrodite, and thereby solace his exclusion from the conjugalities of class, convention, and family. He became a lover-in-waiting, comparing himself to the window prostitutes of Hamburg and Amsterdam. Fragments like lovers have beginnings only: they do not tell of their end. Yet as a writer Barthes excluded himself through the force of a gift that he knew his lover could not embrace like talk which indeed touches the flesh directly without binding it to conventions of passion, sincerity, and desire. Writing, however, begins only with the lover's absence: therefore he made himself mother and child of his own desire in order to bear the wound of *a lover* writing:

Faced with the death of his baby son, in order to write (if only scraps of writing), Mallarmé submits himself to parental division:

> Mère, pleure
> Moi, je pense
> Mother, weep
> While I think.

But the amorous relation has made me into an atopical subject—undivided: I am my own child: I am both mother and father (of myself, of the other): how would I divide the labor? (RB)[22]

The writer can no more live with a passive reader than with a passive lover; the writerly text demands to be manhandled, misread, fragmented, and rewritten, step-by-step, from any point and always open to digressions.

In *S/Z* Barthes *pluralizes* a text of Balzac. In other words, he overwhelms the paternal and proprietary culture of the classical text in a riot of reading/writing that rushes in on the text from all sides thereby destroying its orderly confrontation. Barthes's plural readings require the fragmentary method, chopping up the sacred text into any number of *lexias,* which then function to tell a story like an astrological reading which cannot be told without one body perusing another; fragments of life furnishing fragments of meanings from day to day.[23] Thus a text can no more be sensibly read *as a whole* than it would make sense to read one's horoscope *for the year,* rather than to read oneself into it according to one's moods, hopes, and fears; for the fun of it, even. But daily, since the sense of each fragment, like a haiku, is in what we bring to it, not in its relation to other fragments. The horoscope is therefore an *autoscope;* and the self is not read otherwise than from day to day. Reading therefore does not deliver our lives; it is living that makes us readers. Once our readings are free from the practices to totalization, unity, and survey, we are at liberty to read things together in our own fashion. Hence Barthes can collect Sade, Fourier, and Loyola despite their differences and without benefit of any conventional colligation. In each figure, Barthes treats the text as a pretext for challenging interpretative stereotypes which otherwise function to censor the underlying *literary joy* in the Ignatian, Fourierist, and Sadean texts whereby they achieve coexistence:

Reading texts and not books, turning upon them a clairvoyance not aimed at discovering their secret, their "contents," their philosophy, but merely their *happiness of writing,* I can hope to release Sade, Fourier, Loyola from their bonds (religion, utopia, sadism); I attempt to dissipate or elude the moral discourse that has been held on each of them; working, as they themselves worked, only on languages, I unglue the text from its purpose as a guarantee: socialism, faith, evil, whence (at least such is the theoretical intent of these studies) I force the displacement (but not to suppress; perhaps even to accentuate) of the text's social responsibility. (RB)[24]

Barthes's literary subversions displace the pleasures of the social contract—security, house, province, family—indeed, the pleasures of classical culture. This literary criticism therefore upsets the estab-

lished, progressive history of literary monuments. Its goal is to re-
store the *body of literature* to its blissful exercise by destroying *the
myth of the disembodied reader/writer* whose pleasure is returned
through the observance of our cultural dualisms of male/female,
mind/body, power/weakness. Hence his fascination with the *transi-
tional*, the neither/nor, with tenderness, grace, charm, childhood, between vanity and lucidity. And so throughout *S/Z* the sexual con-
stellations revolving around the castrato La Zambinella are starred
for the story's fortune, its reversals of shape, grammar, and discourse
whose instability foretells the death of Sarrasine while serving the
narrator with a necessary delaying device with which to thicken, suspend, and finally deliver his story. In this way, the storyteller exchanges desire for a body with desire for the textual body, each receiving the other's wound.

The textual body fascinates with a promised but undeliverable
unity, like the arms, legs, eyes, hair of the striptease artist who never
goes beyond a ritual of fetishized somemes.[25] The reality she promises
us, like that of literature, is the splendid deception of the man/
woman, La Zambinella, more beautiful than any woman—even in the
eyes of women. With truth and beauty, the desire to abide with the
spectacle is stronger than the rationalist striptease, whatever philosophers think. To see things true and beautiful is to see truth and
beauty; for disappointment is always on hand, and more easily enter-
tained. The castrato, being castrated, reveals not his own condition
(who cannot identify with a limited being?) but the excessive condition of the woman beyond men-and-women whom both love (can so
love themselves) to love. Hence the spectacle of La Zambinella fright-
ened by a snake! We love her, and when we can no longer be de-
ceived by her, we shall die, like Sarrasine, or go home.

In my view, the fragmentary method pursued by Barthes pushes
reading and writing into the closest possible relation. It is a risk that
has fascinated several remarkable writers. It should be noted that
Barthes's alphabetical table of contents plays upon Flaubert's *Dictionary of Received Ideas*. It may also be worthwhile, then, to specu-
late upon Barthes's fragmentary method as an exercise in which he
played his own Bouvard to Pécuchet, lovingly tying reading to writing
and writing to reading, thereby turning the world into a library, or a
single copybook. The encyclopedic labors of Bouvard and Pécuchet,
like Flaubert's own unremitting labor in the research for this work,
as well as the *Dictionary*, destroy the realistic version of knowledge

by pushing it to its logical extreme: removing choice and composition in deference to the authority of realist science.[26] The chimera of organized knowledge turns into the fantasia of the library as a labyrinth of internal references from which the reader cannot retrieve his steps.[27] Indeed, in Borges's reflections on this theme the reader might as well be blind:

In my eyes there are not days. The shelves stand very high, beyond the reach of my years, and leagues of dust and sleep surround the tower. Why go on deluding myself? The truth is that I never learned to read, but it comforts me to think that what's imaginary and what's past are the same to a man whose life is nearly over, who looks out from his tower on what was once city and now turns back to wilderness.[28]

Like the modern university, the library externalizes the world's knowledge but is incapable of generating the creative subjects it dooms to wander through its texts; except as they retreat into Xeroxing. Paradoxically, these literary clones are indeed guilty of plagiarism, if by that we understand reproduction without the bodily labor and love of the copyist. The latter may seem more foolhardy. Yet he is the model for Flaubert, for Barthes and Borges, each superficially repeating himself and others without end; each wasting efforts upon works that might be judged below their literary and scientific talents. But this is less likely, if we give a moment's reflection to the demonic side of writing. I have in mind the desperation quickened by fitting fragments to a whole; to a chapter, to a book; to the next book. The anxiety in modern writing does not derive from its concern with the achievement of realism but rather from the mirroring of the text as intertext, like the self's discovery of its intrinsically othering mirror image.[29] The book that opens up the world opens up the world of books. For a while, sainthood surrenders to ignorance and stupidity multiplies. But Bouvard and Pécuchet *learn not to learn* from their reading and joyously return to themselves—copyists twinned in the pleasures of the text.[30]

   Like Flaubert, Barthes wished to destroy the concept of literature as a museum by dissolving its archeological presuppositions, its placement of texts according to genre, specimen, and period.[31] His study of Racine, in particular, challenged the literary establishment by shifting the temporality of texts out of the literary museum into the lived time of the literary body whose thematics are opposed to the official anthropocentrism of the cultural establishment. Thus, while Barthes's fragments superficially resemble the fragments of the museum, they are radically indifferent to its chronology and catalogue. They are rather morsels or tidbits, things cherished in the literary corpus, to be enjoyed by the reader/writer as one body enjoys another.

In the modern period language is sharply divided between prose and poetry.[32] This division reflects the struggle between art and society, between pleasure and utility. It serves the liberation of literary production—its danger, however, is that it easily turns over into the literary alienation of art for art's sake. Alternatively, it may be employed to turn the study of literary production to the embodied work of reading and writing, and to the patient effort of integrating literary labor with literary pleasure. Here we witness the metamorphoses of man and writer—*homotextuality*—with a limit, we would argue, in the embodied grounds of literary praxis: a man reading and writing. Thus, as we have seen, Barthes never separated the text from its corporeal thematics, its radical biography. Though without privilege—being a familied body—the literary body is the theater upon which the totalitarian and subversive powers of language and poetry are played out.

In this struggle, the sketch, phase, fragment, parenthesis, and unfinished work clings to life, to the renewable body, rejecting the literary monument, the literary corpse of received ideas, motive, character. In this conflict the fragment as used by Barthes does not destroy the body of literature; it renders it polymorphous, pleasurable, at once readerly and writerly, coproductive of literary community. Ultimately, therefore, Barthes escapes the intransitivity to which poetry is condemned through the simple contrast with prosaic reference.[33] The bodily praxis of literature is inconceivable on the theory that the author is wholly metamorphosed into the writer. This is the old ghost returned to the word machine. Rather, all language is half prose, half poetry, like the embodied soul whose emblem it is. No central, official self, to be sure. Yet not totally empty. Embodied, moved, fixed, drifting, androgyne, prostitute, lover, writer. Like Montaigne earlier, Barthes disclaimed any literary strength, or scholarly endurance. He could demean himself as little better than a copyist, without voice or center; a literary eunuch. Yet Barthes never surrendered to the literary system. He remained an outsider in the way a child must live outside his mother's body, fascinated. No other incorporation, no other patrimony ever removed him from this margin. Even when he chose a lover, he remained on the outside of a body he knew writing could never possess. All of his other bodies, drifting in literary promiscuity, were flights from our uterine body, expectant, faithful:

(as a child, I didn't forget: interminable days, when the Mother was working far away; I would go, evenings, to wait for her at the Ubis bus stop, sèvres-Babylone; the buses would pass one after the other, she wasn't in any of them.) (RB)[34]

. . . . .

A Response to John O'Neill

Gayatri Chakravorty Spivak

. . . . .

I am suspicious of the theoretical privileging of the unmediated body that seems to inform John O'Neill's reading of *Fragments d'un discours amoureux, Le plaisir du texte,* and *Roland Barthes par Roland Barthes.*[1] Such a privileging of the body seems to depend on concepts of self-identity that are shared by the most mind-y of idealisms. I will concentrate on a few moments in O'Neill's text where a privileging of the body necessarily brings in concepts of the mind. I will then look at the beginnings of *Fragments, Pleasure,* and *RB,* to show where a reading such as O'Neill's might oversimplify Barthes.

O'Neill's very first sentences privilege body over mind in so uncritical a way that they serve to legitimize the body-mind opposition: "We read books with our bodies. We write with our bodies too." The legitimation operates through the resolute exclusion of the mind from the operations of reading and writing. (It might have been more interesting to observe that we read and write with bodies and minds, and the line between the two cannot be fixed.) Further, O'Neill adduces the family and society as proofs of our being *embodied* beings: "the writer dwells in language precisely because he or she is an embodied being; familied and thereby social." Why suppress and exclude the fundamental institutionality of both?

Such an exclusion or denegation operates also on the textual level. After "Fragment (RB)" we have, presumably, the first footnote. As we see, it is in fact a new section of the essay, entitled "Footnote," which carries its own note 1. A footnote is secondary in its institutional definition. To raise it to the level of "the text proper" can in fact be a reminder that text and note, like body and mind, are each other's parasites. But O'Neill is, once again, interested in denying the dependency, secondariness, and institutionality of the note. He bestows upon his note the supreme ontic privilege and writes, in the note to "A Footnote": "This, then, is an example of itself." It is not, of course. It is merely a legitimation of the text-note hierarchy, where the text must pretend to be a footnote in order to prove that a footnote is as good as the text.

If I seem to insist upon small points, it is because, as I will argue later, admirers of French poststructuralism, by ignoring the implications of their gestures, allow their less adventurous students and colleagues once again to forget the historical, political, economic, and sexual vulnerability of bodies.

Thus it is that O'Neill can attribute to Barthes an adequation of interpretation to body: "Barthes improvised a further state in the physiology of literature, lodging interpretation *once and for all* in the literary body" (italics here are mine). For most of us the figure of Nietzsche looms up with any invocation of the physiology of the text. Nietzsche couples "philology" and "physiology" in a rather specific way, where indeed physiology may be called a protohistorical script which predetermines philosophy insofar as it is the effect of the grammatical function of language. That is a far cry from positing "a literary body" by a foreclosed analogy with the body as a place of unmediated pleasure. "The strange family resemblance between all Indian, Greek and German philosophizing is explained easily enough. . . . The spell of determined [*bestimmt*] grammatical functions is ultimately the spell of *physiological* value judgments [*Werturtheile*] and racial conditions."[2]

Indeed, in the simplest possible way, O'Neill's untroubled discourse already "proves" that unmediated bodies need the support of much-mediated historical topoi and thus such bodies contravene their status of being unmediated. For example, the "literary body" must invoke the "*conception* of the literary body," which cannot hang onto "an *unrevised conception* of language." One must have a foot in the institution of philology to speak of conceptions, of revised conceptions, and, even more, of unrevised ones. The historical itinerary traced by such words cannot be accommodated to an unmediated body. Thus, O'Neill's unproblematic views of a "pure" physiology (already differentiated from the pure body) of literature can only be sustained by the often revised but fundamentally traditional opposition between thought and language: mind (thought) becomes body (incarnation) in the word (verb).

There is a complicity not only between the privileging of the body and idealism in the broadest sense, but also between "literary realism," which O'Neill repudiates in every way, and "literary body"-ism. If "literary realism . . . cannot tell of its alliance with the unreality of language through which it works its very realism," the ideology of literature as body does not seem to be able to tell, in O'Neill's essay at least, of its alliance with the institutionality that is the condition—*and effect*—of its possibility. To be able to work toward the telling of such a double complicity one would, incidentally, need to understand the word "deconstruction" somewhat differently from its modish use as "dismantling" as reflected in the following statement: "the structuralist activity" is "a movement of deconstruction in order to reproduce the function of structure: the production of meaning and value."

Briefly, "deconstruction" as I see it, is not a methodology of disclosing liminated functions. It is rather a morphology for disclosing complicities in place of oppositions—including the complicity of body and idea, of "body"-ism and "realism." Acknowledgment of the critic's complicity in the ruses of such an enterprise might lead to a more affirmative general practice.[3] But that is another argument. Here it is sufficient to point at a few more complicities-in-oppositions in O'Neill's essay.

When "the lover's discourse" is described as "exclamatory rather than descriptive of what loving he experiences," it is only the putative narrative allegory of such a discourse that is in fact disclosed: that the *Fragments* tells the story of exclamation rather than description. This story is complicit with the conduct of the book's language; which shows, in turn, that exclamation and description are themselves complicit. *Ex*-clamation (calling or voicing *out*) shares an obvious structure of self-division with *de*-scription (writing *down*). They are also both designated components of institutionalized discourse.

Thus the alphabet, designating its alpha and omega, is neither an "absolutely insignificant order," nor an avoidance of "the institutional sirens." Barthes himself discusses the "motivated" nature of the alphabet in the play between S and Z in *S/Z* (O'Neill alludes to this but does not draw the unavoidable conclusions). In fact, even if the alphabet were to be seen as the opposite of all motivated institutionality, the Table of Contents of *Fragments,* seemingly arbitrarily alphabetical, would show the encroachment of re-flexivity, that most motivated of gestures, the encroachment of the self as the other's *mark* rather than its own em*bodi*ment. For the first entry of *Fragments* cannot in fact begin with an "a." It is "*s'abîmer,*" meaning precisely the feeling of the self turning into nothing! (the English version of the book translates it as "to be engulfed"). The curious splintered "s' " gives the arbitrariness of the alphabet and the nothingness of the self the lie, since it is the mark of the self's reflex for the entry of the institutionalized subject.

The enchanted space of Barthes's apparently "insignificant" Table of Contents is framed by a certain significant use of the alphabet in yet another way. It is framed by the codes of the book trade, where the content or gestures of the book become trivialized, not through a deliberately *arbitrary* but through a *political* facticity, a price fixing whose network lies elsewhere. The privileged example of such a trivializing of any attempt to pretend that the alphabet were "insignificant" would, of course, be the letters of the ISBN.

Searching for a body free of institutionality, O'Neill must present every desire as its own fulfillment:

Instead of recognizing the theoretical fictionality—as of Freud's "primary process"—of "that so-called subnature of expression where the first coition of words and things takes place," O'Neill not only makes Barthes accede to that "corporeal infralanguage" but allows him to locate select members of literary history there: Flaubert, Michelet![4] Indeed, whatever might have been Barthes's intention, the historical burden of the Holy Trinity is such that we cannot simply say, as does O'Neill: "In Sade, Fourier, and Loyola, he discovered the same pleasure in segmentation (the body of Christ, the body of the victim, the human soul). He intended nothing transcendental in this trinity: merely three fetishisms of the text." We cannot grant, unproblematically, that "as a writer [Barthes] *applied* a certain method to himself," when what Barthes says is "were I writer, and dead, how I would love it if my life, through the pains of some friendly and detached biographer, were to reduce itself to a few details . . . to 'biographemes' . . . [which] might go beyond any fate." Indeed, the curious fact is that this reduction happens anyway, all the time, to all "lives," although we cannot accede to a special or unique desire for this fate. That is why, although we cannot say

"*Barthes* never wrote a book," we are obliged to say that no one ever writes one.

Here are a few of Barthes's beginnings, pre-mises, putative origins, to show that the institution of self-division (in the supposed preinstitutionality of the body) is never far from the offing.

Although the project of the *Fragments* is artfully constituted under the rubric of the disinterested alphabet, it is also described as the appropriation (indeed *re*-appropriation) of what has fallen into nongregariousness. This avowal, which is punningly called the *subject* of the book, carries, then, the mark of the institution of history. The "dramatic" method of the book, which supposedly rests on nothing but the action of language, is divided from that action by the simple fact of miming it. It must also presume a mute institutionalized other for purposes of its own monologic burden. This is figuration—the lover at work—and the denegation of the rhetorical meaning of "figuration," like the denegation of the "clinical" meaning of "anguish," remains caught precisely within a rhetorical topos.

Similarly in *RB*, speaking in the third person, the project of reading is named by default as the intellectual *redoing* of a cut. *Plaisir du texte* invokes the *trace* of a citation to begin with, a citation that itself describes the pleasure of the text as a turning *away* of the glance—a "looking away"—a troping of a citational origin that has no specificity in Barthes's text but the double negative of the "jamais rien" [never anything]. Here again what we encounter is the moment of a monumental desire which we should on no account confuse with an accomplished fact: the wish to be free of that old specter of logical contradiction.

Why should one wish to overlook the troping in the text, to declare declarations of desire as fulfillments? It is because we wish, above all, to homogenize the text, even as we speak of "sanctioned Babel[s]" (*Pleasure*, p. 4). This has some connection with our desire to self-marginalize.

Thus O'Neill homogenizes not only his author's text, but also groups of people who should be recognized as differentiated by at least race, class, and sex: "We" read, "we" write, "poets" celebrate, "writers" discover themselves, ending, appropriately, in a laid-back acceptance of history: "What is done is done. . . . *we* have built this world much as *we* have fenced our fields, built our homes and all the other machinery of our living" (italics mine). (Once again, a cozy idiom ameliorates, unbeknownst to the author, the relentless constitution of the history of political economy, where the active "we" and the excluded "they" mark together an irreducible discontinuity.)

The impulse toward such a homogenization—to give the name of "man" to what one imagines oneself to be, to create an atopical "we"—is of course a millennial impulse.[5] The more recent manifestation, among literary critics especially, is to homogenize for purposes of apparent self-marginalizations, the margin slowly transforming itself into a sort of center: "the struggle between art and society," O'Neill writes, "serves the liberation of literary production. . . . it may be employed to turn the study of literary production . . . to the patient effort of integrating literary labor with literary pleasure." We must intensify our cloistered efforts, in other words, in the little place or topos granted us by the struggle between art and society, and blithely name it our very special a-topia.

Yet who *can* marginalize himself in this way? Perhaps *because* of the desires crosshatched in Barthes's Inaugural Address, we cannot afford to forget that it is of a member of the prestigious Collège de France that the following marginalizing remarks are made: "Barthes disclaimed any literary strength, or scholarly endurance. He could demean himself as little better than a copyist, without voice or center; a literary eunuch. Yet Barthes never surrendered to the literary system. He remained an outsider in the way a child must live outside his mother's body, fascinated. No other incorporation, no other patrimony ever removed him from this margin." It is not to deny Barthes his just rewards and his excellence if we compare this to the saint's obsession with sin, and to locate it as a gesture whereby the center, wishing to marginalize itself, contributes to the centralization of the margin.

This tendency toward self-marginalization has a darker side. What is this place of pleasure to which Barthes must seduce us? There is no personal stake in this seduction scene, for the reader remains without a face: "I must seek out this reader (must 'cruise' him) without knowing where he is" (*Pleasure*, p. 4). As long as we play in that margin of alienated and anonymous seduction, the imaginary topos

of homogenization will preserve us from the brutal heterogeneities
of the differential of race(s), class(es), and sex(es). The place of that
preservation is marked in O'Neill's text by the absence of the word
"technology," between the two homogeneous items "arts" and "sciences." "The life of the arts and sciences cannot be confined to retailing their achievements." (It must, of course, also be asked: Who
says so?)

The intellectual elite of post-Heisenbergian science is entering
the hallowed marginal space of philosophical speculation. The advent
of probability statistics, theories of entropy, and particle physics has
"transformed the object of science."[6] What advanced technology is
making of such a transformation, however, is the semiconductor,
leading to smaller and more sophisticated computers in the service
of the extraction of surplus value from people who cannot afford or
accede to the *pleasure* of the readable text in the narrow sense by
virtue of their *place* in the writable text of "the world."[7] The literary
critic's blindness to the text of technology is demonstrated by his use
of the concept of surplus value as a synonym for the inexhaustible
excess of the text in the narrow sense. I have discussed elsewhere
the results of a perception of the "specificity" of that term.[8]

(In "Les Morts de Barthes," Derrida writes: "Time: metonymy
of the instantaneous, the possibility of the *recit* by its own limit. The
photographic instantaneous would itself be no more than the most
striking metonymy in the technical modernity of its apparatus."[9] In
La carte postale, Derrida suggests that there is a similar supplementary
complicity between old-fashioned letters and telecommunication.[10]

There is nothing wrong with such suggestions, of course. Yet I
would wish that Derrida might take a strategically asymmetrical stand
with the neutralizing complicity discourse of deconstruction on this
point: "that *strategic dissymmetry* that must ceaselessly check [*con-
trôler*] the neutralizing moments of any deconstruction. This dissymmetry has to be minutely calculated, taking into account all the
analyzable differences within the topography of the field in which it
operates."[11] It would be much more important and to the point to
follow the ethico-economic agenda that operates the oppositions—
between *recit* and photograph as between letter and computer—in
the interest of the differences between absolute and relative surplus
value, postmodern and comprador economies. I have written on this
issue in the context of the Figure of Woman in Derrida.)[12]

On page 18 of the English translation of *Roland Barthes* there is a facsimile of a note of hand. The caption below it troubles me: "Has not writing been for centuries the acknowledgment of a debt, the guarantee of an exchange, the contract [*seing*] of a representation? But today writing gradually drifts toward the cession of bourgeois debts, toward perversion, the extremity of sense [*sens*], the text. . . ." Just as "technology" was the absent word in O'Neill's passage about the arts and sciences, "bureaucracy" is the absent word here. It should be recognized that the "unlearning of the pleasure of writing" which is bureaucracy is indeed a gift of the "today" that spans the last two centuries. Because it does not recognize this, Barthes's caption—yesterday the contract, today the text—might find its distorted origin in, let us say, Woodrow Wilson's writings on public administration.[13] Here Barthes himself seems to declare fulfilled, with a suspicious ease, the desire to abandon the bourgeois norm. I look for that other book, *Kafka on Barthes*. In its absence, the "pleasure of the text" remains complicit with that very Xeroxing and much, much more (as the television commercials say) that John O'Neill deplores.

Flaubert does not make this "mistake." With a judgment that is not, of course, favorable, he carefully places Bouvard and Pecuchet's class fix; for O'Neill, the various activities of the two old guys can be seen as nothing more than a simple and joyous participation. And indeed, I would suggest that, in moving from Flaubert to Barthes, O'Neill makes this kind of flattening miscalculation. Barthes himself, in *Roland Barthes*, describes himself as "assigned to an (intellectual) site, to residence in a caste (if not in a class)" (*RB*, p. 49). Barthes's autobiographical work develops *against* this irreducible heterogeneity, working up an *atopia*, an interior doctrine that has something like a relationship with the unique individualism of that very bourgeoisie he deplores, rather than with the uncritical homogenization of collective nouns that I point out in O'Neill's essay.

Thus it becomes impossible not to ask yet another vulgar question: Who reads Barthes? In the United States, almost exclusively academics in search of advancement. I have recently heard a mainstream American feminist suggest that American feminist literary criticism should occupy itself with the sort of semiotic spot analysis Barthes was doing in the middle and late fifties, later to be put together as *Mythologies*.[14] When I was invited as an afterthought to speak at the Annual Semiotics Congress at the International Center at Urbino, I was told, when proposing Barthes as one of my possible lecture topics, that he had really been worked over and that my other topic sounded more interesting. As I write these lines in Paris, the readers of *Poétique,* including myself, are eagerly awaiting the September [1981] issue, which will contain Derrida's essay on Barthes, reputedly a positive articulation. Barthes is hardly available outside the circuit loosely outlined by my anecdotes. Thus it becomes a little dubious to say that "the fragment, as used by Barthes . . . renders [the body of literature] polymorphous, pleasurable, . . . coproductive of literary community." The word "community" blandly hides the competitive, often pusillanimous, quietly desperate, ideology-reproductive, international-neighborhood market where Barthes-as-a-commodity changes hands so that the "true" Barthes may be revealed.

Of course O'Neill's Barthes seems to have no history. It should at least be mentioned that Barthes himself marked out a certain historical "line" in his own work: semiology through semioclasm (printed as the 1970 introduction to *Mythologies*) to semiotropy (announced in the Inaugural Address at the Collège de France). Each stage seems to reflect, to reproduce, and, finally, to transform (all these verbs to be used with caution, of course) something that, in such brief compass, I am obliged to call the air of the times: the rage for legitimation through scientific systematization in the sixties, the mood of ideology critique at the end of the sixties, the quest for apolitical innocence after the mid-seventies.

Up to a certain point, the Other that must be excluded as such, so that O'Neill's text can define its inner space and its Barthes, remains the specter of "positivist history," or what O'Neill calls "the literary monument, the literary corpse of received ideas." My critique implies that the privileging of the body, deliberately blind to the complexity of institutions, can lead to a variety of undisclosed positivism. Thus, to think of the fragment as unmediated exclamation is deliberately to ignore that it is a remains (*reste*) as well, and that denegating that exquisite corpse that has done its work at least since Heraclitus seems to signal cryptomania.[15] "History" creeps in through the back door when O'Neill writes: "the writer dwells in language precisely because he or she is an embodied being; familied and thereby social," for we hear the echo of an idea that has been received at least since the fashionably melancholy tones of a Villiers de l'Isle-Adam: "As for living? Our servants will do that for us."[16]

But there is an Other as such in O'Neill's text that lies beyond

"positivist history." It relates to that millennial impulse, the creation
of a "we-men." According to O'Neill, "the sexuality" of Barthesian
"writing . . . would not be the phallocentric expressions of the violence between the sexes (in accordance with legal convention)."[17] But
the desire for the mother, implicated in a legal convention and yet
standing outside it, cannot be put aside merely "with a vision of the
feminine flood." The first image in *Roland Barthes* is of the Mother,
off-centered.

The picture of the eternal feminine that is taken for granted in
O'Neill's paper is indeed phallocentric. Barthes the demystifier of
fashion might not have accepted what seems a *sub specie aeternitatis*
description: "Literary fragments reveal the writer the way a woman's
dress reveals her body." The political economy of female sexuality
and the ideological prohibition of women's pleasure must be ignored
in order to say: "like lovers, both reader and writer want to get to
their satisfaction *any way they can*" (italics mine). The violence and
parasubjective productivity of the uterine code cannot be appropriated and displaced simply by claiming "a gentle hemorrhage which
flows from *no specific point* in my body" (quoted by O'Neill; italics
mine). There is no mistaking what "point" that lack of specificity
must deny.

Benevolent and unwitting masculinists give us our greatest pangs
of conscience, for they are unquestionably full of personal good will.
It is therefore with ambivalence and reluctance that I rewrite John
O'Neill's title as Luce Irigaray would: "Hommo-textualite."[18] Nearly
all the points that I have questioned in his essay are epitomized in the
following sentence: "Style . . . is the corporeal bond between *the
man* and his text" (italics mine).[19]

Let us extract a sentence from above: "As I write these lines in
Paris, the readers of *Poétique*, including myself, are eagerly awaiting
the September [1981] issue, which will contain Derrida's essay on
Barthes, reputedly a positive articulation." That response now reads
as an unwitting travesty of Derrida on Barthes. It appears that Derrida's piece was already in existence as I wrote: "Where," Derrida
writes, "does this desire, to date these last lines (14 and 15 September
1980), come from? The date, and it is always a bit of a signature,
reveals the contingency or insignificance of an interruption . . . but
no doubt it also speaks another interruption" (MRB, p. 289). It remains

for me to add a postscript to situate my "Response to John O'Neill" as a palimpsest in reverse. It is appropriate that I find words for Derrida's role here from his own text, where he speaks of individual "subjects" who seem to inhabit their "contemporaneity" authoritatively:

a certain way of divesting themselves of authority . . . a certain liberty, an avowed relationship with their own finitude confers upon them, by a sinister and rigorous paradox, such as excess of authority . . . that one always wonders, more or less virtually: what does he or she think of it? . . . Not that one awaits a verdict or one believes in a lucidity without weakness, but, even before one looks for it, the image of an evaluation, a glance, an affect imposes itself. (MRB, 284–85)

My commentary on the status of my text as palimpsest will take the form of a tabulation of Derrida's elegiac palimpsest on Barthes.

"Why should one wish," one of my questions had been, "to overlook the troping in the text, to declare declarations of desire as fulfillment?" Derrida's entire eulogy is given in terms of what he desired to achieve and avoid, a desire necessarily not to be fulfilled. He goes as far as to declare: "for him I would have wished, *without succeeding*, to write at the limit, at the closest proximity to the limit but also beyond 'neutral,' 'white,' 'innocent' writing, whose historical novelty and infidelity *Writing Degree Zero* shows at once" (MRB, p. 275; italics mine). He cites Barthes immediately to admonish himself: "Unfortunately there is nothing less faithful than a white writing; automatisms elaborate themselves in the very place where there was at first a freedom" (MRB, p. 276). My point had been that O'Neill had not heeded Barthes's admonitions against desires seeming to entail their automatic fulfillment.

Like O'Neill, Derrida too decides to write about Barthes in the fragment form. I fault O'Neill for ignoring the remains or historical sediment that the fragment leaves behind. Derrida invokes both fragments and remains at the outset: "I no longer know and it matters little at bottom if I know how to explain why I must leave these thoughts for Roland Barthes in a fragmentary state, nor why I favor incompleteness even more than fracture. . . . If not to speak of Barthes's singular clarity I would like at least to give an idea of it, as that which remains for me" (MRB, pp. 269, 270).[20] At the end of the essay, he regards this fragmentary endeavor as having inevitably occasioned the regular argument (*enchainement* = linking together) of prose, and imagines a merely writable text which he as unwittingly perpetrated between its interstices (MRB, p. 292).

In counterpoint to this (unfulfilled) desire for self-fragmentation, Derrida chooses to treat the Barthesian corpus as if it did have a beginning and an end. He rereads Barthes's first and last books— *Degree Zero* and *Camera Lucida*—and weaves Barthes's history or story as the complicity between the origin and the end.

In my response, I speak of deconstruction as the disclosure of complicity. "Les Morts de Roland Barthes" would be an example of mourning as the disclosure of complicity between the subject and the lost object, here Derrida and Barthes. Derrida fabricates this complicity by reinscribing his own thematics in his eulogy.[21] Here one is reminded of *Glas*, where mourning (fathers) had involved incorporation in the sense of eating up. Learning to mourn a mother, Derrida in *Glas* had made himself complicit with the celebrated homosexual son of a mother, Jean Genêt. Barthes is another such son. It is thus worth noting how Derrida works with the mother's place in Barthes's last text. Caught by what seemed O'Neill's gynephobia, I had earlier remarked: "But the desire for the mother, implicated in a legal convention and yet standing outside it, cannot be put aside merely 'with a vision of the feminine flood.' The first image in *Roland Barthes* is of the Mother, off-centered."

Derrida gives us no legend of mothering as such, of course. He becomes complicit with, implicates himself in, Barthes's desire for *his* mother. He suggests that the Mother's picture in the Winter Garden is the utopia where wishes *are* fulfilled. The mother's radiant smile, neither hiding nor revealing itself, remains unique and is yet pluralized in the text of *Roland Barthes*. Indeed, by choosing Barthes's first and last works, he establishes something like a relationship with Barthes's mother. The following sentence begins with the words that entitle his own essay: "Les morts de Roland Barthes [the deaths of Roland Barthes]: *his* deaths, the dead and deaths, his own who are dead and whose death had to inhabit him, situate the grave places and agencies, of oriented tombs in his interior space (his mother in the end and no doubt in the beginning)" (MRB, p. 282). By the grace of a metaphoric matronymic gesture (first and last books of Barthes, first and last deaths of the mother, as all of Barthes's life, all his deaths) Derrida's subject matter too would be Madame Barthes.

Thus Derrida rehearses the historical gesture of the son toward the mother, to want to be and have her as one and all. In the Genêt section of *Glas* she is seen as the mother of fetishism. Trying to catch the Name of that Mother, as the patronymic chain enables the son to grasp the Name of the Father, *Glas*'s writer gives up in frustrated jealousy.[22] Here the tone is calmer, although the generic model for identifying and identification—complicity as mourning and reading—remains the homosexual son. Barthes does not want the Face/Figure-of-the-Mother, the mother in the Symbolic, within the (conventional) circuit of the Signifier. (How the displacement of Name into Face/Figure relates to the Levinasian rather than the Lacanian Other, the Jewish mother rather than the Christian father, might take us as far back as "Violence and Metaphysics.")[23] He only wants his singular and unsymbolic mother: "Not the Figure of the Mother, but his mother. There should not be, there should not-be, any metonymy in that case, love protests . . ." (MRB, p. 279). But Derrida gently reminds us of the conduct of Barthes's text and points out: "He was right to protest against the confusion between she who was his mother and the Figure of the Mother, but the metonymic power (part for the whole or a name for an other, etc.) will always come to inscribe the one and the other in that relationship without relation" (MRB, pp. 286–87).

The metonymic complicity between part and whole has long been one of Derrida's deconstructive concerns. Here he re-casts it as "composition." Making Barthes make like Derrida—an avowedly complicitous reading creating a com-position—he suggests that when Barthes capitalizes the contrast between Nature and History, for example, "he made the concepts that are apparently frontally opposed and opposable play one *for* the other, in a metonymic composition" (MRB, p. 271). I locate my complicity with Derrida here in the substance of my argument about Barthes's beginnings where he seems to insist that one should not forget the (historical) institutionality of the (natural) body.

The chief example of metonymic composition in "Les Morts" is Barthes's opposition between *stadium* and *punctum*—continuity and the instant—in *Camera Lucida*. The dynamic reserve of the point makes it a metonym of continuity—thus Derrida plots the relationship between time and narrative. By referring to *stadium* and *punctum* as S and P—Subject and Predicate—Derrida tacitly composes the Barthesian pair with his own long-standing occupation with the copula supplement—that the copula ("is") between Subject and

Predicate in any proposition is also an open-ended "and" (a supplement—additive and complementary): "between the two concepts the
relationship is neither tautological, nor oppositional, nor yet oppositional, nor dialectical, nor in any way symmetrical, it is supplementary
and musical (contrapuntal)" (MRB, p. 286).[24] When he insists that
P (*punctum* or predication) rhythms S (*stadium* or subject) all the
arguments about the work of spacing or the norming of theory by
practice come to mind, and we see how, by weaving in versions of
his own themes in Barthes's text, Derrida is trying to "find himself
in Barthes," "make Barthes his own," or, as he says, "I searched *like
him* like him" (MRB, p. 272). When he points out that, according to
Barthes, S *and* P—*stadium* and *punctum*—"carry truth only within
an irreplaceable musical composition" (MRB, p. 275), it reminds us that
for Derrida S *is* P—truth as the proposition "Subject is Predicate"—
is in the same case.

The most striking example of the rhythming of the subject
(*stadium*) by predicate (*punctum*) is when the "I" ("Derrida") of the
"Les Morts de Roland Barthes" is normed by his predication as
Barthes's eulogist through a simple French pun: "la valeur d'*intensité*
dont je suis la piste . . ." (MRB, p. 287; Derrida's italics). "Je suis"
here can mean both "I am" and "I follow." It is sufficiently self-
problematizing to say I am the pathway of an intensity value. If even
that subject avowal takes place in the place of the declaration "I follow (rather than am) such a path . . . leading to the theme of Time"
then the narrative begins to mime Freud's masterful anaseme of "I
am" (*ich bin*): "where it was there shall I be(come)" (*wo es war soll
ich werden*)—"Derrida" in search of "Barthes" as "himself." I had
a similar scenario in mind when I had asked O'Neill to attend to the
role of the institutional subject-of-the-reflexive in "s'abîmer."

The final Derrida-Barthes composition that I shall touch refers to
the referent. Barthes insists upon the "photographic referent" in
Camera Lucida. Derrida invokes the prevailing argument of "The
Double Session": "Suspend like a chandelier [il-lustrate] the referent
(not reference) everywhere that it is produced . . . and of suspend-
ing a naive concept of the referent" (MRB, p. 279). In "The Double
Session," Derrida's argument runs that the reference structure (a
structure of difference from and pointing to) metaleptically produces,
by way of an entailing "interest," referents that are contingent and
shifting. We can read the following sentences as composing with such

an argument. "Should one say reference or referent? The analytical minutiae should here be a measure with the stake, and photography puts it to the proof: the referent is visibly absent, suspendable, disappeared in the once of the past of its event, but the reference to that referent, let us say that the intentional movement of that reference (since Barthes has recourse in this book precisely to phoneomonology)"—Barthes's particular "interest" in this case—"also irreducibly implies the having-been of a unique and invariable referent" (MRB, p. 283). But just as, according to Derrida in "The Double Session," Mallarmé problematized the referent by choosing figures such as the blank and the fold, so, according to Derrida in "Les Morts de Roland Barthes," does Barthes by choosing the figure of death. "Basically," Derrida cites Barthes, "what I am at [vise] in a photo that one takes of me (the 'intention' according to which I look at it) is Death: Death is the eidos of that photo" (MRB, p. 283). In *Mimique*, Mallarmé's pirouetting ballerina had mimed for Derrida the constant operation of the reference structure, not resting on a transcendental referent but situating each referent as she turned on her *pointe*—Mallarmé's "i," Barthes's *punctum*. In the following passage it is as if Derrida's Barthes composes with Mallarmé's ballerina and takes the dance floor: "Carried by this relationship," Derrida continues, "by the reference to the spectral referent, he traversed periods, systems, modes, 'phases,' 'genres,' marked and punctuated their *stadium, crossing*, phenomenology, linguistics, literary mathesis, semiosis, structural analysis, etc. His first movement was to recognize their necessity or their fecundity, their critical value also, their light and then to turn them against dogmatism" (MRB, p. 284).

But if the spectral referent is a "return to the dead" (MRB, p. 283) Derrida too is involved in the same dance as an eulogist. The ballerina had been alone, this is a composition. Derrida's task has been to pluralize Barthes's unique ghost. We begin to understand the opening musical metaphor, saying, of the title: "How to accord this plural? To whom?" (MRB, p. 269).

Deconstruction, then, is a disclosure of complicity rather than a dismantling. It would not be possible to privilege the body (or indeed the mind) as O'Neill does in my view. One must see mind and body as each other's asymmetrical metonyms.

And indeed it is after all these deconstructive gestures that Derrida tries to catch Barthes's body, fleetingly, poignantly (MRB, p. 289), before passing to a consideration of the impossible sentence "I am dead," which allows him to compose his own early work, *Speech and Phenomena,* with the ghost of Barthes.[25]

I have attempted to situate my "Response to John O'Neill" as a proleptic shadow and to suggest my point of difference with Derrida.

. . . . .

Surviving Figures

Gary Lee Stonum

. . . . .

I must first apologize for my title, which is all too obviously one of those tedious plays with language that are so common in the new scholasticism. What is worse, I find that the title contradicts the very point I intend to argue. My bias is for the constitutive indeterminancy of figures of speech, not in a hard Derridean or Godelian sense whereby they produce rigorously undecidable statements but in a softer and perhaps more sentimental sense whereby their effects are always underdetermined and hence incalculable. This is a bias rather than a demonstrable proposition, because it presents a negative thesis of the inherently unprovable sort, like "there is no Easter bunny" or "man will never get to the moon."

By titling my paper according to a rhetorical mode that is now unmistakably a cliché, however, I have apparently succumbed to the pervasive calculus of tropology. As a figure of speech, "surviving figures" does not survive the power of rhetorical criticism to ascertain its nature and its use. Indeed, it reinforces the proudest, boldest claim of tropological analysis: that identifiable rhetorical patterns inevitably prestructure all discourse. Furthermore, by beginning with an excursus on the title, I have succumbed a second time to a wholly familiar, predictable figuration, this one more syntagmatic than paradigmatic.[1] The first cliché, I assure you, was not originally intended to exemplify my theme; the title was invented several weeks before the opening words were written. In contrast, the second one, the coy reflection on my own opening maneuver, was fully premeditated. It makes no difference, however. My intentions can hardly alter the deadening effects of both clichés.

Fresh or inventive tropes are said to be lively, but the cliché, according to a well-established and no doubt accurate metaphor, is deadly. Itself a dead image, it kills interest. On the other hand, the cliché obviously continues to live on in some sense, for it is precisely the likelihood of repetition that defines it as cliché and assures it of survival. Depending on how they are viewed then, clichés are both dead and alive. Rhetoricians would call this crisscrossing of life and death, good figure and bad figure, a chiasmus. So indeed it is. My purpose, however, is to ask what we have learned or gained once that identification is made.

The imagery of life and death, the concept of the trope, and the field of textual hermeneutics converge in an old and now widely reiterated proposition: more than truth, more than representational power, and more than the expression of subjectivity, figurality is the life of the text. Indeed, again according to a widely repeated truth, it is figurality (along with historical distance) that typically calls for, justifies, and perhaps even necessitates hermeneutic activity. The letter kills, but the spirit gives life, as few hermeneutical theories fail to remind us.

More than any other modern theorist, Paul Ricoeur has insisted that figurality is a central challenge and a prime justification for the theory of interpretation. He also recognizes that figurality, understood as life, calls for an especially open, generous form of hermeneutics. Ricoeur's own patient, receptive reflections are explicitly set in motion by what he calls the symbol, a term that covers most paradigmatic or connotative kinds of figurality. Rather than establishing a normative reading that would definitively manifest the symbol's import or liberate its essential truth, Ricoeur aims to prepare the way for listening to its vital kerygma. The practical outcome of this, in the book on evil or the one of Freud, is to remind us forcefully that even the most archaic symbols remain alive in and for us.[2]

One finds a similar respect for figural vitality in many non-hermeneutic modes of interpretive theory. The revival of tropology is a strikingly common feature of much contemporary criticism, linking the various antihermeneutical arguments of Harold Bloom and Paul de Man, the more traditionally formalist work of Gerard Genette, the historiographical investigations of Hayden White, and the widespread renewal of interest in Kenneth Burke. I have no wish to minimize the hostility that many revisionist critics display toward a hermeneutics descended from Schleiermacher or early Heidegger. In fact, I share the suspicion that texts are more apt to feign kerygmatic force than to embody it. Nevertheless, both camps agree that figurality is a central locus for such life as the text has.

Modern tropological criticism often goes beyond figures of speech, as such, in part following the lead of Burke. As one example, de Man's most recent work insists upon a gap between rhetoric as a system of tropes and rhetoric as an instrument of persuasion. As another, Bloom enlarges the idea of trope as one that emphasizes psychic stances and defenses more than language. Nevertheless, the starting point and the diction of their work certify it as endorsing the taxonomies of classical rhetoric. Bloom, because he is explicitly concerned with the force or value of literary texts, takes up the traditional imagery of life and death, and he can therefore serve as an example of how such images characterize the trope.[3] Later, I will refer a related topic to a text by de Man.

The consistent, insistent telos of Bloom's multifold rhetorical mapping—the calculus of images, defenses, revisionary ratios, and cabalistic isometrics—is poetic strength. Strength, I take it, is a figure for life in both the intensive and extensive senses: both vitality and survival. According to Bloom poetic strength is vitality itself. Furthermore, achieving poetic strength assures the survival of one's poem, primarily by obligating its canonization. Thus do post-Miltonic poets bid for the immortal life that their ancestors once bartered to princes and warriors.

Bloom admits that for the poet such vitality can only be a lie, albeit a brave one. John Milton is quite dead, after all. Yet the inseparability of poetry and lying does not thereby discredit the life of the poem or render it merely fictional. To the reader or to the late-coming ephebe, the poem exerts a living force that is entirely real.

Bloom vacillates somewhat about the extent to which this life can be attributed to the poem's verbal figures and their power to outshout rival tropes. He is obviously happier to make life a function of the poem's stance—the strategic genealogy of its tropes—than of its language. Yet according to his theory and in clear keeping with his readings of specific poems, stance cannot be separated from figures of speech.

There is no such equivocation or uncertainty about death. "If death ultimately represents the earlier state of things, then it also represents the earlier state of meaning, or pure anteriority; that is to say, repetition of the literal, or literal meaning. Death is therefore a kind of literal meaning, or, from the standpoint of poetry, *literal meaning is a kind of death*."[4]

Bloom goes on to say: "[Psychoanalytic] *defenses can be said to*

*trope against death rather in the same sense that tropes can be said
to defend against literal meaning.*" This is confusing. Although Bloom
elsewhere rightly insists that Freudian defenses work against change,
tropes by definition turn from a literal meaning. In other words, if
the precursor poem's deadening quasi-literality—its ability to perpetuate its own glory by resisting revisionary misprision—has genuinely influenced the ephebe, then the ephebe's defensive troping will
work for rather than against change. The steady state would be his
helpless, perhaps silent, recognition of belatedness. One possible
clarification—it would be faithful to Freud—would consider the precursor text a wholly unconscious and *Trieb*-like phenomenon, against
whose representatives the ephebe's ego sought to defend its pride.
However, such a clarification would require Bloom to complicate beyond recognition his already complex stage of the Scene of Instruc-
tion. Nor is it certain that a revised staging would suffice. The confusion ultimately derives from an incompatibility between the two
thermodynamic principles at work in Freud's notion of death in-
stincts: the principle of equilibrium or constancy on the one hand
and the entropic tendency toward a null state on the other.

The associations that Bloom endorses—of the literal with death
and of the figurative with life—are entirely traditional. The pairings
lead to another chiasmus, however, one whose import had best be
spelled out in advance. The chiasmus is not very startling or informative in itself; the crossing of terms only reproduces in tropological
form a well-known tenet of romantic ideology, one that Bloom explicitly avows. In the course of seeing how this chiasmus operates,
however, we will find that the polarities on which it is based do not
simply change places but tend to collapse into one another. The collapse is emphatically not an instance of rhetoric slyly deconstructing
itself, at least not in the de Manian sense of anticipating its own
aporia. Rather it comes from a power that tropology regularly claims
for itself, the one that largely defines tropology as such: an ability to
distinguish and categorize how figures of speech function. According
to the values represented in the imagery of life and death, this power
amounts to a literalizing and hence a deadening of the most audacious
tropes.

If there is a scandal here, it does not arise from the abundant and
fairly evident confusion in our ideas about life and death. Bloom has
relied more and more upon Freud's speculations concerning the warfare of Eros and Thanatos. And as Jean Laplanche points out, noting

the thermodynamic concepts I have mentioned, the ambiguities of life and death in Freud's texts themselves take the form of a chiasmus.[5] Yet these ambiguities or downright confusions in Freud are not so much errors that we might safely avoid as accurate representations of a deeply complex issue.

The problem, in other words, is not that Bloom's psychopoetics needs to be disengaged from the outmoded science in Freud. Nor is it that we have somehow stumbled in the initial association of figuration with life and death, however the latter are understood. We are not, to put it facetiously, in need of an analytic philosopher to unplug our semantic drains. Rather, the life and death imagery seems to me entirely appropriate, for it reflects and thus helps to reveal a darkness in the supposedly simpler or at least less melodramatic project of tropology.

To make the chiasmus visible, a working definition of literal usage and literal meaning is required. From a theoretical or transcendental standpoint there may be no such thing as the literal. Indeed, it is usually a simple exercise to show that any particular instance of allegedly literal usage rests on a figurative base, through its etymology, for example.[6] Nevertheless, to say that all language is figurative vacates the concept of the trope, which only makes sense in comparison to a putative literality. Moreover, genealogical or transcendental considerations make little practical difference, for the literal turns out to be defined by contingency and epiphenomenality.

In plain words, literal usage is common usage, as everyone already knew. In other and not much fancier words, literality is stipulated in the transitory semantic agreements of those who share a dialect. (*Mutatis mutandis*, the group's agreements constitute its members as speakers of a dialect with specified rules of literality.) This description follows Aristotle's identification of the literal and the colloquial, but it strongly insists that literality cannot be defined according to exact, universal standards or even those of an otherwise reasonably homogeneous culture. The idea of a language group is always an approximation or a serviceable fiction; a great many persons may share the same grammar, but I doubt that any two persons share an identical semantic field. Nevertheless, despite the absence of definitional rigor, literal meaning can still be equated with that which is communicated in everyday discourse. Literal usage is instrumental usage, the approximations that are understood according to the codes and conventions of the day.

The romantic poet's objection to the literal is exactly this: the arbitrary and drearily uniform conventionality by which a predictable sign automatically calls forth a predictable meaning. Bloom expands this dread of automatism to include the ephebe's anxiety in the face of earlier poetry's authority, but the principle remains the same. The deadliness and deathliness of the literal is its obedience to what exceeds the power of the living self, especially to the impersonal codes of public discourse. Such language is a self-oiling and eternally prior species of mechanism. Although like most machines it is therefore useful, it threatens to make the user into a servo-mechanism. Even linguistic democrats like Emerson can therefore only admire literal speech as an instance of fossilized poetry, usage whose expired figurative life must be restored or reinvented.

The main lines of the chiasmus should now be obvious, especially since the crossing pattern is identical to the one already noticed in clichés. What a poet would consider the dead language of literality is precisely what survives in most discourse. The crossing occurs between the values of the poet and the tribe; life for one is death for the other. The chiasmus thus reproduces a familiar (and dubious) tenet of romantic individualism: that the poet's demand for a word of his own alienates him from the group, which generally requires reliable communication in order to conduct its business and so perpetuate itself.

This simple polarity between the literal and the figurative or the polarized opinions about which one makes for expressive vitality should obviously not be taken too seriously. Most romantics argue, for example, that the poet's language ultimately serves the welfare of the group. Yet the polarities do reflect the widespread poetic abhorrence of the banal, the shopworn, and the mechanical in language. The difficulty arises when one seeks to locate and describe tropologically a variety of rhetoric that would avoid these deadly qualities. According to the chiasmus and indeed according to common agreement, the living words ought to be found among vigorous, innovative figures of speech. Yet actual poetic figures are not easy to distinguish tropologically from the baldest of clichés and colloquialisms. From the point of view of the rhetorician, all figures of speech are defined by properties that closely resemble the mechanisms of literality. Literal language is characterized by semantic automatism and by the working of impersonal codes of signification; to the extent that their forms and operations are regular, predictable, and classifiable, so are figures of speech. Thus, just as the expression "full count" must be counted as literal to the baseball fan, so within a thorough tropological system all tropes must be said to be literal. I am not simply playing with words. Literal signification seems definable only by means of semantic codes, and the taxonomy of rhetorical figures is precisely a codification of figurative usages. The two sorts of conventionality are hardly identical, of course, but neither are they all that easy to disassociate. Furthermore, although the proposition that all discourse is figurative seems objectionably empty, this would not be true of the opposite. Defining the figurative as a turn from the literal does not assure that the former actually exists.

The main question is the kind of mechanism that tropology manifests, in comparison to the mechanisms of literal signification. Two sorts of codificability seem to be applicable to tropes. The first is like what we find in clichés; the more important second one resembles the workings of literal discourse.

The first derives from the notable and probably inevitable conservatism of poetic imagery. Birds, rivers, flowers, the sun, and so forth stock the common fund of images on which, as always, poets continue to draw. (This may be why Bloom prefers to identify strength with stance rather than with imagery.) It is frequently easy enough to distinguish familiar poetic images from the clichés we forbid in freshman composition or snicker at in political oratory; clichés largely operate without witting reference to the sensory image, and they accordingly often lend themselves to hilariously mixed metaphors. On the other hand, poetic commonplaces closely resemble clichés and literalism in their deployment of a time-honored sign to represent, more often than not, a time-honored meaning. That is presumably why images like the sun get used again and again with much the same meaning, because they effectively signify that valuable meaning. The selection of such images is not necessarily automatic, but their effects depend upon the same kind of mechanism as literality. If anything, the partly translinguistic and transcultural power of the signifying mechanism in poetic imagery has a more impressive permanence than the relatively fleeting conventions of the boardroom, the barroom, and the bedroom.

Images per se are not tropes, for the same image can enter into a wide range of figurative uses. Tropology, furthermore, includes a much wider range of expressive forms than the image: syntactic figures like hyperbaton ("backwards roll the sentences until reels the mind") and even morphemic ones like metaplasm (*"différance"* à la Derrida or "o'er" à la metric elision). Thus the persistence of height as an image of glory or majesty may well be less significant than the variety of tropological uses—hyperbolic versus metaphoric, for example—to which the image can be put. If the repetition of an image does testify to the continuing power of a code of signification, that coding mechanism need not be tropological. The more strictly rhetorical sort of literality within figurative language would have to automate the way in which an expression is used.

This second kind of coding, much more than a dictionary of images, is tropology as such. Tropological analysis defines itself as an explanation or rationalization of why and how a figure displaces a literal usage. It speaks directly of the rhetorical codes alleged to govern the trope.

Unlike the grammatical and lexical codes of literal signification, which describe an automatic functioning of the language, tropological codes often seek to explain an initially puzzling usage. (To be more precise, they seek to do this for those of us who have not had the sort of rhetorical training that would allow us to process specific tropes as readily as we do specific grammatical forms.) Furthermore, knowing or saying that "X is a metonymy" differs from the capacity to understand an expression literally. Signifier and signified have a presumably unbreakable bond in the latter case; "code" is no more than an uninformative synonym for the nature of that bond. On the other hand, one can fail to recognize a metonymy, even while more or less grasping the meaning of the figure. Proper names, for example, are largely metonymic in our culture, but one need not even tacitly recognize that relation in order to call the children to supper.

Tropology names and explicates the relation. In doing so, it dispels the mystery of how an understood expression functions, or it decodes the enigma that a baffling expression presents. It thus can work to determine both the meaning and how the meaning is generated.

At the far end of that working, one might fantasize a utopian tropology that would do this for any and every piece of figurative discourse. I suspect, however, that we are still too close to the collapse of literary structuralism to entertain seriously the notion of a closed, systematic, and exhaustive calculus of tropes. Moreover, unlike the relatively well-ordered tools that structuralism borrowed from linguistics, the existing system of tropes is obviously an ad hoc affair and thus hardly a proper system at all.[7]

Even as an ad hoc assemblage, however, tropology claims the not insignificant power to codify and thus literalize most figures of speech. The very existence of useful categories like synechdoche, metalepsis, and the rest testifies that most figures of speech succumb to a regularity of form and function. Barring the unlikely possibility that the would-be strong poet had invented an utterly new trope, the tropologist can always say to him: "Aha! That's a parabasis [or whatever]. You have fallen once again into the mechanical patterns that my science predicts. Your fresh coinage is just one more literality to me."

Even the most valiant attempt at lively figuration, one that might dazzle the rhetorically untutored, can thus be expected to reveal the deathly cogs of a tropological automaton. The situation does not, of course, call for banning tropology. At some ionospheric level of generality, language may be a prison house; if so, even the Bloomian poets have learned to live within its walls. The issue is the explanatory powers of a tropological determination. Simply to call a trope a catachresis, i.e., an abuse of metaphor, is plainly a matter more of name calling than of substantive definition. But for the most important and prevalent figures of speech, the tropological name specifies nontrivial information about the figure's operation.

I have already stated my opinion, that figures of speech are underdetermined in their functioning. If so, then most or all identifications of a given figure should fail to specify its workings sufficiently. You shouldn't, in other words, be able to tell the metonymies from the metaphors. The example is hardly innocent. Roman Jakobson's famous and influential suggestion that metaphor and metonymy form the two fundamental poles of discourse has had an unhappy history. As a master concept, the distinction has proven so embarrassingly slippery that its official discrediting is now well under way.[8] But Jakobson to an extent and his followers to a larger one were under the sway of structuralist imperialism. They believed in universal, rigorously definable categories of discourse. In contrast, few ancient or modern rhetoricians have claimed that tropology could or should approach mathematical rigor.

Even within the confines of an appropriately modest tropology, however, significant claims are made. Examining those claims thoroughly would require analyzing the concepts and categories of every significant system of tropes. That task is obviously impractical, but some inkling of the likely result may be seen in the quarrels between rival systems. Bloom, for example, loudly disagrees with Jakobson's argument, claiming that the crucial polarity lies between synechdoche and metonymy. Neither Bloom nor Jakobson would be happy with the common assumption in modern Anglo-American analysis that metaphor by itself is the exemplary case of all figurality.[9] Needless to say, the precise definitions of these figures (and hence the classification of any given expression) differ somewhat from rhetorician to rhetorician.

Short of an exhaustive demonstration that tropological analysis regularly produces a bestiary of incoherent, overlapping, and arbitrary categories, the best evidence I can offer is a specific example. Paul de Man's work offers the fairest and most promising instance of sophisticated tropological interpretation, in part because his commitment to tropology has been both wary and fervent. On the one hand, he has been sharply critical of tropology's pretensions to rigor, exhaustiveness, or even compatibility with other modes of analysis. On the other, he has clearly been the most prominent and influential contemporary advocate of rhetorical reading.

In his latest book de Man carefully investigates the figurative language in a brief passage from Proust.[10] His chief aim is to question the interpretive use of rhetorical categories, first by pitting rhetoric against its enemy brother, grammar, and second by locating the passage's specific tropological subterfuge. In order to do this, however, de Man must endorse the possibility and value of identifying the figures in the text. More specifically, in order to argue that the thematic priority of metaphor in Proust gets undercut by the text's rhetorical practices (which depend centrally on metonymy), de Man is obliged to perform two kinds of tropological analysis: he must make the distinction between metaphors and metonymies, and he must correlate the function of each figure with the values argued for in the text. Close attention to one example from de Man's lengthy reading will show that neither act can claim much certainty. The example comes from the following passage in *Swann's Way*:

The sensation of the light's splendor was given me . . . by the flies executing their little concert, the chamber music of summer: evocative not in the manner of a human tune that, heard perchance during the summer, afterwards reminds you of it but connected to summer by a more necessary link: born from beautiful days, resurrecting only when they return, containing some of their essence, it does not only awaken their image in our memory; it guarantees their return, their actual, persistent, unmediated presence. [de Man's translation]

Although de Man points out that an outrageously unlikely chain of substitutions governs the lines immediately following this excerpt, he accepts without comment Proust's flies and music as contrasting figures of summer. Specifically, he agrees that flies are a true metaphor, although not without a nervous footnote in which he argues that the synechdochal, part-for-whole relation of flies to summer is superceded by a metaphorical bond. Metaphor, as Proust suggests without using the term, is defined by the necessary link between the two relata. Parts often have necessary links with wholes, so synechdoche can be a variant of metaphor. And because the necessity here is stronger and more universal than the part-for-whole of, say, Astroturf and baseball, metaphor is the more accurate term. The trouble is already evident in the footnote, however, where de Man admits that classical rhetoric generally makes synechdoche a version of metonymy (as my baseball example certainly is). He concludes somewhat weakly by arguing that synechdoche is a borderline figure that creates an ambivalent zone between metaphor and metonymy. Thus, to the admitted extent that flies are synechdochal, they blur the distinction between metaphor and metonymy.

Metonymy, however, is the trope that Proust clearly wants to deprecate in contrast to metaphor, so de Man obligingly calls "not illegitimate" the distinction that structures Proust's text, the wholly traditional dichotomy between contingency and necessity. Flies are indeed necessarily—i.e., biologically—linked to summer (to spring and fall as well, in warm climates), but Marcel's summer day is less a phenomenon of natural science than aesthetic experience. If flies contain some of the essence of beautiful days, the shared aspect is not by most standards of taste the beauty itself. Indeed, one of the most striking things about this passage is the bizarre choice of flies as a metaphor of summer. Birds, for example, would nicely serve the purpose of supplying a conventionally pleasant sound that could penetrate Marcel's darkened room.

My quarrel seems to be with the narrator's associations, as if I were complaining to Melville that whales aren't all that big. Yet it is the narrator who contrasts necessary links to subjectively associational ones. The problem may be that I have considered the flies in isolation from Proust's specific context. If flies are not in themselves all that persuasive as metaphor, perhaps the necessity will seem greater by contrast to the human tune.

That sound is clearly an associational metonym, something heard only by chance on a summer's day rather than on a winter's night or not at all. Such music has no necessary link to summer, I agree, but only on the condition that calling the buzzing of flies "the chamber music of summer" likewise weakens their link to the season. In other words, the more closely one looks at the tropological relays in this passage—among flies, summer days, chamber music, and the human tune—the more the terms resemble one another and hence equivocate about the distinctions in whose service the text clearly employs them.

The figural zigzagging of the passage may settle down a bit if instead of necessity and contingency—Proust's obviously interested and highly ideological criteria—we make use of analogy and contiguity. De Man seems to feel that the latter pair is more fundamental, and it is certainly more appropriately formal. In addition to beauty, which seems only perversely analogous to the flies, the features of summer emphasized elsewhere in the passage are warmth, light, and activity. The sound of flies, which according to Marcel's claim brings metaphorical warmth and light into his room, offers no obvious analogy with either. Granted, it results from activity, but so does the human tune. By activity Marcel chiefly means playing outdoors, the pastime against which he is defending his preference for reading. If anything, music then supplies the better analogy, because it is human, voluntary, and a kind of play, although less frequently an outdoor phenomenon than the flies. (As evidence of hermeneutic good faith, I resist making anything of the buzzing as *chamber* music.)

Contiguity is no sure help in distinguishing flies from the tune either, because it is so embracing a criterion as to suggest that both are metonymies. Whereas neither flies nor music displays a good analogy to the summer's day, both have spatial and temporal connections to it. The tune is heard on a summer's day and therefore suffers the merely positional relation that the narrator deplores. But flies are even more surely related by contiguity, a necessary contiguity, in fact. They can thus be counted among the fragments that, a few lines below, Proust speaks of as the lamentably metonymic experiences one meets in taking a summer's walk. There as earlier he seeks to contrast the total and essential summer available in his room with the scattered, accidental experiences waiting outside.

Thus, even by the conceivably stricter and more formal criteria of analogy and contiguity, the contrasting images in Proust's text cannot be authoritatively given the tropological identifications that de Man makes. The problem is not that de Man's analysis is in error; his determinations of Proust's figures seem no more and no less certain than my counterreadings. Indeed, if I had to choose, I would choose de Man's reading, on the extratropological grounds that it better represents the entirety of Proust's text. One is obliged to choose, however, only if the choice does not appear empty, only, that is, if a tropological analysis provides reliable and substantive insight. But the criteria that distinguish the main figures of speech— the ones here as well as most other paradigmatic tropes—are always eminently debatable. Furthermore, many figures of speech can be matched with the criteria of several, ostensibly distinct tropological categories. A sufficiently manic or maniacal reader could probably interpret a given figure as serving dozens of tropological functions. All his readings might not be convincing, but there would be no assured tropological standard by which his wackiest claims could be discredited.

In sum, as de Man approvingly cites Burke and Peirce for arguing, figurative language is an incalculable element in any text. It is in principle not controlled by the author's intentions, and, more important, it is not wholly constrained by context or by the verification that repeated uses and thematizations may provide. Emerson in fact worries that these other hermeneutically respectable factors may inhibit or override the disseminative operations of the figure. "An imaginative book renders us much more service at first by stimulating us through its tropes than afterward when we arrive at the precise sense of the author."[11] (Notice that Emerson allows for both extravagant associations and a definitive interpretation.)

My conclusion is not that tropological analysis should be discarded as hopelessly incoherent. Nor is it that we should happily indulge in (or glumly resign ourselves to) every wandering turn that a figure might call up. It is rather that tropology is at best a heuristic, a provisional, and an approximate set of notions that allows us to begin the work of describing how some figure operates. Ultimately every reading must appeal to extratropological standards in order to put a practical limit on the volatility of the figure. The most common

of such grounds are the hypothesis of textual coherence, the sur-
mised intent of the author, and the plausibility of the text's representations, all of which the stimulating power of the trope may ex-
ceed. By itself no figure of speech can say enough to determine its
own effects, and therefore no tropology can do so either. The mistake,
like believing that life and death are self-evident, mutually exclusive
notions, would be to treat a tropological interpretation as the fatal
literalizing of the figure.

. . . . .

3

Social Science and Hermeneutics

. . . . .

. . . . .

Hermeneutics and Social Theory

Anthony Giddens

. . . . .

I have to begin my discussion with a qualification. I want to cover a wide range of issues in this essay. It follows that I shall not be able to deal with them all in the detail they warrant; I shall aim to be provocative rather than precise. My objectives are to sketch-in some of the ways in which hermeneutics is relevant to social theory and to trace through the implications of this account for current debates in social analysis.

The Background: The Demise of Orthodox Consensus

I think it would be true to say that it is only fairly recently that "hermeneutics"—the theory of interpretation—has become a familiar term to those working in the social sciences, at least in the English-speaking world. On the face of it this is an oddity, for the hermeneutic tradition stretches back to the late eighteenth century; and the term "hermeneutics" derives from the Greeks. But the circumstance is less odd than it appears, because the hermeneutic tradition was most firmly established in Germany and many of the key texts remained untranslated into English. The concept of *verstehen*, the unifying notion of the hermeneutic tradition, became most widely known in the English-speaking world through its adoption by Max Weber. As such, it was subject to scourging attack by those associated with what I shall call the "orthodox consensus."[1] The controversy about *verstehen* in the English-speaking literature,[2] however, largely by-passed some of the most significant questions raised by the hermeneutic tradition. Weber was only influenced in some part by that tradition, drawing his methodological ideas more strongly from the work of Rickert and the Marburg School.

But the principal factor explaining the relative lack of influence of the hermeneutic tradition in the Anglo-Saxon world has been the dominance of views of social science drawing their inspiration from positivistic or naturalistic philosophies of natural science. Such views were one of the main foundations of the orthodox consensus, an orthodoxy that dominated sociology, politics, and large sectors of the social sciences in general in the postwar period. There are three characteristics of the orthodox consensus I think it particularly important to emphasize. First, there is the influence of positivistic philosophy as a *logical* framework. This influence was itself twofold. The conceptions of science portrayed by philosophers such as Carnap, Hempel, and Nagel were accepted (often in simplified or inaccurate form) as adequate versions of what the natural sciences are like. But it was also emphasized that the social sciences should be modeled upon the natural sciences: that the aim of the former should be to parallel, in the study of human behavior, the achievements of the natural sciences. The object was to produce what Radcliffe-Brown once called a "natural science of society."

Second, on the level of *method*, there is the influence of functionalism. In the writings of Comte, Durkheim, and many others in the nineteenth and early twentieth centuries, functionalism stood in easy and close connection with the thesis that sociology should be a "natural science of society." The widespread use of organic analogies in social analysis encouraged, and in some part derived from, the conception that biology stands in direct line of association with social science. Functional conceptions of a similar kind seemed appropriate to both. In the more recent period, the affiliation between functionalism and the belief that sociology should adopt the same logical framework as the natural sciences has proved more ambiguous. Modern positivist philosophers have been suspicious of the claims of functionalism, and have examined its logical status with a skeptical eye.[3] But if the marriage between contemporary positivism and functionalism was not a case of love at first sight, the relation was at least consummated. From their side, the philosophers have given grudging recognition to functionalist concepts as legitimate parts of the apparatus of science. Many of those working in the social sciences saw such recognition as providing an up-to-date formulation of the traditional ties between functionalism and the advocacy of a "natural science of society."

Third, on the level of *content*, there is the influence of the conception of "industrial society" and of "modernization theory" more generally. I shall not have much to say about these in this paper. However, I think it very important to bear in mind that logical and methodological debates in the social sciences can rarely if ever be severed completely from more substantive views or theories with which they are intertwined. The concepts of "industrial society" and "modernization" belong to what can be called the theory of industrial society. By this I mean they belong to a particular set of views concerning the development of the "advanced" societies, affiliated to liberal political ideas. According to proponents of the theory of industrial society, industrialism is the main motive force transforming the contemporary world. In the postwar period, at a time of apparently stable growth rates in the Western economies, the theorists of industrial society foresaw the prospect of an indefinite period of prosperity, equalization of wealth and income, and the expansion of equality of opportunity. Industrialism provided the guiding thread for this progressive movement of history, both inside the West and in the rest of the world.

Combining these three elements, the orthodox consensus provided a body of "mainstream" opinion for sociology, and in some degree for the social sciences in general. Of course, it would be easy to underestimate the diversity of views within this consensus, and it never went unchallenged. In particular it had its critics from the Left. Throughout the period of its ascendancy, the orthodox consensus was challenged by authors influenced by Marx—although many such critics, such as Mills, Dahrendorf, Lockwood, and Rex, did not regard themselves as Marxists. In retrospect, the influence of Max Weber on their work seems more pronounced than that of Marx. But whatever the disagreements of these critics with the orthodox consensus, it provided a terrain for debate. There was some sort of unity to sociology, even if only in the form of a common series of battlegrounds upon which issues were fought out, and even if the results of such confrontations were hardly ever decisive.

Today the orthodox consensus is no more, for it has given way to dissidence and disarray. The dissolution of the orthodox consensus has been substantially brought about by the critical attacks that have been mounted against positivism in philosophy and the social sciences, and against functionalism.[4] But its demise is certainly not something to be explained solely in terms of intellectual critique. The changes that swept through the social sciences reflected transmutations in the social world itself, as the period of stable Western eco-

nomic growth was interrupted by fresh reversals, crises, and conflicts. The seemingly secure domain staked out by the theorists of
industrial society collapsed like a house of cards. Although I shall
not be examining here the implications of this directly, logical, methodological, and substantive problems are closely bound up with one
another in my thinking. The issues discussed here can be related
directly to the concrete analysis of transformations in society.[5]

Hermeneutics, Positivism, Social Theory

Interest in hermeneutics is one response—among various others—to the toppling of the orthodox consensus, on the levels of the
logic and method of social science. The English-speaking reception, or
recovery, of the hermeneutic tradition has been considerably facili-
tated by the post-Wittgensteinian movement within British and
American philosophy. Writers influenced by the later Wittgenstein,
most notably Peter Winch, have proposed views of the social sciences in sharp contrast to those of the orthodox consensus. In suggesting that there is a radical dislocation between the social and
natural sciences, that the understanding of "meaningful action" is
discrepant from the explanation of events in nature, post-Wittgensteinian philosophy converged with themes that have been the persistent concerns of hermeneutics. Winch's short book, *The Idea of a
Social Science*,[6] has been a focal point of debate among philosophers
for some twenty years, since its first publication. Most of those working in the social sciences, however, either ignored it or dismissed
Winch's claims as untenable. Only relatively recently has the book
been regarded in a more favorable light.

In *The Idea of a Social Science*, Winch argued that the subject
matter of the social sciences is above all concerned with discovering
the intelligibility of human action. To grasp why human beings act
as they do, we must understand the meaning of their activity. To
understand the meaning of conduct, according to Winch, is to grasp
the rules that actors follow in doing what they do. Meaningful action
is activity oriented to rules, where knowledge of those rules provides
the actors "reasons" for the conduct they engage in. Understanding
meaning and reasons, for Winch, involves relating observed behavior
to rules. Rules are not "laws," in the sense in which that term is
applied in the natural sciences. Neither the formulation of laws nor
causal analysis has any place in social science. Social science is thus

an interpretative, or hermeneutic, endeavor; a logical gulf separates
such an endeavor from the logic and method of the natural sciences.

Winch thus produces a contemporary version of the dichotomy,
long-established in the hermeneutic tradition, between *verstehen* and
erklären. *Verstehen*, the understanding of meaning, and the foundation of what were often called the "human sciences" (*Geisteswissenschaften*) was contrasted by Droysen, Dilthey, and others with *erklären*, the causal explanation of natural phenomena. Several things
separate Winch's account from the characteristic preoccupations of
hermeneutics. Winch does not employ the terminology of *verstehen*.
More important, he is unconcerned with history. One of the main
differences between positivistic and hermeneutic traditions has been
the continuing involvement of the latter with history. For hermeneutic
authors, history—not as the elapsing of time but as the capability of
human beings to become aware of their own past and to incorporate
that awareness as part of what their history is—has always been at
the center of the social sciences.

I do not wish in this context to offer a critical evaluation of
Winch's work and that of post-Wittgensteinian philosophy more
generally.[7] Neither do I want to consider at any length the differences
between these and Continental hermeneutics.[8] I do want to claim
that, in social theory, a turn to hermeneutics cannot in and of itself
resolve the logical and methodological problems left by the disappearance of the orthodox consensus. Winch's views cannot be sustained
as they stand, and it would be a mistake to attempt to revive the
differentiation of *verstehen* and *erklären*. This latter point, of course,
is agreed upon by some of the leading contemporary exponents of
hermeneutics, such as Gadamer and Ricoeur. But I think it equally
wrong merely to dismiss the relevance of hermeneutics to social
theory out of hand, as positivistically inclined writers have tended to
do. I want to argue instead for what I propose to call a "hermeneutically informed social theory." I think it is essential in social theory
to pay attention to the revitalization of hermeneutics in the hands of
the post-Wittgensteinian philosophers, Gadamer, Ricoeur, and others.
But at the same time I want to counsel caution; the ideas of such
authors have to be received critically.

In most of my discussion I chose to use the term "social theory,"
rather than "sociology"—or, even worse, "sociological theory." "Social theory," in my view, spans social science. It is a body of theory
shared by all the disciplines concerned with the behavior of human

beings. It concerns not only sociology, therefore, but anthropology, economics, politics, human geography, psychology—the whole range of the social sciences. Neither is social theory readily separable from questions of interest to an even wider set of concerns: it connects with literary criticism on the one hand, the philosophy of natural science on the other. The very importance of hermeneutics in social theory signals this state of affairs: contemporary hermeneutics is very much in the forefront of developments in the theory of the text, and yet at the same time has relevance to current issues in the philosophy of science.[9] There is something new in all this, in what Geertz calls the "blurred genres" of modern thought.[10] Some years ago, it was common enough to call for "interdisciplinary" studies that would seek to overcome the conventionally recognized boundaries of academic disciplines. Such studies rarely amounted to very much. Today, however, real and profound convergences of interests and problems are occurring across broad spectra of intellectual life. Social theory is at the very center of these convergences, having both to contribute to and to learn from them. To talk of the "blurring" of erstwhile separate frames of reference or contexts of discussion is to employ an appropriate term in more than one sense. For the occurrence of a convergence of approaches has not always provided clarification of the matters at issue; it has also fogged them. In the wake of the collapse of the orthodox consensus, as far as the social sciences are concerned, there has come about something of a centrifugal dispersal of vying theoretical approaches. I have argued elsewhere[11] that this seeming intellectual disarray should not lead anyone interested in social theory—as indeed I think we all have to be—to throw his or her hands up in despair. The current phase of development of social theory is one demanding reconstruction on several fronts. Such a process of reconstruction, in my opinion, is already under way, although it is unlikely perhaps to recapture the consensus of the old orthodoxy. Indeed, it would be foreign to the spirit of contemporary social thought to attempt to do so.

Under the somewhat ungainly heading of a hermeneutically informed social theory I would include a number of basic ideas. There are two sets of questions I want to concentrate upon here, however. Each represents a reaction to the first two elements of the orthodox consensus that I have referred to previously: positivism and functionalism. I wish to develop an approach to social theory in which the concept of "function" has no place; in my view the notions of "functional analysis" or "functional explanation" should also be dispensed with altogether, as resting on false premises. However, the contributions of functionalism (in its various guises) to social theory cannot be merely laid to rest in peace. It would not do to forsake Robert K. Merton in favor of Winch. One of the most significant limitations of Winch's "hermeneutic social theory" is that it makes no mention of what has always rightly been a primary concern of functionalism: the unanticipated conditions, the unintended consequences, of action. In this respect Winch's account of the method of the social sciences is inferior to that of Weber, whom on the whole Winch refers to in an approving way.[12] A hermeneutically informed social theory, such as I wish to propose here, and have sought to develop in some detail in recent publications, would recognize the need for connecting an adequate account of (meaningful) "action" (which, I think, Weber did not manage to do)[13] with the analysis of its unanticipated conditions and unintended consequences. In place of functionalism I want to offer what I call the "theory of structuration."

As regards the logic of the social sciences, I want to emphasize a different aspect of the relevance of hermeneutics to social theory. Modern hermeneutics has come together with phenomenology in accentuating the importance of everyday beliefs and practices, the mundane and the "taken for granted" in the constitution of social activity. The social sciences, however, or so I wish to argue, involve a rather special type of hermeneutical phenomenon in the conceptualization of their subject matter. A major objective of the positivistic standpoint involved in the orthodox consensus was the replacing of ordinary everyday language with a technical vocabulary of the social sciences—a technical vocabulary of a parallel kind to those employed in the various areas of natural science.[14] However, the relation between ordinary language, the forms of life in which its use is implicated, and the technical languages of the social sciences, proves to be considerably more complex and significant than was supposed in the pre-existing orthodoxy. Hermeneutics, in fact, enters in in a twofold way here—which is why I refer to my second theme as that of the "double hermeneutic." The social scientist studies a world, the social world, which is constituted as meaningful by those who produce and reproduce it in their activities—human subjects. To describe human behavior in a valid way is in principle to be able to participate in the forms of life that constitute and are constituted by that behavior.

This is already a hermeneutic task. But social science is itself a "form of life," with its own technical concepts. Hermeneutics hence enters into the social sciences on two related levels; this double hermeneutic proves to be of basic importance to the postpositivist reformulation of social theory.

The Theory of Structuration

I have outlined the elements of the theory of structuration in some detail elsewhere,[15] and therefore shall offer only a brief outline here. In working out a conception of structuration, I attempt to meet several desiderata that have been brought to the fore in current debates in social theory. First, I address the demand for a "theory of the subject," as posed primarily by those working within structuralist traditions of thought. The call for a theory of the subject involves a defined break with positivistic standpoints in philosophy, and with the Cartesian *cogito*. "Consciousness," as a property of human beings, is not to be taken as a given, a phenomenon which is a starting point for analysis. But while correctly posing the requirement for a theory of the subject, and in turn arguing that this involves a "de-centering" of the subject, structuralist thought has tended to dissolve subjectively into abstract structures of language. A de-centering of the subject must at the same time *recover* that subject, as a reasoning, acting being. Otherwise the result is an objectivist type of social theory, in which human agency appears only as the determined outcome of social causes. Here there is a strong similarity between structuralism (including most varieties of so-called poststructuralism) and functionalism—neither entirely surprising nor purely fortuitous, for each has its origins in some part in Durkheim.[16]

Second, I address the demand that a theory of the subject which avoids objectivism should not slide into subjectivism. A relapse into subjectivism was precisely one of the main tendencies in early reactions to the dissolution of the orthodox consensus. Subjectivist conceptions on the whole have not offered an *explication* of the origins of subjectivity, even while stressing the creative components of human behavior. In the theory of structuration, I argue that neither subject (human agent) nor object ("society," or social institutions) should be regarded as having primacy. *Each is constituted in and through recurrent practices.* The notion of human "action" presupposes that of "institution," and vice versa. Explication of this relation thus comprises the core of an account of how it is that the structuration (production and reproduction across time and space) of social practices takes place.

The notion of action has been much debated by philosophers, and has given rise to considerable controversy. I take the concept to refer to two components of human conduct, which I shall call "capability" and "knowledgeability." By the first of these I mean that, whenever we speak of human action, we imply the possibility that the agent "could have acted otherwise." The sense of this well-worn phrase is not easy to elucidate philosophically, and it would hardly be possible to seek to elaborate upon it here; but its importance to social analysis is very pronounced, since it connects in an immediate way to the significance of *power* in social theory.[17] By the second term, "knowledgeability," I mean all those things that the members of the society know about that society and about the conditions of their activity within it. It is a basic mistake to equate the knowledgeability of agents with what is known "consciously," where this means what can be "held in mind" in a conscious way. An explication of subjectivity must relate "consciousness" in this sense (discursive consciousness) to what I call "practical consciousness," and to the unconscious. Lack of a conception of practical consciousness, I think, is again common to functionalist and structuralist traditions of thought alike. By practical consciousness I mean the vast variety of tacit modes of knowing how to "go on" in the contexts of social life. Like "knowledgeability," "capability" must not be identified with the ability of agents to make "decisions"—as is posited in game theory, for example. If it refers to circumstances in which individuals consciously confront a range of potential alternatives of conduct, making some choice among those alternatives, decision making is no more than a subcategory of capability in general. Capability, the possibility of "doing otherwise," is generally exercised as a routine, tacit feature of everyday behavior.

By institutions, I mean structured social practices that have a broad spatial and temporal extension, that are structured in what the historian Braudel calls the *longue durée* of time, and that are followed or acknowledged by the majority of the members of a society. In the theory of structuration, "structure" refers to rules and resources instantiated in social systems, but having only a "virtual existence." The structured properties of society, the study of which is basic to explaining the long-term development of institutions, "exist" only in their instantiation in the structuration of social systems, and in the memory traces (reinforced or altered in the continuity of daily social life) that constitute the knowledgeability of social actors. But institutionalized practices "happen," and are "made to happen" through the application of resources in the continuity of daily life. Resources are structured properties of social systems, but "exist" only in the capability of actors, in their capacity to "act otherwise." This brings me to an essential element of the theory of structuration, the thesis that the organization of social practices is fundamentally *recursive*. Structure is both the medium and the outcome of the practices it recursively organizes.

Thus formulated, the theory of structuration seems to me to depart very considerably both from the sort of viewpoint developed by Winch, in respect to human action, and from the objectivism of functionalist theories. The latter theories fail to treat human beings as capable knowledgeable agents. Winch makes these factors central to his version of social science (although not in a wholly satisfactory way), but institutions only tend to appear in his analysis—like in that of Wittgenstein, his mentor—as a shadowy backdrop against which action is to be interpreted. However, we cannot leave matters here, for the discussion so far does not make it clear where the unacknowledged conditions, and unintended consequences, of action figure in this scheme. Among the unacknowledged conditions of action, there should be included unconscious sources of conduct. Unconscious sources of cognition and motivation form one "boundary" to the knowledgeability/capability of agents. But the "bounded" character of knowledgeably reproduced practices also necessarily implicates social analysis in a continuing concern with the prime focus of functionalist approaches: social reproduction via feedback relations of unintended consequences. Here the unintended consequences of action are simultaneously unacknowledged conditions of system reproduction.

It is certainly necessary to insist upon the importance of such feedback relations in social theory. But the concept of "function" is a hindrance rather than a help in conceptualizing them. The notion of "function" only has plausibility as a part of the vocabulary of the social sciences if we attribute "needs" to social systems (or "prerequisites," "exigencies," or other synonyms). However, social systems have no needs, and to suppose that they do is to apply an illegitimate teleology to them. In the theory of structuration, "social reproduction" is not regarded as an explanatory term: it always has itself to be explicated in terms of the bounded and contingently applied knowledge-ability of social actors.

One consequence of the preceding arguments is that the personal, transient encounters of daily life cannot be conceptually separated from the long-term development of institutions. The most casual exchange of words involves the speakers in the long-term history of the language by which their words are formed, and simultaneously in the continuing reproduction of that language. There is more than an accidental similarity between Braudel's *longue durée* of historical time and the *durée* of daily social life to which Schutz, following Bergson, draws our attention.

The double hermeneutic

As I have mentioned previously, some of the leading hermeneutic philosophers of today are critical of the contrast between *verstehen* and *erklären* drawn by earlier writers in the hermeneutic tradition. One reason for this is that which Gadamer in particular concentrates upon: the tendency of Dilthey and others to represent *verstehen* as a "psychological" phenomenon.[18] In other words, *verstehen* was taken to involve "reliving," or "reexperiencing" the mental states of those whose activities or creations were to be interpreted. In place of the "psychological" version of *verstehen*, Gadamer locates the concept squarely in language, language being the medium in which "understanding" is fundamental to human life. Here there is a major point of connection between Continental hermeneutics and the philosophy of the later Wittgenstein. Insofar as Winch follows Wittgenstein, he cannot be regarded as advocating a "psychological" version of *verstehen*. Nonetheless, he does produce a latter-day rendition of the differentiation between *verstehen* and *erklären*, not as a result of his conception of the understanding of action itself, but as a result of his view of natural science. In his own day, Dilthey was strongly influenced by positivistic notions of science, and derived his view of the logic of the natural sciences substantially from John Stuart Mill. Winch's conception of natural science, which really only appears in his book as a foil to his discussion of the social sciences, seems to be derived directly from positivist philosophy, including that of Mill, to whom he devotes some attention. He questions Mill's view that "all explanations . . . have fundamentally the same logical structure" in both the social and the natural sciences.[19] But he does not dispute Mill's account of natural science.

Current issues in social theory, however, cannot be divorced from the rapid changes that have affected the philosophy of natural science. The orthodox consensus, as I have pointed out, not only involved the supposition that the social sciences should be modeled after the natural sciences, but accepted what itself has been called the "orthodox model"[20] of natural science—that is, the liberalized version of logical positivism worked out by Carnap and others. The orthodox model of natural sciences is now itself no more. The writings of Popper, Kuhn, Toulmin, Hesse, Feyerabend, and many others have successfully broken away from the ideas that dominated positivistic models of science. The "newer philosophy of science" seems far from resolving the issues that its leading figures have brought to the fore. But it is clear that these developments cannot be ignored in social theory, even if we no longer sustain the view that our objective should be to construct a "natural science of society." In the social sciences today, as it were, we have to attempt to rotate two axes simultaneously. In rethinking the character of human action, institutions, and their relations, we have at the same time to bear in mind the transmutations in the philosophy of science.

Positivistic conceptions of science emphasized the anchoring of theories in observation statements, verification, and prediction as the elemental logical components of scientific activity. The writings of Kuhn and other contemporary philosophers such as those mentioned above are still, of course, in some degree concerned with these matters. But they have made it plain that science is as much about "interpreting" the world as about "explaining" it; and that these two forms of endeavor are not readily separable from one another. The relation between the "paradigms" (a word that has been so abused that it surely should now be discarded), or the frames of meaning, in terms of which scientific theories are couched, involves translation problems close to those that have long been a primary concern of hermeneutics. The problems raised here are of direct concern to theories developed in the social sciences, but there are some issues that are specific to the social sciences. One is precisely the question of the double hermeneutic. The hermeneutics of natural science are to do only with the theories and discourse of scientists, analyzing an object world which does not answer back and which does not construct and interpret the meanings of its activities.

The double hermeneutic of the social sciences involves what Winch calls a "logical tie" between the ordinary language of lay actors and the technical terminologies invented by social scientists. Schutz refers to much the same issue, borrowing a term from Weber, when he says that the concepts of the social observer must be "adequate" to those employed by actors whose activity is to be described or analyzed. Neither author, however, gives an especially convincing explication of the relation they thus point to. Winch's version, I think, is more accurate than that of Schutz, although its implications remain undeveloped. According to Schutz's view, technical terms in the social sciences are "adequate" only if the mode of activity analyzed in a "typical construct" is "understandable for the actor himself" in terms of that actor's own concepts.[21] But this is not a defensible standpoint. Consider the example Winch takes in his discussion: the use of the concept of "liquidity preference" in economics. Why should we suppose that the "adequacy" of such a notion is governed by whether or not a street trader understands, or can be led to understand, what it means? How well would that individual have to grasp the concept for it to be declared an "adequate" part of the vocabulary of economics? Schutz has actually got things the wrong way around. The "logical tie" implicated in the double hermeneutic does not depend upon whether the actor or actors whose conduct is being described are able to grasp the notion which the social scientist uses. It depends upon the social scientific observer accurately understanding the concepts whereby the actors' conduct is oriented. Winch is right to say of "liquidity preference" that "its use by the economist presupposed his understanding of what it is to conduct a business, which in turn presupposes his understanding of such business concepts as money, cost, risk, etc."[22]

The implications of the double hermeneutic, however, stretch much further, and are considerably more complex, than such a statement suggests. The technical language and theoretical propositions of the natural sciences are insulated from the world they are concerned with because that world does not answer back. But social theory cannot be insulated from its "object world," which is a subject world. Those influenced by the orthodox consensus, of course, were aware of this, but being under the sway of the idea that prediction, on the basis of laws, is the main task of the social sciences, they sought to duplicate such an insulation as far as possible. The double hermeneutic was understood only in relation to the prediction, in the

shape of "self-fulfilling" or "self-denying" prophecies. The tie between ordinary language, daily social life, and social theory was
specifically regarded as a nuisance, something that gets in the way
of testing the predictions whereby generalizations are validated.
Winch's discussion indicates the logical limitations of such a standpoint; but it fails to demonstrate its poverty as a way of expressing
the relations between the social sciences and the lives of the human
beings whose behavior is analyzed. The double hermeneutic entails
that these relations, as Gadamer insists, are dialogical. The fact that
the "findings" of the social sciences can be taken up by those to
whose behavior they refer is not a phenomenon that can, or should,
be marginalized, but is integral to their very nature. It is the hinge
connecting two possible modes in which the social sciences connect
to their involvement in society itself: as contributing to forms of
exploitative domination, or as promoting emancipation.

Conclusion

Many problems are raised by the developments I have described
in the foregoing sections. I shall conclude by indicating what some
of these are.

First, there are still quite basic issues to be resolved in the post-
positivistic philosophy of natural science. Substantial objections have
been raised against the views of each of the major authors whose
work has helped undermine the orthodox model. The attempt of
Popper, for example, to draw a distinct line of demarcation between
science and nonscience, or "pseudo-science," on the basis of his doctrine of falsificationism, has turned out to be untenable. In *The Structure of Scientific Revolutions* and subsequent publications, Kuhn
raised—but has not been able satisfactorily to cope with—fundamental issues concerning relativism and truth in science. A modified
realist theory of science, such as proposed in variant forms by Hesse
and Bhaskar, may have most to offer here.[23] The implications for the
social sciences have yet to be fully explored, but seem compatible
with a viewpoint that draws from hermeneutics without succumbing
to the historicism of Gadamer. Bhasker's "transformative model" of
social activity in particular arrives independently at a conception of
the social sciences having a great deal in common with my account
of structuration.

Second, we have to reformulate pre-existing conceptions of the significance of causal laws in the social sciences. The logical status of causal laws in the natural sciences is by no means an uncontested matter. However, neither the positivistic view that laws in natural and social sciences are logically identical, nor the hermeneutic notion that causal laws have no place in the social sciences at all, are acceptable. I have argued elsewhere that there is a basic logical difference between laws in social and natural science.[24] Laws in the social sciences are intrinsically "historical" in character: they hold only given specific conditions of "boundedness" of knowledgeably reproduced systems of social interaction. The causal relations involved in laws refer to conjunctions of intended and unintended consequences of reproduced action; these conjunctions can be altered by the dialogical application of social analysis itself. The type case here is Marx's analysis of the "laws of the market" in competitive capitalism. The "laws of the market" hold only given a lack of overall understanding and control of economic life by producers in the context of the "anarchic" conditions of capitalist production. The connections they express are mutable in the light of action taken on the basis of knowledge of those connections. This having been said, we have to avoid the error self-confessedly made by Habermas in *Knowledge and Human Interests:* knowledge acquired in the process of "self-reflection" is not a sufficient condition of social transformation.[25] Knowledgeability plus capability—each is implicated in the continuity or change of social systems.

Third, if the traditional differentiation of *verstehen* and *erklären* must be abandoned, we have to recognize the distinctive features of social life singled out by hermeneutic philosophies. I have accepted that it is right to say that the condition of generating descriptions of social activity is being able in principle to participate in it. It involves "mutual knowledge," shared by observer and participants whose action constitutes and reconstitutes the social world. Again, however, there are a variety of questions at issue here: how we are to decide what counts as a "valid" description of an act or form of action, for example; or how the beliefs involved in alien cultures may be subjected to critique. In respect of the conceptualization of action, nevertheless, one thing is clear: deterministic views of human agency, which explain human action as the result of social causes, are to be rejected. It should be evident, in the light of my earlier remarks, that this does not imply that causal laws have no place in the social sciences.

Fourth, social theory is inevitably critical theory. I do not mean by this to defend either a version of Marxism in general, or the specific accounts of critical theory associated with Frankfurt social thought in particular. I do want to insist that those working in the social sciences cannot remain aloof from or indifferent to the implications of their theories and research for their fellow members of society. To regard social agents as "knowledgeable" and "capable" is not just a matter of the analysis of action; it is also an implicitly political stance. The practical consequences of natural science are "technological"; they have to do with the application of humanly attained knowledge to a world of objects that exists independently of that knowledge. Human beings, however, are not merely inert objects of knowledge, but agents able to—and prone to—incorporate social theory and research within their own action.

· · · · ·

Comments on Giddens

Fred R. Dallmayr

· · · · ·

I am strongly impressed by Giddens's general approach. Being sympathetic to many of his arguments, I cannot generate drama by launching a broad-scale offensive against his views. To be sure, there are disagreements between us; but these have the character more of a domestic skirmish than of a battle between opposed camps.

First, a few words of praise. On the whole, I find persuasive Giddens's portrayal of what he calls the "orthodox consensus" in the social sciences and also his account of its demise. As he shows, the orthodox consensus was held together by logical, methodological, and substantive commitments: with positivism supplying the logic of inquiry, functionalism, the methodological apparatus, and the notion of "industrial society," the vision of human and social development. The demise or disintegration of the orthodox consensus calls into question all three of these components and thus can be traced to intellectual as well as social-economic crises and countertrends. Although in his paper Giddens concentrates mainly on intellectual or theoretical aspects, he surely cannot be said to ignore the broader social-economic transformations occurring in our world today. "In my thinking," he writes, "logical, methodological and substantive problems are closely bound up with one another." This kind of balanced outlook strikes me as eminently plausible and commendable (although, on other occasions, the relation between the components may have to be spelled out in greater detail).

Equally praiseworthy, in its general outline, is the proposal for a reorientation of "social theory"—as this term is used in the essay. In my view, Giddens is one of a handful of social theorists today who are attentive not only to the "postpositivist," but also the "postmetaphysical" condition of contemporary thought—that is, to the progressive, though frequently subterranean, erosion of traditional "metaphysics" seen as a "spectatorial theory of knowledge" rooted in human subjectivity or in "an inner glassy essence" of man (to use

Richard Rorty's vocabulary). In his recent writings—particularly in *Central Problems in Social Theory: Action, Structure and Contradiction in Social Analysis* (London: Macmillan, 1979)—Giddens has taken to heart the problems surrounding modern "humanism" and the attacks leveled at subject-centered philosophical premises by Heidegger and contemporary "poststructuralist" writers (such as Foucault, Derrida, and Lacan). At the same time, however, he realizes that social theory must in some fashion deal with the role of human beings (viewed singly or in groups) as actors, and thus with the issues surrounding human agency and "social action." Agency, in turn, is broadly related to such notions as purpose, intentionality, and human responsibility, that traditionally have been termed "freedom." As a result, Giddens has seen himself faced with a momentous challenge: the challenge of incorporating the lessons of ontology and poststructuralism *without* abandoning concern with the "knowledgeability" and accountability of actors; more ambitiously phrased: the task of moving beyond subjectivist metaphysics *without* relinquishing some of its insights, and especially *without* lapsing into objectivism and determinism.

As outlined in the essay and other writings, Giddens's response to this challenge takes the form of a "hermeneutically informed social theory"—a theory that is neither purely hermeneutical in the sense of the traditional *Geisteswissenschaften,* nor a refurbished brand of positivism dressed in interpretive garb. In his words, such a theory pays "attention to the revitalization of hermeneutics in the hands of the post-Wittgensteinian philosophers, Gadamer, Ricoeur, and others," while at the same time treating hermeneutical views "critically" and with caution. Designed as a reply to the orthodox consensus, the proposed perspective provides antidotes to the two main ingredients of that consensus—functionalism and positivism—without canceling their valid contributions. On the level of methodology, functionalism is replaced by what Giddens calls the "theory of structuration," whose chief aim is to link "an adequate account of (meaningful) action with the analysis of its unanticipated conditions and unintended consequences." In the domain of the logic of inquiry, positivism is corrected and overcome through the notion of a "double hermeneutic"—an approach that recognizes that social science is basically an interpretive enterprise dealing with social "forms of life" which, in turn, are webs of meaningful, preinterpreted activities and relationships.

In the following I would like to take a somewhat closer look at Giddens's "hermeneutically informed social theory" and at its two main components: the "theory of structuration" and the "double hermeneutic." As his essay points out, the first component owes its inspiration to a number of demands or *desiderata* prominent in contemporary social theory: particularly the demands for a "theory of the subject" and for a methodological strategy by-passing both objectivism and subjectivism. Taking its cues from structuralist and poststructuralist arguments, the "theory of the subject" involves a break with the Cartesian *cogito* and with the modern focus on consciousness and subjectivity—but a break that simultaneously seeks to recover the human subject as a "reasoning, acting being." The methodological strategy connected with this outlook insists that "neither subject (human agent) nor object (society or social institutions) should be regarded as having primacy," since "each is constituted in and through recurrent practices." Concerning agency and social action, the essay concentrates chiefly on the two aspects of "capability" (option to act otherwise) and "knowledgeability"—with the latter term comprising both "discursive" and "practical consciousness" and being differentiated from the Freudian domain of the unconscious. Elsewhere—in *Central Problems in Social Theory* (pp. 56–59, 123)— Giddens speaks of a "stratification model" of human agency, a model connecting intentionality (or the "reflexive monitoring of conduct") with preconscious motivational factors which in turn are tied to the "unacknowledged conditions" and "unintended consequences" of action. "A 'stratified' model of personality," he notes there, "in which human wants are regarded as hierarchically connected, involving a basic security system largely inaccessible to the conscious subject, is not at all incompatible with an equivalent stress upon the significance of the reflexive monitoring of action, the latter becoming possible only following the 'positioning' of the actor in the Lacanian sense."

In addition to human agency, structuration involves the role of social "institutions" defined as "structured social practices that have a broad spatial and temporal extension"—that is, as practices that, apart from operating concretely in time and space, also exhibit a paradigmatic "structure." In the essay, the term "structure" is explicated as referring to "rules and resources instantiated in social systems, but having only a 'virtual existence.'" Helpful pointers regarding the meaning of these formulations can be gleaned from *Central Problems in Social Theory* (pp. 2–3). There, Giddens differentiates more clearly between "system" and "structure," portraying social systems as practices concretely "situated in time-space," while depicting structure as "non-temporal and non-spatial," as "a *virtual order of differences* produced and reproduced in social interaction as its medium and outcome." As features of concrete social systems, social institutions are basically practices through which the "structured properties of society"—rules and resources—are instantiated and applied in the spatial-temporal setting of daily life. Against this background, "structuration" signifies the continuous instantiation of the virtual existence of structure—a view that undergirds the essay's thesis that "the organization of social practices is fundamentally *recursive*," in the sense that "structure is both the medium and the outcome of the practices it recursively organizes."

As it seems to me, the chief aim as well as the chief merit of the "theory of structuration" lies clearly in the reinterpretation and novel correlation of agency and structure. The structural perspective championed by Giddens has distinct advantages over competing functionalist and systemic frameworks, while salvaging their main analytical assets. The accentuation of rules and resources as structural properties strikes me as potentially fruitful and as an advance over the well-worn "subsystems" familiar from functionalist analysis. Despite these and other accomplishments, however, I find Giddens's conception of structure and structuration somewhat vacillating and ambivalent; differently phrased, his approach seems reluctant at points to draw the full implications from the adopted perspective. As he has conceded in other contexts, his theory of structuration is indebted at least in part to Derrida's notion of the "structuring of structure"; his portrayal of structure as a "virtual existence," a "virtual order," or an "absent set of differences" is likewise reminiscent of Derrida's construal of *"différance."* As employed by Derrida, however, the latter concept involves not only a factual differentiation of elements but also a more basic ontological (or ontic-ontological) difference; as a corollary, structuration in its radical sense injects into social analysis a profoundly nonpositive or, if one prefers, "transcendental" dimension. Against this background, Giddens's treatment appears at times halfhearted. In some passages, the notion of a "virtual order" seems to imply no more than the contingent and essentially remediable constellation of "present" and "absent" factors— or at least a constellation in which absent factors can always readily be "instantiated" or applied. Seen in this light, "structure" tends to merge imperceptibly with "system": the virtual order of structural properties shades over into Robert K. Merton's distinction between "manifest" and "latent" functions.

Instantiation construed as the translation of latent into manifest properties is particularly evident in the case of "resources" through whose application institutionalized practices are said to "happen" or be "made to happen" in the continuity of everyday life. In the case of "rules" the translation process seems less evident or intelligible. The theoretical difficulties surrounding Wittgenstein's notion of "rule-governed" behavior are notorious (some of them have been elucidated by Wittgenstein himself). Giddens's portrayal of rules is not exempt from these difficulties. Viewed as ingredients of a virtual order, it is not entirely clear how rules can be "both the medium and the out-come" of recursive social practices; at least further argument seems required to pinpoint the status of rules in the process of structuration.

Ambiguities also surround the notion of "agency" and its rela-tion to structuration—despite many attractive features of Giddens's perspective as articulated in his paper and elsewhere. In a formula-tion that (I think) can serve as yardstick for future inquiries in this area, Giddens noted in *Central Problems* that the concept "cannot be defined through that of intention, as is presumed in so much of the literature to do with the philosophy of action; the notion of agency, as I employ it, I take to be logically prior to a subject-object differ-entiation" (p. 92). Depicted in this manner, "agency" undercuts or transcends the customary bifurcation between subjectively intended activity and externally stimulated reactive behavior—a bifurcation that in large measure permeates Weberian and post-Weberian soci-ology. Given this overall theoretical thrust, one is surprised to find in Giddens's treatment again an occasional halfheartedness or vacilla-tion—manifest in his tendency of tying agency closely to everyday conduct understood as "activity" or "doing." His paper presents the notion of action as referring mainly to "two components of human conduct," namely capability and knowledgeability. As mentioned, capability is defined as the actor's possibility of acting or "doing otherwise." Practical consciousness, construed as one form of knowl-edgeability, is said in the paper to denote "the vast variety of tacit modes of knowing how to 'go on' in the contexts of social life"; in *Central Problems*, the same concept is circumscribed as "tacit knowl-edge that is skillfully applied in the enactment of courses of conduct" (p. 57). In a similar vein, social institutions are described as struc-

tured social practices, that is, as modes of social interaction in which
structural properties are implemented in a temporal or spatial setting.

What is obscured in this presentation is the claimed status of
agency beyond the poles of intentional activity and reactive behavior;
more sharply put: what tends to be ignored is the peculiar nexus of
action and nonaction within agency itself. If the latter notion is really
"logically prior to a subject-object differentiation" and (as stated in
Central Problems) even adumbrates the "connection of *being and action*" (p. 39), then social theory has to make room for a certain
"openness to being" and remain attentive not only to "doing" but
also to human "suffering" understood as an experience actors
undergo (and not merely in the sense of reactive behavior). Against
this background, one cannot completely assent to the assertion, put
forth in *Central Problems*, that social theory today needs "a grasp of
'what cannot be said' (or thought) as *practice*" (p. 44). The mentioned difficulty or ambiguity, it seems to me, cannot entirely be resolved through reference to the "unacknowledged conditions" and
"unconscious sources" of action: as long as such conditions or
sources are depicted simply as "boundaries" to the "knowledgeabil-
ity/capability of agents," reliance on functionalist types of explanation does not seem far-fetched or illegitimate.

So far I have pointed to some ambiguities or quandaries besetting Giddens's notions of structure and agency and their correlation
in his theory of structuration. I would like to turn now to another
feature of his perspective which is probably no less problematical: his
conception of the "double hermeneutic" and its relationship to structuration. As presented in the essay, hermeneutics serves mainly as a
substitute for positivism on the level of epistemology or the logic of
inquiry; seen in this light, its relevance is not restricted to the humanities and social sciences but extends to the philosophy and epistemology of natural science. In Giddens's words, "the orthodox model
of natural science is now itself no more"; in the wake of the writings
of Thomas Kuhn, Stephen Toulmin, and others, it is "plain that science is as much about 'interpreting' the world as about 'explaining'
it, and that these two forms of endeavor are not readily separable
from one-another." What is distinctive about the humanities and social sciences is that hermeneutics operates, so to speak, on two levels:
"The hermeneutics of natural science are to do only with the theories
and discourse of scientists, analyzing an object world which does not
answer back"; by contrast, "the double hermeneutic of the social sci-

ences involves what Winch calls a 'logical tie' between the ordinary language of lay actors and the technical terminologies invented by social scientists." In the latter case, hermeneutics thus signifies the interpretation of preinterpretations—an aspect lacking in the study of nature: "The technical language and theoretical propositions of the natural sciences are insulated from the world they are concerned with because that world does not answer back. But social theory cannot be insulated from its 'object world,' which is a subject world."

The implication of these comments is that natural and social sciences are unified through their logic of inquiry, and differentiated only in terms of their diverse "object worlds" or targets of investigation. To be sure, unity is no longer predicated on the model of a "unified science" extolled by logical positivism, but rather on the common adherence to hermeneutics seen as a framework of interpretation and intersubjective discourse. In stressing the linkage between natural and social sciences, Giddens seems to endorse, albeit hesitantly, the notion of a "universal hermeneutics" as articulated by Hans-Georg Gadamer—and perhaps even the thesis of the "unsurpassability of hermeneutics" put forth at one point by Paul Ricoeur. Discussion about the relation between modes of inquiry, one might add, is not restricted to Continental thinkers. Something akin to the concept of "unsurpassability" seems to be involved in Richard Rorty's emphasis on "conversation" as the common bond among disciplines—where "conversation" is basically identified with hermeneutics. One difficulty conjured up by this accent on a common logic of inquiry is how it can be squared with Giddens's critical reservations regarding hermeneutics and his broader ambition to overcome the *verstehen-erklären* dichotomy. "I do want to claim," he asserts in one passage, "that, in social theory, a turn to hermeneutics cannot in and of itself resolve the logical and methodological problems left by the disappearance of the orthodox consensus." In focusing on the interpretive dimension of all disciplines, Giddens seems bent not so much on transcending the *verstehen-erklären* conflict as on resolving it in favor of understanding, particularly reciprocal understanding. Thus, assessing the relations between the social sciences and the concrete human agents under investigation he states: "The double hermeneutic entails that these relations, as Gadamer insists, are dialogical."

Another difficulty arising in the same context concerns the connection between logic of inquiry and methodology, that is, between hermeneutics and the theory of structuration. Given the claim that human agency—as a major ingredient of structuration—is somehow "logically prior to a subject-object differentiation," it is not clear how, under the heading of the double hermeneutic, the object world or target area of social science can simply be described as a "subject world." More broadly phrased, it is far from self-evident how hermeneutical exegesis can penetrate to the "virtual existence" or "virtual order" of structural properties. The problems surrounding the relation between logic of inquiry and methodology affect also the status of history in Giddens's outlook and its relevance for social science. In his paper he affirms that "laws in the social sciences are intrinsically 'historical' in character." The same point is stated more boldly in *Central Problems* where we read that "there simply are no logical or even methodological distinctions between the social sciences and history—appropriately conceived" (p. 230). Whatever the import of the last qualifying phrase may be, the linkage between social science and history inevitably brings to the fore the age-old antimony between nature and history—and thus, in a new disguise, the contrast between natural science and hermeneutics.

The difficulties besetting the relation between hermeneutics and structuration are not unique to the essay under review. Actually, Giddens deserves praise for wrestling with the relevant issues in an imaginative manner and thus for bringing them into sharper focus. Readers of "poststructuralist" literature cannot fail being sensitized to the same issues. In light of the Nietzschean maxim that "everything is interpretation"—a maxim endorsed by most poststructuralists—the question inevitably arises how interpretation can grant access to epistemic structures and, more generally, yield a "theory of the subject" bypassing the *cogito* and traditional subjectivity.

. . . . .

Conflicting Interpretations in History: The Case of the English Civil War

W. H. Dray

. . . . .

In this essay I shall review four significantly different interpretations of a controversial object of study, the English Civil War and its origins, which have been prominent in recent historical writing. I shall then discuss certain philosophical issues that are implicit in what their protagonists often have to say in support of them, and are, indeed, sometimes explicitly referred to by them. What I shall be considering is thus historians' interpretations of *events*, not of evidence (to the extent that these are separable questions). And what I shall be concerned with is their interpretations of a selected *stretch* of the past, not of the historical process as a whole (again to the extent that these are separable questions).

The English Civil War is the kind of event, or grouping of events, that virtually invites controversy. According to one authority on the whole period, Lawrence Stone, what we have to do with here is "the central events of modern English history."[1] According to another, Conrad Russell, hunting down its causes is "the traditional blood-sport of English historians."[2] That sport in fact began shortly after the war itself with the now famous, partly apologetic account offered by the earl of Clarendon, a prominent figure on the losing side; and it is really quite breathtaking to find that over three hundred years after Clarendon wrote, and after some of the greatest luminaries of English historiography have had their say, one is almost certain to find in some major historical journal or other, in a given quarter, an article promising a new approach to the problem of the war's origins, if not a whole new interpretation. The four interpretations that I shall begin by sketching have all flourished in the present century, although one really had its heyday in the nineteenth, and

anticipations of others can be found then as well. In order of their
flourishing, they are the Whig, the Marxist, what I shall call the social
interpretation (although it has also been referred to as sociologized
Whig), and one that, being latest on the scene, generally styles itself
and is generally styled revisionist.

Essential to the Whig interpretation in any form is an emphasis
upon political and constitutional development as the main theme of
the several decades of English history that culminated in the war, and
more specifically, upon the growth of an ever more effective opposition to royal power, especially in the House of Commons, interpreted
as one aspect of a "struggle for sovereignty" that was eventually lost
by the king and won by Parliament. Also essential is a strong tendency to look at the early Stuart period chiefly as the prehistory of
present-day English political and constitutional achievements, both it
and the intervening years being regarded, approvingly, as having
been progressive in the sense of having protected, transmitted, and
enlarged the "liberties of Englishmen." However, there are variations
on these tendencies that suggest theories differing in concept and
methodology, the differences not always being clearly signaled in the
literature. With a view to indicating more precisely the nature of recent Whiggism—I think particularly of a historian like J. H. Hexter,
who does not flinch at having a term like "Whig" applied to him[3]—
let me contrast three variations on the Whig approach.

At one extreme is the idea that a revolutionary confrontation
with the king was part of a deliberate policy followed over a considerable period of time by those on the parliamentary side who
eventually took up arms. This view might be called *conspiratorial*
Whig. Perhaps as just stated, it is so extreme that it would be difficult
to find any historian fully committed to it. But one gets at least approximations to it in earlier Whiggish rhetoric: for example, in that
of Macaulay; and it is easily suggested by the highly voluntaristic
language used by many Whigs in describing early Stuart parliaments:
for example, Wallace Notestein's phrase "the winning of the initia-
tive by the House of Commons,"[4] which to many of his critics has
seemed quintessential Whiggism. At the other extreme (and here one
can point at least to passing remarks and innuendo of nineteenth-
century historians like S. R. Gardiner), the idea is rather that in the
seventeenth century, English members of Parliament, common law-
yers, Puritan divines, and so on, had the good fortune to be born into
a historical process that was, in political and constitutional matters,

and perhaps also in religious ones, inherently progressive. On this view—which might perhaps be designated *Hegelian* Whig—the "liberties of Englishmen" are seen as having been realized by means of a social and political process whose inner "logic" transcended the aims and knowledge of the individuals concerned. English institutions are taken to have had something like a rational principle of development in them—an idea put by David Hume as their having been "prognostic of the establishment of liberty."[5]

Recent Whiggism has fallen somewhere between these two extremes, although nearer to the first than to the second. It is allowed that there was something like a political and constitutional conspiracy in the reigns of James I and Charles I; but this is not conceived as aiming at anything as catastrophic as a revolution or a resort to arms. The latter were simply unfortunate results of liberty's persistent defense that right-thinking men and women nevertheless steeled themselves to endure. This view finds expression in a response by Hexter to those—mainly revisionists—who find little continuity, and certainly no formed opposition in the parliaments that preceded the so-called Long Parliament of 1640. Declares Hexter, the English gentry who, in the twenties and thirties resisted illegal taxation, arbitrary arrest, and other abuses of prerogative power, knew exactly wha: they were doing: they *willed* the preservation of liberty—and not just their own, but that also of their descendants.[6] The Whig interpretation has often been described by historians as "teleological." Only this middle position, however, seems to me both to make sense as teleology—its logic being that of a joint enterprise—and to have some empirical plausibility (although historians will certainly dispute how much). Hexter adds that the continuity of the opposition, both in Parliament and country, was not absolute, but more like that of a rope. It involved, not an identity, but an overlap, of particular issues and persons over a considerable period of time—a paradigm case of what W. H. Walsh, arguing for what he called historical "colligation," described as people "taking up each other's work."[7]

The second interpretation, the Marxist, regards the events of the years following the calling of the Long Parliament as a full-blown revolution, of which the Civil War itself was only an aspect. Whigs, too, have often talked at least of a political and constitutional revolution. Others have seen signs of a social revolution as well—if only an abortive one—in such developments as the proparliamentary demonstrations of the London apprentices in 1641, the infiltration of the

New Model Army by Leveller ideology in the early years of the war, or the direct assault on private property by the Diggers soon after it. For the Marxists, however, what occurred was much more than just *a* social revolution; it was the first great social revolution of the West—indeed, the first *bourgeois* revolution.[8] That implies, of course, that it involved vast political and social changes made necessary by economic developments of the preceding century or more: developments which doomed the remnants of a feudal ruling class, saw the rise of a new class to the brink of political power, and thus launched what *must* have been a class war.

Since its introduction into the historiography of the English Civil War in a crude but splendidly forthright form in the middle 1930s, the Marxist interpretation has waged a spirited but not conspicuously successful battle with recalcitrant historical facts: for example, the fact, ruefully admitted by the quasi-Marxist R. H. Tawney, that although the Civil War may indeed be called a bourgeois revolution, it was unfortunately one in which the bourgeoisie fought on both sides.[9] In fact, Marxist thought on this matter has gone through three stages, all found in the writings of the dean of Marxist interpreters, Christopher Hill. At first it was claimed that the revolution was actually *led* by bourgeois elements; then that, although parliamentary as well as royalist leaders were admittedly drawn almost entirely from the landed classes, the *success* of the parliamentary cause was nevertheless due largely to bourgeois *support*—for example, to City money; and finally that, whatever part the bourgeoisie did or didn't play in it, the war's long-term *results*, at least—the permanent weakening of an over-regulating central government, for example—were clearly in bourgeois *interests*.[10] I am less concerned at the moment with the empirical adequacy of any of these stages of interpretation (or, for that matter, in what the third does to the Marxist idea of the primacy of economic over the political), than I am in the general nature of the Marxist approach by contrast with the others. The fundamental way in which, in all its versions, it differs from any of them is in being an attempt to apply to the English Civil War a systematic general theory of the historical process. As its opponents have often complained, its empirical difficulties are doubtless to a large extent due to that theory's having been derived originally from what went on, not in the seventeenth century, but in the nineteenth. Not that those opponents have generally denied the signal service performed by Marxist thought in drawing attention to causally relevant factors that earlier writers tended not to notice: for example, the way tax refusals by groups below the level of what then constituted the "political nation" aided Parliament in 1639; or the element of genuine class hostility that expressed itself in some of the mutinies in Charles's army during his campaigns against the Scots.[11] Recognizing the relevance of such facts, however, is considerably less than accepting the Marxist interpretation of the war.

The third interpretation, the social, is spelled out most magisterially by Lawrence Stone.[12] As on the Marxist view, there is a claim to find social as well as political revolution, a concern with deep structures when looking for causes, and a direct appeal to what is regarded as scientific knowledge of society. However, there is no strait jacket of a single general theory: the social sciences are simply "plundered" for relevant generalizations and bright ideas: or, as Stone himself puts it when responding to a critic who thought him too respectful of recent sociological theories of revolution, he simply "picks over the dump."[13] One of the generalities Stone claims to find useful is "relative deprivation theory": the idea that people become aggressive, not when absolutely deprived, but when reality falls short of their expectations—which he thinks was true of many "rising" gentry in England in the seventeenth century, who were seeking an outlet for their frustrations in parliamentary opposition to the court. Another is the concept of "multiple dysfunction": a way of saying that almost everything in a society is going wrong at once—which, again, he is prepared to say of Stuart England. In fact, as Stone's critics have sometimes pointed out, what he actually takes from the generalizing social sciences seems to provide little more than a perhaps fashionable verbal veneer for conclusions he is quite capable of reaching independently. What really distinguished his approach is not his use of social science, but his attempt, taking account of a wide range of heterogeneous considerations, and in deliberate reaction against what he calls "monocausal" economic determinism, to give something like a comprehensive social explanation of the events of the 1640s and their aftermath.

What Stone looks for is an accumulation of events occurring and conditions obtaining without which the Civil War or Revolution could hardly have happened, or at any rate, could hardly have happened as it did. Each is conceived as adding a degree of probability to the result, although perhaps not a strictly quantifiable one. The conditions seen as explanatory in fact reach back into the preceding

century, although scarcely further than to that disposal of seized monastic lands by Henry VIII which is held to have initiated crucial
long-term changes in the relative economic and, eventually, political
power of the Church, the Crown, and, most important, the gentry.
But Stone sees no inevitable process, only a cumulation of probabili-
ties, which continued right up through the reign of Charles I until
certain final events (to use his own language) "triggered" the revolution. The nearest thing to system in his account is an attempt to clas-
sify his causal factors into long-term *preconditions* which made the
outcome no more than possible, shorter-term *precipitants* (up to a
dozen years in length) which began to make it probable, and, finally,
triggers in the form of particular events or human decisions which
were decisive in the end.[14] I shall have something to say later about
these causal categories. Here I would simply point out how different
is such a cumulative and comprehensive account of the war's origins
from both the application of unitary theory offered by the Marxists
and the overall teleological sort favored by the Whigs. Stone's own
interpretation has been characterized as "teleological" by some historians—as, indeed, has the Marxist; but it is hard to see much justification for this. Of course, like all explanations of outcomes, both
look back from a chosen event or state of affairs to discover what led
up to it; but this clearly doesn't require its representation as something sought and achieved, or even as a goal toward which events
progressed. It is true that the Marxists, unlike Stone, make rather
free with the language of "progressive" and "reactionary"; but if
teleology implies purpose rather than simply predictability coupled
with increasing value, it is surely straining it to call their view "teleological."

The interpretation offered by the fourth group, the revisionists,
resembles that of the Whigs in calling for a stepwise narrative, in
placing emphasis on political affairs, and in taking great pains to determine the precise motivations, problems, and opportunities of the
various human agents involved. But it tells a very different story of
what happened. According to the revisionists—of whom Russell is
perhaps the most eminent[15]—the war was to a large extent an accidental one. It was neither inherent in long-term social and economic
trends converging in the 1640s, nor something that even entered people's heads as a real possibility until just months or even weeks before it occurred. Its causes are thus to be sought, it is claimed, in what
on Stone's interpretation are seen as mere triggers. One example is

Charles's rash involvement early in 1641 in an Army Plot, which had all the appearance of an unsuccessful attempt to overawe Parliament by force. Another is the Irish Rebellion later in that year, which created a sudden fresh need for an English army under conditions of anti–Roman Catholic hysteria and suspicion of the king's intentions which made it almost impossible for the Protestant gentry to accept even the traditional exercises of the royal prerogative in matters military. Revisionists sometimes refuse to look for causes even as close to the final outcome as the Scottish risings of 1638–39—this despite their having bankrupted the English treasury, made it clear that the government could not count on the militia, and confronted Charles with a demand for the summoning of the English Parliament that he could not refuse, all this ensuring at least the collapse of his personal government.

A recurring theme of the revisionists has been that most other interpretations make the fundamental historical mistake of "reading the past backwards"—that is, of projecting back upon earlier periods what was true only of later ones. Thus the Whigs are accused of being so determined to find an opposition movement that they project back into 1640–41, and even into the twenties and thirties, a hostility to the king on the parliamentary side which really existed by 1647 or 1648, after years of fighting and fruitless negotiations, but hardly before; or, on a grander scale, of interpreting shifting groups of MPs airing specific grievances, often in alliance with equally shifting groups at Court, as opposing political parties on the model of nineteenth-century politics. The social interpretation, to the extent that it points to a long economic and political decline of the aristocracy as a cause of the Civil War, itself seen as the work of a concomitantly rising gentry, is accused of reading back into a period when aristocratic manipulation was still the dominant fact of political life such later developments as the exclusion of peers from military command in 1644, or the abolition of the House of Lords after the execution of the king in 1649, developments that occurred under very different circumstances from those that existed before the war and that involved very different people. The Marxist interpretation, especially in its more dogmatic phase, is convicted rather more easily of projecting back upon the seventeenth century, not only an anachronistic bourgeoisie, but even a proletariat. Concern to clear away such errors sometimes makes it easier to say what the revisionists think the causes of the Civil War were not than to say precisely what they think they were. What comes through clearly, however, is their insistence that the answer to *why* the war broke out is to be sought in *how* it did. For a real understanding of what occurred, Russell avers, chronology is of the essence—as is a determination to "read history forwards." Whereas for Hexter narrative is required to show explanatory *continuity*—in particular, the "cumulative fury" of the parliamentary gentry as their relations with the early Stuarts ran their course[16]—for Russell it is needed to show *discontinuity*. In his view, little that happened in England in the first three decades of the seventeenth century, and even earlier, sheds much light on what happened in 1642.

What I have done so far is identify, characterize to some extent, and compare four interpretations of the Civil War and its origins which seem to me not only different in substance, but different in methodology in interesting ways. These, in turn, represent what occurred as an accepted consequence of the pursuit of a deliberate political and constitutional policy, as a necessary stage in the working out of an exorable economic and social mechanism, as the breakdown of a social and political structure due to heterogeneous but cumulating strains, and as an unwanted and unexpected result of a sudden political and military crisis. In the remainder of this essay I shall examine more closely a single issue that divides especially the third and fourth of these interpretations, although it is of some concern for the other two as well. This is the question of whether the war is to be seen as resulting from long-term or short-term causes. I shall begin by looking again at what Stone has to say about causes as preconditions, precipitants, and triggers, and then go on to consider the relevance to this problem of Russell's claim that coincidence, and even chance, in part caused the war.

Perhaps the first thing that strikes one about Stone's causal trichotomy is its appearance of arbitrariness, especially in its inclusion of the middle group called precipitants. Historians have long made use of a fairly serviceable distinction between immediate and underlying causes. This distinction, too, is somewhat vague; but at least it aligns itself with a rather clearer one between trends or movements, on the one hand, and actions or events, on the other. Stone attempts no such correspondence. The promulgation in 1630 of the Book of Orders, an administrative directive, he classifies as a precipitant, along with Laud's ecclesiastical policy, which lasted a decade. Elizabeth's attitude to the clergy he calls a precondition along with the doubling of the population during the century that preceded the war. The basis of the distinction is apparently just pairs of dates. Yet even then, items spill over from one category to another. For example, the reaction of Scotland to the imposition of the English prayer book in 1637 is called a trigger, which is natural enough since it initiated a fairly compact series of events leading to the calling of the Long Parliament. But triggers are not supposed to appear until 1640. The intrinsic nature of the factor thus, at times, overrides the chronological scheme.

Stone suggests, although only in passing, two ways in which his trichotomy might be thought to rest on something more than dates. The first is that while preconditions and precipitants can be compared and theorized about, and perhaps incorporated eventually into general theories of revolution, triggers cannot; they are too unpredictable, too variable, unique.[17] But the unpredictability of triggers would have no bearing on the question of whether, when they do occur, given certain other conditions, they were invariably followed by revolutions; and the sense in which their uniqueness is supposed to raise a problem for theory construction is also rather obscure. According to Stone, Elizabeth's attitude to the Puritans is a precondition, not a trigger; yet, *as described*, it is surely something unique (since there was only one Elizabeth and Puritans are a uniquely identifiable historical group). The queen's attitude can certainly be generalized about in various ways: for example, it can be described as a temporizing policy on the part of a sovereign. But so can an alleged trigger like the Irish Rebellion, which has *in fact* been related to an embryo theory of revolution by H. G. Koenigsberger as a revolt in an outlying subordinate kingdom—apparently a recurring phenomenon in civil wars of the seventeenth century.[18]

The second way in which Stone may seem to give a more than chronological status to his three causal categories is his reiterated claim that preconditions merely make a result possible, precipitants make it probable, and triggers make it inevitable. But the way this fails to work is even more serious for any claim that his scheme has general application. For a long-term condition can surely render a civil war probable, not just possible. Indeed, it seems plausible to say that in the period before the Tudors, the structural relations of Crown and magnates, in which the threat of "overmighty subjects" was endemic, made civil wars probable at almost any time. Certainly they didn't fail to occur. Nor is it clear why triggers must make a result inevitable. Stone doesn't mean that they do this individually; all that any of them do in themselves (with the possible exception of the last) is provide further increments of probability. On the other hand, to say that they render the result inevitable when taken together with all the other relevant conditions would not distinguish them from what falls into the other two categories.

Associated with Stone's division of causes into three main categories are two claims that seem even more questionable. These relate to how causes are to be weighted: how we are to judge which are the more important ones. Stone begins by conceding that historians can only weight causes "intuitively," at any rate "in the last resort."[19] But he goes on to argue that this embarrassment can be reduced by recognizing that it is in any case impossible in principle to contrast the weights of causes falling into the different categories of preconditions, precipitants, and triggers. To cite one of his examples: the untrustworthiness of Charles (a precipitant) cannot intelligibly be said to have been a more or less important cause of the war than the rise of Puritanism (a precondition).

I cannot pretend to be able to settle the general problem of whether historians possess reasonably coherent criteria for judging the relative importance of causes. But I should like at least to question Stone's contention that it is any more dubious to weight causes *across* his categories than it is *within* them. To begin with, the only reason he gives for holding this view is that the three sorts of causes do not coincide in time—as if first the preconditions do their work, and then, successively, the precipitants and the triggers.[20] But this is surely misleading. The three groups of causes must overlap in time if they are to be conceived as, in the end, jointly bringing about the result. If the doubling of the population was really a condition necessary for the war's occurrence (it supposedly became an influence because, among other things, it made parliamentary seats more competitive, and thus MPs more responsive to county opinion, which was often anticourt), then when Charles furnished triggers by actions that enraged the House of Commons in 1641–42, the doubled population must still have been a causal factor. We trace its development back over a stretch of time only because such a factor *takes* a certain time to obtain. Only if the three groups of causes were seen as parts of a process in which the earlier produced the later could they be thought not to overlap in time—a view into which Stone occasionally falls, as when he describes Charles's decision in 1629 to embark on a policy of "law and order" in church and state as "no more than one step in a long anterior chain, an almost Pavlovian response to previous aggressions by the Parliamentary opposition," the "ultimate causes" of which lie in the previous century.[21] If this is to be Stone's model, however, his precipitants and triggers will lose the status of independently necessary conditions for the final result; and the notion of their contributing to a gradually increasing probability will itself be undermined.

In fact, except when he formally sets out his three groups of causes—in which case, oddly enough, apart from distinguishing "salient" from "secondary," he does little weighting even *within* the categories—Stone invariably judges various factors to be more or less important without specifying whether he means *as* a precondition, *as* a precipitant, or *as* a trigger. For example, he just says, without qualification (as would most historians), that the "basic cause" of substantial opposition to the king in the House of Lords was "dislike of Charles' religious and political objectives"; or that what "largely" caused the defeat of the English in the Scottish wars was "the unwillingness of the English troops and their leaders to fight."[22] What in this unlabeled way he selects as "most important" causes are, in fact, seldom events, and are usually conditions of some duration. And this, despite his own warnings against weighting across the categories, suggests an implicit theory that longer-term causes are in general more important than shorter-term ones—a way in which he has often, in fact, been read.

With a view to resisting such a theory, let me juggle a little with two causal factors which not only Stone but most historians now writing about the Civil War would recognize as such. These are, on the one hand, the relatively long-term difficulties of the English Crown in raising money, and on the other, the sudden exhaustion of the royal treasury by the wars against the Scots. Both, I will assume, are necessary conditions of the collapse of the English government at the end of the thirties. Had the king had more substantial sources of revenue, he might have survived the sudden crisis; had he avoided conflict with the Scots, he might also have survived it (or so a number of historians have argued). Now suppose it is accepted that the Crown's financial difficulties, although certainly not negligible, were such that any reasonably efficient seventeenth-century government ought to have been able to cope with: that with normal prudence, the king could still have "lived of his own," and that it took an extraordinarily foolish monarch, involving himself in entirely unnecessary wars, to turn a problem into a catastrophe. It seems to me that in this case—which is fairly close to the way Charles's own situation has actually been regarded by many historians—it would be natural to regard the king's own actions as a more important cause of the break-down than his long-term financial problem. It would be quite the con-trary, however, if those problems were judged to be so overwhelming that it would have taken something like a royal prodigy to ride them out.

What this points to is at least the beginnings of a theory of *prin-cipled* judgment with regard to the relative importance of causes, a theory (and not an unfamiliar one) that would relate causal impor-tance to the degree of abnormality of the factors involved. Given such a theory, however, there would be no reason for expecting long-term causes to be *in general* more important than short-term ones; every situation would have to be examined individually. Not that I would regard this weighting principle as one that historians always do, or even always ought to apply; in fact, a kind of case for which it seems inappropriate immediately springs to mind. Take, for exam-ple, Margaret Judson's contention that before the first session of the Long Parliament was well under way, distrust of Charles had become "the single most important factor" influencing the actions of the par-liamentary leaders.[23] The issue here seems simply to be what con-sideration was uppermost in those leaders' minds—what was their most important reason for acting—which is something to be deter-mined by motive analysis of a sort that historians have long prac-ticed. Hexter talks in this connection of discovering the agents' "priorities"—for example, by searching parliamentary agendas for evidence of the relative strengths of MPs' disaffections.[24] Neither in the case of Charles's financial imprudence, however, nor in that of the parliamentary leaders' distrust, would the historian, as Stone would have it, simply "intuit" the relative importance of causes.

When one turns to the revisionists, it is easy to get the impres-sion that an assumption is at work that is the precise opposite of the one I have been tempted to attribute to Stone, namely, that it is short-term causes, especially triggers, that are generally the more im-portant ones. In fact, as was noted earlier, most revisionists go on to deny that, in the case of the English Civil War, at least, there were any long-term causes at all.[25] They seem sometimes to concede that if a genuine revolution had occurred, especially one going beyond mere political and constitutional change, long-term causes could be assumed—causes involving changes of social and economic structure of the sort that Stone and the Marxists claim to find. But a mere rebellion against a particular king—which is what the revisionists, echoing Clarendon, hold the Civil War to have been—would, according to them, need only short-term causes. One should at any rate applaud here one of the most salutary emphases of the revisionists: their insistence that causes not be sought for things that never happened, or never happened as envisaged.[26] The question "What really happened?" is clearly prior to the question "What were its causes?" But is it correct to say that a mere rebellion against a particular king would require only short-term causes?

Revisionists sometimes link their rejection of long-term causes with their contention, already mentioned, that the war was *unintended*. The crux of their argument here is the denial that there existed any concerted opposition to the king either in Parliament or in the country before the late thirties, their opponents' penchant for "reading history backwards" thus having led to a causal mistake. Behind this strategy of argument lies a recognition of a philosophical principle of importance, namely, that people are properly said to cause things when, with a view to attaining a certain end, they act in such a way as to furnish the conditions necessary for that end's coming into being. Of course, they can never accomplish their ends without certain "enabling conditions" which may lie in varying degrees beyond their control. For example, if I am to cause further controversy about the Civil War by writing this essay, there will have to be on the part of readers a capacity to understand what I am saying. But if the controversy I aim at does follow, their understanding me will hardly be called the cause of it.

The conception of a cause as what has intended consequences has, I think, played a considerable role in most causal investigations of wars by historians. For example, it has been at the center of some recent disagreements over the causes of the Second World War, the problem centering upon different reconstructions of the intentions of Hitler, those who, like A. J. P. Taylor, wish to downplay the latter's contribution to bringing on the war feeling obliged to argue that war was far from Hitler's intentions, a situation simply having got out of hand.[27] In the historiography of the English Civil War, the same principle seems to lie behind the emphasis placed by Stone on the aspirations of the Levellers, as if revolutions have to be brought about by revolutionaries,[28] or Hill's taking the trouble to assure us that the bourgeoisie were "much less confused" about what they were doing than non-Marxists often suppose[29]—even though, for him, their causal role may only be that of a stand-in for economic forces. It seems to be appealed to implicitly even in the perhaps half playful speculation of Geoffrey Elton that, since as late as December 1641 the king was the only one actually considering fighting, some historian ought to take seriously the hypothesis that Charles caused the war himself.[30] From the standpoint of revisionist apologetic, the trouble with this general line of argument is that it is fully effective only against the interpretation offered by the Whigs, and perhaps only against a highly conspiratorial version of Whiggism at that. The degree to which the war, or even a serious confrontation, was unintended, almost to the end, has little bearing upon the acceptability of the social interpretation as such, or even that of Marxists in its more refined versions. It is not surprising that some of the reviewers of Russell's most recent book have pointed this out.

But the revisionists have another line of argument: that the transition to actual warfare from the relative tranquility of Stuart England up to about 1637 (which their opponents, of course, accuse them of exaggerating), or even from the period of determined parliamentary reform that began late in 1640, required such a series of untoward events, extraordinary decisions, and unforeseeable coincidences that longer-term factors, however much part of the total situation and in various ways relevant to what ensued, can hardly be said actually to have caused it. What this comes to is the judgment that what some would call the immediate causes were in this case of such a nature as drastically to reduce the claim of longer-term conditions to be considered causes at all. It seems to me that this, once again, expresses a philosophical insight—or, at any rate, acknowledges a deeply entrenched feature of the causal concept we all normally employ and expect historians to employ—namely, that the search for causes ought not to go back to the Creation: that causal accounts have *natural beginnings* as well as *prescribed endings;* or, perhaps better, that causal processes have *points of origin* as well as *ultimate results.* One aspect of any attempt to interpret a historical event in terms of its causes is thus to determine an appropriate point of origin. And the fact that, when historians offer causal accounts, this is one of the things they think worth arguing about suggests that *criteria* are involved, if perhaps not very precise ones.

Not only philosophers, but also historians, have sometimes denied that there are such criteria. Charles Beard, for example, maintained that once a causal investigation in history begins, there can
never be any reason, except sheer exhaustion, for giving up the
search for causes behind causes.[31] In fact, what might be called the
intrusiveness of certain events or conditions, meaning their extreme
abnormality or their consisting of deliberate and relatively unpredictable interventions by strategically placed human agents, is generally regarded as providing such a reason.[32] Even Stone, in making
the case for some of his long-term causes, in effect acknowledges this
principle—for example, in regarding the highly intrusive actions of a
particular king, Henry VIII, as an appropriate point of origin for
those economic and social developments which he takes to be causes
of the Civil War. Russell and most other revisionists are more sensitive to the intrusiveness of events and actions closer to the final outcome; and on the principle of tracing back *to*, but not *through*, such
events, regard them as points of causal origin. A good example is the
emphasis placed by Russell on what he considers Charles's quite arbitrary, and certainly imprudent, decision in the late twenties—a
"feat of incompetence,"[33] in his view, and quite the opposite of a
"Pavlovian response"—to back the Arminians against the Calvinists
in the English Church, thereby driving into increasing hostility to the
government a Puritan movement that was not inherently antagonistic
to authority. This, of course, falls within Stone's allotted time for
precipitants; but it is a relatively short-term cause, and it is selected
for what it begins.

Russell describes Charles's preference for the Arminians as a
crucial "coincidence";[34] and both he and other revisionists also talk
of finding a place for *chance* in their accounts of the origins of the
Civil War. This may raise some hackles; but it should raise fewer if
it is remembered what chance commonly means in historical studies.
As Nagel and others have pointed out,[35] it has little to do with predictability in principle, or with indeterminism as philosophers normally conceive it. The death early in 1641 of the earl of Bedford, a
reform leader whom some historians have considered a possible architect of a compromise solution, is a good example of what revisionists have seen as an element of chance at work in the final stages
of the drift toward war. That doesn't mean that they think Bedford's
death had no determining conditions. It means rather that they regard those conditions, being physiological, as lying beyond the his-

torian's purview, so that the event remains unpredictable from what the historian considers his normal subject matter. One might say that, lacking *historical* causes, it is, from the historian's standpoint, *as good as undetermined*. There are similar, although not identical reasons for Russell's regarding the timing of the Irish Rebellion as a matter of chance. This event occurred just at the point when, the invading Scots having gone home, and the reforming aims of the Long Parliament having been largely achieved, the parliamentary leaders were in the dangerous positions of lacking both allies and popular issues. Panic about an impending "popish" invasion played an essential part in the final crisis. Of course, the Irish Rebellion, unlike Bedford's death, did have historical causes; but they were located outside the mainstream of English history—and revisionists stress their "externality." From the standpoint of a person tracing English political and constitutional developments, they, too, therefore (although in a weaker sense), were *as good as undetermined*. Chance events or coincidences, so conceived, will naturally be judged disruptive. They are therefore especially open to selection as points of causal origin.

Besides insisting on chance, revisionists generally deny in explicit terms the *inevitability* of the war—which they consider all other interpretations to be committed to in one way or another. In fact, only the Marxist account seems to me clearly open to this charge; and even it may assert no more than that a change of ruling class, not an actual war, was inevitable, given the supposed rise of the bourgeoisie during the Tudor period. If the Whig view implies inevitability, it can surely be only in what I called its *Hegelian* version, which, by locating the drive toward liberty in institutions rather than in people, makes it somewhat easier to talk of inevitable progress. Inevitability would not, at any rate, be entailed by the retrospective discovery that a movement toward political confrontation, and perhaps war, was in fact constituted by the actions of a series of agents choosing to defend their "liberties" and prepared to accept the consequences. It is true that middle-position Whigs sometimes talk metaphorically about king and Parliament having been on a "collision course." But this presumably means no more than that *if* neither changed their policies, then civil war, or something like it, was almost sure to follow.

Stone's interpretation has sometimes been thought to commit itself to inevitability simply because of its preoccupation with long-term causes.[36] If there were such causes, it has been argued, the result

must have been determined from the moment they came into existence. But as was noted, Stone's view of long-term causes is only that
they make a certain result possible, or at most, probable; their existence is not supposed to imply that there was a set of conditions sufficient for that result before the triggers supervened. Stone himself,
at one point, observed that a revolution is *never* inevitable—adding
somewhat paradoxically, "the only evidence of its inevitability is that
it actually happens."[37] Oddly enough, it is Russell, the revisionist,
who is found saying at least that, from a certain point on, the war
could hardly have been *avoided*.[38] That point, according to him, was
the king's departure from London early in 1642 after his unsuccessful
attempt to arrest John Pym and other parliamentary leaders, about
seven months before the actual fighting began.

If any thesis that the war was truly inevitable is to be of enough
interest to be blazoned forth, it would need to indicate, as Russell's
judgment does, the point at which inevitability is supposed to set in;
and the point indicated would need to be at some appreciable interval
before the war's outbreak—which is not true of the one Russell mentions. What would be interesting would be a claim, say, that civil
war or revolution became inevitable once Henry VIII distributed
monastic lands, given the certainty that the gentry would be the principal beneficiaries; or once James I ascended the throne, given his
own character and the constitutional legacy of Elizabeth; or once his
son Charles opted for the Arminians, given the expectations of the
Puritans. The cited conditions could, in each case, be thought of as
completing a set of coexisting conditions, some perhaps left unmen-
tioned, which would eventually bring about the result deemed inevitable. But if still further conditions, *later in time,* are allowed also to
have been necessary for that result (certain triggers, perhaps), clearly
no judgment of inevitability would be justifiable unless those conditions (as is the case on one interpretation of Stone's position) were
themselves thought to follow necessarily from conditions already obtaining at the point of inevitability. The danger, of course, is that, because historians have the advantage of hindsight, the inevitability of
a certain result will be asserted, assuming that later events which are
known to have happened were *going* to happen. It may thus be sus-
pected—and certainly Russell suspects[39]—that when Whigs come at
least close to deriving inevitability from king and Parliament having
been on a "collision course," hindsight has not in fact been excluded.

Russell's chief prescription for avoiding what he considers the

illusion of inevitability is "reading history forwards." By this he
seems to mean giving an account of it from the standpoints of the
original agents, in the sense both of excluding at every stage what
those agents did not themselves know, and of conceiving what was
happening as it was conceived by the agents themselves. And as far
as what is at issue is understanding the reasons for which various
agents acted, such exclusion both of foreknowledge and of the historian's own interpretive concepts is doubtless correct. When it comes
to understanding why the Long Parliament demanded the death of
Strafford, or why John Hampden and others refused to pay ship
money, what matters is how *they* saw their situation, not how the
historian does.

For purposes of causal analysis, however, while the exclusion of
foreknowledge still holds, the demand that we adopt the agent's own
interpretation of what was happening surely doesn't. To revert to
that favorite issue of the revisionists, the question whether there was
an opposition movement among the parliamentary gentry in the
twenties and thirties (a prima facie cause of the Civil War if it existed) is not settled by the much emphasized fact—and it seems to
have been a fact—that no contemporary MP would have admitted to
participating in such a movement so characterized, or even genuinely
saw himself as participating in one—the idea of opposing "the king's
government" (according to the revisionists at least) being beyond the
mental horizons of early Stuart Englishmen. The activities of MPs
may have *constituted* an opposition movement whether or not they
were so conceived at the time; and, as such, they may have been
likely to lead to war as their implications became clearer—for example, as attacks only on the king's "evil counsellors" were gradually
replaced by a recognition that the problem was the king himself. This
is not to say, revisionists' protests notwithstanding, that, for purposes of causal analysis if not for that of the explanation of actions
by agents' reasons, historians may indulge in the historical sin of
anachronism: the reading back into the past of what was not in fact
there. It is rather to say that, in seeking correctly to characterize what
was there, they may apply concepts that the original agents would
have rejected, and perhaps (as in cases like "bourgeois revolution"
or "inflation") would not even have understood.

For still other purposes—for example, that of making clear the
historical significance of what was happening—even knowledge of
what was *going* to happen cannot be excluded; for without it, his-

torians would be prevented from saying even that in 1642 the Civil War at last broke out, or that in November 1640 the Long Parliament assembled for the first time.[40] Thus although "reading history backwards" certainly has its hazards, revisionists cannot, without qualifications, label it as a historical sin. Nor can they count on reading it "forwards" to conjure away inevitability.[41]

.....

On Dray's "Conflicting Interpretations in History: The Case of the English Civil War"

Rex Martin

.....

An account of the disagreement of historians about causes, not causation in general but, rather, the causes of a particular occurrence, is a subject that belongs in the general domain of hermeneutics. An account will have significance in that domain only if it offers a coherent and cogent interpretation of the disagreement. William Dray's essay is an attempt to provide such an account with respect to historians' disagreements about the origins of the English Civil War, a complex event in the decade of the 1640s.[1]

In the present essay, while providing a resumé of Dray's presentation, I want to identify what I take to be the main lines of his interpretation of the disagreement. Then I will generalize this interpretation somewhat by indicating the sort of causal structure or form of thinking that it embodies. Finally, I will suggest an overall assessment of Dray's account.

Dray identifies four main historical stances toward the origins of the war: the Whig, the Marxist, the social, and the revisionist. Each deserves at least a word.

The variant of the Whig approach that he emphasizes is the one associated with the work of J. H. Hexter. On this view, the origins of the war are tied in with attitudes, specifically with those that affirm the importance of maintaining certain prerogatives or powers of the House of Commons and of maintaining liberties, both political and personal, of subjects, that is, of Englishmen taken individually. There was no conspiracy, no deliberate policy to advance these aims at the cost of war (or, perhaps, through war) but there was a firm commitment to them on the part of many politically active people. Because they had similar or overlapping aims, these people were able to make joint enterprise in furthering their goals. The Commons' cause was a common cause. And this cooperative prosecution of mutual aims surely counts as one of the main contributing causes of the war.

The Marxist approach, like the Whig approach, has a distinguished nineteenth-century pedigree. Indeed, it is closely tied in not only with Karl Marx's general materialist theory of history, what with its doctrines of politics as class struggle and of the emergence of bourgeois society out of feudal society, but also with his designation of the English Civil War as the first bourgeois revolution. It would be an interesting thought experiment to ask whether this particular interpretation of the English Civil War, as a bourgeois revolution, would have purchase even if Marxism had never developed in nineteenth- and twentieth-century Europe. Suppose that the main lines of the subsequent development of Hegel's philosophy had emphasized, not his doctrine of civil society, but his conception of the state and that, accordingly, his political side (in particular his emphasis on civil rights) had been brought to the fore. Suppose, in sum, that T. H. Green had been as powerful a thinker as Marx and that his theories had become ascendant to the same degree Marx's have, but in a situation in which there were—in counterpoint to Greenism—virtually no Marxism. (Marx, we could imagine, for reasons of historical circumstance only slightly different from those that actually obtained, had remained in Germany as a relatively obscure left-Hegelian critic of Christian theology and German political arrangements.) There would still be available, we might note—in such places as the writings of James Harrington[2]—important sources of an economic interpretation of political revolutions whereby one social class gained dominance, by virtue of its economic leverage, at the expense of a previously dominant class. Still, it is not likely that the question whether the English Civil War was a bourgeois revolution, let alone the *first* such revolution, would be addressed with such insistence, as it has been by Christopher Hill, C. B. Macpherson,[3] and others, if there had been no disposition to that conclusion in a well-formed general social theory. (Here I agree with Dray.)

Dray, without delineating Marx's own role in the case at hand, identifies three stages that Marxist historiography has gone through in twentieth-century Britain respecting the Civil War. But it is worth noting that only two of these concern the *origins* of the conflict. The third and most recent stage concerns, rather, the *results* of the conflict, specifically, that the "interests" of the bourgeois class were served by the "war's long-term results." The significance of this shift, from origins to results, is easily missed. I would like to fix attention here by suggesting that it is a mistake to *identify* what Marx called a revolution with such things as armed struggle or civil war. Armed struggle—meaning a sequence of such things as barricade incidents, pitched battles, and a Yorktown ending—is only a part, a phase, of a Marxist social revolution (as Dray notes). It is not odd, then, to identify the bourgeois revolution in England with a sequence having the Civil War as *one* of its members and, as further members, such events as the Glorious Revolution, the Bill of Rights of 1689, and the Act of Settlement of 1701. All these contribute to the progressive embourgeoisification of English political life (at least as seen from the perspective of the present century and of the nineteenth). This revolution is datable, but its dates are not confined to the 1640s. What is odd, though, is the implicit claim that *after* the Civil War was over the bourgeois class was politically dominant in England (just as the proletariat class is going to be, it is said, after the next phase—the phase of socialist revolution—is initiated). The Marxist interpretation would seem to stand or fall with the validity of this particular claim in the case of the English Civil War and its political aftermath (during the remainder of the seventeenth century).[4]

The social interpretation, especially in the hands of its leading practitioner, Lawrence Stone, attempts to take "account of a wide range of heterogeneous considerations," including some long-term but mounting social changes, that together suggest "a comprehensive . . . explanation of the events of the 1640s and their aftermath" (says Dray). Among these social changes are such trends as the one(s) initiated by Henry VIII's "disposal of seized monastic lands." Other examples of significant social trends would be "the doubling of the population during the century that preceded the war" and the "rise of Puritanism."

Stone proposes a complicated schema for organizing these heterogeneous considerations into three classes: (1) long-term preconditions, (2) shorter-term precipitants, and (3) particular events or human decisions near in time to the main event(s) under study. The schema defines a chronological sequence: thus, long-term preconditions begin before the other considerations and last—or continue to have effect—throughout the sequence; the shorter-term precipitants (which can last as long as a dozen years) begin later and are not necessarily continuing at the time of the outbreak; the "triggers" are events that occur when these other tides are flowing or have flowed, with cumulative effect, and set off, or help set off, the outbreak of the war. As triggers they must be relatively close in time to that outbreak, say 1640 or thereafter and no earlier than 1637.

Dray criticizes this particular schema, I think, quite effectively. I do, though, doubt one of the arguments he conducts.[5]

However, Stone's main point could be put more simply, as Dray notes. The point is: some factors are more important, some less. And in general, the longer-term factors (most of them cumulative and continuing social trends) are among the more important. I presume this means that if these factors were varied significantly then there would have been no event like the English Civil War. But the "precipitants" or the "triggers" could be varied considerably (some even omitted) without affecting the larger event in the gross. When we say this latter thing do we mean that *all* the precipitants and triggers could be altered (suppose all of them omitted, for example) without significantly altering the war—its outbreak and its general course? Surely not. And do we mean, in talking of the longer-term factors, that no *one* of them could be altered, even though the others stayed the same, without significantly altering the war? An answer here is not self-evident. What if Henry's "disposal of seized monastic lands" had occurred in a Buddhist context rather than a Christian one? It is not wholly clear what will count as a *significant* alteration. Nonetheless, it is clear that the sheer omission of any such long-term factor would appear to go too far. The long-term social trends have the status of important necessary conditions; they constitute a necessary framework for the occurrence of the war, under the characterization that it has.

The issue is not whether these important necessary conditions *as a set* have greater weight than the *set* of "precipitants" and "triggers" (after it is allowed that factors in this latter set are individually alterable and that no one of them is sufficient, as described). For put this way, it is not obvious that the issue could even be joined. It is, perhaps, best to say, then, that all the factors conjointly made the occurrence of the event (under the description it bears) highly probable and that, among the factors, all the long-term ones, certainly the social trends, are weighty and none omittable and that some of the "precipitants" and "triggers" are also weighty. Which ones? The ones that are necessary to the event. If the event itself—its occurrence or general course—would be significantly altered by a significant alteration, or the omission, of one of these factors then that factor is necessary. What about the *other* "precipitants" and "triggers," the ones that are not *necessary* to the event? They are included if their presence in sum with the other factors increases the probability of the occurrence of that focal event.

The tone of Stone's analysis is to give preponderance to the *necessary* factors in the overall causal mix and this tends to favor the long-term factors, especially the social trends, for all of these are, under the descriptions they have, clearly necessary to the event. It is this point that the revisionists dispute: their position seems to be, according to Dray, that "it is generally short-term causes, especially triggers, that are the most important ones." Indeed, their position could be rendered as the flat denial that there are any long-term causes of the English Civil War at all. And this denial would range them against Stone and the Marxists and, perhaps, the Whigs as well.

The main claim of the revisionists, put positively now, is that the war "was to a large extent an accidental one." They tend, echoing Clarendon, says Dray, to identify the Civil War as "a mere rebellion against a particular king." Since they are inclined to characterize the war as an armed outbreak and not as a social revolution, and since they are seeking the origins of this narrower event, a closely datable one, they can trace the origins of this event to proximate triggers. As Dray says, "What comes through clearly . . . is their insistence that the answer to *why* the war broke out is to be sought in *how* it did."

Behind this rather bland facade lies a point of considerable methodological importance. An event, even a complex event like the English Civil War of the 1640s, can be explained only under some particular description. That is, to be explained it must be characterized—interpreted, understood—in some definite way.[6] Once it is described, that description will affect, will control to some extent, what can be said in the way of explanation of that event. For example, no event can be explained in the form "*A* because *A*." For here *A* is simply not explained. So if an event is described as *A* then it cannot also be explained essentially using *A*. But a more important point to note is that the characterization of the event to be explained suggests the level, and sets constraints, for what is going to count as the explanation.[7] What is true of explanations here is also true of causal accounts. No event can be *said* to be caused except under a description. And that description affects, controls, what is going to be counted as the cause of the event in question. For example, no event can be caused in the form "*E* is caused by *E*." For there is no cause of *E* stated here. And, again, the way in which an event is characterized suggests the level, and sets constraints, for what is going to be said as to its causal origins.[8]

Thus, a man might react to a nasty comment by throwing a punch, or a drink; the nasty comment is said to trigger the event and would be, colloquially, regarded as its cause. But if we described the event in question differently we might seek for different origins. If we wanted to explain the jumpiness of the aggrieved man, or his bad mood, we might go to his job, his sex life, or his insomnia. If it wasn't the nasty comment that put him in a bad mood, then it could hardly be described as the cause of that bad mood. By the same token, if he threw the punch because he was in a mood to do so, then the nasty remark seems no more than an occasion, a catalyst. Again, if we wanted to say what caused the man's explosive reaction to Jake, throwing the drink at *him*, we might go to his hostility to Jake in particular, as the cause, or to his hostility to Notre Dame alumni, at least male ones, in general. The same remark, then, by Lisa (a University of Kansas graduate) would have brought no more than a wince or a snarl; so it wasn't the remark as such that caused the incident.

Dray notes the importance of what has been sketched here when he says, "The question 'What really happened?' is clearly prior to the question 'What were its causes?'" But he does not, I think, sufficiently emphasize that the way in which an event is characterized—interpreted—internally affects any causal account that can be given of it. It is not merely a question of what is so but, more profoundly, of how what is so is described.

Thus, one important differentiating principle that distinguishes the various causal interpretations is the different ways in which they initially characterize the Civil War itself. Causal accounts will necessarily differ if one *characterizes* the war as one stage in a sequence of bourgeois revolution—characterizes the war, that is, by reference to this long-term result—as distinct from, say, characterizing it as part of a long-range joint enterprise designed to maintain parliamentary prerogatives and the liberties of subjects. The revisionist characterizes the war as a kind of military action, as a particular and localized rebellion against a particular king. We should expect his account of

causal origins to reflect this characterization and to differ from accounts that characterize that war in ways significantly different from
this.

The program of the revisionist has three foundations. One is the
restriction of the event they want explained, which is captured in the
restrained description of it as a particular rebellion, an outbreak of
armed struggle, against a particular king. The second is the interesting contention that, insofar as this outbreak can be correctly characterized as a war with a definite long-term outcome or as a revolution
(characterizations that are themselves debatable), the outbreak *so
characterized* was *unintended*. Hence the Whig interpretation is especially vulnerable.

The relevant reasoning goes roughly as follows: people, acting
individually or jointly, are properly said to be causes only when, with
a view to a certain end or outcome, they act so as to bring about this
end or, at least, so as to "furnish the conditions necessary for the
coming into being of that end." In sum, the conception of agent
causation here advanced sees the action as being undertaken as a
means, direct or indirect, to an intended end. What the Whig and
the revisionist have in common is this conception of agent causation,
as the preferred *form* for explanations. Where they differ is on the
facts. Each would agree, though, that *if* the agents had no such ends
in view, no such intentions as are ascribed by, say, the Whigs, then
clearly their actions—as means—could not be traced to such ends. We
would have to look elsewhere than to a structure of well-defined
political grievances and a program either of taking over from the king
or of advancing the liberties of Parliament as a body and of subjects
individually.

The third and final ground of revisionist historiography is the
concept of *chance*. Dray addresses this point in a somewhat round-
about way. He adduces two principles: (1) "the search for causes
ought not to go back to the Creation" and should stop at a well-
determined point of origin for any given cause; (2) the determination
of such a point is made, at least in part, by reference to *criteria*,
albeit not very precise ones. One criterion that Dray mentions, for
instance, is the "intrusiveness" of certain events or conditions. So we
reach the notion of a finite causal sequence, which has a determinate
beginning in time. Such a view of causal sequences, as finite and determinate, represents the normal revisionist outlook. Now, these sequences as finite are relatively independent of one another. Nonethe-

less, two of them can coincide or cross at some given point. Such a crossing is called "chance" or "accident." The claim here is not that the normal end events in each sequence are undetermined; it is, rather, that the coincidence of the two sequences, or their coincidence at that time, is undetermined in either sequence. Thus, the death early in 1641 of the earl of Bedford, a potential architect of compromise between king and Parliament, coincided with unsettling political events. It is this very coincidence, or its timing, that is undetermined, but not the happening of the events themselves.

This emphasis on chance or coincidence, on the importance attached to intersecting finite causal sequences, which are otherwise independent, also explains the revisionists' hostility to generalized talk of inevitability or large-scale determinism. If one is to talk of inevitability (recall the description of the American Civil War as the Irrepressible Conflict),[9] he must find and precisely identify a point from which, or after which, the occurrence of the focal event is said to be inevitable. Dray does not, by the way, regard contentions of inevitability as interesting ones if the point selected is in time too close to the event in question. Interesting claims, about the English Civil War, for example, must select a point "at some appreciable interval before the war's outbreak"—say the distribution of monastic lands by Henry VIII.

Let us turn now from the details of Dray's account to a sketching-out of some of its general, structural features. We might begin by noting, though the matter is not entirely clear, that Dray inclines on the whole to favor the revisionist perspective. Let us grant next, for the sake of argument, that the revisionist approach can be suitably generalized to cover a fairly wide range of historical events and problems. (It appears less likely that the revisionist approach could be generalized than it does that the other three—the Whig, the Marxist, and the social—could be; nonetheless, I think the exercise a profitable one.) The question is, would Dray tend to support this *generalized* revisionist stance or not? I would suggest, on the strength of things he says in his essay, that he would. Here I have in mind the several causal paradigms that he identifies, explicitly discusses, and seemingly endorses, as he goes along.

I have already mentioned two of these: first, the conception—or explanation *form*—that I have called agent or intentionalistic causation; second, the favorable emphasis given by Dray to the notion of finite and independent causal chains. These two views together, by the way, tend to define the *generalized* revisionist stance and, if insisted on, would serve to distinguish that stance from the generalized versions of the other three—the Whig, the Marxist, and the social.

The other causal paradigms introduced by Dray have roughly the same character: they tend to support the revisionist stance especially. The most notable of these paradigms is introduced by Dray as "at least the beginnings of a theory of *principled* judgment with regard to the relative importance of causes"; it is the theory "that would relate causal importance to the degree of abnormality of the factors involved."[10] Some of Dray's other descriptions of causal force follow this lead. We find him speaking of the "intrusiveness" of certain events or conditions, of their character as abnormal or as "unpredictable interventions";[11] it is this feature that guides us in identifying something as a *significant* cause or in determining the significant beginning point of a finite causal sequence. At a later point, where Dray is discussing chance events or coincidences, he tells us that these are, or naturally appear, "disruptive." Thus, coincidences are "especially open to selection as points of causal origin." Why? Because they are disruptive, intrusive, in a word "abnormal."

It should be stressed that Dray's theory here speaks to the questions, How do we weight a cause or determine it to be significant? and How do we determine beginning points of causal sequences? But we should note that weighting causes, as to significance, or determining a point of origin for a given causal chain presupposes that causes are independently identifiable, presupposes that a characterization of the cause is antecedently available or, at least, that it is logically distinct from the weighting of significance or the determining of a point of origin.

On this interpretation Dravian abnormalism is not a theory of causes but of causal *importance* or, alternately, of the important beginning point of a causal sequence. And I am suggesting that Dray subscribes to this theory of causal *importance*. But what theory of causes, if any, does Dray subscribe to?[12]

We have already noted that he seems to favor the notion of finite causal sequences. But one can hold to the idea of finite sequences without any commitment to the kind(s) of cause that might be involved. The notion of finite sequence suggests merely that causes, whatever they are, don't go backwards forever, in the way that a Baptist sermon in Georgia might take us back to the New Testament and, if we don't watch out, back to the Fall of our original parents and even to the Creation itself.[13] But are there any *kinds* of causes that Dray seems inclined to favor in principle, as it were? Any kinds that he would identify as specially suited to be causes in history?

I would suggest that here the other paradigm mentioned earlier comes into play. I refer to the conception of agent causation, of intentionalistic action. In this paradigm, action is seen as a means, direct or indirect, to the realizing of an intended end, or is seen as part of achieving some such end. I want to claim that this is Dray's preferred paradigm.[14]

One qualification is, perhaps, in order; for we are required to put this paradigm into what might be called a revisionist harness. For the paradigm must be consistent with the occurrence of *unintended* consequences, with coincidences (as we have seen), and so on. The combination of the paradigm of agent causation with that of finite causal chains, a combination that largely defines what we have called the "generalized" revisionist stance, seems especially suited to achieve, precisely, this desired consistency. And I take Dray's discussion at the end of his essay to indicate the importance he attaches to the notion of unintended consequences.

In general, the reasons paradigm in harness with that of finite causal sequences can handle the fact of unintended consequences, that is, consequences that the agent did not foresee—or, if he did, did not intend. Such consequences, nonetheless, can be admitted as effects of the agent's doing what he did intend. Always, though, such unintended effects are secondary in that if the agent had never done what he did intentionally, or tried to do, he would never have brought about what he did bring about, unintentionally, as an effect of what he did intentionally.

The thing brought about—whether intentionally or unintentionally—can itself be a starting point for the original agent's or another agent's intentional response. For example, a medieval siege captain might have the decaying carcass of an animal tossed over the wall into a city or a fortress. The inhabitants might respond to the action-effect directly, for instance, by spreading lye on the carcass and burying it or, again, by throwing it back. Or the siege captain's action might have its intended effect: disease would spread and the inhabitants would have to respond to that, if they could. They might choose ultimately to surrender. Such sequences—where an action (throwing a decayed carcass over the wall of a besieged city) has causal effects (disease spreads in the town) and these effects are, in turn, responded to intentionally (the inhabitants surrender)—are called quasi-causal by von Wright.[15] They are *causal* insofar as the relationship between two intentional actions is mediated by a causal effect of the first action (an effect that then provides the situational setting and motivation of the second action). But the relationship is only *quasi*-causal because the second action is not a mere causal effect of the first, as the inhabitants' simply dying from the disease would have been, but is itself an intentional action.

Variations on the pattern just discussed are possible. The causal effect might actually be unforeseen or otherwise unintended. Thus, intensive planting or a poor choice of crops might lead to erosion or some other barrenness of the soil (as it did in Paloma, in Peru, one of the earliest inhabited sites in America), making further agricultural use of the area impossible. The inhabitants then abandon the locale, or are forced to. Such a description—where the first action (intensive agriculture) leads to an effect (depletion of the soil), which in turn is responded to intentionally (the site abandoned)—still conforms to the quasi-causal model, even though the mediating causal effect is itself unintended, so long as the responding action is an intentional one. The causal efficacy of unintended consequences often depends on their arousing such intentionalistic responses.

Sometimes, though, the causal efficacy of such consequences is *merely* causal in that no responding action—or at least none that is intentional—is initiated. An unintended result could evoke a response that was wholly within the "course of nature," as we call it: thus, a stray bullet could dislodge a heavy tile which, in turn, kills a bypasser or knocks him out. Or it could evoke a behavioral but nonintentionalistic response: a dog, or child, startled or panicked by the falling tile, could run off. And, as before, the chain of events could be lengthened somewhat: thus the child could be startled, to the point of running off in panic, by coming upon the unconscious bypasser who had earlier been knocked out by the falling tile. In none of these cases do we conform to von Wright's quasi-causal model (for none of the responses is an intentional action). Even so, each is a possible finite causal sequence initiated *by* an intentional action (we presume in each case that the original bullet was fired intentionally) and, thus, each comes within the purview of the generalized causal model for actions, held in common by Dray and the revisionists, that we have been examining.

I believe it is Dray's view that the normal or basic paradigm for causation in history is that of agent causality, which involves, essentially, the performance of intentional actions. And we have seen that the concept of agent causation in league with that of finite causal chains can give rise to a number of interesting variations: quasi-causal patterns, unintended consequences, intersecting chains (as when the by-passer walked under the falling tile), and so on. Dray's commitments here—to intentional action and to finite, often intersecting, causal sequences—are consistent with and could even be said to lead to the criterion of abnormality, by which he assesses causal *importance*. It should also be obvious that, given these commitments, Dray, like the revisionists, is quite amenable to talk of historical chance or accident.

But these commitments do not rule out all talk of events happening with inevitability in history. Much that appears inevitable there does so only because people have intentionally—predictably, perhaps, but not inevitably—gone on to do the things they did with whatever result, intended or unforeseen, their doing had. And so on. But such things are, nonetheless, to be understood as done intentionally. Remove what is done intentionally and there is no inevitability. So, in these cases at least, there is compatibility between talk of intentional action and talk of inevitability and no threat is posed to the former by the latter. Of course, it is still possible that some events (like the cooling of the sun) might be established as inevitable and, probably, this would indicate that they were nonintentional—though there is no logical entailment here to that conclusion.

Such events are not ruled out by Dray's commitments. It's just that they would not account, in all likelihood, for a very large number of the events historians set themselves to study. More important, the study of these things *as inevitable* would proceed on principles different from those we have considered in this essay. Such a study would represent a different way of discoursing, in a different idiom, about things that are discussed by historians, typically, in the intentionalistic mode.[16]

.....

Notes

.....

Introduction

1 Wayne C. Booth, *Critical Understanding: The Power of Pluralism* (Chicago: University of Chicago Press, 1979); Denis Donoghue, *Ferocious Alphabets* (Boston: Little, Brown, 1981); Gerald Graff, *Literature Against Itself: Literary Ideas in Modern Society* (Chicago: University of Chicago Press, 1979); Geoffrey Hartmann, *Criticism in the Wilderness* (New Haven: Yale University Press, 1980); W. J. T. Mitchell, ed., *The Politics of Interpretation* (Chicago: University of Chicago Press, 1983).
2 Graff, *Literature Against Itself*, pp. 174–75.
3 Hartmann, *Criticism in the Wilderness*, pp. 227–28.
4 Richard Rorty, *Philosophy and the Mirror of Nature* (Princeton: Princeton University Press, 1979), p. 360.
5 Karl-Otto Apel, *Charles S. Peirce: From Pragmatism to Pragmaticism*, trans. John Michael Krois (Amherst: University of Massachusetts Press, 1981), p. 1.
6 Hans-Georg Gadamer, *Truth and Method*, trans. Garret Barden and John Cumming (New York: Continuum, 1975), p. 466.
7 See the recent book on Foucault by Dreyfus and Paul Rabinow, *Michel Foucault: Beyond Structuralism and Hermeneutics* (Chicago: University of Chicago Press, 1982).
8 Theodor W. Adorno, *Against Epistemology*, trans. Willis Domingo (Cambridge: MIT Press, 1983).

The Epistemological Problem of Understanding

1 This concept of sensible forms is rendered by H. Lipps, *Untersuch. z. e. hermeneut. Logik*, pp. 110, 111, with the expression *"Versinnlichungen"*; by Br. Snell, *Der Aufbau der Sprache* (1952), p. 29, with the term *"Sinnformen"*; by H. Freyer, *Soziologie als Wirklichkeitswiss.* (1930), p. 15, with the term *"sinnhaltige Formen,"* without, however, arguing for the scientific development of the concept itself.
2 By continuing to use this qualification, we consciously take a position against that recent tendency that conceives of music as a totally asemantic art: a conception that, rigorously pursued, would lead to making it an art without meaning, resistant to interpretation.
3 What is meant here is expressed in German by the word *"Haltung"*: Rothacker, *Geschichtsphil.* (1934), pp. 46 ff., 82 ff.; Bollnow, *Wesen der Stimmungen*, 2d ed. (1943), pp. 135–41; Triepel, *Stil des Rechts* (1947), pp. 62–63; Porzig, *D. Wunder d. Sprache*, 257.

4   This situation is rendered in Rilke's lyric poem, *Werke*, 3: 452: "Es winkt zu
    Fühlung fast aus allen Dingen. . . ."

5   The clear distinctions are pointed out by Seneca, *ad Lucil.*, 102, 15: "Non ad
    vocem referunt, sed ad sententiam"; 16: "Non verba, sed iudicia promittimus";
    Humboldt, *Werke*, 6: 120 ("Blosse Schällen); 154 ("Nur Zeichen von Tonen");
    7: 66; Paul., D. 44, 7, 38 (where he contrasts to the "figura literarum" the
    "oratio, quam exprimunt literae," and makes what "scriptura" means equal
    to "quod vocibus lingua figuratis significaretur"); Husserl, *Logische Untersu-
    chungen*, 2d ed., 2, 1: 66: "Es erscheint uns nicht bloss ein sinnlicher Zug auf
    dem Papier, sondern das physisch Erscheinende gilt als ein Zeichen, das wir
    verstehen. Und indem wir in seinem Verstandnis leben, vollziehen wir nicht
    ein Vorstellen oder Urteilen, das sich auf das Zeichen als sinnliches Objekt
    bezieht, sondern ein ganz anderes und andersartiges, das sich auf die bezeich-
    nete Sache bezieht. Also im sinngebenden Aktcharakter, der ein ganz anderer
    ist, je nachdem das Interesse auf das sinnliche Zeichen oder auf das mittels
    des Zeichens vorstellig gemachte (wenn auch durch keinerlei Phantasie-vor-
    stellungen verbildlichte) Objekt gerichtet ist, liegt die Bedeutung": Spranger,
    in "Festschrift für Völkelt" (1918): 382; Kraft, *Wiener Kreis*, p. 56.

    For the distinction between countersigns and symbols, see Cassirer, *Saggio
    sull'uomo*, p. 57.

6   It might seem superfluous to insist here on such an elementary distinction,
    were it not that a widespread bad habit and recurrent materialistic prejudice
    still leads some to confuse, for example, the statement with the document in
    which it is incorporated (thus, Schlossmann, *Irrtum*, p. 33; R. Sacco, *Concetto
    di interpretaz.* [1947] p. 59), or to qualify as "document" the "text" of the
    statement itself (Friedrichs, *Der allgemeine Teil d. Rechts* [1927], pp. 123–89;
    Giannini, *Interpr. atto ammin.*, p. 60). Sometimes even certain writers who
    have the merit of having distinguished clearly between the statement and the
    document destined to represent it nonetheless confuse representational form
    and material support. Thus, Carnelutti, in *Riv. trim. dir. pubbl.* (1951), p. 300,
    when he affirms that "words are symbols, but also (!) sounds," and asks him-
    self "what mysterious relationships might exist between symbol and sound."
    The answer is that words in one respect are symbols—that is representational
    forms—which are linguistic in character, and in another respect are articu-
    lated sounds, that is figures of sound (*Lautformen*, Humboldt would say) to
    which a sense of language is linked (*Sprachsinn*). Carnelutti's question seems
    to derive from the preconception that identifies the word with the graphic sym-
    bol, that is, with its having been written, with the documenting that sets its
    visible symbol into a material support.

7   The discrepancy specially attracts the attention of linquistics: thus: De Saus-
    sure, *Cours de linguistique générale*, p. 170, cf. p. 29; G. Ipsen, "Gespräch u.
    Sprachform," in *Blätter f. dtsche Philos.* 6 (1932–33): 69, remarks that the con-
    figuring of sounds (*das Lauten*) is not at all a simple physical, or even physio-
    logical, phenomenon, but a quality of figure (*Gestalt*) in the order (*Gefüge*) of
    a given sphere of linguistic articulation, and it is then essentially determined
    by the ordering of this sphere. Br. Snell, *Der Aufbau der Sprache*, p. 45, notes
    that the more man becomes man, the more the urge to expression (*Ausdrucks-*

ruf) detaches itself from and rises above the rigid connection to excitation and to interior movement (p. 45), and that multiple forms of *Synästhesien* may determine the phonetic value of and impress themselves on the phonemes of words (p. 53). A. Pagliaro, "Logica e grammatica," in *Ricerche linguistiche* 1 (1950): 19, n. 8, points out that the dynamic quality of languages originates in an imbalance, which is perennially created between the content of the consciousness of the one who speaks, and the language as a complex of distinct signifieds (from which a form suited to distinguish its content adequately does not come forth to meet the consciousness of the speaker), and to an imbalance that is perennially re-created. Rothacker, *Gesch. phil.*, p. 73, is in agreement.

8   Thus, W. M. Urban, *Language and Reality* (1939), pp. 121–22.

9   Baratono, "Il mio paradosso," in *Filosofi ital. contemporanei* (1947), estr. 24–25; *Arte e poesia* (1945), p. 175, cf. pp. 135–36, where Rilke, *Aug. Rodin*, in *Ges. Werke* (1927), 4: 382: "Ob nicht alles Oberfläche ist, was wir auslegen und deutern" is recalled. Cf. also Segond, *Psychologie*, nn. 68–69; Roland Manuel, *Plaisir de la musique* (1947), 1: 274 ff.; W. M. Urban, *Language and Reality*, p. 121 (who calls representational forms "expressions"). The concept of representational forms has another precedent. An analogous concept of "representamen" had been elaborated by C. S. Peirce, *Collected Papers* (1931), 1: 564; he wrote "since 'representation' is the character of a thing, in virtue of which it can stand in the place of another in order to produce a certain mental process or thought, so we propose to call: (a) the thing endowed with that character 'representamen,' (b) the mental process its 'interpretant' (which means: a parte subjecti, 'interpretive key'; a parte objecti, 'stimulus'), (c) the thing in place of which it stands, its 'object' (or the objectivity or alterity, to which the sense is referred)." Cf. ibid., p. 541 in Morris, *Signs, Language, and Behavior* (1946), pp. 289–90.

10   See A. H. Gardiner, *Theory of Speech and Language*, p. 100; H. Lipps, *Die menschliche Natur* (1941), p. 28; Br. Snell, *Aufbau der Sprache*, p. 18.

11   *Wissenschaft der Logik*, 2d ed. (1841), 1: 119–22; *Encyklopädie*, sec. 91. See N. Hartmann, *Problem d. geist. Seins*, pp. 144, 365, 387, 425, 448, *Grundleg. d. Ontologie*, 3d ed., pp. 85, 152 ff.

12   See my "Teoria gener. d. negozio giur." (2d ed.), sec. 3 (52), sec. 10 (126); also Carnelutti, *Sistema d. dir. proc. civ.* (1938), 2: 159–68, nn. 456, 457, 458; *Teoria gener. d. dir.*, 3d ed., n. 124.

13   Dilthey, *Ges. Schr.*, 5: 318; Wach, "Festschr. Goetz": *Kultur- u. Universalgesch.* (1927), p. 380, n. 1; *Sociology of Religion*, 6th ed. (1951), pp. 28 ff., 375 ff. On the deaf mute and blind: Humboldt, *Werke*, 6: 120, 153 ff.; cf. 7: 66, 100; Segond, *Psychologie*, pp. 184 ff.; Gardiner, *Theory of Speech and Language*, p. 67; Baratono, *Prima grammatica*, 2d ed. (1947), pp. 53–54; Maeterlinck, *Les aveugles*; Rilke, *Werke*, 2: 154.

14   Cf. Augustine, *Confessions*, 10: 18, 2.

15   Hanslick, *Vom Musikalisch-Schönen*, 6th ed. (1881), pp. 64, 78; Baratono, *Arte e poesia*, pp. 36 ff., 93 ff., 201 ff.; Hartmann, *Problem d. geist. Seins*, pp. 378, 381 ff.

16   Cf. Carnelutti, *Teoria gener. d. dir.*, p. 386, n. 150; 2d ed., 268, n. 119.

17   Humboldt, *Werke,* 7: 170; 5: 381–2; Steinthal, *Einleitung in d. Psychol. u. Sprachwiss.* (1871), 1: n. 512; Meusel, *Hegel u. das Problem d. phil. Polemik* (1942), p. 40; Jhering, *Geist d. rom. Rechts,* 2: 444 ff.; W. M. Urban, *Language and Reality,* pp. 234 ff.

18   Cf. Humboldt, *Werke,* 6: 182–83; 7: 64 ff.

19   Carnelutti, *Teoria gener. d. dir.,* sec. 148; cf. 2d ed., sec. 116: pp. 264 ff.

20   Humboldt, *Werke,* 7: 56 ff.; 6: 177; Hartmann, *Problem d. geist. Seins,* pp. 394–96; cf. p. 232.

21   Goethe, letter to Zelter, November 7, 1816; cf. Humboldt, *Werke,* 7: 56–58; Nietzsche, *Menschliches Allzumenschl.,* 2: 126; Lipps, *Untersuch. z.e. hermeneut. Logik,* p. 86.

22   Matt., 13: 3–15; Mark 4: 3–12; Luke, 8: 4–15; Cf. Matt., 13: 18–23.

23   Cf. esp. 1 Cor. 1:15.

24   Carnelutti, *Teoria gener. d. diritto,* 2d ed., p. 356.

25   Cf. Urban, *Language and Reality,* p. 115; and my "Hermeneut. Manifest," n. 9.

26   J. Wach, *Verstehen,* 2: 16; Droysen, *Historik,* p. 180; Litt, *Individuum u. Gemeinschaft,* 3d ed., pp. 182 ff.; Löwith, *Das Individuum in der Rolle des Mitmenschen* (1928), pp. 103, 123–26; Hartmann, *Problem d. geist. Seins,* pp. 216 ff.; Kahler, *Deutscher Charakter in der Gesch. Europas,* p. 13; Snell, *Aufbau der Sprache,* p. 29; K. Engisch, *Logische Studien* (Heidelbg. Akad., 1943), pp. 67–68. Also my "Hermeneut. Manifest," n. 8a; 9a,b,c.

27   For example H. Lipps, *Hermen. Logik,* p. 112; J. R. Weinberg, *Examin. of Logical Positivism,* Hahin translation (1950), p. 255; Snell, *Aufbau der Sprache* (1952), p. 19; O. Dittrich, *Probleme der Sprachpsychologie* (1913), pp. 38–52; J. Stenzel, "Sinn, Bedeutung, Begriff, Definition," in *Jahrbuch f. Philologie* 1 (1925): 160–201.

28   C. G. Jung, *Seelenprobleme der Gegenwart* (1946), p. 323.

28   Cf. Lipps, *Hermen. Logik* (1938), pp. 77, 102, 104.

29   Cf. Lipps, *Hermen. Logik* (1938), pp. 77, 102, 104.

30   Cf. Hatschek, *Englisches Staatsrecht* (1906), 2: 638 ff.; Savekouls, *Das Englische Kabinettsystem* (1934).

31   Oppo, *Profili di interpretazione oggettiva,* pp. 32 ff. Also [Italian law] art. 1362 capov. c. civ.

32   Manigk, *Willenserkl.,* 419; Schleiermacher, *Werke,* 3, sec. 3, 201; Lipps, *Hermen. Logik,* p. 77; N. Hartmann, *Teleol. Denken* (1951), p. 104.

33   My *Teoria del negozio giur.,* sec. 14; sec. 11, sec. 34 bis, n. 3; and *Dir. proc. civ. it.,* p. 434, n. 32; Manigk, *Willenserklärung u. Willensgeschäft,* pp. 418 ff., 425; Schreier, *Interpretation,* pp. 56 ff., 88. Also A. Gardiner, *Theory of Speech and Language,* pp. 195 ff.; W. Kayser, *D. sprachl. Kunstwerk,* pp. 282 ff.

34   Droysen, *Historik,* pp. 37 ff., 62, 65; Bernheim, *Lb. d. histor. Methode,* 6th ed., pp. 255–58, 466–67, 470–71; 503–4, 569; Albers, *Man. d. propedeut. stor.* (1909), pp. 62 ff., 81–2; Droysen, *Historik,* pp. 38, 50, 61, 64; Hartmann, *Problem d. geist. Seins,* p. 398; Carnelutti, *Lezioni dir. proc. civ.,* 2, n. 150; *Prova civile* (1915), nr. 22; *Teoria gener. d. dir.* (2d ed.), n. 167; *Lezioni sul proc. penale* 1 (1949), n. 149. Rather confused and not useful is the generic notion of "documents" which Croce proposes, *Storia come pens.* (1938), 109–10.

35 Eisele, *Archiv f. d. civ. Praxis* 69 (1886): 281; Schreier, *Interpretation d. Gesetze u. Rgesch.*, p. 56; Titze, in *Zschr. f. ausland. u. internat. Privatrecht*, 13 (1941): 980; my "Interpretazione d. legge," pp. 161 ff., 278 ff.; Husserl, *Logische Untersuchungen*, 2d ed. 2, 1: pp. 61–66; H. Lipps, *Untersuch. z.e. hermeneut. Logik*, 89.

36 Droysen, *Historik*, sec. 7: 328; sec. 51: 347; cf. Wach, *Verstehen*, 1: 38, n. 1; 3: 162, n. 2.

37 Droysen, *Historik*, pp. 187–273 ff.; Freyer, "Festschr. Goetz" (1927), pp. 494–96; cf. Segond, *Tr. de psychologie*, nn. 84; 86–88.

38 But cf. Feldkeller, *Das unpersonliche Denken* (1949): 47–50.

39 Urban, *Language and reality*, pp. 109 ff.; Snell, *Aufbau der Sprache*, p. 18; my "Hermen. Manifest," nn. 9, 16.

40 Most of the material analyzed and criticized by Betti in this section is drawn from Morris, *Signs, Language and Behavior* (1946); W. M. Urban, *Language and reality* (1939, 1949); Ogden and Richards, *The Meaning of Meaning* (1923).—Trans.

41 In this section, Betti draws primarily upon Peirce, *Collected Papers*, vols. 1, 2, 4, 5, 6, as well as Morris, and Ogden and Richards. He also uses G. W. Cunningham, "Perspective and Context in Meaning-Situations," *University of California Publications in Philosophy* 16 (1935): 29–52.—Trans.

42 Morris, *Signs, Language and Behavior*, p. 93.

43 Ducasse, "Symbol, Signs and Signals," *Journal of Symbolic Logic* 4 (1939).

44 Tolman, *Purposive Behavior in Animals and Men* (1932).

References

Betti's bibliographical information is fragmentary in the original. The titles and authors presented here amount to about 90 percent of those he had in mind; the others remain unidentified.

Baratono, Adelchi. *Arte e Poesia*. Milan: V. Bompiani, 1945.

———. "Il mio paradosso." *Filosofi ital. contemporanei*, 1947.

———. *La prima grammatica*. 1942; 2d ed. Florence: G. C. Sansoni, 1947.

Bernheim, Ernst. *Lehrbuch der historischen Methode*. Leipzig: Duncker and Humblot, 1889.

Betti, Emilio. *Diritto processuale civile Italiano*. 2d ed. Rome: Societa editrice del "Foro Italiano," 1936.

———. *Interpretazione della legge e degli atti giuridici teoria generale e dogmatica*. Milan: Giuffore, 1949.

———. *Teoria generale del negozio giuridico*. 2d ed. Turin: Unione tipografico-editrice torinese, 1950.

Bollnow, Otto. *Das Wesen der Stimmungen*. 2d ed. Frankfurt: V. Klostermann, 1943.

Carnelutti, Francesco. *La prova civile*. Rome: Athenaeum, 1915.

———. *Lezioni di diritto processuale civile*. Padua: "La Litotipo," editrice universtaria, 1920.

————. *Sistema di diritto processuale civile*. Padua: A Milani, 1936.

————. *Teoria generale del diritto*. 2d ed. Rome: Fora italiano, 1946. (3d ed., 1949.)

————. *Lezioni sul processo penale*. 2d ed. Rome: Edizioni dell'Ateneo, 1949.

Croce, Benedetto. *La Storia come pensiero e come azione*. 2d ed. Bari, Gius: Laterza and Figli, 1938.

Cunningham, G. W. "Perspective and Context in Meaning-Situations." *University of California Publications in Philosophy*, no. 16, 1935.

Dilthey, Wilhelm. *Gesammelte Schriften*. 11 vols. Leipzig: Teubner, 1923–1958.

Dittrich, Ottmar. *Die Probleme der Sprachpsychologie und ihre gegenwaertigen loesungsmoeglichkeiten*. Leipzig: Quelle and Meyer, 1913.

Droysen, Johan Gustav. *Historik: Vorlesungen ueber Enzyklopaedia und Methodologie der Geschichte*. Edited by R. Huebner. Munich and Berlin: R. Oldenbourg, 1937.

Ducasse, C. J. "Symbol, Signs, and Signals." *Journal of Symbolic Logic* 4 (1939).

Engisch, Karl. *Logische Studien zur Gesetzesanwendung*. Heidelberg: C. Winter, 1943.

Feldkeller, Paul. *Das Unpersoenliche Denken*. Berlin: W. de Gruyter, 1949.

Freyer, Hans. *Soziologie als Wirklichkeitswissenschaft*. Leipzig and Berlin: B. G. Teubner, 1930.

Friedrichs, Karl. *Der allgemeine Teil des Rechts*. Berlin and Leipzig: W. de Gruyter, 1927.

Gardiner, Alan H. *The Theory of Speech and Language*. Oxford: Clarendon Press, 1932.

Giannini, Massimo. *L'Interpretazione dell'atto amministrativo e la teoria giuridica generale dell' interpretazione*. Milan: Giuffre, 1939.

Hanslick, Eduard. *Vom Musikalisch-Schoenen*. 6th ed. Leipzig: J. A. Barth, 1881.

Hartmann, Nicolai. *Das Problem des geistigen Seins*. Berlin and Leipzig: W. de Gruyter, 1933.

————. *Zur Gründlegung der Ontologie*. Vol. 1 of *Ontologie*. 3d ed. Meisenheim an Glan: A. Hain, 1948.

————. *Teleologisches Denken*. Berlin: W. de Gruyter, 1951.

Hatschek, Julius. *Englisches Staatsrecht*. 2 vols. Tuebingen: J. C. B. Mohr, 1905–06.

Hegel, G. W. F. *Encyklopaedie der philosophischen wissenschaften im Grundrisse*. Heidelberg: A. Oswald, 1817.

————. *Wissenschaft der Logik*. 2d ed. Leipzig: F. Meiner, 1951.

Humboldt, Wilhelm Freiherr von. *Gesammelte Schriften*. 17 vols. Berlin: B. Behr, 1903–36.

Husserl, Edmund. *Logische Untersuchungen*. 2d ed. 2 vols. in 3. Halle: M. Niemeyer, 1913–22.

Ipsen, Gunther. "Gespraech und Sprachform." *Blaetter fur deutsche Philosophie*, 1932–33.

Jhering, Rudolf von. *Geist des romischen Rechts*. 3 vols. Leipzig: Breitkopf and Hartel, 1852–58.

Jung, Carl G. *Seelenprobleme der Gegenwart*. Zurich: Rascher, 1946.

Kahler, Erich. *Der deutsche Charakter in der geschichte Europas*. Zurich: Europa-Verlag, 1937.

Kayser, Wolfgang. *Das sprachliche Kunstwerk*. Bern: A. Franke, 1948.

Notes 277

Kraft, Viktor. *Der wiener Kreis, der Ursprung des Neopositivismus.* Vienna: Springer-Verlag, 1950.

Lipps, Hans. *Untersuchungen zu einer hermeneutischen Logik.* Frankfurt: V. Klostermann, 1938.

Litt, Theodor. *Individuum und Gemeinschaft.* 3d ed. Leipzig: B. G. Teubner, 1926.

Loewith, Karl. *Das Individuum in der Rolle des Mitmenschen.* Munich: Drei Masken Verlag, 1928.

Maeterlinck, Maurice. *Les Aveugles.* Brussels: Paul Lacomblez, 1890.

Manigk, Alfred. *Willenserklaerung und Willengeschaeft.* Berlin: Vahlen, 1907.

Meusel, Anton. *Hegel und das Problem der philosophischen Polemik.* Berlin: Junker and Duennhaupt, 1942.

Morris, Charles W. *Signs, Language and Behavior.* New York: Prentice-Hall, 1946.

Nietzsche, Friedrich. *Menschliches, allzumenschliches.* 2 vols. New ed., Chemnitz: E. Schmeitzner, 1878; Leipzig: E. W. Fritzsch, 1886.

Ogden, C. K., and I. A. Richards. *The Meaning of Meaning.* New York: Harcourt, Brace, and Co., 1923.

Oppo, Giorgio. *Profili dell'interpretazione oggettiva del negozio giuridico.* Bologna: N. Zanichelli, 1943.

Pagliaro, Antonio. "Logica e grammatica." *Ricerche Linguistiche,* 1950.

Peirce, C. S. *Collected Papers.* Cambridge: Harvard University Press, 1931–58.

Porzig, Walter. *Das Wunder der Sprache.* Bern: A. Francke, 1950.

Rilke, Ranier Maria. *Auguste Rodin.* Berlin: Julius Bard, 1903. (In *Ges. Werke.* Vol. 4. Leipzig: Insel-Verlag, 1927.)

Roland, Manuel (also Manuel, Roland). *Plaisir de la musique.* 3 vols. Paris: Editions du Seuil, 1947–51.

Rothacker, Erich. *Geschichtsphilosophie.* Munich: R. Oldenbourg, 1934.

Sacco, Rudolfo. *Il concetto di interpretazione del diritto.* Turin: G. Giappichelli, 1947.

Saussure, Ferdinand de. *Cours de Linguistique Générale.* Lausanne: Payot, 1916.

Schleiermacher, Friedrich. *Saemmtliche Werke.* 30 vols. Berlin: G. Reimer, 1835–64.

Schlossmann, Siegmund. *Der irrtum ueber wesentliche eigenschaften der person und den sache nach dem buergerlichen gesetzbuch.* Jena: Fischer, 1903.

Schreier, Fritz. *Die Interpretation der Gesetze und Rechtsgeschaefte.* Leipzig: F. Deuticke, 1927.

Segond, Joseph Louis. *Traité de Psychologie.* Paris: A. Colin, 1930.

Seneca, Lucius. *Ad Lucilium Epistulae Morales.* 2 vols. Rome: Typis Regiae Officinae Polygraphicae, 1931.

Snell, Bruno. *Der Aufbau der Sprache.* Hamburg: Claassen Verlag, 1952.

Steinthal, Hermann. *Einleitung in die Psychologie und Sprachwissenschaft.* Berlin: Duemmler, 1871.

Stenzel, Julius. "Sinn, Bedeutung, Begriff, Definition." *Jahrbuch fuer Philologie,* 1925.

Titze, Heinrich. *Zeitschrift fuer ausland. und internat.* Privatrecht. 1941: 13.

Tolman, Edward C. *Purposive Behavior in Animals and Men.* New York: The Century Co., 1932.

Triepel, Heinrich. *Vom Stil des Rechts.* Heidelberg: L. Schneider, 1947.

Urban, Wilbur M. *Language and Reality.* London: George Allen and Unwin, 1930.

Wach, Joachim. *Das Verstehen*. 3 vols. Tuebingen: J. C. B. Mohr, 1926–33.
————. *Sociology of Religion*. Chicago: University of Chicago Press, 1951.
Wartburg, Walther von. *Einfuehrung in Problematik und Methodik der Sprach-wissenschaft*. Halle: M. Niemeyer, 1943.

Beyond Hermeneutics

1   Michel Foucalt, *The Order of Things* (New York: Vintage Books, 1973), p. 373.
2   Michel Foucault, *The Birth of the Clinic* (New York: Vintage Books, 1975), p. xvi.
3   Martin Heidegger, *On the Way to Language* (New York: Harper and Row, 1971), p. 51.
4   Ibid., p. 12.
5   Martin Heidegger, *Nietzsche II* (Pfullingen: Verlag Gunter Neske, 1961), p. 415.
6   Martin Heidegger, *What is Called Thinking* (New York: Harper & Row, 1954), p. 159ff.
7   Martin Heidegger, *Being and Time* (New York: Harper and Row, 1962), p. 62. All references are to the standard English translation. I have modified the translation wherever I thought necessary to preserve the sense.
8   Ibid., p. 60.
9   Heidegger, *On the Way to Language*, p. 51.
10 Heidegger, *Being and Time*, p. 60.
11 Ibid., pp. 61, 38.
12 W. Caudill and H. Weinstein, "Maternal Care and Infant Behavior in Japan and in America," in *Readings in Child Behavior and Development*, ed. C. S. Lavatelli and F. Stendler (New York: Harcourt Brace, 1972), p. 78.
13 Heidegger, *On the Way to Language*, p. 33.
14 Ibid., p. 36.
15 Harold Garfinkel, *Studies in Ethnomethodology* (Englewood Cliffs, N.J.: Prentice-Hall, 1967).
16 See especially Taylor's article, "Interpretation and the Sciences of Man," in *Interpretive Social Science*, ed. P. Rabinow and W. Sullivan (Berkeley: University of California Press, 1979).
17 Clifford Geertz, *The Interpretation of Cultures* (New York: Harper and Row, 1973).
18 Thomas Kuhn, *The Essential Tension* (Chicago: University of Chicago Press, 1977).
19 Heidegger, *On the Way to Language*, pp. 11, 28.
20 Heidegger, *Being and Time*, p. 38.
21 Ibid., p. 359.
22 Ricoeur blurs his classification by including Nietzsche, who, indeed, does not take our practices at face value, among those who practice the hermeneutics of suspicion. According to Foucault's more rigorous and illuminating classification, however, Nietzsche, while questioning our cultural self-interpretation, is not practicing hermeneutics because he does not assume that the interpre-

tation in our cultural practices is the result of a deliberate cover up. The *Genealogy of Morals*, for example, questions the validity of Western morality and metaphysics but it does not trace these practices back to a refusal to face a deep truth (as Freud does) or even the refusal to face the fact that there is no deep truth (as Heidegger does). As Foucault points out, for Nietzsche our current self-interpretation is not in the service of a deliberate cover up, but rather is the result of many local power struggles: "If interpretation is the violent or surreptitious appropriation of a system of rules, which in itself has no essential meaning, in order to impose a direction, to blend it to a new will, to force its participation in a different game, and to subject it to secondary rules, then the development of humanity is a series of interpretations. The role of genealogy is to record its history" ("Nietzsche, Genealogy, History," in *Language, Counter-Memory, Practice*, ed. Donald F. Bouchard, [Ithaca, N.Y.: Cornell University Press, 1977], pp. 151, 152).

23   Martin Heidegger, "The Way Back into the Ground of Metaphysics," in *Existentialism from Dostoevsky to Sartre*, ed. Walter Kaufman (New York: Meridian Books, 1957), p. 211.

24   Martin Heidegger, "What Are Poets For?" in *Poetry, Language, Thought* (New York: Harper and Row, 1971).

25   Martin Heidegger, *Discourse on Thinking* (New York: Harper and Row, 1959), p. 55.

26   Martin Heidegger, "The Age of the World Picture," in *The Question Concerning Technology and Other Essays* (New York: Harper and Row, 1977), p. 131.

27   Martin Heidegger, "The Origin of the Work of Art," in *Poetry, Language, Thought*, p. 61.

28   Martin Heidegger, "The Question Concerning Technology," in *The Question Concerning Technology and Other Essays*, p. 16.

29   Michel Foucault, *Power/Knowledge*, ed. Colin Gordon (New York: Pantheon, 1980), p. 186.

30   For a detailed study of this method, which Foucault calls archaeology and its difficulties, see Hubert L. Dreyfus and Paul Rabinow, *Michel Foucault: Beyond Structuralism and Hermeneutics* (Chicago: University of Chicago Press, 1982), pt. 1.

31   For a discussion of this revised method, its relation to archaeology, and its use of something like paradigms, see ibid., pt. 2.

On the Transcendability of Hermeneutics

1   The papers and discussions from this meeting were subsequently published in the *Review of Metaphysics* 34 (Sept. 1980): 3–55.

2   Charles Taylor, "Interpretation and the Sciences of Man," *Review of Metaphysics* 25 (1971): 3–51.

3   Rorty, *Philosophy and the Mirror of Nature* (Princeton: Princeton University Press, 1979).

4   Heidegger, *Unterwegs zur Sprache* (Pfullingen: Neske, 1959), p. 98.

5 This is documented in *Hermeneutik und Ideologiekritik*, a collection of essays by Karl-Otto Apel et al. (Frankfurt: Suhrkamp, 1971); key essays, translated, appear in Josef Bleicher, *Contemporary Hermeneutics: Methodology, Philosophy, Critique* (London: Routledge and Kegan Paul, 1980).

Transcendental Philosophy and the Hermeneutic Critique

1 Immanuel Kant, *Critique of Pure Reason*, A 346 = B 404.
2 For (1), see *Critique of Pure Reason*, A xiii, B xxxviii, A 67 = B 92; for (2), see ibid., B xxv; (3) underlies the entire transcendental enterprise.
3 G. W. F. Hegel, *Introduction to Phenomenology of Mind*, trans. J. B. Baillie (New York: Harper and Row, 1967), p. 132.
4 Cp. B. Stroud, "Transcendental Arguments," *Journal of Philosophy* 65 (1968): pp. 241–56.
5 Hegel, *Phenomenology of Mind*, p. 162.
6 Ibid., p. 141 ("all we are left to do is simply and solely to look on"); p. 144 ("to us, who watch the process").
7 Edmund Husserl, "Kant and the Idea of Transcendental Philosophy," trans. Ted Klein and William Pohl, *Southwestern Journal of Philosophy* 5, no. 3 (1974), esp. p. 22.
8 Cp. *Critique of Pure Reason*, A 146–47 = B 185–87; A 240–41 = B 299–300; A 244–45.
9 Cp. Martin Heidegger, *Sein und Zeit*, ¶43 (a).
10 Eugen Fink, "Operative Begriffe in Husserls Phänomenologie," *Zeitschrift für philosophische Forschung* 11 (1957): 321–37.
11 H-G. Gadamer, "The Phenomenological Movement," in Gadamer, *Philosophical Hermeneutics*, trans. and ed. David E. Linge (Berkeley: University of California Press), pp. 130–81, esp. p. 169.
12 Ibid., p. 148.
13 Ibid., p. 156.
14 For more on this, see my "Intentionality and the Mind/Body Problem," in *Organism, Medicine and Metaphysics: Essays in Honor of Hans Jonas*, ed. Stuart F. Spicker (Dordrecht: D. Reidel Publishing Co., 1978), pp. 283–300.

Phenomenality and Materiality in Kant

1 Michel Foucault, *Les mots et les choses* (Paris: Gallimard, 1966), p. 255.
2 Immanuel Kant, *Kritik der Urteilskraft*, vol. 10 of *Werkausgabe* (Frankfurt am Main: Suhrkamp, 1978), ed. Wilhelm Weischedel, p. 90. Subsequent references to this work cite two page numbers. The first refers to this edition; the second reference (here pp. 17–18) is to the English translation (*Critique of Judgment*, trans. J. H. Bernard [New York: Hafner Press, 1951]). I have occasionally made slight changes in the English version. References to other works by Kant are from the same Suhrkamp *Werkausgabe*; the translations are my own.

3   Pascal, *Pensées*, ed. Louis Lafuma (Paris: Editions du Luxembourg, 1951), 1: 199–390, 138.
4   *Logik* in *Werkausgabe*, 6: 457.
5   *Betrachtungen über das Gefühl des Schönen und Erhabenen* in *Werkausgabe*, 2: 875.
6   Denis Diderot, *Lettre sur les sourds et muets* in *Oeuvres complètes*, ed. Roger Lewinter (Paris: Le Club français du livre, 1969–73), 2: 573–74.
7   *Kritik der reinen Vernunft* in *Werkausgabe*, 4: 696.
8   See Paul de Man, "Aesthetic Formalization: Kleist's *Ueber das Marionetten-theater*," in *The Rhetoric of Romanticism* (New York: Columbia University Press, forthcoming).

The Problem of Figuration in Antiquity

1   Luther, "Answer to the Hyperchristian, Hyperspiritual, Hyperlearned Book by Goat Emser in Leipzig—Including Some Thoughts Regarding His Companion, the Fool Murner" (1521), *Luther's Works*, ed. Eric W. Gritsch (Philadelphia: Fortress Press, 1970), 39: 177–81.
2   A good way for a modern reader to approach Philo's hermeneutics of figuration is by way of Heidegger's conception of the as structure of human understanding. See *Being and Time*, trans. John Macquarrie and Edward Robinson (New York: Harper and Row, 1962), pp. 188–95. One could say that Heidegger's conception of understanding and interpretation is really modeled on the allegorical practices of the ancients, in which nothing is taken to make sense in itself but only as it can be taken as something other.
3   *Origen on First Principles, Being Koetschau's Text of the De Principiis*, trans. B. W. Butterworth (New York: Harper and Row, 1966), p. 282. Reference here and below is to the translation from the Greek version.
4   Maimonides, *The Guide of the Perplexed*, trans. Shlomo Pines (Chicago: University of Chicago Press, 1963), 1: 6–7: "Hence you should not ask of me here anything beyond the chapter headings. And even those are not set down in order or arranged in coherent fashion in this Treatise, but rather are scattered and entangled with other subjects that are to be clarified. For my purpose is that the truths be glimpsed and then again concealed, so as not to oppose and which has concealed from the vulgar among people those truths especially requisite for His apprehension."
5   Origen, *Homélies sur Josué*, the Latin text with a French translation by Annie Jaubert (Paris: Les Editions du Cerf, 1960), pp. 258–60. The Joshua text intoxicated Greek-speaking Christians, because the Hebrew *Joschua* is rendered as *Iesous* in Septuagint. The figure of Christ as *hermeneus* must be seen against the tradition of *pesher* interpretation, or interpretation on the model of promise and fulfillment, which was widely practiced by various sects in the intertestamental period. See Geza Vermes, "The Qumran Interpretation of the Scripture in Its Historical Setting," in *Post-Biblical Jewish Studies* (Leiden: E. J. Brill, 1975), pp. 37–49.

6   *The Gospel of the Egyptians*, trans. Alexander Bohling and Frederick Wisse
    (Grand Rapids: W. B. Eerdmans, 1975), p. 205.
7   See Erich Auerbach's essay, "Figura," in *Scenes from the Drama of European
    Literature* (New York: Meridian Books, 1959), esp. pp. 28–60.
8   See Erich Auerbach, *Literary Language and Its Public in Late Antiquity and
    in the Middle Ages*, trans. Ralph Mannheim (New York: Pantheon Books,
    1965), p. 65.
9   The notion that the plain must be used to elucidate the obscure is a common-
    place in nearly every hermeneutical tradition. Augustine himself may have in
    mind the wonderful passage in Mark 12:29–31, in which Jesus responds to a
    question as to which is the greatest of the laws. Jesus answers by citing, first,
    Deuteronomy 6:4–5 ("Listen, O Israel; the Lord is our God, the Lord alone; so
    you must love the Lord your God with all your mind and all your heart and
    all your strength") and, second, Leviticus 19:18 ("You must not avenge your-
    self, nor bear a grudge against the members of your own race, but you must
    love your fellow as one of your own"). In other words, Christ reinscribes all
    the Law in terms of its parts, figuring it thereby as a law of charity.
10 Gadamer, *Truth and Method* (New York: Seabury Press, 1975), pp. 264–65.
    The point is that there can never be an individual understanding of a text that
    falls entirely outside a tradition in which the text and its meaning are handed
    down, even though it is always the case that an individual interpretation never
    merely reproduces a traditional meaning.
11 See Bernardin Schneider, "The Meaning of St. Paul's Antithesis: 'The Letter
    and the Spirit,' " *The Catholic Biblical Quarterly* 15 (1951): 163–207.
12 A good deal of study has yet to be done before we can begin to understand
    the ancient notion of literalness. The Greek word that usually gets translated
    as "literal" is *"kurios,"* that is, "authorized," "primary," "exact," "common,"
    "familiar," and so on. Augustine's notion of "literal" implies the idea of the
    proper name, or what a thing would call itself were it able to speak. A whole
    mythology of names lies behind ancient concepts of literal and figurative
    usage, but there seems to have been almost no inquiry into this subject.
13 Augustine, *On Dialectic*, trans. B. Darrell Jackson (Dordrecht, Holland: D.
    Reidel, 1975), pp. 88–91.
14 Hartman, *Criticism in the Wilderness: The Study of Literature Today* (New
    Haven: Yale University Press, 1980), p. 31. "Hermeneutics," Hartman says,
    "has always inquired into the scandal of figurative language, when that was
    extraordinary and transgressive." My argument would be that, on the con-
    trary, it is only on the basis of a complicated series of Enlightenment presup-
    positions (mainly having to do with a desire for a philosophical language, or
    a system of logical designations) that figuration becomes something scan-
    dalous. From the standpoint of traditional rhetoric and poetics, of course,
    figurative utterances are said to be licensed rather than authorized, as the
    speech of fools, lovers, and poets is licensed and contrasted to the authorized
    teachings of philosophy and theology. There is nothing transgressive, how-
    ever, about figuration as an ancient hermeneutical practice.
15 See, for example, the concept of figurality in Paul de Man, *Allegories of Read-
    ing: Figural Language in Rousseau, Nietzsche, Rilke, and Proust* (New Haven:

Yale University Press, 1979), esp. pp. 103–18. The concept of figurality here presupposes at every turn Enlightenment conceptions of a philosophical language, or a language of designations.

16 A perfect illustration of our easy disregard of the ancients is to be found in a recent (and otherwise fine) essay by Michael Ermarth, "The Transformation of Hermeneutics: 19th Century Ancients and 20th Century Moderns," in the *Monist* 64 (1981): 175–93. On this historical model, Philo, Origen, and Augustine would have to be considered as preancient or pretraditional—or, let us say, prehistoric: the great dinosaurs of hermeneutics!

Homotextuality: Barthes on Barthes, Fragments

1 This, then, is an example of itself. The following notes are more dutiful. Like pallbearers, they carry the weight of the literary corpus honored through them. Think, then, of the internal citations (RB) as the caryatids of temple literature.

2 Sandra M. Gilbert, "Costumes of the Mind: Transvestism as Metaphor in Modern Literature," *Critical Inquiry* 7, no. 2 (Winter 1980): 391–417.

3 George Steiner, "Eros and Idion," in *On Difficulty and Other Essays* (New York and London: Oxford University Press, 1978), p. 117.

4 John O'Neill, *Essaying Montaigne: A Study of the Institution of Writing and Reading* (London and Boston: Routledge and Kegan Paul, 1982).

5 *The Pleasure of the Text*, trans. Richard Miller (New York: Hill and Wang, 1975), pp. 16–17.

6 John O'Neill, *Perception, Expression and History: The Social Phenomenology of Maurice Merleau-Ponty* (Evanston, Ill.: Northwestern University Press, 1970); Maurice Merleau Ponty, *Signs*, trans. Richard C. McCleary (Evanston, Ill.: Northwestern University Press, 1964), p. 96.

7 *Système de la mode* (Paris: Editions du Seuil, 1967).

8 Lévi-Strauss, *Mythologiques: Le cru et la cuit* (Paris: Librairie Plon, 1964); *Mythologiques: Du miel aux cendres* (Paris: Librairie Plon, 1967); *Mythologiques: L'origine des manières de table* (Paris: Librairie Plon, 1968).

9 "Literature Today: Answers to a Questionnaire in *Tel Quel*," in *Critical Essays*, trans. Richard Howard (Evanston, Ill.: Northwestern University Press, 1972), pp. 151–61.

10 "Science versus Literature," in *Introduction to Structuralism*, ed. Michael Lane (New York: Basic Books, Publishers, Inc., 1970), pp. 410–16; citation from p. 413.

11 "The Structuralist Activity," in *Critical Essays*, pp. 213–20.

12 Harold Bloom, *A Map of Misreading* (New York: Oxford University Press, 1975).

13 *Writing Degree Zero and Elements of Semiology*, trans. Annette Lavers and Colin Smith (Boston: Beacon Press, 1970), p. 10.

14 *On Poetic Imagination and Reverie: Selections from the Works of Gaston Bachelard*, trans. with an introduction by Collette Gaudin (Indianapolis: The Bobbs-Merrill Company, Inc., 1971).

15 *Critical Essays*, pp. xi–xxi.

16 *Sade/Fourier/Loyola*, trans. Richard Miller (New York: Hill and Wang, 1976).

17 Ibid., p. 9.

18 "La Sorcière," in *Critical Essays*, pp. 103–15. Linda Orr, "A Sort of History: Jules Michelet's 'La Sorcière,'" *Yale French Studies* 59 (1980): 119–36.

19 "La Sorciere," in *Critical Essays*, p. 146.

20 *A Lover's Discourse: Fragments*, trans. Richard Howard (New York: Hill and Wang, 1978), p. 7.

21 *Pleasure of the Text*, pp. 10–11.

22 Ibid., p. 99.

23 *S/Z*, trans. Richard Miller (New York: Hill and Wang, 1974). The method of "starring" the text can be found in Jean-Pierre Richard, *L'univers imaginaire de Mallarmé* (Paris: Aux Editions du Seuil, 1961).

24 *Sade/Fourier/Loyola*, p. 9 (my emphasis).

25 "Striptease," in *Mythologies*, selected and trans. Annette Lavers (London: Jonathan Cape Ltd., 1972), pp. 84–87.

26 Jorge Luis Borges, "Of Exactitude in Science," in *A Universal History of Infamy*, trans. Norman Thomas di Giovanni (New York: E. P. Dutton and Co., Inc., 1972).

27 Jorge Luis Borges, *The Book of Sand*, trans. Norman Thomas di Giovanni (New York: E. P. Dutton, 1977).

28 Jorge Luis Borges, "The Keeper of the Books," in *In Praise of Darkness*, trans. Norman Thomas di Giovanni (New York: E. P. Dutton and Co., Inc., 1974), p. 75.

29 Jacques Scherer, *Le "Livre" de Mallarmé: Premiers recherches sur des documents inédits* (Paris: Gallimard, 1957).

30 Michel Foucault, "Fantasia of the Library," in *Language, Countermemory, Practice: Selected Essays and Interviews*, ed. Donald F. Bouchard (Ithaca: Cornell University Press, 1980), p. 109.

31 Eugenio Donato, "The Museum's Furnace: Notes Toward a Contextual Reading of *Bouvard and Pécuchet*," in *Textual Strategies: Perspectives in Post-Structuralist Criticism*, ed. Josué V. Harari (Ithaca: Cornell University Press, 1979), pp. 223–24.

32 John O'Neill, "Language and the Voice of Philosophy," introduction to Maurice Merleau-Ponty, *The Prose of the World*, trans. John O'Neill (Evanston, Ill.: Northwestern University Press, 1973), pp. xxv–xxvi.

33 For a comparison of Barthes and Blanchot in these terms, see Tzvetan Todorov, "Reflections on Literature in Contemporary France," *New Literary History* 10, no. 3 (Spring 1979): 511–31.

34 *A Lover's Discourse*, pp. 14–15. In his last book, *La Chambre Claire*, Barthes deals with his mother's death. This work was not available to me. See Tzvetan Todorov, "The Last Barthes," *Critical Inquiry* 7, no. 3 (Spring 1981): 449–54.

A Response to John O'Neill

1 Roland Barthes, *Fragments d'un discours amoureux* (Paris: Seuil, 1977); *Plaisir du texte* (Paris: Seuil, 1973); *Roland Barthes par Roland Barthes* (Paris: Seuil, 1975); English translations: *A Lover's Discourse: Fragments*, trans.

Richard Howard (New York: Hill and Wang, 1978). *The Pleasure of the Text,*
trans. Richard Miller (New York: Hill and Wang, 1975); *Roland Barthes by
Roland Barthes,* trans. Richard Howard (New York: Hill and Wang, 1977).
Cited in my text as *Fragments, Pleasure, RB.* Page references are to the English translations.

2 Friedrich Nietzsche, *Werke,* ed. Giorgio Colli and Mazzino Montinari (Berlin:
de Gruyter, 1968), vol. 6, pt. 2, p. 29; English translation: *Beyond Good and
Evil: Prelude to a Philosophy of the Future,* trans. Walter Kaufman (New
York: Vintage, 1966), pp. 27–28. It is to belabor the obvious that the problem-
atics of the physiology of interpretation in Nietzsche are not exhausted by a
single quotation out of context.

3 The more authoritative definition of deconstruction—"the impossibility to
evaluate positively or negatively the inescapable evaluation that [the word]
implies" (Paul de Man, *Allegories of Reading: Figural Language in Rousseau,
Nietzsche, Rilke, and Proust* [New Haven: Yale University Press, 1979], p. x)
would also question O'Neill's usage.

4 For a discussion of the theoretical fictionality of Freud's "primary process,"
see Sigmund Freud, "The Interpretation of Dreams," in *The Standard Edition
of the Psychological Works,* trans. James Strachey (London: Hogarth Press,
1953), 5: 603; *Gesammelte Werke* (Frankfurt am Main: Fischer, 1960), vol. 3.

5 See Jacques Derrida, "Les fins de l'homme," in *Marges;* English translation:
"The Ends of Man," trans. Edouard Morot-Sir et al., in *Philosophy and Phenomenological Research* 30 no. 1 (1969): 35.

6 Ilya Prigogine and Ilya Stengers, *La nouvelle alliance* (Paris: Gallimard,
1979).

7 If taken out of a merely literary context, the writable [*scriptible*] text can be
understood as a name for the intricate and micrological dynamics of "history,"
"politics," "economics," "psychology," "sexuality," within which we are
written, for which each "individual" is a pluralized reference point, but
which we cannot read. The argument, in a less developed form, is launched in
Barthes, *S/Z* (Paris: Seuil, 1970); English translation: *S/Z,* trans. Richard
Miller (New York: Hill and Wang, 1974), pp. 3–6. This notion can be made
to relate to the notion of the Symbolic Order as developed in the writing
and practice of Jacques Lacan. In this connection, it should be emphasized
that "l'imaginaire" in Barthes, following Sartre and Lacan (in the latter's
work the Imaginary Order is entailed by the Symbolic), should be translated
"the Imaginary," with perhaps a footnote, rather than "image-repertoire."

8 Spivak, "Il faut s'y prendre en se prenant à elles," in *Les fins de l'homme,* ed.
Phillippe Lacoue-Labarthe and Jean-Luc Nancy (Paris: Galilee, 1980).

9 Jacques Derrida, "Les morts de Roland Barthes," *Poétique* 47 (September
1981): 288. Hereafter cited in my text as MRB, followed by page number. Translations are my own.

10 Jacques Derrida, *La carte postale* (Paris: Flammarion, 1980), p. 115.

11 Jacques Derrida, "La double séance," "The Double Session," in *Dissemination,*
trans. Barbara Johnson (Chicago: University of Chicago Press, 1981), p. 207 n.

12 "Feminism and the Critical Tradition," in collection, ed. Pauls Treichler
(Urbana: University of Illinois Press, forthcoming).

13   Woodrow Wilson, "The Study of Administration," *Classics of Public Administration*, ed. Jam M. Shafritz and Albert C. Hyde (Oak Park, Ill.: Moore Publishing Co., 1978).

14   Barthes, *Mythologies*, 2d ed. (Paris: Points, 1971); English translation, *Mythologies*, trans. Annette Lavers (New York: Hill and Wang, 1972).

15   The political implications of collective cryptomania form a part of my current work. The relevant text here is Maria Torok, "Maladie du devil et fantasme du cadavre exquis," *Revue Française de Psychanalyse* 4 (1968).

16   Villers de l'Isle-Adam, *Axel* (Paris: Quantin, 1890); English translation: *Axel*, trans. Marilyn Gaddis Rose (Dublin: Dolmen Press, 1970), p. 170.

17   I quote from an earlier version of O'Neill's paper which he read at the conference on hermeneutics.

18   Irigaray, "Le Marché des femmes," *de Sexe qui n'en est pas un* (Paris: Minuit, 1977), p. 168.

19   At the conference itself, John O'Neill sincerely responded to my final critique: "But it goes without saying that I was thinking of women as well!" Needless to say, it is what goes without saying that outlines the limits of strategic exclusions.

20   For "remains" (*restance*), see Jacques Derrida, *Limited Inc abc* (Baltimore and London: The Johns Hopkins University Press, 1977); English translation by Samuel Weber, *Glyph* 2 (1977): 188–89.

21   All talk of thematics in Derrida should reckon with the cautionary words in "La double séance," *Disseminations* (Paris: Seuil, 1972); "The Double Session," *Dissemination*, pp. 245–51.

22   See Spivak, "Displacement and the Discourse of Woman," which is included in a forthcoming collection from Indiana University Press, edited by Mary Drupnick.

23   "Violence et métaphysique," *L'écriture et la différence* (Paris: Seuil, 1967); "Violence and Metaphysics," *Writing and Difference*, trans. Alan Bass (Chicago: University of Chicago Press, 1978).

24   "Le Supplement de copule: la philosophie devant la linguistique," *Languages* 24 (December 1971); "The Supplement of Copula: Philosophy Before Linguistics," trans. James Creech and Josué Harari, in Josué Harari, ed., *Textual Strategies: Perspectives in Post-Structural Criticism* (Ithaca, N. Y.: Cornell University Press, 1979).

25   *La voix et le phénomène: Introduction au problème du signe dans la phénoménologie de Husserl* (Paris: Presses universitaires de France, 1972); *Speech and Phenomena: And Other Essays on Husserl's Theory of Signs*, trans. David B. Allison (Evanston: Northwestern University Press, 1973).

Surviving Figures

1   For the sake of clarity I use this distinction rather than the sometimes similar one that various rhetoricians have proposed between "trope" and "scheme." Likewise, I use "trope" and "figure" interchangeably, although rhetoricians have argued for a number of ways of distinguishing them.

2 Paul Ricoeur, *The Symbolism of Evil* (New York: Harper and Row, 1967) and
   Freud and Philosophy (New Haven: Yale University Press, 1970).

3 I draw chiefly on the following works by Bloom: *A Map of Misreading* (New
   York: Oxford University Press, 1975); *Poetry and Repression* (New Haven:
   Yale University Press, 1976); "Freud's Concept of Defense and Poetic Will,"
   in *The Literary Freud*, ed. Joseph H. Smith (New Haven: Yale University Press,
   1980), pp. 1–27; and "Freud and the Poetic Sublime: A Catastrophe Theory of
   Creativity," *Antaeus* 30/31 (Spring 1978): 355–77.

4 Bloom, *A Map of Misreading*, p. 91 (Bloom's italics).

5 Jean Laplanche, *Life and Death in Psychoanalysis* (Baltimore: The Johns Hopkins University Press, 1976). See also Anthony Wilden, *System and Structure*
   (London: Tavistock, 1972), chaps. 6 and 12.

6 Recourse to etymology has become a fairly common hidden-ball trick by
   which revisionary critics put in question the appeals to common sense and
   representational norms. See, for example, J. Hillis Miller's rejoinders to
   Wayne Booth and M. H. Abrams in "The Limits of Pluralism," *Critical Inquiry* 3 (Spring 1977): 407–47.

7 There has been a number of attempts to make rhetoric a formal system or at
   least to regularize and rationalize its categories. The most interesting recent
   venture of this sort is the *Rhétorique générale* produced by Groupe μ. (Jacques
   Dubois et al. [Paris: Larousse, 1970, 1976]). This is now available from The
   Johns Hopkins University Press in a translation by P. Burrell and E. M.
   Slotkin.

8 See Maria Ruegg, "Metaphor and Metonymy: The Logic of Structuralist Rhetoric," *Glyph* 6 (1979): 141–57. Jakobson's original article, "Two Aspects of
   Language and Two Types of Aphasic Disorders," first appeared in *Fundamental of Language*, written with Morris Halle (The Hague: Mouton, 1956).

9 See I. A. Richards, *Philosophy of Rhetoric* (New York: Oxford University
   Press, 1936) or Samuel Levin, *The Semantics of Metaphor* (Baltimore: The
   Johns Hopkins University Press, 1977).

10 Paul de Man, *Allegories of Reading* (New Haven: Yale University Press,
   1979), pp. 3–19, 57–78.

11 "The Poet," *Selected Writings of Ralph Waldo Emerson*, ed. Brooks Atkinson
   (New York: Modern Library, 1940).

Hermeneutics and Social Theory

1 For further discussion, see Giddens, *Central Problems in Social Theory:
   Action, Structure and Contradiction in Social Analysis* (London: Macmillan,
   1979), chap. 7.

2 See M. Truzzi, *Verstehen: Subjective Understanding in the Social Sciences*
   (Reading, Mass.: Addison-Wesley, 1974).

3 See Carl G. Hempel, "The Logic of Functional Analysis," in *Aspects of Scientific Explanation* (New York: Free Press, 1965).

4 See my retrospective analysis in "Functionalism: après la lutte," in *Studies in
   Social and Political Theory* (London: Hutchinson, 1977).

5   See *A Contemporary Critique of Historical Materialism* (London: Macmillan, 1981), vol. 1.

6   Peter Winch, *The Idea of a Social Science* (London: Routledge and Kegan Paul, 1958).

7   See, however, Giddens, *New Rules of Sociological Method* (London: Hutchinson, 1976), chap. 1.

8   Cf. K. O. Apel, *Analytical Philosophy of Language and the Geisteswissenschaften* (New York: Reidel, 1967).

9   Kuhn has accepted this. See T. S. Kuhn, *The Essential Tension* (Chicago: University of Chicago Press, 1977).

10 Clifford Geertz, "Blurred Genres: The Refiguration of Social Thought," *American Scholar* 49 (1980).

11 *Central Problems in Social Theory.*

12 Winch, *The Idea of a Social Science*, pp. 111ff.

13 Giddens, *Studies in Social and Political Theory*, pp. 179ff.

14 For one of the clearest statements of this position, see C. W. Lachenmeyer, *The Language of Sociology* (New York: Columbia University Press, 1971).

15 *Central Problems in Social Theory.*

16 Ibid., chap. 1.

17 See "Action, Structure, Power," in Anthony Giddens, *Profiles and Critiques in Social Theory* (London: Macmillan, 1982).

18 Hans-Georg Gadamer, *Truth and Method* (London: Sheed and Ward, 1975).

19 Winch, *The Idea of a Social Science*, p. 71.

20 See Herbert Feigl, "The Origin and Spirit of Logical Positivism," in *The Legacy of Logical Positivism*, ed. Peter Achinstein and Stephen F. Barker (Baltimore: Johns Hopkins University Press, 1969).

21 Alfred Schutz, "Common-Sense and Scientific Interpretation of Human Action," in *Collected Papers* (The Hague: Mouton, 1967), 1: 37.

22 Winch, *The Idea of Social Science*, p. 89.

23 Mary Hesse, *The Structure of Scientific Inference* (London: Macmillan, 1974); Roy Bhaskar, *A Realist Theory of Science* (Leeds: Leeds Books, 1975).

24 *Central Problems in Social Theory*, chap. 7.

25 See Habermas's "auto-critique" in Jürgen Habermas, "Introduction: Some Difficulties in the Attempt to Link Theory and Practice," in *Theory and Practice* (London: Heinemann, 1974).

Comments on Giddens

1   Stone, *The Crisis of the Aristocracy, 1558–1641*, abridged ed. (London: Oxford University Press, 1967), p. 13.

2   Russell, *Parliaments and English Politics, 1621–29* (New York: Oxford University Press, 1979), p. 4.

3   Hexter, "The Not-So-New Men," *New York Review of Books*, December 18, 1980, p. 61.

4   See Notestein's article thus entitled in *Proceedings of the British Academy* 11 (1924–25): 125–75.

5 Hume, *The History of England* (New York, 1880), 4: 315, cited by R. Zaller in "The Concept of Opposition in Early Stuart England," *Albion* 12 (Fall 1980): 211.

6 Hexter, "The Not-So-New Men," p. 58. See also his "Power Struggle, Parliament, and Liberty in Early Stuart England," *Journal of Modern History* 48 (1978): 47.

7 Walsh, "Colligatory Concepts in History," in *Studies in the Nature and Teaching of History*, ed. W. H. Burston and D. Thompson (London, 1967), p. 74.

8 See, for example, J. A. C. Hill, *The English Revolution, 1640* (London: Lawrence and Wishart, 1940), *The Century of Revolution, 1603–1714* (London: Thomas Nelson and Sons, 1961), and B. S. Manning, *The English People and the English Revolution, 1640–49* (London: Heinemann, 1976).

9 Quoted in R. C. Richardson, *The Debate on the English Revolution* (London, Methuen, 1977), p. 97.

10 "Christopher Hill and Lawrence Stone discuss with Peter Burke the English Revolution of the Seventeenth Century," the *Listener*, October 4, 1973, p. 448.

11 Conrad Russell, ed., *The Origins of the English Civil War* (London, 1973), p. 26.

12 See especially Stone, *The Causes of the English Revolution, 1529–1642* (London: Routledge and Kegan Paul, 1972).

13 In Stone's reply to a review of his *Causes of the English Revolution*, by H. G. Koenigsberger, *Journal of Modern History* 48 (1974): 108 .

14 Stone, *Causes of the English Revolution*, pp. 57, 146.

15 See especially Russell, *The Crisis of Parliaments* (Oxford: Oxford University Press, 1971) and his *Parliaments and English Politics*.

16 Hexter, *On Historians* (Cambridge: Harvard University Press, 1979), pp. 205–6.

17 Stone, *Causes of the English Revolution*, pp. 8, 37.

18 Koenigsberger, review of Stone, *Causes of the English Revolution*, p. 104.

19 Stone, *Causes of the English Revolution*, p. 58 .

20 Ibid.

21 Ibid., p. 146.

22 Ibid., pp. 229, 135.

23 Margaret Judson, *The Crisis of the Constitution* (New Brunswick: Rutgers University Press, 1949), p. 161.

24. Hexter, "Power Struggle, Parliament, and Liberty," p. 31.

25 I am not sure that historians recognize a firm distinction, in practice at least, between the contrasts more/less important causes and causes/relevant but noncausal conditions; but I shall not attempt to deal with this problem in this paper.

26 See, for example, Russell, *Crisis of Parliaments*, p. 339.

27 See, for example, my *Perspectives on History* (London: Routledge and Kegan Paul, 1980), chap. 4.

28 *Causes of the English Revolution*, p. 48.

29 J. A. C. Hill and E. Dell, *The Good Old Cause: The English Revolution of 1640–1660* (London: Lawrence and Wishart, 1949), pp. 19–21.

30 Elton, in his review of Russell, *Origins of the English Civil War*, *Historical Journal* 17 (1974): 213.

31 Charles Beard, *The Discussion of Human Affairs* (New York: Macmillan, 1936), p. 79 .

32 As has been persuasively argued by H. L. A. Hart and A. M. Honore in *Causation in the Law* (Oxford: Clarendon Press, 1959).

33 Russell, *Origins of the English Civil War*, p. 24.

34 Ibid., pp. 12, 23.

35 Nagel, "Determinism in History," in *Ideas of History*, ed. R. H. Nash (New York, 1969), 2: 340ff.

36 See, for example, Russell, *Origins of the English Civil War*, p. 4.

37 Stone, *Causes of the English Revolution*, p. 11.

38 Russell, *Crisis of Parliaments*, p. 339. In talking of the war's "avoidability," however, he may wish only to address the question whether, without giving up their whole positions, there was anything the principal actors could have done to avert it—that is, the *practical* question of whether any possibility of reasonable compromise remained (this was suggested to me by Professor B. H. McCullagh).

39 See, for example, Russell's "Parliamentary History in Perspective, 1604–1629," *History* 209 (1976): 1.

40 A feature of historical reconstruction brought forcefully to the attention of philosophers of history by Arthur Danto in his *Analytical Philosophy of History* (Cambridge: Cambridge University Press, 1965).

41 This paper was written during the tenure of a Killam Research Fellowship and a Research Grant from the Canadian Social Sciences and Humanities Research Council. I am grateful to these bodies for their assistance.

Conflicting Interpretations in History

1 An excellent guide to the bibliography of items under discussion in Dray's essay and my own is provided in the annotated bibliography in J. P. Kenyon, *Stuart England* (London: Allen Lane, 1978), pp. 357–72. I owe this reference to Dr. Margaret Bricke.

2 Harrington, *Oceana* (1656).

3 C. B. Macpherson, *The Political Theory of Possessive Individualism: Hobbes to Locke* (Oxford: Oxford University Press, 1962), esp. chaps. 2–4.

4 Such a claim is strongly suggested in one of Marx's famous *mots*: "When the real aim had been achieved, when the bourgeois transformation of English society had been accomplished, Locke supplanted Habakkuk" (*Eighteenth Brumaire of Louis Bonaparte*).

5 Dray appears to argue (1) that Stone denies a temporal overlap between the three kinds of factors and (2) that, therefore, the factors are not *independently* necessary, with the result that the gradual increase in probability values would be undermined. This is doubtful. Even if Stone wished to deny the overlap, a point that is not itself clear, it would not follow that a temporally defined sequence, of the sort Dray here ascribes to Stone, could not exhibit in-

creasing probability value. If the *order* in which certain antecedent events occurred can affect the probability of some subsequent event's occurring, then this is sufficient to establish the point Stone is concerned to make. The issue of independent necessity is not raised in any case, for, clearly, some of the antecedent events will be sufficient but not necessary conditions of the subsequent event's occurring.

6   An event or deed to be explained must always be explained *under some particular description;* one never explains the event or deed per se. This point is drawn from Arthur Danto, *Analytical Philosophy of History* (Cambridge: Cambridge University Press, 1965), pp. 218–19.

7   See Rex Martin, *Historical Explanation: Re-enactment and Practical Inference* (Ithaca, N.Y.: Cornell University Press, 1977), pp. 161, 167.

8   G. H. von Wright emphasizes that entities in a causal relation must be logically independent of one another, as follows: if *C* is the cause of *E*, then it must be *logically* possible that *C* is instantiated (is true) when *E* is not; von Wright refers to this relationship as "humean connection." (See his *Explanation and Understanding* [Ithaca, N.Y.: Cornell University Press, 1971], pp. 93, 195, n. 18; also pp. 18, 139.) Many philosophers have argued, as well, that if *C* is the cause of *E*, then there must be a law that includes *C* and *E* or from which they could be derived.

9   William H. Seward coined this memorable phrase. For discussion see William H. Dray, "Some Causal Accounts of the American Civil War," *Daedalus* 91 (1962): 578–92.

10 The leading advocate of an abnormalist criterion for causation is Morton G. White. See, in particular, his *Foundations of Historical Knowledge* (New York: Harper and Row, 1965), pp. 107–8, 115–33.

11 Important "interventionist" accounts of causality are given in von Wright, *Explanation and Understanding,* chap. 2, and in his *Causality and Determinism* (New York: Columbia University Press, 1974). Earlier accounts, still of considerable philosophical interest, are found in R. G. Collingwood, *An Essay on Metaphysics* (Oxford: Oxford University Press, 1940), pt. 3; and D. Gasking, "Causation and Recipes," *Mind* 64 (1955): 479–87.

12 Dray's most general discussion of causes in history is found in chap. 4 ("A Controversy Over Causes: A. J. P. Taylor and the Origins of the Second World War") of his book *Perspectives on History* (London: Routledge and Kegan Paul, 1980), pp. 69–96. The reader should refer to this chapter in order to round out and confirm what I say about Dray in the present essay.

13 The example is drawn from Charles Beard, as Dray notes. This particular view of Beard's perhaps lay behind his ultimate reluctance to allow talk of causes in history at all. (See Charles A. Beard, note to Proposition Ten, in *Theory and Practice in Historical Study: A Report of the Committee on Historiography.* Social Science Research Council, Bulletin 54 [1946], pp. 136–137 n.)

14 That Dray's preferred paradigm, for talk of causation in history, is that of agent causality (a term I have taken over from Roderick Chisholm) should be clear from the following works by Dray: *Laws and Explanation in History* (London: Oxford University Press, 1957), esp. chap. 5; *Philosophy of History* (Englewood Cliffs, N.J.: Prentice-Hall, 1964), esp. chap. 2; "The Historical Ex-

planation of Actions Reconsidered," in *Philosophy and History*, ed. Sidney Hook (New York: New York University Press, 1963), pp. 105–35; and *Perspectives on History*, esp. pp. 58–60.

15 See von Wright, *Explanations and Understanding*, pp. 142–43 and 85–86 esp. For further discussion see my paper, "Explanation and Understanding in History," in *Essays on Explanation and Understanding*, ed. J. Manninen and R. Tuomela (Dordrecht: D. Reidel, 1976), esp. pp. 315ff and 327.

16 See Dray, "Historical Explanation of Actions Reconsidered," pp. 131–33.

Bibliography

Abrams, M. H. "How to Do Things with Texts." *Partisan Review* 64 (1979): 566–88.

Alexander, Edwin. "Hermeneutical Violence: Heidegger's Kant-Interpretation." *Philosophy Today* 25 (Winter 1981): 286–306.

Allison, David. "Destruktion/Deconstruction in the Text of Nietzsche." *boundary 2* 8 (Fall 1979): 197–222.

Althusser, Louis, and Etienne Balibar. *Reading Capital*. Trans. by Ben Brewster. London: New Left Books, 1972.

Altieri, Charles. "The Hermeneutics of Literary Indeterminancy: A Dissent from the New Orthodoxy." *New Literary History* 10 (Autumn 1978): 72–99.

———. *Act & Quality: A Theory of Literary and Humanistic Understanding*. Amherst: University of Massachusetts Press, 1981.

Antoni, Carlo. *From History to Sociology: The Transition in German Historical Thinking*. Trans. by Hayden White. London: Merlin Press, 1962.

Apel, Karl-Otto. *Analytic Philosophy of Language and the Geisteswissenschaften*. Trans. by H. Holstelilie. Dordrecht: D. Reidel, 1967.

———. "Szientifik, Hermeneutik, Ideologie-Kritik." *Man and World* 1 (1968): 37–63.

———. *Hermeneutik und Ideologiekritik*. Frankfurt: Suhrkamp, 1971.

———. "The A Priori of Communication and the Foundation of the Humanities." *Man and World* 5 (1972): 3–37.

———. "Communication and the Foundations of the Humanities." *Acta Sociologica* 15 (1972): 7–26.

———. "From Kant to Peirce: The Semiotical Transformation of Transcendental Logic." In *Kant's Theory of Knowledge*, ed. L. W. Beck. Dordrecht: Reidel, 1974.

———. "The Problem of Philosophical Fundamental-Grounding in Light of a Transcendental Pragmatics of Language." *Man and World* 8 (1975): 239–75.

———. "Causal Explanation, Motivational Explanation, and Hermeneutic Understanding." *Ajatus* 37 (1977).

———. "Types of Social Science in the Light of Human Interests of Knowledge." *Social Research* 44 (Autumn 1977): 425–70.

———. "The Common Presuppositions of Hermeneutics and Ethics: Types of Rationality Beyond Science and Technology." *Research in Phenomenology* 9 (1979): 35–53.

———. *Towards a Transformation of Philosophy*. Trans. by Glyn Adey and David Frisby. Boston: Routledge and Kegan Paul, 1980.

Apel, Karl-Otto, J. N. Mohanty, and Anthony Quinton. "Discussion: Theories of Meaning in the Analytic and Continental Traditions." *Graduate Faculty Philosophy Journal* 7 (Spring 1978): 79–105.

Aquinas, St. Thomas. *Aristotle: On Interpretation (Commentary by St Thomas and Cajetan: Peri Hermenias)*. Trans. by Jean T. Oesterle. Milwaukee: Marquette University Press, 1962.

Ast, Friedrich, *Grundlinien der Grammatik, Hermeneutik und Kritik*. Landshut: Thomann, 1808.

Auerbach, Erich. *Scenes from the Drama of European Literature*. New York: Meridian Books, 1959.

Bachelard, Gaston. "Preliminary Critique of the Concept of Epistemological Frontiers." *Graduate Faculty Philosophy Journal* 6 (Fall 1977): 201–208A.

———. "Discursive Idealism." *Graduate Faculty Philosophy Journal* 7 (Spring 1978): 3–13.

Bahti, T. "Vico, Auerbach, and Literary History." *Philological Quarterly* 60 (Spring 1981): 239–55.

Barthes, Roland. *Writing Degree Zero/Elements of Semiology*. Trans. by Annette Lavers and Colin Smith. Boston: Beacon Press, 1970.

———. *Mythologies*. Trans. by Annette Lavers. New York: Hill and Wang, 1971.

———. *Critical Essays*. Trans. by Richard Howard. Evanston: Northwestern University Press, 1972.

———. *The Pleasure of the Text*. Trans. by Richard Miller. New York: Hill and Wang, 1975.

———. *S/Z*. Trans. by Richard Miller. New York: Hill and Wang, 1975.

———. *Sade/Fourier/Loyola*. Trans. by Richard Miller, New York: Hill and Wang, 1976.

———. *Image Music Text*. Trans. by Stephen Heath. New York: Hill and Wang, 1977.

———. *On Racine*. Trans. by Richard Howard. New York: Hill and Wang, 1977.

———. *Roland Barthes*. Trans. by Richard Howard. New York: Hill and Wang, 1977.

Bauman, Zygmunt. *Hermeneutics & Social Science*. London: Hutchinson, 1978.

Benson, John Edward. "Schleiermacher's Hermeneutics." Ph.D. diss., Columbia University, 1967.

Benton, Ted. *Philosophical Foundations of the Three Sociologies*. London: Routledge and Kegan Paul, 1977.

Bernstein, Richard J. *The Restructuring of Social and Political Theory*. Philadelphia: University of Pennsylvania Press, 1978.

———. "From Hermeneutics to Praxis." *Review of Metaphysics* 35 (1982): 823–45.

Betti, Emilio. *Teoria Generale della Interpretazione*. 2 vols. Milan: Istituto di Teoria della Interpretazione, 1955. Trans. by the author into German: *Allgemeine Auslegungslehre als Methodik der Geisteswissenschaften*. Tuebingen: J. C. B. Mohr, 1967.

———. *Die Hermeneutik als allgemeine Methode der Geisteswissenschaften*. Tuebingen: J. C. B. Mohr, 1962 (2d ed., 1972). Trans. by Josef Bleicher in *Contemporary Hermeneutics*.

Black, Max. "Meaning and Intention: An Examination of Grice's Views." *New Literary History* 4 (Winter 1973): 257–79.

Blasi, Anthony; Fabio Dasilva; and Andrew J. Weigert. *Toward an Interpretive Sociology*. Washington: University Press of America, 1978.

Bleicher, Josef. *The Hermeneutic Imagination: Outline of a Positive Critique of Scientism and Sociology.* Boston: Routledge & Kegan Paul, 1982.

————, ed. *Contemporary Hermeneutics: Hermeneutics as Method, Philosophy, and Critique.* Boston: Routledge and Kegan Paul, 1980.

Bloom, Harold. *A Map of Misreading.* New York: Oxford University Press, 1975.

Bloom, Harold, Paul de Man, Jacques Derrida, Geoffrey Hartmann, and J. Hillis Miller. *Deconstruction and Criticism.* New York: Seabury Press, 1979.

Blumenberg, Hans. *The Legitimacy of the Modern Age.* Trans. by Robert Wallace. Cambridge: MIT Press, 1983.

Boeckh, August. *On Interpretation and Criticism.* Trans. by John Paul Pritchard. Norman: University of Oklahoma Press, 1968.

Bollnow, Otto Friedrich. *Die Lebensphilosophie.* Berlin: Springer Verlag, 1958.

————. "What Does It Mean to Understand a Writer Better Than He Understood Himself?" *Philosophy Today* 23 (Spring 1979): 16–28.

Bourgeois, P. *Extension of Ricoeur's Hermeneutics.* The Hague: Nijhoff, 1975.

Brown, P. L. "Epistemology and Method: Althusser, Foucault, Derrida." *Cultural Hermeneutics* 3 (1975): 147–63.

Bruns, Gerald. *Inventions: Writing, Textuality and Understanding in Literary History.* New Haven: Yale University Press, 1982.

Bubner, Ruediger. "Theory and Practice in the Light of the Hermeneutic-Criticist Controversy." *Cultural Hermeneutics* 2 (1975): 337–52.

————. "Is Transcendental Hermeneutics Possible?" In *Essays on Explanation and Understanding,* ed. Juha Manninen and Raimo Tuomela. Dordrecht: Reidel Pub. Co., 1976.

Buck, Guenther. "The Structure of Hermeneutic Experience and the Problem of Tradition." *New Literary History* 10 (Autumn 1978): 31–47.

————. "Hermeneutics of Texts and Hermeneutics of Action." *New Literary History* 12 (Autumn 1980), 87–96.

Bultmann, Rudolf. "The Problem of Hermeneutics." In *Essays Philosophical and Theological.* New York: Macmillan, 1955.

————. *Jesus Christ and Mythology.* New York: Charles Scribner's and Sons, 1958.

————. "Is Exegesis without Presuppositions Possible?" In *Existence & Faith: Shorter Writings of Rudolf Bultmann.* New York: Meridian, 1960.

Cain, W. E. "Authors and Authority in Interpretation." *Georgia Review* 34 (Fall 1980): 617–34.

Calinescu, M. "Hermeneutics or Poetics." *Journal of Religion* 59 (1979): 1–17.

Chabot, C. B. "Fates of Interpretation." *Georgia Review* 34 (Fall 1980): 639–57.

Child, Arthur. *Interpretation: A General Theory.* University of California Publications in Philosophy, vol. 36. Berkeley: University of California Press, 1965.

Collins, James. *Interpreting Modern Philosophy.* Princeton: Princeton University Press, 1972.

————. "Interpretation: The Interweave of Problems." *New Literary History* 4 (Winter 1973): 389–403.

Cooper, Barry. "Hermeneutics and Social Science." *Philosophy of the Social Sciences* 11 (1981): 79–90.

Coreth, Emrich. "From Hermeneutics to Metaphysics." *International Philosophical Quarterly* 11 (1971): 249–59.

Corngold. S. "Error in Paul de Man." *Critical Inquiry* 8 (Spring 1982): 489–513.

Corrington, Robert S. "Horizontal Hermeneutics and the Actual Infinite." *Graduate Faculty Philosophy Journal* 8 (Spring 1982): 36–97.

Cotgrove, Stephen. "Styles of Thought: Science, Romanticism, and Modernization." *British Journal of Sociology* 29 (1978): 358–71.

Crowley, Charles B. *Universal Mathematics in Aristotelian-Thomistic Philosophy: The Hermeneutics of Aristotelian Texts Relative to Universal Mathematics.* Washington: University Press of America, 1980.

Dallmayr, Fred R., and Thomas A. McCarthy, eds. *Understanding & Social Inquiry.* Notre Dame: University of Notre Dame Press, 1977.

Danto, Arthur C. "Deep Interpretation." *Journal of Philosophy* 78 (1981): 691–706.

De George, Richard T., and M. Fernande, eds. *The Structuralists: From Marx to Lévi-Strauss.* Garden City, N.Y.: Anchor Books, 1972.

de Man, Paul. *Allegories of Reading.* New Haven: Yale University Press, 1979.

Den Hengel, John W. Van. *The Home of Meaning: The Hermeneutics of the Subject of Paul Ricoeur.* Washington: University Press of America, 1982.

Derrida, Jacques. *Of Grammatology.* Trans. by Gayatri Spivak. Baltimore: Johns Hopkins University Press, 1976.

———. "Fors." *Georgia Review* 31 (Spring 1977): 64–116.

———. *Writing & Difference.* Trans. by Alan Bass. Chicago: University of Chicago Press, 1978.

———. *Spurs: Nietzsche's Styles.* Trans. by Barbara Harlow. Chicago: University of Chicago Press, 1979.

Dilthey, Wilhelm. *Gesammelte Schriften.* 18 vols. Goettingen: Vandenhoeck & Ruprecht, 1913–1967 (Vol. 7, *Der Aufbau der geschichtlichen Welt in den Geisteswissenschaften,* 1927). Volumes 1–12 reprinted, Stuttgart: B G Teubner, 1958.

———. *Pattern & Meaning in History: Thoughts on History & Society.* Ed. and intro. by H. P. Rickman. New York: Harper and Row, 1962.

———. "The Rise of Hermeneutics." *New Literary History* 3 (Winter 1972): 229–44.

———. *Selected Writings.* Ed., trans., and intro. by H. P. Rickman. Cambridge: Cambridge University Press, 1976.

Dockhorn, Klaus. "Hans-Georg Gadamer's *Truth & Method.*" *Philosophy and Rhetoric* 13 (Summer 1980): 160–80.

Doyle, Esther M., and Virginia H. Floyd, eds. *Studies in Interpretation, No. 2.* Atlantic Highlands: Humanities Press, 1977.

Dreyfus, Hubert L. "Holism and Hermeneutics." *Review of Metaphysics* 34 (1980): 3–55.

Dreyfus, Hubert, and Paul Rabinow. *Michel Foucault: Beyond Structuralism and Hermeneutics.* Chicago: University of Chicago Press, 1982.

Droysen, Johann Gustav. *Outline of the Principles of History.* Trans. by E. Benjamin Andrews. New York: Howard Fertig, 1967. (Orig. published, 1867.)

Dufrenne, Mikel. *The Phenomenology of Aesthetic Experience.* Trans. by E. Casey; A. Anderson; W. Domingo; and L. Jacobson. Evanston: Northwestern University Press, 1974.

Eco, Umberto. *Theory of Semiotics.* Bloomington: Indiana University Press, 1976.

————. *The Role of the Reader: Explorations in the Semiotics of Texts.* Bloomington: Indiana University Press, 1979.

Empson, William. *Seven Types of Ambiguity.* 3d ed. New York: New Directions,
1953.

Ermarth, Michael. *Wilhelm Dilthey: The Critique of Historical Reason.* Chicago:
University of Chicago Press, 1978.

————. "Historical Understanding in the Thought of Wilhelm Dilthey." *History
and Theory* 20 (1981): 323–34.

————. "Transformation of Hermeneutics: 19th Century Ancients and 20th Century Moderns." *Monist* 64 (1981): 175–94.

Farrar, Frederic W. *The History of Interpretation.* (Bampton Lectures, 1885.) Grand
Rapids: Baker Book House, 1961.

Fekete, John. *The Critical Twilight: Explorations in the Ideology of Anglo-
American Literary Theory from Eliot to McCluhan.* Boston: Routledge and
Kegan Paul, 1977.

Femia, J. V. "Historicist Critique of Revisionist Methods for Studying the History
of Ideas." *History and Theory* 20 (1981): 113–34.

Feyerabend, Paul. *Against Method: Outline of an Anarchistic Theory of Knowledge.* London: New Left Books, 1975.

Forstman, H. Jackson. "The Understanding of Language by Friedrich Schlegel and
Schleiermacher." *Soundings* 51 (Summer 1968): 146–65.

Foucault, Michel. *The Order of Things: An Archaeology of the Human Sciences.*
New York: Pantheon, 1970.

————. *The Archaeology of Knowledge* and *The Discourse on Language.* Trans. by
A. M. Sheridan Smith. New York: Pantheon, 1972.

————. *Language, Counter-Memory, Practice.* Ed. by D. F. Conchard. Ithaca: Cornell University Press, 1977.

Frei, Hans W. *The Eclipse of Biblical Narrative: A Study of Eighteenth and Nineteenth Century Hermeneutics.* New Haven: Yale University Press, 1974.

Funk, Robert W., ed. *History & Hermeneutic* (Journal for Theology and the
Church, Vol. 4). Tuebingen: J. C. B. Mohr, 1967 and New York: Harper & Row,
1967.

————. *Schleiermacher as Contemporary* (Journal for Theology and the Church,
vol. 7). New York: Herder & Herder, 1970.

Gadamer, Hans-Georg. "Notes on Planning for the Future." *Daedalus* 95 (Spring
1966): 572–89.

————. "Schleiermacher als Platoniker" (1969). In *Kleine Schriften III: Idee und
Sprache.* Tuebingen: J. C. B. Mohr (Paul Siebeck), 1972.

————. "Concerning Empty and Ful-filled Time." *Southern Journal of Philosophy*
8 (Winter 1970): 341–54.

————. "The Power of Reason." *Man and World* 3 (1970): 5–15.

————. "The Problem of Language in Schleiermacher's Hermeneutics." In *Schleiermacher as Contemporary,* ed. R. W. Funk.

————. "The Continuity of History and the Existential Moment." *Philosophy Today* 16 (Fall 1972): 230–40.

————. "Hermeneutics and Social Science"; "Summation"; "Response." *Cultural
Hermeneutics* 2 (1975): 307–16, 329–30, 357.

———. "The Problem of Historical Consciousness." *Graduate Faculty Philosophy Journal* 5 (1975): 8–52. Reprinted in *Interpretive Social Science*, ed. Rabinow and Sullivan.

———. *Truth & Method*. Trans. by G. Barden and J. Cumming. New York: Seabury, 1975.

———. *Hegel's Dialectic: Five Hermeneutical Studies*. Trans. and intro. by P. Christopher Smith. New Haven: Yale University Press, 1976.

———. *Philosophical Hermeneutics*. Trans. and ed. by David Linge. Berkeley: University of California Press, 1976.

———. "Theory, Technology, Practice: Task of the Science of Man." *Social Research* 44 (Autumn 1977): 529–61.

———. "The Western View of the Inner Experience of Time and the Limits of Thought." In *Time and the Philosophies*. Unesco, 1977.

———. "Historical Transformation of Reason." In *Rationality Today*, ed. Theodore Geraets. Ottawa: University of Ottawa Press, 1979.

———. *Dialogue and Dialectic: Eight Hermeneutical Studies on Plato*. Trans. by P. Christopher Smith. New Haven: Yale University Press, 1980.

———. *Reason in the Age of Science*. Trans. by Frederick Lawrence. Cambridge: MIT Press, 1982.

Gadamer, Hans-Georg, and Leo Strauss. "Correspondence Concerning *Wahrheit und Methode*." *Independent Journal of Philosophy* 2 (1978): 5–12.

Gardner, Howard. *The Quest for Mind: Piaget, Lévi-Strauss, and the Structuralist Movement*. New York: Vintage Books, 1974.

Geras, Norman. "Literature of Revolution." *New Left Review*, nos. 113–14 (Jan.–April 1979): 3–42.

Gerhart, Mary. "Imagination and History in Ricoeur's Interpretation Theory." *Philosophy Today* 23 (Spring 1979): 51–68.

Giddens, Anthony. *New Rules of Sociological Method: A Positive Critique of Interpretive Sociologies*. New York: Basic Books, 1976.

———. *Studies in Social & Political Theory*. London: Hutchinson, 1977.

———. "Mediator of Meaning." *Times Literary Supplement*, no. 4118, March 5, 1982, 240.

Glowinski, Michel. "Reading, Interpretation, Reception." *New Literary History* 11 (Autumn 1979): 75–82.

Graff, Gerald. *Literature Against Itself*. Chicago: University of Chicago Press, 1979.

Graham, Gordon. "Can There be a History of Philosophy?" *History and Theory* 21 (1982): 37–52.

Gras, Vernon, ed. *European Literary Theory and Practice*. New York: Delta Books, 1973.

Green, Bryan S. "On the Evaluation of Sociological Theory." *Philosophy of the Social Sciences* 7 (March 1977): 33–50.

Habermas, Jürgen. "A Review of Gadamer's *Truth & Method*" (1967). In *Understanding and Social Inquiry*, ed. Dallmayr and McCarthy.

———. "Zur Logik der Sozialwissenschaften." *Philosophische Rundschau* 5 (1967): 149–76.

———. "The Hermeneutic Claim to Universality" (1971). In *Contemporary Hermeneutics*, ed. Bleicher.

Hamlin, Cyrus. "Conscience of Narrative: Toward a Hermeneutics of Transcendence." *New Literary History* 13 (Winter 1982): 205–30.

Hartmann, Geoffrey. "The Interpreter: A Self-Analysis." *New Literary History* 4 (Winter 1973): 213–27.

———. "Centaur: Remarks on the Psychology of the Critic." *Salmagundi*, no. 43 (Winter 79): 130–39.

Heelan, Patrick. "Towards a Hermeneutic of Natural Science." *Main Currents* 28 (1972): 85–93.

Hinman, L. M. "Quid facti or quid juris?: The Fundamental Ambiguity of Gadamer's Understanding of Hermeneutics." *Philosophy and Phenomenological Research* 40 (1980): 512–35.

Hirsch, Eric D., Jr. "Truth and Method in Interpretation" (review of Gadamer). *Review of Metaphysics* 18 (1965): 488–507.

———. *Validity in Interpretation.* New Haven: Yale University Press, 1967.

———. "Three Dimensions of Hermeneutics." *New Literary History* 3 (Winter 1972): 246–61.

———. *The Aims of Interpretation.* Chicago: University of Chicago Press, 1976.

Hodges, H. A. *Wilhelm Dilthey: An Introduction.* London: Routledge and Kegan Paul, 1944.

———. *The Philosophy of Wilhelm Dilthey.* London: Routledge and Kegan Paul, 1952.

Holborn, Hajo. "Wilhelm Dilthey and the Critique of Historical Reason." *Journal of the History of Ideas* 2 (1950).

Hookway, Christopher, and Philip Pettit, eds. *Action & Interpretation.* Cambridge: Cambridge University Press, 1978.

Horkheimer, Max. "The Relation Between Psychology and Sociology in the Work of Wilhelm Dilthey." *Studies in Philosophy and Social Science* 8 (1939): 430–43.

How, Alan R. "Dialogue as Productive Limitation in Social Theory: The Habermas-Gadamer Debate." *Journal of the British Society for Phenomenology* 11 (1980): 131–43.

Howard, Roy J. *Three Faces of Hermeneutics: An Introduction to Current Theories of Understanding.* Berkeley: University of California Press, 1982.

Hoy, David Couzens. *The Critical Circle: Literature, History, and Philosophical Hermeneutics.* Berkeley: University of California Press, 1978.

———. "Hermeneutic Circularity, Indeterminacy, and Incommensurability." *New Literary History* 10 (1978): 162–73.

———. "Forgetting the Text: Derrida's Critique of Hermeneutics." *boundary 2* 8 (Fall 1979): 223–35.

———. "Taking History Seriously: Focault, Gadamer, Habermas." *Union Seminary Quarterly Review* 34 (Winter 1979): 85–95.

———. "Must We Say What We Mean?" *Review of the University of Ottawa* 50 (1980): 411–26.

Humboldt, Wilhelm von. *Linguistic Variability and Intellectual Development.* Trans. by George Buck and Frithjof A. Raven. Philadelphia: University of Pennsylvania Press, 1972.

Ihde, Don. *Hermeneutic Phenomenology.* Evanston: Northwestern University Press, 1971.

———. "Interpreting Hermeneutics." *Man and World* 13 (1980) : 325–44.

Ingarden, Roman. *The Cognition of the Literary Work of Art.* Trans. by Ruth Crowley and Kenneth Olson. Evanston: Northwestern University Press, 1973.

———. *The Literary Work of Art: An Investigation of the Borderlines of Ontology, Logic, and Theory of Literature.* Trans. by George Grabowicz. Evanston: Northwestern University Press, 1973.

Iser, Wolfgang. "The Current Situation of Literary Theory: Key Concepts and the Imaginary." *New Literary History* 11 (Autumn 1979) : 1–20.

Jameson, Fredric. *Marxism and Form: Twentieth-Century Dialectical Theories of Literature.* Princeton: Princeton University Press, 1974.

———. *The Prison House of Language: A Critical Account of Structuralism and Russian Formalism.* Princeton: Princeton University Press, 1974.

———. "Magical Narratives: Romance as Genre." *New Literary History* 7 (Autumn 1975) : 135–63.

———. "Figural Relativism, or the Poetics of Historiography." (Review of Hayden White's *Metahistory*) *Diacritics* 6 (Spring 1976) : 2–9.

———. "On Goffman's *Frame Analysis*." *Theory and Society* 3 (1976) : 119–33.

———. "Ideology, Narrative Analysis, and Popular Culture." *Theory and Society* 4 (1977) : 543–59.

———. "Ideology & Symbolic Form," *Critical Inquiry* 5 (Winter 1978).

———. "Marxism and Historicism." *New Literary History* 11 (Autumn 1979) : 41–73.

———. *The Political Unconscious: Narrative as a Socially Symbolic Act.* Ithaca: Cornell University Press, 1981.

Jauss, Hans Robert. "The Idealist Embarrassment: Observations on Marxist Aesthetics." *New Literary History* 7:1 (Autumn 1975) : 191–208.

———. "Alterity & Modernity of Medieval Literature." *New Literary History* 10 (Winter 1979) : 181–227.

———. "The Limits and Tasks of Literary Hermeneutics." *Diogenes*, no. 17 (1980) : 92–119.

———. *Aesthetic Experience & Literary Hermeneutics.* Trans. by Michael Shaw. Minneapolis: University of Minnesota Press, 1982.

Jensen, Bernard. "The Recent Trend in the Interpretation of Dilthey." *Philosophy of the Social Sciences* 8 (1978) : 419–38.

Johnson, Patricia, ed. "Hermeneutics." *University of Dayton Review* (1983).

Juhl, P. D. *Interpretation: An Essay in the Philosophy of Literary Criticism.* Princeton: Princeton University Press, 1980.

Jung, Hwa Jol. "A Hermeneutical Accent on the Conduct of Political Inquiry." *Human Studies* 1 (1978) : 48–82.

Kelly, Louis G. *The True Interpreter: A History of Translation Theory and Practice in the West.* Oxford: Basil Blackwell, 1979.

Kermode, Frank. *The Genesis of Secrecy: On the Interpretation of Narrative.* Cambridge: Harvard University Press, 1979.

———. "Institutional Control of Interpretation." *Salmagundi*, no. 43 (Winter 1979) : 72–86.

Kimmerle, Heinz. "Introduction." In Schleiermacher's *Hermeneutics.*

Kinneavy, James. *Theory of Discourse.* Englewood Cliffs: Prentice-Hall, 1971.

Kirkland, Frank M. "Gadamer & Ricoeur: The Paradigm of the Text." *Graduate Faculty Philosophy Journal* 6 (Winter 1977): 131–44.

Kisiel, Theodore. "The Happening of Tradition: The Hermeneutics of Gadamer and Heidegger." *Man and World* 2 (1969): 358–85.

———. "Ideology Critique and Phenomenology: The Current Debate in German Philosophy." *Philosophy Today* 14 (Fall 1970): 151–60.

Klemm, David E. *The Hermeneutical Theory of Paul Ricoeur.* Lewisburg: Bucknell University Press, 1983.

Kockelmans, Joseph. "On Myth and Its Relationship to Hermeneutics." *Cultural Hermeneutics* 1 (1973): 47–86.

———. "Toward an Interpretive or Hermeneutic Social Science." *Graduate Faculty Philosophy Journal* 5 (Fall 1975): 73–96.

Krieger, Murray. *Theory of Criticism: A Tradition & Its System.* Baltimore: Johns Hopkins University Press, 1976.

Kristeva, Julia. *Desire in Language: A Semiotic Approach to Literature & Art.* Trans. by Thomas Gora and Alice Jardine. New York: Columbia University Press, 1980.

Kuhns, Richard. *Structures of Experience: Essays on the Affinity Between Philosophy & Literature.* New York: Harper and Row, 1974.

LaCapra, Dominick. "Political Unconscious." *History and Theory* 21 (1982): 83–106.

Laslett, Peter. "The Wrong Way Through the Telescope: A Note on Literary Evidence in Sociology and in Historical Sociology." *British Journal of Sociology* 27 (1976): 319–42.

Lawrence, Fred. "Dialectics & Hermeneutic: Foundational Perspectives on the Relationship Between Human Studies and the Project of Human Self-Constitution." *Stony Brook Studies in Philosophy* 1 (1974): 37–59.

———. "Gadamer and Lonergan: A Dialectical Comparison." *International Philosophical Quarterly* 20 (1980): 25–47.

Lecourt, Dominique. *Marxism & Epistemology: Bachelard, Canguilhem, and Foucault.* Trans. by Ben Brewster. London: New Left Books, 1975.

Legrand, Michael. "How New is 'New Hermeneutics'?" *Journal of Dharma* 5 (1980): 94–108.

Lemert, Charles. "Language, Structure, and Measurement: Structuralist Semiotics and Sociology." *American Journal of Sociology* 84 (1979): 929–57.

———. *Sociology and the Twilight of Man.* Carbondale: Southern Illinois University Press, 1979.

Lentricchia, Frank. *After the New Criticism.* Chicago: University of Chicago Press, 1980.

Lund, A., and Luce, A. *Hermeneutics.* Life Publishers International, 1979.

Maimonides, Moses. *The Guide for the Perplexed.* 2d ed., trans. by M. Friedlaender. 1904; New York: Dover Publications, 1956.

Makkreel, Rudolf A. *Dilthey: Philosopher of the Human Studies.* Princeton: Princeton University Press, 1975.

Marino, Adrian. "Two Hermeneutical Circuits: Part/Whole and Analysis/Synthesis." *Dialectics and Humanism* 3 (1976): 125–34.

Marle, Rene. *Introduction to Hermeneutics.* New York: Herder and Herder, 1967.

Mazzeo, Joseph Anthony. *Varieties of Interpretation.* Notre Dame: University of Notre Dame Press, 1978.

MacCannell, Dean, and Juliet Flower MacCannell. *The Time of the Sign: A Semiotic Interpretation of Modern Culture.* Bloomington: Indiana University Press, 1982.

McCarthy, Thomas A. "A Theory of Communicative Competence." *Philosophy of the Social Sciences* 3 (1973): 135–56.

————. "The Problem of Rationality in Social Anthropology." *Stony Brook Studies in Philosophy* 1 (1974): 1–21.

McIntosh, Donald. "Habermas on Freud." *Social Research* 44 (Autumn 1977): 562–98.

McKnight, Edgar V. *Meaning in Texts: The Historical Shaping of a Narrative Hermeneutics.* Philadelphia: Fortress Press, 1978.

MacLean, M. J. "Johan Gustave Droysen and the Development of Historical Hermeneutics." *History and Theory* 21 (1982): 347–65.

Medina, Angela. *Reflection, Time and the Novel: Toward a Communicative Theory of Literature.* Boston: Routledge and Kegan Paul, 1979.

Meiland, Jack W. "Interpretation as a Cognitive Discipline." *Philosophy and Literature* 2 (1978): 23–45.

Metscher, Thomas. "Literature and Art as Ideological Form." *New Literary History* 11 (Autumn 1979): 21–39.

Minogue, K. R. "Method in Intellectual History: Quentin Skinner's *Foundations.*" *Philosophy* 56 (1981): 533–52.

Misgeld, Dieter. "Critical Theory and Hermeneutics: The Debate Between Habermas and Gadamer." In *On Critical Theory,* ed. O'Neill.

Morawski, Stefan. *An Inquiry into the Fundamentals of Aesthetics.* Boston: MIT Press, 1974.

Mueller-Vollmer, Kurt. *Towards a Phenomenological Theory of Literature: A Study of Wilhelm Dilthey's Poetik.* The Hague: Mouton, 1963.

————, ed. *Hermeneutics Reader.* New York: Continuum Books, 1983.

Murphy, E. A. "Stochastic, the Heuristic, and the Hermeneutic." *MLN* 96 (1981): 981–1001.

Murray, Michael. "The New Hermeneutic and the Interpretation of Poetry." *Review of the University of Ottawa* 50 (1980): 374–94.

Niebuhr, Richard R. *Schleiermacher on Christ and Religion: A New Introduction.* New York: Charles Scribner's Sons, 1964.

O'Hara, Daniel T. *Tragic Knowledge: Yeat's Autobiography and Hermeneutics.* New York: Columbia University Press, 1981.

————, ed. "Why Nietzsche Now?" *boundary 2* 9, no. 3 (Spring 1981), and 10, no. 1 (Fall 1981).

Olson, Alan. *Transcendence and Hermeneutics.* Boston: Kluwer, 1979.

O'Neill, John. *Essaying Montaigne: A Study of the Renaissance Institution of Writing and Reading.* Boston: Routledge and Kegan Paul, 1982.

————, ed. *On Critical Theory.* New York: Seabury, 1976.

Orr, Leonard. "The Hermeneutic Interplay." *Journal of Thought* 16 (Winter 1981): 85–98.

————. *De-Structuring the Novel: Essays in Postmodern Hermeneutics.* Troy, N.Y.: Whitston Pub., 1982.

Otto, Eckart. "Die Applikation als Problem der Politischen Hermeneutik." *Zeitschrift fuer Theologie und Kirche* 71 (1974).

Otto, Rudolf. *The Idea of the Holy: An Inquiry into the Non-rational Factor in the Idea of the Divine and Its Relation to the Rational.* Trans. by John W. Harvey. Oxford: Oxford University Press, 1923.

Outhwaite, William. *Understanding Social Life: Verstehen.* London: Allen and Unwin, 1975.

Palmer, Richard E. *Hermeneutics: Interpretation Theory in Schleiermacher, Dilthey, Heidegger, and Gadamer.* Evanston: Northwestern University Press, 1969.

————. "Hermeneutics & Methodology." *Continuum* 7 (Winter–Spring 1969): 153–58.

————. "Toward a Postmodern Interpretive Self-awareness." *Journal of Religion* 55 (1975): 313–26.

————. "Postmodernity & Hermeneutics." *boundary 2* 5 (Winter 1977): 363–93.

Pannenburg, Wolfhart et al. *History & Hermeneutic.* New York: Harper & Row, 1967.

Parsons, Arthur. "Interpretive Sociology: The Theoretical Significance of Verstehen in the Constitution of Social Reality." *Human Studies* 1 (April 1978): 111–37.

Pavolic, K. R. "Science & Autonomy: The Prospects for Hermeneutic Science." *Man and World* 14 (1981): 127–40.

Pettit, Philip, ed. *Action & Interpretation: Studies in the Philosophy of the Social Sciences.* Cambridge: Cambridge University Press, 1978.

Pilotta, Joseph J., ed. *Interpersonal Communications: Essays in Phenomenology and Hermeneutics.* Washington: University Press of America, 1982.

Rabinow, Paul, and William Sullivan, eds. *Interpretive Social Science.* Berkeley: University of California Press, 1979.

Radnitzky, Gerard. *Contemporary Schools of Metascience: Anglo-Saxon Schools of Metascience/Continental Schools of Metascience.* Chicago: Henry Regnery, 1973.

Ramm, Bernard L. *Hermeneutics.* Grand Rapids: Baker Book House, 1971.

Rasmussen, David. "Ricoeur: The Anthropological Necessity of a Special Language." *Continuum* 7 (Winter–Spring 1969): 120–30.

Rauhala, Lauri. "The Hermeneutic Metascience of Psychoanalysis." *Man and World* 5 (1972): 273–97.

Reagan, Charles E., ed. *Studies in the Philosophy of Paul Ricoeur.* Athens: Ohio University Press, 1979.

Rickman, H. P. *Wilhelm Dilthey: Pioneer of the Human Studies.* Berkeley: University of California Press, 1980.

Ricoeur, Paul. "Existence & Hermeneutics" (1965). In Bleicher's *Contemporary Hermeneutics.*

————. *Freud and Philosophy: An Essay on Interpretation.* Trans. by Denis Savage. New Haven: Yale University Press, 1970.

————. "The Model of the Text: Meaningful Action Considered as a Text." *Social Research* 38 (1971): 529–62.

————. "Ethics and Culture: Habermas and Gadamer in Dialogue." *Philosophy Today* 17 (1973): 153–65.

————. "The Hermeneutical Function of Distanciation." *Philosophy Today* 17 (1973): 129–41.

————. *The Conflict of Interpretations: Essays in Hermeneutics.* Ed. by Don Ihde. Evanston: Northwestern University Press, 1974.

————. "Phenomenology & Hermeneutics." *Nous* 9 (1975): 85–102.

————. *Interpretation Theory: Discourse and the Surplus of Meaning.* Fort Worth: Texas Christian University Press, 1976.

————. "Introduction." In *Time and the Philosophies.* Unesco, 1977.

————. *The Rule of Metaphor: Multi-disciplinary Studies of the Creation of Meaning in Language.* Trans. by R. Dzerny. Toronto: University of Toronto Press, 1977.

————. "Schleiermacher's Hermeneutics." *Monist* 60 (1977): 181–97.

————. *The Philosophy of Paul Ricoeur.* Ed. by Charles Reagan and David Stewart. Boston: Beacon Press, 1978.

————. *Hermeneutics and the Human Sciences.* Ed. by John Thompson. New York: Cambridge University Press, 1981.

Riffaterre, M. "Interpretation and Undecidability." *New Literary History* 12 (1981): 227–42.

Robinson, James M., and John B. Cobb, Jr., eds. *The New Hermeneutic.* New York: Harper and Row, 1964.

Rorty, Richard. *Philosophy & the Mirror of Nature.* Princeton: Princeton University Press, 1979.

————. *Consequences of Pragmatism.* Minneapolis: University of Minnesota Press, 1982.

Rurak, James. "The Imaginative Power of Utopias: A Hermeneutic for Its Recovery." *Philosophy and Social Criticism* 8 (1981): 183–206.

Ryan, Michael. *Marxism and Deconstruction: A Critical Articulation.* Baltimore: Johns Hopkins University Press, 1982.

Said, Edward W. *The World, The Text, The Critic.* Cambridge: Harvard University Press, 1983.

Sandkuehler, Hans Joerg. *Praxis und Geschichtsbewusstsein: Fragen einer dialektischen und historisch-materialistischen Hermeneutik.* Frankfurt: Suhrkamp, 1973.

Sapir, J. David, and J. H. Crocker. *Social Use of Metaphor: The Anthropology of Rhetoric.* Philadelphia: University of Pennsylvania Press, 1977.

Savile, Anthony. "Historicity and the Hermeneutic Circle." *New Literary History* 10 (Autumn 1978): 49–70.

Schleiermacher, F. E. D. *Schleiermacher's Introductions to the Dialogues of Plato.* Trans. by William Dobson. New York: Arno Press, 1973 (reprint of 1836 edition).

————. *Brief Outline of the Study of Theology,* with Reminiscences of Schleiermacher by Friedrich Luecke. Trans. by William Farrer. Edinburgh: T & T Clark, 1850.

————. *The Life of Schleiermacher as Unfolded in his Autobiography and Letters.* 2 vols. Trans. by Frederica Rowan. London: Smith, Elder, and Co., 1860.

————. *Brief Outline on the Study of Theology.* Trans. by Terrence N. Tice. Atlanta: John Knox Press, 1966.

————. *Hermeneutics: The Handwritten Manuscripts.* Ed. by H. Kimmerle. Trans. by J. Duke and J. Forstman. Missoula: Scholars Press, 1977.

————. "The *Hermeneutics*: Outline of the 1819 Lectures." *New Literary History* 10 (Autumn 1978): 1–16.

Schochet, Gordon. "Quentin Skinner's Method." *Political Theory* 2 (1974): 261–76.

Schrijver, G. de. "Hermeneutics and Tradition." *Journal of Ecumenical Studies* 19 (Spring 1982): 32–47.

Schuckman, Paul. "Aristotle's Phronesis and Gadamer's Hermeneutics." *Philosophy Today* 23 (Spring 1979): 41–50.

Schweitzer, Albert. *The Quest of the Historical Jesus: A Critical Study of Its Progress from Reimarus to Wrede.* New York: Macmillan, 1948 (reprint of 1910 edition).

Seebohm, Thomas M. "The Problem of Hermeneutics in Recent Anglo-American Literature." Parts 1, 2. *Philosophy & Rhetoric* 10 (Summer, Fall 1977): 180–209, 263–75.

————. "Reflexion, Interpretation, and Dialectic." *Graduate Faculty Philosophy Journal* 7 (Spring 1978): 15–34.

————. "Review Essay: Paul Ricoeur's *Interpretation Theory.*" *Graduate Faculty Philosophy Journal* 7 (Winter 1978): 257–72.

Seung, T. K. *Structuralism and Hermeneutics.* New York: Columbia University Press, 1982.

————. *Semiotics & Thematics in Hermeneutics.* New York: Columbia University Press, 1982.

Seigfried, Hans. "Phenomenology, Hermeneutics, and Poetry." *Journal of the British Society for Phenomenology* 10 (1979): 94–100.

Shapiro, Michael J. *Language and Political Understanding: The Politics of Discursive Practices.* New Haven: Yale University Press, 1981.

Sheehan, Thomas. "Heidegger: Philosophy and Propaganda." *Salmagundi*, no. 43 (Winter 1979): 173–84.

Siemak, Marek. "Marxism and the Hermeneutic Tradition." *Dialectics and Humanism* 4 (1975): 87–103.

Singleton, Charles, ed. *Interpretation: Theory & Practice.* Baltimore: Johns Hopkins University Press, 1969.

Skinner, Quentin. "Meaning and Understanding in the History of Ideas." *History and Theory* 8 (1969): 3–53.

————. "Motives, Intentions, and the Interpretation of Texts." *New Literary History* 3 (Winter 1972): 393–408.

————. "Social Meaning and the Explanation of Social Action." In *Philosophy, Politics, and Society*, 4th series. Ed. Peter Laslett et al. Oxford: Basil Blackwell, 1972.

————. "Some Problems in the Analysis of Political Thought and Action." *Political Theory* 2 (1974): 277–303.

————. "Hermeneutics and the Role of History." *New Literary History* 7 (Autumn 1975): 209–32.

Smith, P. Christopher. "Gadamer on Language and Method in Hegel's Dialectic." *Graduate Faculty Philosophy Journal* 5 (Fall 1975): 53–72.

Spanos, Wm. V., ed. *Martin Heidegger and the Question of Literature: Toward a Postmodern Literary Hermeneutics.* Bloomington: Indiana University Press, 1980.

Steiner, George. *After Babel: Aspects of Language and Translation.* New York: Oxford University Press, 1975.

————. *On Difficulty and Other Essays.* New York: Oxford University Press, 1978.

Sullivan, William, and Paul Rabinow. "The Interpretive Turn: Emergence of an Approach." *Philosophy Today* 23 (1979): 29–40.

Sutherland, David Earl. "The Factor of Hermeneutics in Habermas' Critical Theory." In *Research in Sociology of Knowledges, Sciences, and Art.* Westport, Conn.: JAI Press, 1979.

Symposium. "Hermeneutics and Critical Theory." *Cultural Hermeneutics* 2 (1975): 307–90.

Symposium. "Hermeneutics, Post-Structuralism, and Objective Interpretation." *Papers on Language and Literature* 17 (1981): 48–87.

Szondi, Peter. "Introduction to Literary Hermeneutics." *New Literary History* 10 (Autumn 1978): 18–29.

Tate, P. D. "Comparative Hermeneutics: Heidegger, the pre-Socratics, and the Rgveda." *Philosophy East and West* 32 (1982): 47–59.

Taylor, Charles. "Interpretation and the Sciences of Man." *Review of Metaphysics* 25 (1971): 3–51.

————. "Understanding in Human Science." *Review of Metaphysics* 34 (1980): 25–55.

Thompson, John B. *Critical Hermeneutics: A Study in the Thought of Paul Ricoeur and Juergen Habermas.* Cambridge: Cambridge University Press, 1981.

Topolski, Jerzy. *Methodology of History.* Dordrecht: Reidel, 1976.

Turner, Stephen, and David Carr. "The Process of Criticism in Interpretive Sociology & History." *Human Studies* 1 (1978): 138–52.

Todorov, Tzvetan. *The Poetics of Prose.* Trans. by Richard Howard. Ithaca: Cornell University Press, 1977.

Van Til, Cornelius. *The New Hermeneutic.* Grand Rapids: Baker Book House, 1974.

Velkley, Richard. "Gadamer and Kant: The Critique of Modern Aesthetic Consciousness in *Truth & Method.*" *Interpretation* 9 (1981): 353–64.

Virkler, Henry A. *Hermeneutics: Principles and Processes of Biblical Interpretation.* Grand Rapids: Baker Book House, 1979.

Wach, Joachim. *Das Verstehen: Grundzuege Einer Geschichte Der Hermeneutischen Theorie im 19. Jahrhundert.* 3 vols. Hildesheim: Georg Olm's Verlagsbuchhandlung, 1966 (reprint of 1926 edition).

Weinsheimer, Joel. " 'London' and the Fundamental Problem of Hermeneutics." *Critical Inquiry* 9 (1982): 303–22.

Wellmer, Albrecht. "Communication and Emancipation: Reflections on the 'Linguistic Turn' in Critical Theory." *Stony Brook Studies in Philosophy* 1 (1974): 75–101. Reprinted in *On Critical Theory,* ed. O'Neill.

West, Philip. "The Redundant Labyrinth." *Salmagundi*, no. 46 (Fall 1979) : 58–83.

Westphal, Merold. "Hegel, Pannenburg, and Hermeneutics." *Man and World* 4 (1971) : 276–93.

White, Hayden. "Foucault Decoded: Notes from Underground." *History and Theory* (1973) : 23–54.

———. "Interpretation in History." *New Literary History* 4 (Winter 1973) : 281–314.

———. *Metahistory: The Historical Imagination in Nineteenth-Century Europe*. Baltimore: The Johns Hopkins University Press, 1974.

———. "The Problem of Change in Literary History." *New Literary History* 7 (Autumn 1975) : 97–111.

———. *Tropics of Discourse: Essays in Cultural Criticism*. Baltimore: Johns Hopkins University Press, 1978.

Wiener, Jonathan. "Quentin Skinner's Hobbes." *Political Theory* 2 (1974) : 251–60.

Wolf, Friedrich August. *Vorlesung ueber die Enzyklopaedia der Altertumswissenschaft*. Leipzig: Lehnhold, 1831.

Wolff, Janet. *Hermeneutic Philosophy and the Sociology of Art*. London: Routledge and Kegan Paul, 1975.

Wolff, Kurt. *Surrender & Catch: Experience and Inquiry Today*. Boston Studies in the Philosophy of Science, vol. 51. Dordrecht: Reidel, 1976.

Wollheim, Richard. "The Cabinet of Dr. Lacan." *New York Review of Books*, January 25, 1979.

Wood, Charles Monroe. *Theory and Religious Understanding: A Critique of the Hermeneutics of Joachim Wach*. Missoula: Scholars Press, 1975.

Wood, Michael. "Deconstructing Derrida." *New York Review of Books*, March 3, 1977.

Contributors

· · · · ·

EMILIO BETTI. Before his death Betti was a leading theorist of law in Italy, as well as an internationally known expert in hermeneutic theory. Except for one small handbook on interpretation, none of his works is in English. Susan Noakes's forthcoming translation of his major work will fill this gap.

GERALD BRUNS is a professor of English at the University of Iowa and is the author of *Modern Poetry and the Idea of Language* and of *Inventions: Writing, Textuality and Understanding in Literary History.*

FRED DALLMAYR is a professor of government and international studies at the University of Notre Dame. He is the author of *The Twilight of Subjectivity* and co-editor of *Understanding and Social Inquiry,* with Thomas McCarthy. He has also written numerous articles in English and German.

PAUL DE MAN is a professor of comparative literature at Yale University and the author of *Blindness and Insight, Allegories of Reading,* and of many papers.

WILLIAM DRAY is a professor of philosophy at the University of Ottawa and is the author of *Laws and Explanation in History, Philosophy of History, Perspectives on History,* and of many papers.

HUBERT DREYFUS is a professor of philosophy at the University of California-Berkeley. He is the author of *What Computers Can't Do* and of *Michel Foucault: Beyond Structuralism and Hermeneutics* (with Paul Rabinow).

HANS-GEORG GADAMER is a professor of philosophy at Heidelberg University. He also teaches annually at Boston College. His books in English include *Truth and Method, Philosophical Hermeneutics, Dialogue and Dialectic, Hegel's Dialectic,* and *Reason in the Age of Science.*

ANTHONY GIDDENS is a lecturer in sociology at King's College, Cambridge University. He is the author of *Politics and Sociology in the Thought of Max Weber, Capitalism and Modern Social Theory, Class Structure of the Advanced Societies, Studies in Social and Political Theory, New Rules of Sociological Method,* and *Central Problems in Social Theory.* He is the translator and editor of *Durkheim,* and editor of *Positivism and Sociology.*

REX MARTIN is a professor of philosophy at the University of Kansas. He is the author of *Historical Explanation: Re-enactment and Practical Inference* and of many articles.

J. N. MOHANTY is George Lynn Cross Research Professor of Philosophy, University of Oklahoma. He has written *Husserl and Frege, Edmund Husserl's Theory of Meaning,* and many other books and articles on phenomenology and Oriental philosophy.

SUSAN NOAKES is an associate professor of French and Italian at the University of Kansas. She has published a number of articles on Dante and Renaissance learning. Her complete translation of Emilio Betti's *General Theory of Interpretation* will appear soon.

JOHN O'NEILL is a professor of sociology and comparative literature at York University. He is the author of *Expression and History: The Social Phenomenology of Merleau-Ponty, Sociology as a Skin Trade, Making Sense Together,* and *Essaying Montaigne.* He has also translated *Studies on Marx and Hegel, Humanism and Terror, Themes from the Lectures at the Collège de France,* and *The Prose of the World.*

RICHARD PALMER is a professor of philosophy at MacMurray College. He is the author of *Hermeneutics* and of many articles.

GAYATRI CHAKRAVORTY SPIVAK is a professor of English at the University of Texas, Austin. Author of *Myself Must I Remake: The Life and Poetry of W. B. Yeats* and of many articles, she has also translated *Of Grammatology.*

GARY STONUM, is an associate professor of English at Case Western Reserve University. He is the author of *Faulkner's Career* and several articles.